CAT
HEALTH
ENCYCLOPEDIA

Edited by Dr. Lowell Ackerman

TS-302

© by Lowell Ackerman, D. V. M.

Distributed in the UNITED STATES to the Pet Trade by T.F.H. Publications, Inc., One T.F.H. Plaza, Neptune City, NJ 07753; on the Internet at www.tfh.com; in CANADA Rolf C. Hagen Inc., 3225 Sartelon St. Laurent-Montreal Quebec H4R 1E8; Pet Trade by H & L Pet Supplies Inc., 27 Kingston Crescent, Kitchener, Ontario N2B 2T6; in ENGLAND by T.F.H. Publications, PO Box 15, Waterlooville PO7 6BQ; in AUSTRALIA AND THE SOUTH PACIFIC by T.F.H. (Australia), Pty. Ltd., Box 149, Brookvale 2100 N.S.W., Australia; in NEW ZEALAND by Brooklands Aquarium Ltd. 5 McGiven Drive, New Plymouth, RD1 New Zealand; in SOUTH AFRICA, Rolf C. Hagen S.A. (PTY.) LTD. P.O. Box 201199, Durban North 4016, South Africa; in Japan by T.F.H. Publications, Japan— Jiro Tsuda, 10-12-3 Ohjidai, Sakura, Chiba 285, Japan. Published by T.F.H. Publications, Inc.

MANUFACTURED IN THE
UNITED STATES OF AMERICA
BY T.F.H. PUBLICATIONS, INC.

CONTENTS

PREFACE 5

SKIN DISORDERS 7
   Alexander H. Werner, VMD and Bonnie E. Werner, DVM

DISORDERS OF THE MUSCULOSKELETAL SYSTEM 47
   Dennis C. Law, DVM and Terry Silkman, DVM

THE FELINE EYE IN HEALTH AND DISEASE 87
   Charles L. Martin, DVM, MS

CARDIOVASCULAR DISORDERS 123
   Debbie Hadlock, DVM

BLOOD DISORDERS 145
   W. Jean Dodds, DVM

DISEASES OF THE RESPIRATORY SYSTEM 161
   Gary D. Norsworthy, DVM

DENTAL PROBLEMS AND CARE 189
   Kenneth Lyon, DVM and Gregg DuPont, DVM

DIGESTIVE TRACT DISORDERS 213
   Minta Keyes, DVM

URINARY TRACT PROBLEMS 231
   Robert B. Koch, DVM

IMMUNE DISORDERS 249
   W. Jean Dodds, DVM

ENDOCRINE (HORMONAL) DISORDERS 257
   Alexander H. Werner, VMD and Bonnie E. Werner, DVM

NUTRITION-RELATED PROBLEMS 269
   Lowell Ackerman, DVM, PhD

FELINE EMERGENCIES 287
   Alexander H. Werner, VMD and Bonnie E. Werner, DVM

PHARMACOLOGY 303
   Lester Mandelker, DVM

INDEX 311

**Lowell Ackerman, DVM, PhD
Diplomate, American College of Veterinary Dermatology**

Director of Clinical Resources
Mesa Veterinary Hospital, Ltd
Mesa, Arizona

PREFACE

Cats are currently the most populous pets in America. There are over 65 million of them in the United States and Canada. And there's a lot of money spent on them; the pet product market in the United States is a multibillion-dollar-a-year reality. With all the attention that cats are getting, you might suspect that they are healthier than ever, and in some respects they are. However, in many areas, cats have not benefited from all of the advancements that have been made. Some segments of the population are still not giving cats the care they deserve. We hope to change that trend somewhat, with this book and its prequel, *Owner's Guide to Cat Health*. Whereas *Owner's Guide* was dedicated to preventive health care, this book examines feline illness on a system-by-system basis, the same method used by veterinarians. And to do this effectively, we have selected internationally renowned experts in their fields to help relay pertinent information. It has been my pleasure to work with these specialists, and I applaud their efforts to bring feline medicine directly to the cat-owning public.

Lowell Ackerman, DVM, PhD
Editor

Cats don't really have nine lives; all they need is one good healthy one!

Dr. Bonnie Werner   Dr. Alexander Werner

Dr. Bonnie Werner graduated from the University of California, Davis, School of Veterinary Medicine, followed by an internship at the Coast Pet Clinic in Hermosa Beach, California. She completed a residency in small animal internal medicine at the Louisiana State University, School of Veterinary Medicine. Both Drs. Werner live in Southern California, where they practice together in a referral specialty clinic.

Dr. Alexander Werner graduated from the University of Pennsylvania, School of Veterinary Medicine, followed by an internship at the California Animal Hospital in Los Angeles, California. He completed a residency in veterinary dermatology at the University of California, Davis, School of Veterinary Medicine, where he met his wife Bonnie. Dr. Alexander Werner is a Diplomate of the American College of Veterinary Dermatology.

SKIN DISORDERS

By Alexander H. Werner, VMD, Diplomate, ACVD
and Bonnie E. Werner, DVM

Animal Dermatology Centers
Valley Veterinary Specialty Services
13125 Ventura Boulevard
Studio City, CA 91604

INTRODUCTION

The skin of cats is similar, though not identical, to the skin of humans. It is not surprising, therefore, that identical skin diseases can occur in cats and humans. Cats have their own ways of demonstrating skin diseases, such as acne and allergy, and they have their own group of important syndromes. Cats are clandestine creatures; they prefer to hide any sign of disease until it is very severe. Many times their fur hides evidence of disease, and their secretive nature prevents the cat owner from seeing them in discomfort. It is common for cats to see the veterinarian for hair loss while the owner insists that the cat never licks or chews at itself. An increased frequency of hairballs or large amounts of hair in the stool should alert the owner to fact that the cat is removing its fur out of the owner's sight.

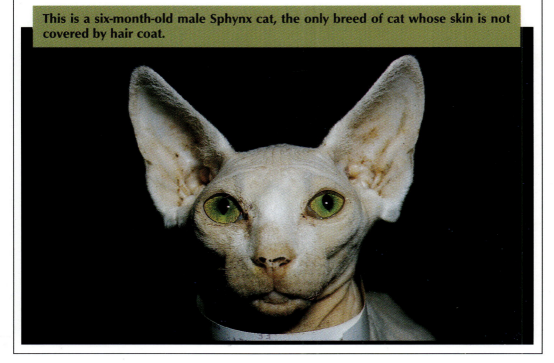

This is a six-month-old male Sphynx cat, the only breed of cat whose skin is not covered by hair coat.

Cat Health Encyclopedia

As varied as the hair coat can appear, the underlying skin is limited in the different ways it can show disease. The hair coat can fall out excessively, fail to regrow, or change in color. The skin can become inflamed, scaly, crusty, or scabby. It can lose its pigment or become excessively pigmented. It can have pimples or bumps; sections of skin can die, leaving depressions or ulcers. Distinguishing between diseases requires an appropriate history and the ability to recognize disease patterns. Specific diagnosis of the cat's skin lesions is required to allow appropriate treatment. There are many different drugs that can be used to resolve an abnormal skin condition. Many people think that the use of cortisone is a safe cure-all for any skin problem. Unfortunately, cortisone (a.k.a. steroids) is neither safe nor a cure-all.

The skin is the largest and one of the most active organs of the body. The skin protects the inside of the body from the outside world. It functions in temperature regulation, immune system function, hormone and other chemical synthesis, and in sensory perception. It does all this while still having sufficient elasticity to permit motion and maintain shape. Perhaps because of the skin's importance to the body, as well as the amount of detective work often required to diagnose specific diseases, there are a group of veterinarians who have had years of advanced training in the diagnosis and treatment of animal skin diseases. These veterinary dermatologists can work with your general veterinarian to provide accurate diagnosis and appropriate treatment for your cat with skin disease.

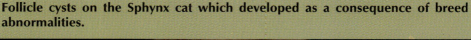

Follicle cysts on the Sphynx cat which developed as a consequence of breed abnormalities.

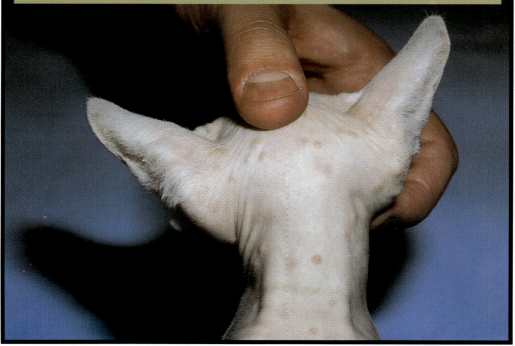

Skin Disorders

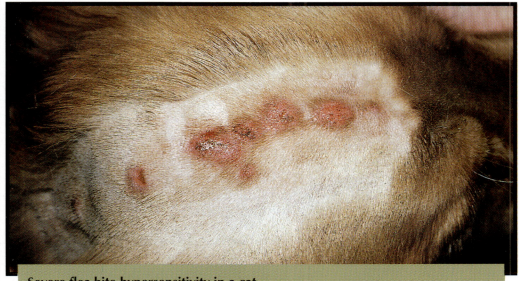

Severe flea-bite hypersensitivity in a cat.

HEREDITARY OR CONGENITAL SKIN DISORDERS

In human and animal medicine, there is growing recognition that a vast majority of diseases have some basis in heredity. As we learn more about the genes that create each of us, we have begun discovering specific markers within the DNA that makes up our genes that can be related to specific diseases. It has long been known that certain breeds of cat are more prone to particular problems. These unwanted problems have become associated with the genes for tendencies we desire (such as hair color or ear shape). Therefore many diseases have a genetic predilection or tendency. Fortunately, these diseases are extremely rare.

Seborrhea is an abnormal accumulation of debris and oil on the skin. It is common in the dog but rare in the cat. Seborrhea has been documented in Persian cats as an autosomal recessive trait, and affected kittens may show signs as early as two days of age. Typically, excessive amounts of scale and grease cause the hairs to paste together, and, eventually, the hair is lost. These accumulations are particularly severe in the ears and facial folds. The diagnosis is made by biopsying the skin. Other than frequent shampooing to remove debris, there is no specific treatment.

Epidermolysis bullosa is a disease in which the connections between the upper layers of the skin (epidermis) and the lower layers (dermis) are absent or abnormal. This results in the loss of the epidermis with minimal trauma. Most often in cats this disease is seen as the complete shedding of all claws at an early age. However, any region of skin that is subjected to movement or trauma can ulcerate, including the mouth and paw pads. A tentative diagnosis can be made by biopsying affected areas. However, examination of tissues under an electron microscope is required to demonstrate the defect of this disease. There is no specific treatment, although reducing trauma and treating secondary infections can permit a more normal life.

Hair follicle and hair shaft disorders define certain breeds. For example, the Sphynx cat is bred for hairlessness. Some of these defects are encouraged by excessive inbreeding, and therefore nutritional deficiencies or poor housekeeping cannot be blamed for the appearance of defects in certain lines. Two specific syndromes have been reported in cats. There are no treatments for these diseases.

Shaft disorder in Abyssinian cats: Affected cats have whiskers and primary hairs that become rough and break easily. An onion-shaped swelling can be seen at the tip of the hair under the microscope.

Congenital hypotrichosis: Described in Birman, Burmese, Devon Rex, and Siamese cats, these kittens are born hairless and may lack whiskers, claws, and the rough projections on the tongue (papillae).

Chediak-Higashi syndrome is an inherited disorder of Persian cats. It is seen only in cats with blue smoke hair color and yellow eyes. Abnormal clumping of pigment granules within the hairs and abnormalities in white blood cell function are seen. Affected cats are highly susceptible to infection, have bleeding disorders, and develop eye abnormalities. There is no specific treatment available.

Cutaneous asthenia is characterized by fragile, loose, and hyperextensible skin. The cause of this disease is an abnormality in the production of collagen. Collagen is crucial to maintenance of skin strength and shape. As a result, animals with collagen defects frequently have skin that tears easily, heals with scarring, hangs in loose folds, and stretches easily beyond normal limits. In cats, most cases occur in Himalayan cats and the domestic short or long-haired breeds. Diagnosis is made by a combination of clinical signs, calculation of excessive skin extensibility, and demonstration of abnormal collagen formation by biopsy. There is no specific treatment for this disease; minimizing trauma to the skin is critical.

Mosquito-bite allergy. The bridge of the nose is scabbed and swollen.

Skin Disorders

Facial dermatitis in a 6-year-old female Himalayan as the result of a food allergy.

IMMUNOLOGIC DISEASE

The immune system is the body's main protection against outside invaders (infections). In protecting the body, the immune system must be able to distinguish what is normal (a part of the body or manufactured molecule such as a hormone), and what is abnormal (an organism or cancer cell). There are three basic ways in which the immune system can malfunction:

1. It can fail to react to something abnormal (immunodeficiency) leading to infection,
2. It can overreact (hypersensitivity or allergy), or it can react to an otherwise normal part of the body (auto-immunity).
3. Cutaneous signs of immunodeficiencies are rare and are most often seen as skin infections (which will be discussed under the topic of infections). Hyper-reactivity (allergy) and aberrant reactivity (auto-immunity) are discussed below.

ALLERGY

Allergy is defined as an excessive immune reaction to substances normally found in the environment. Allergies are a common cause of skin disease in the cat. There are four main groups of allergic reactions that produce skin disease: insect allergy, food allergy, pollen allergy, and contact allergy.

Insect allergy is the most common cause of excessive itching and licking in the cat. In most regions, fleas are the most common culprit. A smaller group of cats show sensitivity to mosquitoes or other insects. Flea allergy can appear in any, or all, of the following patterns.

Like dogs, cats may lick and chew the fur off of the rear half of the body, particularly over the base of the tail and back of the thighs. Many cats continue the pattern of excessive grooming with removal of hair from the groin and belly. In some cats, there may be no signs of inflammation, and cats may remove their hair outside of the owner's

Cat Health Encyclopedia

sight, leading to the false impression that the cat's hair is failing to grow, rather than being pulled out. As in all cats with flea allergy, but especially in this group of cats, it may be impossible to ever see a flea on the body of the cat. This is because these cats are so sensitized to the presence of fleas on their bodies that the instant one bites them they meticulously remove it. Thus, the inability to find fleas is not significant when diagnosing flea allergy.

Many cats develop "miliary dermatitis," named because of the multiple small scabs and crusts that feel like many millet seeds over the entire body. Many of these cats are very itchy and will scratch and bite fur. Their skin feels rough and gritty due to the large numbers of these scabs.

Lesions of the eosinophilic granuloma complex are frequently seen with flea bite allergy.

Flea bite allergy is diagnosed by seeing typical lesions and by excluding other diagnoses. Often, the best way to diagnosis it is by noting a good response to adequate flea control. The use of corticosteroids is acceptable for short-term resolution of lesions in the cat, but only if the primary cause (the flea) is being controlled. Long-term administration of corticosteroids is neither appropriate nor safe. Adequate flea control must involve treating all household animals with frequent flea sprays or rinses, as well as routine premise (house and yard) treatments. For the flea-allergic cat, one flea bite can produce up to two weeks of inflammation and itch. Your veterinarian should be consulted to outline a correct flea control program for your situation. Additionally, a large number of new flea control products are on the market that can have a profound effect on flea control. Your veterinarian or a veterinary

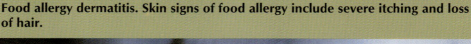

Food allergy dermatitis. Skin signs of food allergy include severe itching and loss of hair.

Skin Disorders

Food allergy dermatitis. Your veterinarian can diagnose food allergies and recommend specific diets to eliminate the symptoms.

dermatologist can provide you with the most up-to-date information on what is available and effective in your area.

Mosquito-bite allergy is a seasonal problem that corresponds to the presence of mosquitoes. Lesions most often affect the face of outdoor cats. Crusting, hair loss, scaling, and swelling of the bridge of the nose and inner aspects of the ear flaps are most common. The diagnosis is made by biopsying the area, or confining the cat indoors and seeing rapid improvement. Because this is a seasonal disease, using steroids is acceptable, but only if mosquito control is impossible by confining the cat or by applying mosquito-repellents.

Food allergy is more common in the cat than in the dog. However, food allergy is often over diagnosed. It is important to distinguish the difference between food allergy and food intolerance. Food intolerance is a non-allergic event caused by the inability to digest or absorb a particular food. Food intolerance causes intestinal signs such as vomiting and diarrhea, but does not cause itching. Food allergy is an immunologic event. The immune system reacts excessively to normal diet components. Gastrointestinal signs of food allergy can appear similar to food intolerance, but skin signs can also be seen. Food allergy most often develops in middle-aged to older cats, although very young food-allergic cats have been reported. Most cats have been fed the same food for a long time before becoming allergic to an ingredient in that food. Skin signs of food allergy include severe, non-seasonal itching of the front half of the body the face, ears, head, and neck. Less often, generalized itching can develop.

A suspicion of food allergy can be derived from a skin biopsy; however, food allergy is diagnosed by feeding a restricted-ingredient (elimination) diet for an extended period. It is highly unlikely that food allergy will be diagnosed by simply changing the diet from one commercial cat food to another. Most commercial diets contain similar basic ingredients, even though the main flavor ingredients differ. Many diets claim to be "hypo-allergenic." However, this is a misleading statement. There is nothing more hypo-allergenic about any one food source over another (i.e., lamb over beef). It is the frequency of exposure to a particular food source that increases the chances that an allergy will develop.

Traditionally, cat foods have contained beef, dairy products, or seafood as the main protein or flavor. It is logical, therefore, that one study demonstrated that these are the most common causes of food allergy in cats. However, as the popularity of lamb- and turkey-based diets increases, allergy to these ingredients has also been on the rise. An adequate elimination diet is one that contains a minimal number of ingredients to provide sufficient nutrition, and utilizes ingredients not commonly found in commercial cat foods. Fortunately, there are several commercially available, prescription-only diets that can be used so that home-cooking is not required. Your veterinarian or veterinary dermatologist can advise you on the proper elimination diet, or give you recipes for home-cooking if you prefer. Elimination diets should be fed for four to eight weeks (as long as required to note improvement). During this time, no other foods or treats can be given. An outdoor cat that travels the neighborhood food circuit will be difficult to diagnose without confinement. When improvement is noted, or after eight weeks of the food trial, the previous food is re-instituted. Food-allergic cats should begin itching and breaking out with new lesions within one week of the food change.

Pollen allergy (atopy) is an under-diagnosed disease of cats. In dogs, the syndrome of facial and foot itch that is diagnosed by allergy skin testing and treated with immunotherapy is well documented. However, in cats, fewer animals are skin tested and treated properly. This may reflect the veterinary dermatology community's lack of experience with this disease, or the hesitation of the cat owner to pursue this diagnosis through extensive

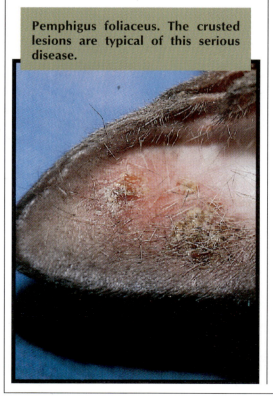

Pemphigus foliaceus. The crusted lesions are typical of this serious disease.

SKIN DISORDERS

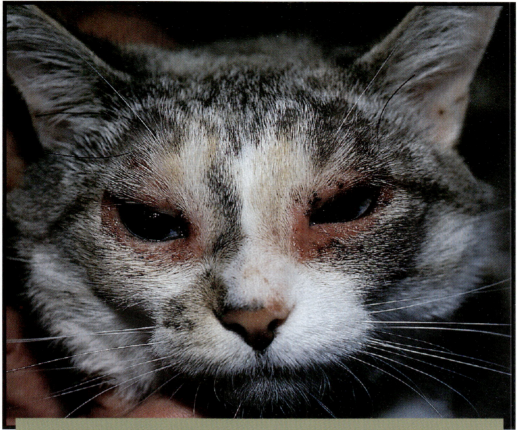

Atopic cat with facial itching and redness due to pollen allergy.

testing. Current thoughts on feline atopy regard this allergy as the second most common cause of itching in the cat. Typically, signs are non-seasonal and develop in the young cat (six months to two years). Clinical signs are similar to food allergy, though tend to be less severe. Itching of the head and neck, excessive grooming, lesions of the eosinophilic granuloma complex, and miliary dermatitis have been documented.

The diagnosis of atopy in the cat is made by excluding the two other main causes of itch in felines (flea bite allergy and food allergy), and by obtaining a positive allergy skin test. Allergy skin testing involves injecting small amounts of various allergens (substances that may cause an allergic reaction) into the skin. Most veterinary dermatologists use between 50 and 70 allergens in their tests. For the procedure, the cat is sedated and a patch of hair is shaved off the side of the chest. In this patch, individual allergens are injected. The injection sites are then observed for reactions. A positive reaction is a raised and reddened spot over the injection site.

There are three aspects to treating the atopic cat. First, if there is a specific source of the allergy (e.g., a particular plant), it can be removed to lessen the cat's exposure; this is rarely practical. Second, immunotherapy is initiated, using injections of the allergens specific for that cat (based on the allergy skin test). With immunotherapy, the immune system can be made tolerant to the allergen. Third, medical control of itchiness is attempted. Using antihistamines is a safe method of itch control in cats. For some cats these drugs are highly effective, while in others there is no response.

Substances that have been reported to induce contact irritant and contact allergy dermatitis include plants, medications, finishes, and cleansers. The difference between a contact allergic reaction and contact irritant reaction is based on the body's response to the causative substance. With contact allergic reactions, the

Intradermal allergy test in an allergic cat. Positive reactions are seen as slightly raised and reddened injection sites (above black dots).

Dietary supplements with essential fatty acids have also shown promise. Unfortunately, some cats do require corticosteroids to control their itch, but these drugs should always be used with great care and always in conjunction with other therapies.

Contact dermatitis is rare in cats. This is because the hair coat protects cats' skin from contacting irritating or allergy-producing compounds.

immune system reacts excessively to even a small amount of a substance which by itself may not be irritating to the skin. With contact irritant reactions, the substance is toxic or irritating to the skin (as in a chemical burn), and the cat's immune system is not directly involved in the reaction. Signs of contact dermatitis are usually non-seasonal, and seen mostly in the non-haired regions of

SKIN DISORDERS

Incessant scratching is not normal. If your cat can't stop scratching, consult your veterinarian. It may be simple to remedy and ignoring the problem only makes it worse in the long term.

the skin because these areas are not protected. In cats, these areas include the chin, inner aspects of the ears, inner aspects of the toes between the pads, and around the anus or scrotum. Less often, the underbelly is affected, especially in short-furred cats. Contact dermatitis from medications is most common in the ears. If any skin condition worsens following topical medication, it should be reported to a veterinarian.

Diagnosis of contact dermatitis is made by excluding other sources of itching, by having compatible skin biopsies, and by a positive reaction to a patch test. A presumptive diagnosis can be made by removing the cat from the environment for seven days with lesions initially healing, then rapidly recurring when the cat is returned to its environment. In patch testing, small amounts of suspicious items are applied individually to the skin under a bandage. These sites of

Cat Health Encyclopedia

contact are then examined at 24 and 48 hours. A positive reaction is seen as redness and swelling at any of the specific sites. Treating contact dermatitis requires removal of the offending substance from the cat's environment; otherwise, unacceptably high dosages of corticosteroids are required to control the itch associated with this disease.

AUTOIMMUNE DISEASE

In autoimmune diseases, the immune system fails to recognize normal constituents of the body and begins to attack specific parts of the body. Autoimmune disease can affect any organ of the body; skin diseases caused by an uncontrolled immune system are not rare. Diagnosing these diseases always requires skin biopsies, as the treatment requires strong medications. There are two main syndromes of autoimmune skin disease in the cat: the pemphigus complex and systemic lupus erythematosus. There are also several less common diseases.

Two diseases of the pemphigus complex have been described in cats. The more common is pemphigus foliaceus. In this disease, the upper layers of the epidermis are targeted by the immune system. Cats of all ages can be affected, although the disease appears most often in the middle-aged cat. Typical lesions are thick crusts that adhere to the skin over the ears, face, and claw folds. In some cats, the region surrounding the nipples may also be affected. Some cats will act sick when lesions are severe, and, in many of these cases, secondary bacterial infection will develop. Lesions may wax and wane, further confusing the diagnosis. The diagnosis of pemphigus foliaceus is based on compatible skin biopsy findings. Only

after the diagnosis is confirmed is therapy instituted to selectively inhibit the immune system's attack on the skin. It is critical to realize that both the disease and the treatment are serious concerns. Untreated cases of pemphigus foliaceus can be fatal, most often because of debilitation or secondary infection. On the other hand, inappropriate treatment or the failure to monitor therapy for potential side effects can cause death. Therefore, once pemphigus foliaceus is diagnosed, the treatment and monitoring protocol set up by your veterinarian or veterinary dermatologist must be strictly adhered to, and all side effects or problems must be reported immediately. With appropriate therapy, cats with pemphigus foliaceus may be well controlled, or even go into remission.

Pemphigus vulgaris is the second disease of the pemphigus complex that has been reported in the cat. Fortunately this disease is very rare, because it is much more severe than pemphigus foliaceus, and is often fatal. The causes of pemphigus vulgaris and pemphigus foliaceus are similar except that the deep layers of the epidermis are attacked in pemphigus vulgaris producing deep ulcers rather than thick crusts. Lesions especially occur in the mouth and in areas of trauma such as claw folds, armpits, and groin. Because these are deeper lesions, secondary infections are common and are often the cause of death. The diagnosis is made by skin biopsy. The treatment program is similar to pemphigus foliaceus but is usually less successful.

Systemic lupus erythematosus (SLE) is very rare in the cat. An increased incidence has been reported in Siamese, Persian, and

SKIN DISORDERS

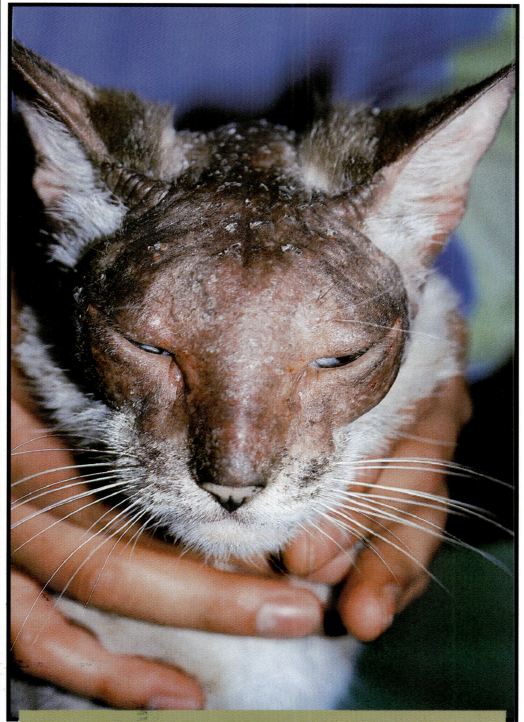

Feline immunodeficiency virus. Infected cats may be asymptomatic for years, but the active disease can involve an array of secondary infections including severe hair loss. Fortunately, it is not transmittable to humans.

Cat Health Encyclopedia

Himalayan cats, although cases have been seen in all breeds and at all ages. SLE is not primarily a skin-related disease; only 20 percent of cases have skin lesions. More commonly, cats with SLE have abnormalities of the blood system, joints, or kidneys. When skin lesions do occur, they may look like any type of dermatosis; thus SLE has been nicknamed "the great imitator." The diagnosis requires compatible skin biopsy findings, the presence of disease in another organ system (hence the name "systemic" lupus erythematosus), and a positive test called an ANA (anti-nuclear antibody). In some early cases it may be difficult to find a second organ system that is affected. Thus, if skin biopsy results are compatible, and other possible diagnoses have been excluded, then treatment for SLE can be initiated. Treatment of SLE is similar to that of the pemphigus group. However, treatment usually surrounds control of disease of the organ systems other than of the skin, as these are often more life threatening than the dermatosis.

Cold agglutinin disease is a rare disease in which the immune system makes antibodies that react at colder temperatures. In cats, this rare disease produces redness, swelling, and loss of skin tissue on the extremities, tail tip, nose tip, and ears (regions generally cooler than the rest of the body). Diagnosis is made by biopsy and by the finding of cold agglutinating antibodies on a blood test. Treatment is aimed at correcting the cause of the antibody production or by immunosuppressing the cat.

Drug reactions that cause skin disease are uncommon. However, any disease that seems to worsen with appropriate medication should have therapy re-evaluated. Drug reactions may be predictable and related to known common side effects of a

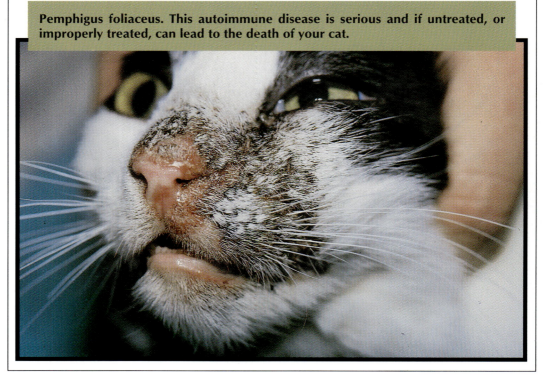

Pemphigus foliaceus. This autoimmune disease is serious and if untreated, or improperly treated, can lead to the death of your cat.

Skin Disorders

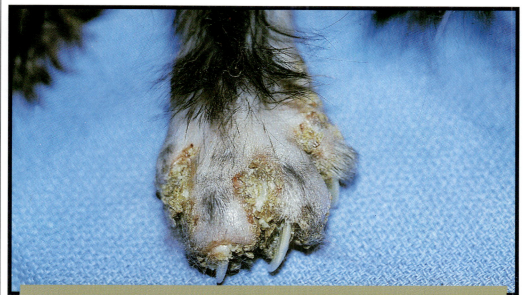

Pemphigus foliaceus. Lesions consist of thick crusts, scabs, and inflammation on the face, ears, and feet.

medication (i.e., hair loss with chemotherapy). These reactions are usually dose-dependent and will stop once the drug is discontinued. Unpredictable drug reactions are produced by an abnormal reaction to a medication and are not dose-dependent. In addition, unpredictable drug reactions may continue well past the time that the particular medication is withdrawn. Drug reactions can look like any form of skin disease. Most often an itchy rash will develop and worsen as medication is continued. In rare instances, severe disease, including the loss of large areas of skin, similar to total body burning, can occur. These types of reactions, from the less severe erythema multiforme to the overwhelming toxic epidermal necrolysis, can be fatal. Drug reaction can be diagnosed by noting improvement or by biopsy confirmation. Challenging a suspected case of drug reaction with the offending drug is dangerous and not recommended. If a drug reaction is suspected, the medication should be discontinued. The cat owner is advised to remind any veterinarian treating his pet of any previous drug reaction so that a repeat prescription is avoided.

Vasculitis is an inflammation of blood vessels and is rare in cats. Vasculitis causes bleeding, hair loss, tissue death, and scarring, particularly in areas containing very small blood vessels or capillaries (feet, tail tip, ears). Vasculitis may also affect tissues other than the skin. Therefore, a multitude of disease signs is possible. Vasculitis is diagnosed by skin biopsy. Treatment is aimed at correcting any underlying cause of the disease and by suppressing the inflammatory immune reaction.

Relapsing polychondritis is a rare disease of cats that causes swollen and painful ears. All cats diagnosed with this condition have been either feline leukemia virus (FeLV)- or feline immunodeficiency virus (FIV)-positive. The diagnosis is made by

Cat Health Encyclopedia

skin biopsy. Treatment is difficult and may require specific drugs to modulate the immune system.

Alopecia areata is a rare disease in which the hair follicles are targeted for destruction. Patches of non-inflamed hair loss are typically seen. The diagnosis is by skin biopsy. The disease is cosmetic and no specific treatment is recommended at this time.

Cutaneous amyloidosis is a rare disease in which specific abnormal proteins are deposited in the skin. Amyloidosis is most often seen as a disease of the kidneys or liver, and may be caused by any disease that causes chronic stimulation of the immune system. In cats, nodular accumulations of these proteins have been seen, most commonly on the ears. Lesions are frequently removed for biopsy, which can result in a cure if any underlying disease (e.g., infection) is controlled.

INFECTIOUS DISEASE

In cats, there are two main classes of infectious disease that cause skin disease: bacterial and fungal. Viral, rickettsial, and protozoal agents are rarely primary causes of skin disease, although the FeLV and FIV viruses can permit secondary skin infections due to their immunosuppressive effects.

Bacterial Skin Disease

The skin is not a sterile canvas. A large number of organisms inhabit the layers and follicles of the skin. These normal organisms, called the resident flora, are crucial for the skin's health because they prevent disease-causing bacteria from invading. Superficial bacterial skin disease is very common in the dog and can develop secondary to any disease that alters or damages the normal environment of the skin. Cats, however, are fairly resistant to

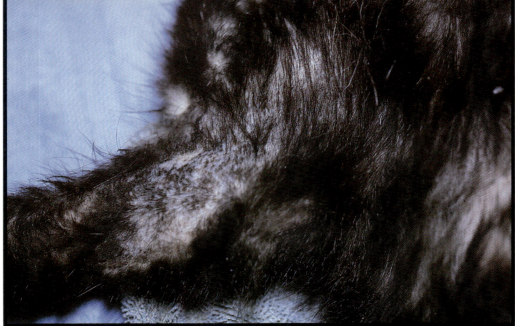

Systemic lupus erythematosus. Lesions in this cat appear as patches of hair loss and scaling on the forearms.

SKIN DISORDERS

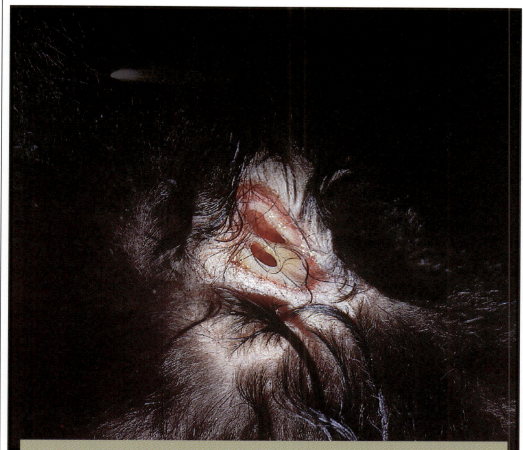

Drained abscess of the abdomen from a penetrating wound. Treatment required flushing of the wound and oral antibiotics.

these infections. The most common bacterial skin disease of cats is the abscess produced by cat bites. In reality, these abscesses are infections of the tissues beneath the skin, but as pus accumulates, the skin overlying the abscess frequently dies, allowing the abscess to drain. Treatment of abscesses involves opening and flushing the abscess cavity and systemic antibiotics to resolve the infection.

Bacterial folliculitis (inflammation of the hair follicles) and furunculosis (destruction of the follicles) are rare in cats, and most often are secondary to allergic skin disease or acne. Diagnosis is made by detecting bacteria in smears from the skin. Treatment is appropriate antibiotics and correcting any underlying cause.

There are unusual bacteria that produce unusual diseases. Cats seem particularly adept at developing these infections. The following paragraphs mention these infections briefly; they are very rare and can be challenging to diagnose.

Cutaneous tuberculosis most often occurs in animals in conjunction with infections in people. There are three organisms that produce most cases of feline tuberculosis: *Mycobacterium tuberculosis*, *Mycobacterium bovis*, and *Mycobacterium avium*. The latter two are more common in cats.

Cat Health Encyclopedia

Siamese cats may be more at risk. Respiratory and digestive tract lesions are more common than skin lesions with these infections. Cats with skin lesions have multiple ulcers, nodules, and abscesses that drain a foul discharge. Most infected cats are obviously sick. The diagnosis of tuberculosis is very difficult in the cat. Testing methods utilized for humans can be unreliable. Treatment is rarely instituted because the infected cat can be a source of infection for humans.

Leprosy is another rare bacterial skin disease. The causative agent is also a member of the *Mycobacterium* family. Signs develop most often from infected bite wounds after a long (several months) incubation. Lesions of feline leprosy appear as single or multiple nodules that may ulcerate, but do not commonly spread. Most cats do not act sick. The diagnosis is made by finding the organisms in smears from nodules, or by biopsy.

The diagnosis is confirmed by growing the bacterium in culture. If there are only a few small nodules, surgically removing these lesions may be curative. There are several different drugs used to treat feline leprosy. All drugs require a lengthy (months) treatment period.

Some opportunistic mycobacterial infections in cats do not respond to medications, leading to chronically draining and open lesions. Although infected cats may feel well throughout their infection, many owners are unwilling to keep a cat with open and draining wounds, and euthanasia is elected.

Actinomycosis is a rare bacterial infection most often caused by contamination of penetrating wounds (i.e., bites or foxtail migration) with *Actinomyces* organisms. Lesions begin as abscesses that drain a thick, foul-smelling fluid. Initially, they may look like the typical cat-fight abscess. However, they fail to respond to

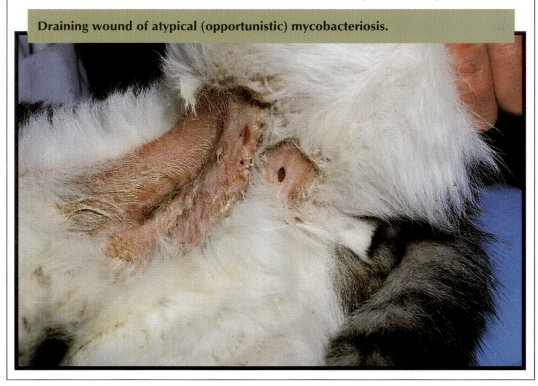

Draining wound of atypical (opportunistic) mycobacteriosis.

Skin Disorders

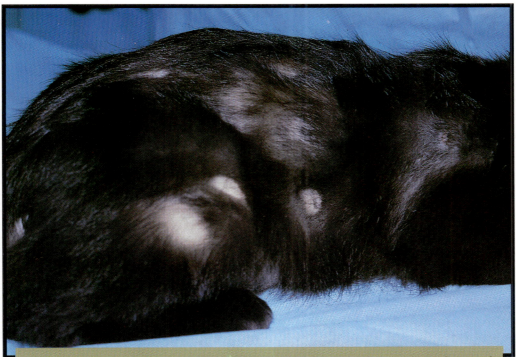

Classical lesions of dermatophyte infection are circular patches of hair loss and scale.

routine therapy. The diagnosis of actinomycosis is made by observing the organisms in biopsies or aspirates, or by culturing the organisms on special media. Treatment involves removing as much infected tissue as possible, and long-term, high-dose antibiotic therapy. Relapses are very common.

Nocardiosis, caused by *Nocardia* bacteria, also appears similar to actinomycosis, but infected cats frequently have respiratory signs as well as skin lesions, and are often ill. Diagnosis requires identification of the organism through cultures or the use of special stains on biopsy tissues. The treatment is similar to that for actinomycosis except that these cats may be more difficult to manage due to the more generalized infection.

Actinobacillosis is caused by infection with *Actinobacillus lignieresii*. Signs are similar to actinomycosis except that the discharge is usually odorless and contains many small yellow granules. The diagnosis is made by biopsy or culture. Treatment requires different medications than those for actinomycosis, which is the reason why identification of the organism is so important. But like actinomycosis, treatment length is long and relapse is common.

Plague is a significant human health hazard. Cats are very susceptible to infection by *Yersinia pestis*, the causative organism. Rodent fleas are the most common vector for this disease (cat and dog fleas are rarely implicated), although transmission by ingestion of an infected rodent is possible. Plague has three forms: bubonic, pneumonic, and septicemic. The bubonic form is the most common, and is seen as enlargement of lymph nodes with eventual abscessation and drainage. The septicemic form occurs with the bubonic form in half of infected cats. The most severe and fatal form, pneumonic plague, is uncommon. Cats infected with plague are usually very ill and develop high fevers; death can occur in 75 percent of cases without appropriate treatment. The diagnosis is made by culturing the organism from discharges. Treatment with the appropriate antibiotics can be very effective.

Fungal Skin Disease

Ringworm is the most common fungal skin infection of the cat. Ringworm is a term coined from the characteristic human lesion of a slowly expanding ring of inflammation. However, ringworm is neither caused by a worm, nor seen as a ring-like lesion in cats. Ringworm is caused by a group of fungal organisms known as dermatophytes. In the cat, almost all cases of dermatophytosis are caused by the fungus *Microsporum canis*. This infection is transmitted by contact with infected animals and people. Fungal spores can also live in the environment for a long time, leading to chronic reinfection. Management of recurrent ringworm infection in catteries can be extremely difficult. Many cats can carry the fungal organisms on their coats without showing signs of disease.

Ringworm infection in the cat does not have one specific appearance. The most common findings are patches of hair loss with fine scaling. Lesions are rarely itchy. Infection of the claws or claw folds can result in the accumulation of debris around or loss of the claws. Some cats will have generalized disease with scabbing and scaling in addition to the hair loss. Persian cats have developed deep nodules of infection, but only

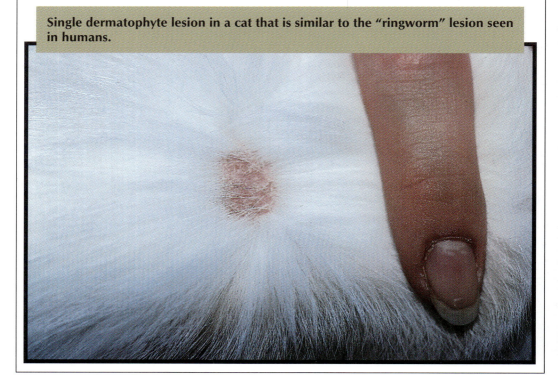

Single dermatophyte lesion in a cat that is similar to the "ringworm" lesion seen in humans.

SKIN DISORDERS

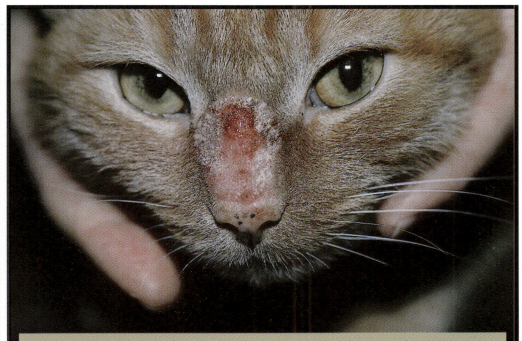

If your pet develops a suspicious skin lesion, consult your veterinarian. Do not handle your pet unless absolutely necessary and wash thoroughly with an antiseptic soap.

rarely. Longhaired cats, especially Persians and Himalayans, are particularly susceptible to ringworm infection.

The diagnosis of ringworm requires fungal culture and identification of the organisms. In about half of the cases of cat ringworm, the hair shafts will glow an apple-green color when exposed to a special black light. Unfortunately, misinterpretation of this glow is common (scales and hair treated with certain medications may glow), leading to frequent over-diagnosis of ringworm. Therefore, growth of the fungus on a culture is necessary. In many instances, especially if the lesions are unusual, dermatophytosis is diagnosed by biopsy.

Treatment of ringworm requires treating the infected animal(s) and the environment. If the environment is not treated, chronic reinfection may develop. Removal of fungal spores from the environment can be challenging. All carpeting, drapery, and furniture should be steam-cleaned thoroughly, paying close attention to maintaining boiling hot water in the machine's chambers. Lukewarm water is not fungicidal. Fungicides, such as bleach or antiseptic solutions, can be added to cleaning solutions (following all equipment manufacturer recommendations). All surfaces and walls should be wiped down with a bleach or antiseptic solution. Air filters should be changed throughout the household. All bedding, grooming devices, cages, and feeding utensils should be disinfected.

Treating ringworm on the animal may be accomplished by either topical therapy, systemic therapy, or both. Topical application of antifungal solutions, based on veterinary directions, can be used to treat milder cases and individual animals. Clipping the hair coat will assist in removing infected material; make sure hair clippers are thoroughly disinfected after the procedure. Topical antifungal rinses should be continued for six weeks, or until all lesions have healed and a negative fungal culture is obtained. Spot treating individual lesions with human antifungal creams and ointments is often disappointing because of the thick hair coat and widespread disease in cats. As a rule, all animals, infected or not, in a household should be treated with topical antifungal therapy. Systemic therapy with oral antifungal drugs should be reserved for severely infected animals and multiple infected animals in a household. Oral antifungal drugs can have severe side effects, therefore appropriate monitoring of cats undergoing therapy is vital. As with topical methods, therapy is continued for six weeks, or until a negative fungal culture is obtained.

Malassezia is a yeast organism that has recently been implicated as a cause of skin disease in cats and dogs. *Malassezia* is normally found in the ear canals and other moist regions of the body. When the skin or ear canal environment is altered, yeast overgrowth may occur. In cats, disease produced by *Malassezia* is most often seen as ear infections, severe chin acne, and generalized redness and scaling. Severe disease may be associated with concurrent FIV infection. Diagnosing *Malassezia* dermatitis requires identifying yeast organisms in exudates from the ears or skin. It may be difficult to find these organisms in biopsy samples, and culturing skin debris may be unreliable since small numbers of this yeast on the skin are considered normal. Treatment may involve topical anti-yeast rinses and/or oral

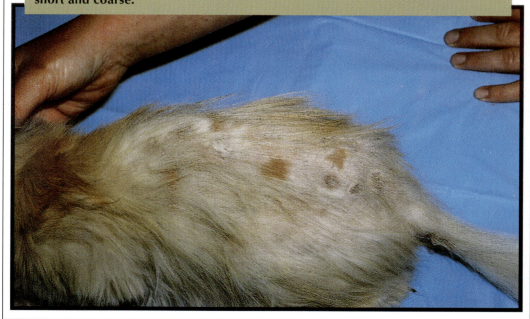

Cats infected with ringworm often experience hair loss on their heads or faces, but hair loss can also occur on other areas of their bodies. Hair that remains is usually short and coarse.

Skin Disorders

antifungal medications. Because most cases of *Malassezia* dermatitis are secondary to an underlying disease, recurrence is common unless the cause can be resolved.

Deep fungal infections are rare in cats. The names for the various types of deep fungal infections are numerous and confusing and are based on the type of organism found. Most deep fungal infections result from inoculation of the organism into the deep tissues from a traumatic wound. Eumycotic mycetoma, phaeohyphomycosis, pythiosis, and zygomycosis are all fungal infections of the deeper tissues caused by different organisms. Cutaneous signs for all deep fungal infections can be similar: singular to several draining tracts with or without adjacent nodules. Systemic signs vary. Diagnosis is made by finding organisms in biopsy tissues, and identifying the organism by culture. Treatment usually requires wide surgical removal of infected tissues. Systemic antifungal medications may help, but response is variable. Recurrence is common.

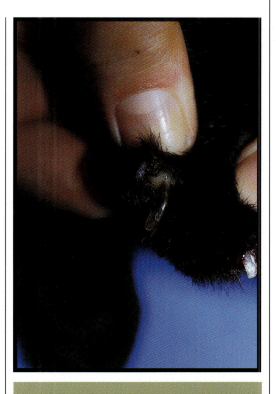

Above: Dermatophyte infection of the nailbeds. Fungal paronychia.

Below: Ulcers of the tongue induced by the feline calicivirus.

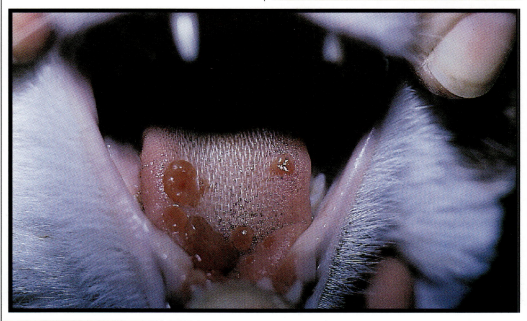

Cat Health Encyclopedia

Sporotrichosis is an uncommon fungal skin infection in cats. However, unlike the above mentioned deeper fungal infections, this disease can be contagious to humans. Infection with the organism, *Sporothrix schenckii*, most often occurs from contamination of traumatic wounds. Lesions in humans often occur from the prick of plants, such as rosebush thorns. Unlike infection in dogs and humans, where the number of fungal organisms is very low, cats harbor massive numbers of fungal organisms and thus are potentially more infective for humans. There have been multiple reports of human infection from contact with infected cats, even without a bite or scratch from the cat.

Sporotrichosis in cats most often appears as non-healing, draining nodules on the head and feet. The disease may generalize, and a rare cat will be ill. Diagnosis is made by finding numerous organisms in smears of discharges or in biopsy tissues. The organism is easily cultured; however, culturing is not recommended as it poses a significant health hazard to laboratory personnel. This disease responds moderately to antifungal therapy.

Cryptococcosis is an uncommon disease, but it is the most common deep fungal infection in cats. Most signs of infection with *Cryptococcus neoformans* involve the respiratory tract, central nervous system, and eyes. Skin disease is found in about 40 percent of cases. When skin disease is present, multiple nodules and draining tracts are seen. Organisms are usually easy to find in discharges. Disease can also be diagnosed by blood tests and by cultures. Treatment with antifungal drugs is often successful though lengthy.

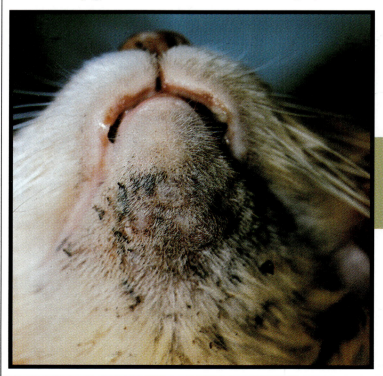

Severe chin acne in a cat. This is a frequent site of *Malassezia* infection.

Skin Disorders

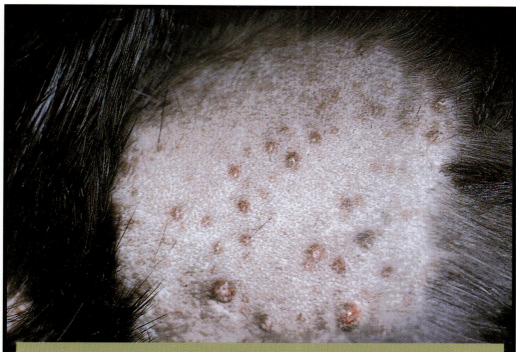

Multiple small, red, and raised skin nodules in a cat with sporotrichosis.

There are several fungal organisms that cause systemic disease, and uncommonly cause skin disease. Therefore, skin infection by one of these organisms assumes a more general infection as well. Blastomycosis, coccidioidomycosis, histoplasmosis, aspergillosis, paecilomycosis, protothecosis, trichosporonosis, and geotrichosis have all been reported in cats. Infections by these organisms most often produce non-healing draining nodules or tracts. Diagnosis requires identification of the organisms from discharges or cultures. Treatment is with antifungal medications for lengthy periods.

HORMONAL CAUSES OF SKIN DISEASE

Many hormones affect the skin. Unfortunately, cutaneous manifestations of abnormalities in these hormones can be very similar. In general, hormonal diseases cause a failure of the hair coat to regrow, a dull, dry hair coat, and regions of hair loss in a symmetric pattern. Without secondary complications, most hormonal diseases do not result in itching or discomfort.

Hyperadrenocorticism ("Cushing's syndrome") is an excess of cortisol (commonly called cortisone or "steroids") in the body. It is rarely seen in cats. The two main causes are excessive production by the body itself, or excessive administration of steroid medications, with the latter being the most common cause of the disease in cats. Signs include thinning of the skin, hair loss, and most importantly, skin fragility. Affected cats can develop large tears and rips in the skin from simple activities such as handling or grooming. Bruising of the skin and curling of the ear tips have also been described. Diagnosis requires measuring cortisol in the blood before

Cat Health Encyclopedia

and after giving drugs intended to either stimulate or suppress the adrenal gland. Depending upon the specific cause, discontinuing cortisone-based medications or surgically removing one or both adrenal glands should eventually allow the skin to return to normal.

Hyperthyroidism is a common hormonal disease in cats. This disease affects older cats and sometimes causes skin disease. In severely affected cats, excessive shedding or matting of the hair coat, hair loss from excessive grooming, thinning and scaling of the skin, and greasiness of the coat have been noted. Diagnosis of hyperthyroidism is based on a high measurement of thyroid hormone in the blood. Treatment is aimed at reducing the thyroid gland's production of hormone. Return to a normal skin and coat should follow appropriate treatment.

Diabetes mellitus is associated with several skin disorders in humans. In cats, however, skin signs are less common. Most often, excessive scaling and shedding are noted, with diabetic cats appearing unkempt. Secondary bacterial skin infections, usually rare in cats, can develop with this disease. Diagnosis and treatment of the diabetes results in normalization of the skin.

Xanthomas are small nodules that result from abnormal lipid (fat) accumulations. They have been associated with both diabetes mellitus in the cat and with other metabolic abnormalities. Diagnosis is made by biopsying the nodules. Treatment is based on correcting the diabetes (if present) or by feeding a low-fat diet.

ABNORMALITIES IN PIGMENTATION

Abnormalities in pigmentation may result from a decrease or loss of

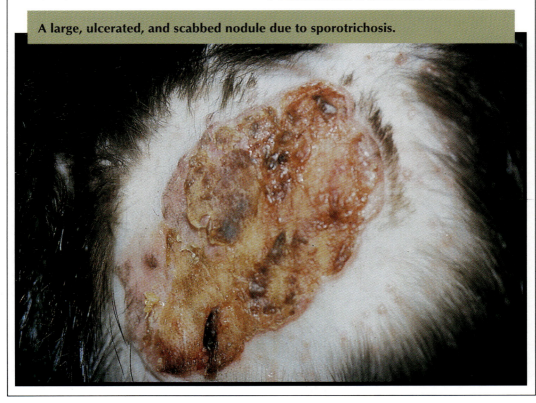

A large, ulcerated, and scabbed nodule due to sporotrichosis.

Skin Disorders

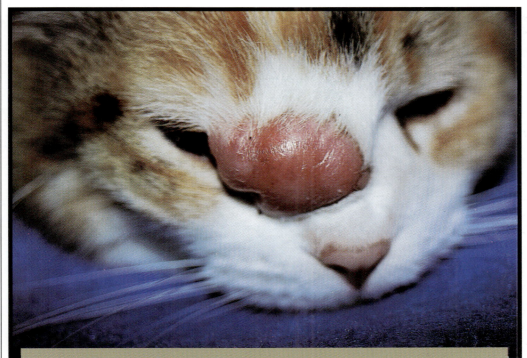

Severe bulbous mass over the nose of a cat due to cryptococcosis.

pigment (hypopigmentation) or an increase in pigmentation (hyperpigmentation). In general, the loss or gain of pigmentation is of little concern to the cat. However, human concerns with skin color changes can result in concerns over pigment changes in their cats.

The most common cause of hyperpigmentation is inflammation in the skin. Any disease that causes hair loss or inflammation can stimulate the pigment-producing cells. Once the stimulation stops, the abnormal pigmentation should also slowly resolve. Sun exposure can induce pigmentation in cats, although this is uncommon due to the protective nature of the cat's hair coat.

Lentigo refers to small patches of excessive pigmentation. These lesions have been described in orange cats and have a genetic basis. Typically, young cats develop small, black spots on the lips, nose, eyelid margins, and mouth. They are not associated with any inflammation or disease and persist throughout the year. No diagnostics or treatments are indicated for this syndrome.

Vitiligo is the loss of pigmentation in normally pigmented skin. A hereditary cause has been described in Siamese cats. Affected cats lose pigment on the nose, lips, and face. Infrequently, pigmentation returns. There is no specific diagnostic test or treatment available.

Waardenburg-Klein syndrome has been described in cats. This inheritable defect in pigment metabolism produces cats with blue eyes, deafness, and a complete lack of pigmentation of the hair coat and skin. There is no treatment currently available; affected animals should never be bred.

Hypopigmentation can develop secondary to any severe trauma to the skin and hair follicles. Burns, severe infections, and radiation therapy are the most common causes of pigmentation loss. Re-pigmentation is unusual in these cases.

Whitening of the hairs around the eyes (goggles) has been described in Siamese cats. Females are more affected than males. This syndrome of periocular whitening is usually transient and resolves within two hair cycles.

PARASITIC SKIN DISEASE

The feline skin is exposed to an environment filled with insects and parasites. In most instances, the cat's meticulous grooming habits remove parasites as they are encountered. However, if large numbers of parasites infest the skin, clinical signs of disease will develop as the cat becomes unable to remove all of the organisms on its skin. Fortunately, except for fleas and mites, parasitic skin diseases in the cat are rare. The basic treatment of all parasitic skin disease is to remove the parasite from the animal (or all animals in the household if the parasite is contagious). In some instances, environmental control is also required.

Fleas are the most common parasites affecting cats, and *Ctenocephalides felis felis* is the main culprit implicated of the 2,000 or so species of fleas found worldwide. Flea allergy was discussed earlier, and this section will discuss effective flea control strategies. To be successful, treatment must be directed not only against adult fleas but against the immature forms (eggs, larvae) as well. Safe and effective products that kill adult fleas include imidacloprid (Advantage™) and fipronil (Frontline®); products containing permethrin can be quite toxic to cats and only those licensed for use on this species should be considered. Products effective against eggs and larvae include the insect growth regulators such as pyriproxyfen and methoprene, and the insect development inhibitor lufenuron (Program®). Outdoor flea control can be achieved with insecticides (e.g., diazinon) and nematodes (microscopic worms such as *Steinernema carpocapsae*). More specific flea remedies are discussed in Dr. Karen Kuhl's chapter in *Skin and Coat Care for Your Cat,* published by T.F.H. Publications.

Arachnids include ticks, mites, and spiders. These are non-winged insects, and several are important parasites of cats. While mites are often species-specific (affecting only one type of animal), ticks are not. The significance of skin disease produced

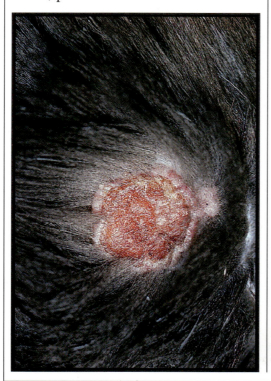

Ulcerated nodule in a cat with cryptococcosis.

Skin Disorders

Pigmented spots of lentigo in a young cat.

Otodectes mites in a smear prepared from ear debris.

by tick infestations varies with the location and environment of the cat. An indoor, urban cat is unlikely to encounter ticks in the home (although some ticks can live indoors). An outdoor cat in the lush foliage regions outside of the city is far more likely to encounter many ticks as it ventures through the underbrush. More important than the local irritation and poor cosmetic appeal of ticks, many diseases are transmitted by ticks as they feed on animals. Diseases such as Lyme, tick paralysis, and various bacterial, rickettsial, viral, and protozoal organisms can be transmitted by ticks to cats. Ticks must be removed from the skin, potential sources (foliage, etc., if possible) must be treated, and then repellent or insecticidal compounds should be applied to the cat. There are several new products on the market that prohibit attachment, encourage disattachment, repel, or kill the tick. Your veterinarian should be

Cat Health Encyclopedia

consulted regarding which products are available in your area and are most likely to be effective for your cat.

The spinous ear tick, *Otobius megnini*, is found in the external ear canals of cats and dogs in the southern United States. The immature forms of this tick feed on secretions in the ear canal. When large numbers of them infest the external ear canal, pain, swelling, and infection can develop. Treatment involves removing ticks from the ear canal, the application of insecticidal ear medications, and treating the environmental source of the infestation.

Mites are small external parasites that are found worldwide. They are a significant cause of parasitic skin disease in cats. In most instances, infested cats display signs of irritation and skin inflammation that may be severe enough to produce death in a very young or ill cat. Rarely, large infestations may cause severe, or even fatal, anemia.

The poultry mite, *Dermanyssus gallinae*, affects cats and people sporadically. In most instances, the cat is infested after exposure to bird nests or to a chicken house. Extreme itching, with crusts and scabs, occurs in infested cats. The diagnosis is made by finding mites on skin scrapings and by discovering the sources of mites. Insecticidal sprays to treat the environment should resolve the infestation.

Fur mites are generally an uncommon parasite of cats in the United States. They have been reported in Texas, Florida, and Hawaii. These mites use their first two legs to grasp and hold onto the cat's hair. They cause little irritation and may not affect more than one animal in a household, but they can be unsightly, producing a salt-and-pepper appearance and a dull hair coat. Treatment involves insecticidal sprays.

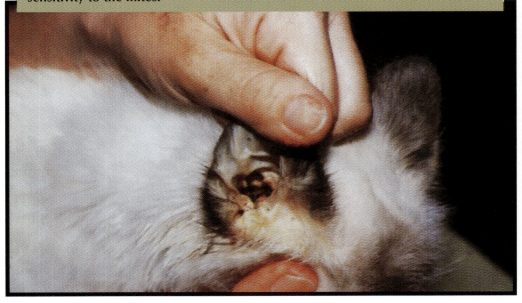

Ear mites are suspected when examination of the ears reveals coffee-ground-like material. The animal may or may not show signs of itching depending on its sensitivity to the mites.

SKIN DISORDERS

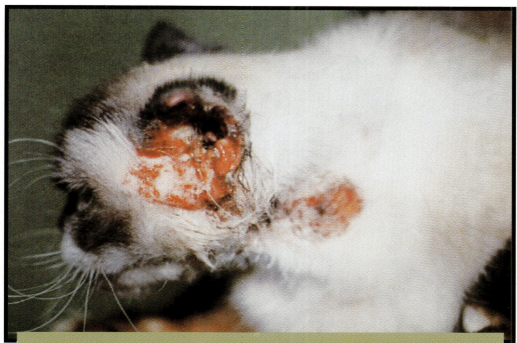

The severe itching and hair loss of this Himalayan cat are not caused by external parasites but by a food allergy.

Chiggers, or harvest mites, cause severe discomfort in summer and fall in endemic areas. These mites are distinguished from other parasites by their vivid red-orange color. They live in decaying vegetation and soil; therefore lesions are found on those areas of the body that have contact with the ground, such as the feet, head, ears, and legs. Intensely itchy lesions develop from the bite of this mite. Treatment involves insecticidal sprays and environmental control.

Otodectes cynotis is the ear mite of cats. The larvae and adults feed on debris and fluid within the ear canal. They do not burrow. As the mites feed, they cause irritation, resulting in the accumulation of wax and blood within the canal, with a classic "coffee ground" appearance. Some cats are sensitive to ear mites, while others are not. Therefore, not all cats with ear mites show signs of discomfort. Conversely, the appearance of "coffee ground" debris in the ear is not proof of mite infestation. Infestation in adult animals is rare because of developing immunity. The introduction of infested animals into the household may precipitate a generalized problem. Mites can wander beyond the ear canals to produce more generalized itching, although this is rare. Diagnosis requires finding mites in smears of ear debris. Treatment should include all animals in the household, whether obviously affected or not. Topical anti-mite insecticidal drops or injection of insecticidal medications are very effective.

The walking dandruff mite is a large mite that can be seen by the naked eye (hence the name, as mites are visible while moving through the hair coat). There are three species that are not host-specific, although *Cheyletiella blakei* is considered the

Cat Health Encyclopedia

species found in cats. These mites live freely on the skin surface, and their entire life cycle is completed on the cat. This mite can bite humans and has been reported as a source of itching in people. In cats, symptoms can range from unnoticeable to intense itching. Excessive scaling frequently develops. Diagnosis is made by finding the mites or eggs on the hairs or in the feces (as cats ingest the mites through grooming). These mites are easily killed by insecticides. Environmental cleanup is suggested. In areas with large flea populations, incidences of Cheyletiellosis are rare because of the sensitivity of mites to routine flea control products.

Demodicosis is rare in cats. This disease is produced by two species of mites, *Demodex cati*, and an unnamed species. The *Demodex* mite is a usual inhabitant of the hair follicles and migrates from the mother to the kittens during nursing. However, the cat's normal immune system effectively controls the number of mites, prohibiting the proliferation necessary to produce disease signs. When mite numbers become large, hair loss and secondary infection develop as the hair follicles become inflamed. Ear disease can occur if large mite populations develop within the ear canals. *Demodex* mites can occasionally be found in lesions of feline acne. Generalized demodicosis is often associated with an underlying disease process such as diabetes mellitus, FeLV infection, cancer, and immunosuppressive therapy. Generalized disease is most commonly reported in Siamese and Burmese cats. The diagnosis is usually made by finding mites on skin scrapings or biopsy. Treatment is aimed at reducing mite numbers through topical insecticides, as well as correcting any underlying disease process.

Notoedres cati producing a thick mantle of crusts in this cat.

Skin Disorders

Thermal facial burn in a cat resulting from a house fire. The hairs of the face and whiskers have been burned.

Feline scabies, also called feline mange, is caused by the mite *Notoedres cati*. This mite is highly contagious from cat to cat. Interestingly, cat scabies is regional in distribution—some areas have high numbers of cases, other adjacent areas have none. This mite causes an intense inflammatory reaction seen as severe crusting, scabbing, hair loss, and itching—primarily of the face, ears, and head. As the mite numbers increase, entire body itching can occur. Severe infestations lead to deterioration in the cat's condition, as it spends a great deal of time scratching rather than eating or sleeping. These mites will bite humans, and can cause inflamed and itchy red bumps on skin areas most in contact with cats (forearms and face), or at clothing edges as mites migrate. The diagnosis of scabies in the cat is relatively easy. Mite numbers on infested cats are high. Simple skin scrapings will demonstrate many mites and mite eggs. Treatment requires application of insecticidal rinses to all cats in the household. Treatment can also involve injections of an insecticidal medication.

Spider bites are more common in cats than in dogs, as cats tend to prowl around wood piles and under buildings, where spiders nest. Spider bites are most common on the face and forelegs. In general, a severe local reaction develops within hours or days of envenomation. Small puncture marks over the site of inflammation are a clue to the lesions' origin. Systemic signs may develop in certain cases. If a spider bite is suspected, immediate examination and treatment by a veterinarian are recommended to ameliorate potentially fatal generalized toxicity.

Lice (pediculosis) produce disease mainly through irritation and scratching. Significant blood loss is unusual. Lice produce signs of generalized itching, an ill-kempt hair coat, excessive scaling, and crusting. Lice infestations are most associated with poor and crowded housing conditions. Diagnosis is made by visualizing the parasite on the hair coat. Treatment is relatively simple through the use of insecticides. All animals in the household should be treated.

PSYCHOGENIC SKIN DISEASES

Psychogenic hair loss (also called neurodermatitis) is caused by constant licking and excessive grooming. The main cause of this syndrome is thought to be from anxiety that results in a displacement behavior toward grooming. Displacement behaviors are a normal activity initiated by an abnormal circumstance. With anxiety, a cat may be unable to address the source of the problem directly, and therefore may begin to groom itself continuously as a way to show its distress. Common causes of anxiety include a new cat in the environment (inside or outside the home), a new member in the family (baby), loss of a family member (animal or human), or moving to a new home. Psychogenic hair loss is not caused by a lack of hair growth. Instead, cats are meticulously removing hairs as they grow. Evidence of this is demonstrated by examining hair shafts for breakage, or by revealing active hair growth within follicles on a skin biopsy. Neurodermatitis lesions occur anywhere that a cat can lick or groom itself. Typically, the belly, outer and inner areas of the thighs, and the front of the forelegs are affected. If the licking is chronic, inflammation of the skin may develop. The characteristic symmetrical pattern of hair loss

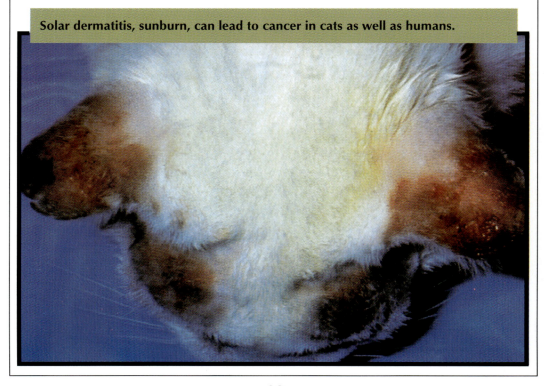

Solar dermatitis, sunburn, can lead to cancer in cats as well as humans.

Skin Disorders

Ulcerated lesions on the upper lip of a cat with indolent ulcer.

should raise the suspicion of a psychogenic cause. The diagnosis of psychogenic hair loss is made by excluding other diseases; the possibility of inflammatory or infectious causes of hair loss must be investigated. Treatment of this disorder is difficult, particularly if the behavior has persisted for any length of time. Even if the original cause of the behavior is removed, the habitual behavior can continue. If the anxiety-producing problem is resolved quickly, anti-anxiety drugs can reduce the excessive grooming, possibly leading to eventual cure.

Tail sucking is a syndrome seen in Siamese cats in which the tail tip is continuously licked. Minimal changes in the skin develop, but the hair is removed, leaving a bald end. Most often associated with boredom, this habit can be eliminated by changes in the lifestyle of the cat.

ENVIRONMENTAL SKIN DISEASE

The hair coat is wonderful protection for the skin. It shields the skin from the sun as well as from many caustic or irritating substances. For this reason, chemical skin inflammation, such as poison oak, is rarely seen in cats. There are specific regions of the skin that are not protected by a thick hair coat, such as the nose, the inner aspects of the ear flaps, eyelid and lip margins, underbelly, anal area, and the bottom of the feet. These areas are more prone to environmental diseases.

Feline solar dermatitis is a form of chronic sunburn and is seen most often in white-haired cats. The eyelids, ears, nose, and lips are most often affected. Constant sun exposure leads to sun damage, which appears as redness, scaling, and eventual hair loss. Chronic sun damage increases the risk of developing squamous cell carcinoma, a skin cancer that can be aggressive and difficult to treat. The diagnosis of both solar dermatitis and skin cancer is made by biopsy. Solar dermatitis can be suspected based on the history and color of the cat. Treating solar dermatitis is accomplished by restricting the cat inside the house during high sun intensity (especially the afternoon hours). Application of sun block is helpful but usually difficult in cats. Aggressive surgical removal of cancers is required. Chemotherapy, radiation therapy, and photodynamic treatment of cancer sites are also utilized.

Burns may be caused by chemicals, electricity, or heat. In cats, burns are most often caused by heat from fires, boiling liquids, hot metals, or excessive blow drying. Heating pads are also a significant cause of burns because temperatures produced by them can fluctuate. As with all burns, the length of exposure, the temperature of the heat source, and the area of skin affected will determine the severity of the burn. In severe burn cases, significant loss of body fluids in addition to overall infection due to the loss of protection by the skin leads to rapid death. The full extent of a cat's burn may not be evident for several days after an incident, as skin that was less severely burned gradually dies. The diagnosis of burns is usually obvious by clinical signs of skin death and a history of heat exposure. Treatment of burns is aimed at maintaining the cat's hydration, reducing pain, encouraging healing of new skin, and preventing or treating infection. Treatment is slow and requires weeks or months of attention.

Frostbite is caused by prolonged exposure to freezing temperatures. Areas of the body most at risk for

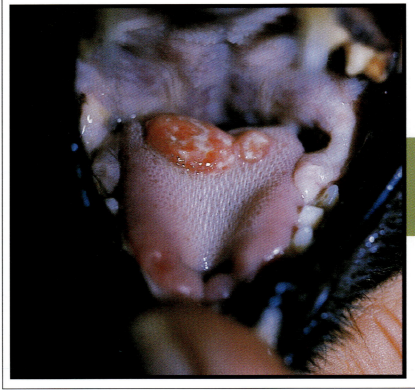

Raised plaques on the tongue in a cat with eosinophilic plaques.

42

Skin Disorders

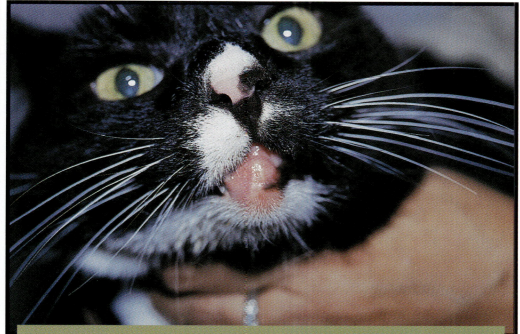

Protruding, swollen, and inflamed chin (pouting) associated with eosinophilic granuloma.

frostbite include the ear tips, tail tip, and digits. After thawing, affected regions may die and slough. In milder cases, loss or whitening of hairs may be seen. In cases of frostbite, gentle warming of the tissues will help to reduce the severity of damage.

Foreign bodies cause skin disease in cats when they induce a tissue reaction or secondary infection. Quills and plant awns are the most common foreign bodies. Lesions from foreign bodies consist of abscess and draining tracts as the object migrates through tissues. Treatment requires removing the foreign body and long-term antibiotics for the secondary infection.

MISCELLANEOUS CONDITIONS

Plasma cell pododermatitis is rare in the cat. The disease starts as a painless swelling of multiple foot pads, especially the large ones. Lameness may occur, but the cat otherwise feels fine. Diagnosis is made by biopsying the affected pads. Treatment is challenging, but oral steroids are most often administered.

Sebaceous adenitis is very rare in the cat. In this disease, an immune response is directed against the sebum-producing glands in the skin, resulting in their destruction. Lesions consist of areas of scale, adherent crust, and hair loss primarily on the head and neck. The diagnosis is made by biopsy. Therapy, other than frequent bathing, is generally nonproductive.

Feline eosinophilic granuloma complex is a group of syndromes that is at best confusing. Three specific lesions have been identified: the indolent ulcer, eosinophilic plaque, and eosinophilic granuloma. Most of these lesions are believed to have an allergic origin, although a heritable basis has also been documented. Distinguishing between the three

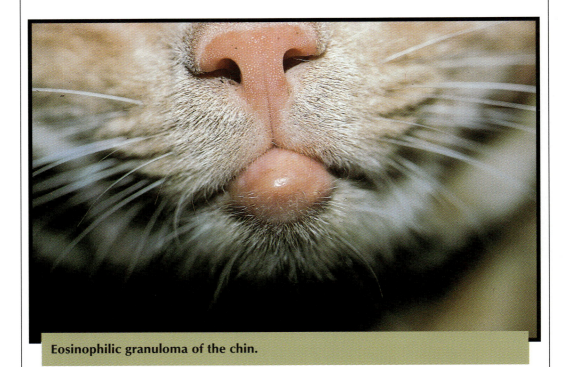

Eosinophilic granuloma of the chin.

lesions is based on clinical signs and biopsy results. Treatment is usually based on attempting to find an underlying allergy, although in many cases none is found. The use of corticosteroids is often required but must be administered with care. Rarely, more powerful chemotherapy drugs are used.

The indolent ulcer is a common skin lesion that is most often seen as thickening of the upper lip near the center. Frequently, the lesions develop ulcerations that are well demarcated and glistening. Rare lesions can develop inside the mouth. Although they look painful, they rarely are; and cats usually show no signs associated with these lesions.

The eosinophilic plaque is the most common lesion in this complex. Most plaques occur on the belly and thighs, but lesions can develop anywhere. They appear as raised, hairless, reddened, and oozing patches.

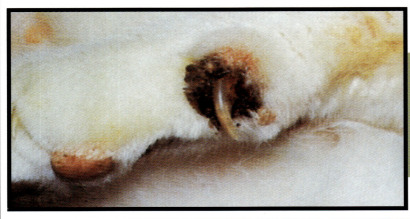

In squamous-cell carcinoma, the skin is dark and thickened.

Skin Disorders

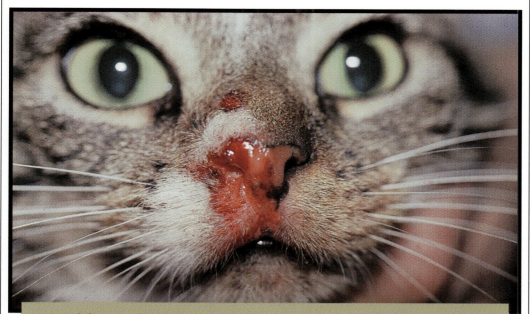

Eosinophilic granuloma involving the nose with bleeding and ulceration. Biopsy is required to differentiate this disease from cancers that develop on the face and nose. It may look painful, but apparently does not usually cause the animal much discomfort.

The eosinophilic granuloma is the third type of lesion in this complex. Two distinct types are seen. The linear granuloma most often develops on the backs of the thighs as a long, thin, raised, inflamed lesion. Overlying scabbing can be seen. The second distribution is seen on the face as swellings and nodules. Cats with this lesion on their lower chins will appear to "pout" or have a chin that sticks out. Any of the three types of lesions can occur in conjunction with the other two forms of the eosinophilic granuloma complex.

Feline ulcerative dermatitis is a rare disease of cats. This lesion develops as a single patch of hair loss and scabbing between the shoulder blades. It is not itchy, although it appears as though the cat might be scratching the area because of the extensive scabbing and ulceration. The cause is unknown. Lesions are usually cured by surgical removal.

Diseases that affect the skin can also affect the ears and claws. Specific syndromes that commonly affect these structures include the autoimmune disorders, allergies, and external parasites. Signs associated with these diseases are mentioned under their appropriate topic. In rare cases, ear or claw lesions may be the only sign of disease in the cat. Polyps, tumors, and foreign bodies are unusual reasons for diseases affecting only the ear. Congenital abnormalities of the claw and infections within the claw bed itself occur rarely. Diagnosis requires a full examination of the ear canals or claw and claw fold, as well as tests such as biopsy or radiographs.

RECOMMENDED READING
Ackerman, L (Ed.): *Skin and Coat Care for Your Cat.* TFH Publications, Neptune City, NJ, 1996, 158pp.

Dr. Dennis C. Law

Dr. Terry Silkman

Dr. Dennis C. Law graduated from Colorado State University with his DVM degree in 1982. He is currently associated with the Cat Clinic and Cottonwood Animal Hospital as a surgeon and does referral mobile surgery at numerous clinics in the greater Salt Lake City area. Dr. Law has had a strong interest in orthopedic surgery and has practiced primarily in general surgery, orthopedic surgery, and spinal surgery since 1987.

Dr. Law has been a member of the Veterinary Orthopedic Society, an international organization of veterinary orthopedic surgeons, for the past 10 years and is currently serving as president of that organization. Dr. Law is also very active in local, state, and national veterinary organizations.

Dr. Terry Silkman received a DVM degree from Colorado State University in 1990. Interest in soft tissue and orthopedic surgery led to a search that brought Dr. Silkman to join the staff of Cottonwood Animal Hospital in 1993. Since joining CAH, Dr. Silkman has continued to pursue interests in orthopedic surgery and medicine, including long bone, pelvic, and spinal surgery as well as general small animal practice. Professional affiliations include membership in the Veterinary Orthopedic Society, the American Veterinary Medical Association, as well as local and state veterinary medical associations. Dr. Silkman is also currently certified with International Canine Genetics in reproduction and the Pennsylvania Hip Improvement Program.

DISORDERS OF THE MUSCULOSKELETAL SYSTEM

By Dennis C. Law, DVM
and Terry Silkman, DVM

Cottonwood Animal Hospital
6360 South Highland Drive
Salt Lake City, UT 84121

INTRODUCTION

Traditionally, feline orthopedics, like many other areas of feline medicine and surgery, has been approached with a rather casual attitude. When dealing with fractures in cats, it is often said that "if the bone fragments are in the same room they will heal." We know that cats do not have "nine lives" and that feline fractures will not always heal without proper treatment; however, these ideas have evolved from centuries of observing cats responding to injury and illness. Cats have an amazing ability to compensate and cope with disease and trauma. This uncanny ability to heal and compensate under less-than-ideal circumstances has led to a potentially blasé approach to feline orthopedics. As veterinarians and feline enthusiasts, we must demand and strictly apply the proper principles and concepts of trauma and disease management to achieve the best results possible for our feline patients.

Most of the general principles of orthopedics are directly applicable to cats. However, as the number of domestic cats increases, a thorough understanding of the conditions unique to cats is essential to everyone associated with feline health care.

The bone structure of cats is different from dogs in that the long

Polyarthritis associated with systemic lupus erythematosus. The cat is painful in nearly all of her joints and reluctant to move about.

bones tend to be narrower and straighter in proportion to length. The cortex, or walls of the bone, also tends to be thinner and more brittle than those of dogs. These points are especially important to consider in fracture management. The feline nature and ability to compensate for physically debilitating problems often lead to advanced disease before discovery and presentation occur. Vigilance and care must be exercised to avoid missing early symptoms that would allow small problems to become more serious.

Proper treatment requires an accurate, concise diagnosis. The diagnosis of orthopedic disease is based on a thorough history, complete physical examination, and effective radiographic evaluation.

Cat Health Encyclopedia

The history most often associated with bone, muscle, and joint diseases is one of an abnormal gait, lameness, or a notable swelling or mass. Details such as age of onset, duration of the signs, and severity are essential in arriving at an accurate diagnosis. Other important factors when taking or providing an adequate history are: geographic location, life style of the cat (indoor vs. outdoor), diet, sex, age, and related family history.

A complete physical exam should include a thorough general physical including temperature, pulse, and respiration. Each system of the body should be evaluated to avoid missing other related or unrelated problems. Particular care must be exercised in evaluating the musculoskeletal system. Localization of pain or discomfort, inhibited range of motion in painful joints, lack of normal stability in bones or joints, or excessive swelling of bone, joints, or muscles are all important signs in the evaluation of a musculoskeletal problem.

The amount of information gained from radiographs in the diagnoses and treatment of feline orthopedic diseases may vary greatly from case to case. In the management of fractures, it is essential to have good-quality radiographs. Joint disease, on the other hand, may or may not have significant radiographic changes. The lack of obvious radiographic changes might indicate soft tissue disease affecting muscle, tendon, or

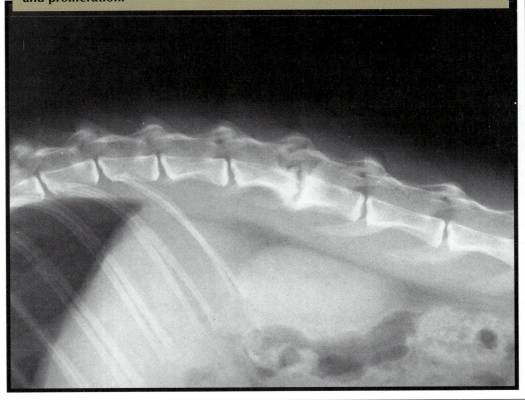

Osteomyelitis in the spine: Diskospondylitis or infection of the inter-vertebral disk and adjacent bone of the vertebral body endplates, demonstrating both bony lysis and proliferation.

Disorders of the Musculoskeletal System

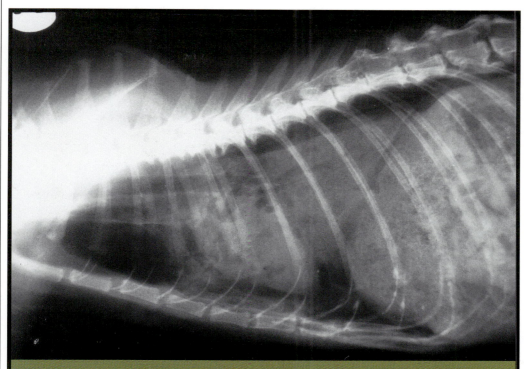

Collapsed lungs secondary to trauma resulting in: a. diaphragmatic hernia (abdominal organs displace into the chest); b. pneumothorax (air in the chest).

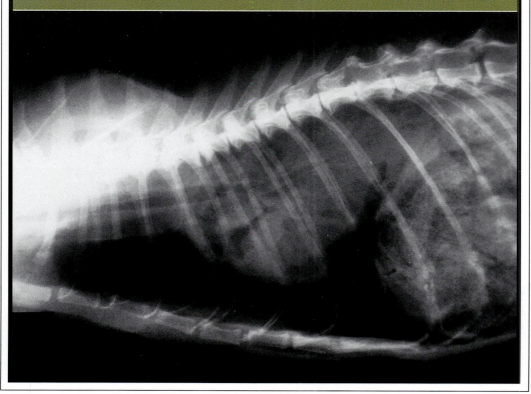

CAT HEALTH ENCYCLOPEDIA

cartilage. The presence and location of a lesion or the complete lack of radiographic changes are both important in the localization and diagnosis of disease in the cat's musculoskeletal system.

INFLAMMATORY DISEASES

Inflammation is an important aspect of most disease processes. In this section we will deal with diseases of the musculoskeletal system in which inflammation is the major component in the development of the signs and symptoms of these diseases. Inflammatory diseases can be divided into two groups based on the cause of the disease: infectious diseases and non-infectious diseases.

Infectious Diseases

Infectious musculoskeletal diseases are the result of the invasion and proliferation of microorganisms, and the body's response to those microorganisms. The organisms most often responsible for causing orthopedic disease in cats are bacteria, viruses, mycoplasmas, and fungi.

In adult cats, bacterial diseases are most often caused by penetrating wounds. Cat bites, gunshot wounds, automobile trauma, and surgery are frequent routes by which bacteria gain access to the musculoskeletal system. Neonates and immune-suppressed cats, such as those with FIV (feline immunodeficiency virus) or FeLV (feline leukemia virus), and cats receiving chemotherapy or corticosteroid therapy are more susceptible to blood-borne bacterial infections.

Viruses, mycoplasmas, and fungi, on the other hand, generally gain access to cats' bones, muscles, and joints via the blood stream after invading the gastrointestinal and/or respiratory systems. Immuno-suppressed cats are generally more susceptible to infections caused by any of these microorganisms.

OSTEOMYELITIS

Osteomyelitis is an infection of the bone. Most commonly it is the result of a bacterial infection introduced through a periodontal infection, penetrating wound, open fracture, or surgical incision. Although aerobic and anaerobic bacteria are the most common agents involved, fungal organisms such as *Coccidioides immitis* are also capable of infecting cats' bones. Surgical or wound-introduced osteomyelitis is usually associated with soft tissue swelling, pain, heat, and sometimes drainage at the site of infection. Radiographic changes in the bone are often much more subtle than in the dog. They may appear to be somewhat osteolytic (bone destroying), with occasional areas of adjacent periosteal reaction and proliferation. Hematogenous (spread by blood) osteomyelitis may occur in several locations simultaneously and tends to affect the medullary, or inner cavity, of the bone. Periodontal osteomyelitis is most often associated with extension of severe gum disease. Radiographs of periodontal osteomyelitis frequently demonstrate lysis (destruction) of the bone surrounding the tooth roots.

The treatment of feline osteomyelitis is based upon the same principles as applied to the treatment of any other infection. First, all devitalized tissue, sequestra (dead bone), loose teeth, and foreign material or loose orthopedic implants must be

Disorders of the Musculoskeletal System

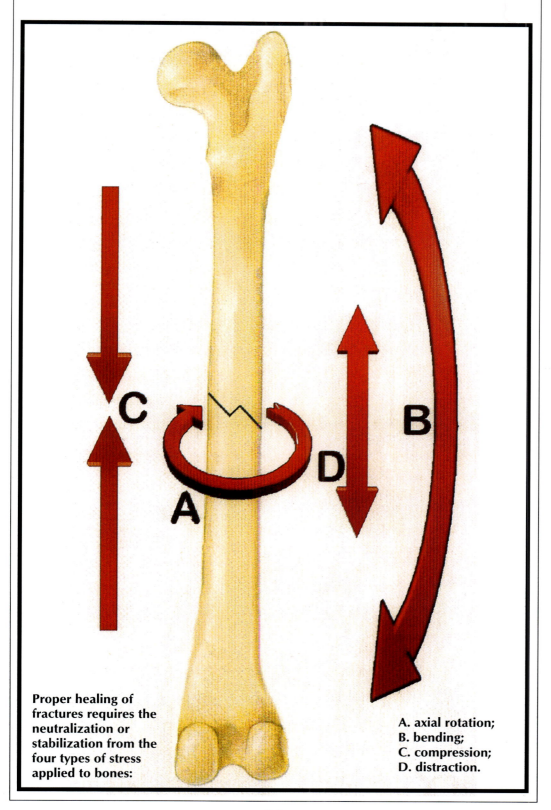

Proper healing of fractures requires the neutralization or stabilization from the four types of stress applied to bones:

A. axial rotation;
B. bending;
C. compression;
D. distraction.

CAT HEALTH ENCYCLOPEDIA

removed. Second, adequate drainage should be provided. Third, proper antibiotic therapy should be initiated. Bacterial culture and antibiotic sensitivity are valuable tools in the selection of an effective antibiotic. The prognosis for feline osteomyelitis is fair to good when all of the above steps can be followed. When osteomyelitis affects the vertebrae or bones where debridement (removal of devitalized and dead tissue) and drainage are not easily achieved, or there is an organism such as *Coccidioides immitis*, long-term prognosis is substantially poorer.

VIRAL-ASSOCIATED BONE DISEASE

Although reports of viral bone infections are uncommon, FeLV-associated bone lesions have been reported. These infections seem to stimulate an osteogenic (bone-forming) reaction, causing increased osteogenesis (growth of new bone) in the trabecular bone and marrow cavity of the long bones of infected cats. A diagnosis must be made on the basis of radiographic changes in light of positive serology for FeLV infection.

SEPTIC ARTHRITIS

Septic (bacterial) arthritis results from bacterial colonization and infection of a joint. In kittens, this disease is usually the result of a blood-borne infection initiated when the mother chews off the umbilicus of the kitten. In adult cats, septic arthritis is more commonly the result of a cat fight or other penetrating wound.

The diagnosis of septic arthritis is based upon history, physical exam, and clinicopathologic data. Septic arthritis is generally a disease of the soft tissue of the joint. Therefore, radiographs generally do not reveal

bone involvement. The history may indicate some type of injury or trauma such as a cat bite, gunshot wound, etc. Lameness, joint swelling, and joint pain are usually part of the presenting picture. Elevated temperature, inappetence, and reluctance to move are also commonly seen. Affected cats may or may not have an elevated white blood cell count.

Joint taps and microscopic analysis of the synovial (joint) fluid aid in the definitive diagnosis of septic arthritis. Joint fluid from affected cats will most often contain white blood cells and bacteria, both of which are generally not found in normal joint fluid. The normal sticky, viscous nature of joint fluid is lost in joints affected with septic arthritis; instead it is a more watery or serous fluid.

The treatment of septic arthritis requires drainage and clearing the affected joint of the lytic destructive fluid caused by the bacteria and inflammation in the joint. Appropriate antibacterial drugs are selected, based on synovial fluid culture and antibiotic sensitivity.

VIRAL ARTHRITIS

Viral arthritis is rare in cats. Chronic progressive polyarthritis has been shown to have a statistical association with feline syncytium forming virus (FeSFV) and feline leukemia virus (FeLV). Even though there is an association with these viruses, chronic progressive polyarthritis is considered to be an immune-mediated disease and is not reproducible with experimentally induced infections of FeSFV and FeLV. Therefore, chronic progressive polyarthritis will be discussed in the section on non-infectious inflammatory disease.

DISORDERS OF THE MUSCULOSKELETAL SYSTEM

Examples of two types of coaptation devices used to stabilize fractures: *Right:* Mason metasplint; *Below:* modified Thompson splint.

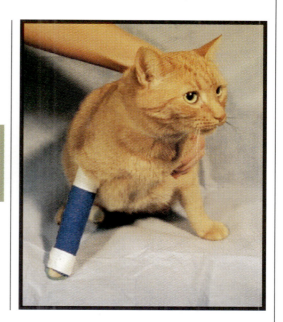

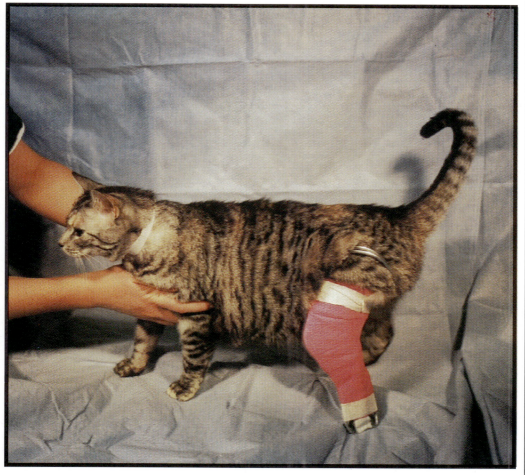

Cat Health Encyclopedia

Some strains of calicivirus are capable of causing viral arthritis in kittens. This disease is generally a mild self-limiting disease characterized by joint pain, fever, reluctance to move, and slight upper respiratory disease. Calicivirus vaccines may not be protective against these so-called "arthralgic" strains of calicivirus.

Mycoplasmal Arthritis

Mycoplasmal arthritis is rare in cats. Mycoplasmas are common in the oropharynx and upper respiratory tract of cats, and may in some circumstances, such as in immune-compromised patients, become opportunistic pathogens causing an infectious arthritis. Diagnosis depends on the isolation and demonstration of *Mycoplasma* from the affected joints. Proper treatment must address any underlying causes as well as provide the proper antibiotic therapy. Mycoplasmal infections are most sensitive to treatment with tetracycline, doxycycline, tylosin, erythromycin, and chloramphenicol.

Fungal Arthritis

Primary fungal infections of the joints of cats are rare. Hematogenous spread of systemic fungal infections or extension of local fungal infections of the bone or skin can cause secondary fungal arthritis. Histoplasmosis and cryptococcosis have both been reported as pathogens affecting the joints of cats.

Diagnosis and treatment of fungal arthritis relies on the identification and culture of the offending fungus from the joint.

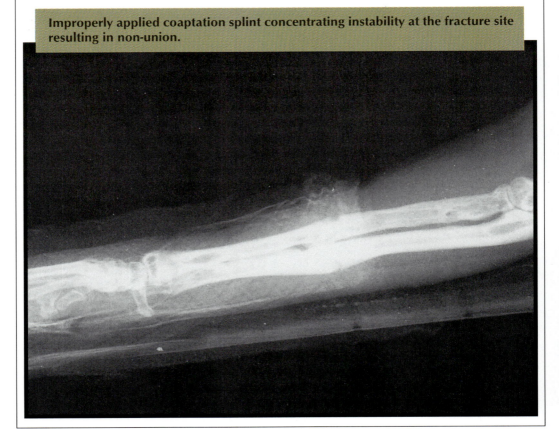

Improperly applied coaptation splint concentrating instability at the fracture site resulting in non-union.

DISORDERS OF THE MUSCULOSKELETAL SYSTEM

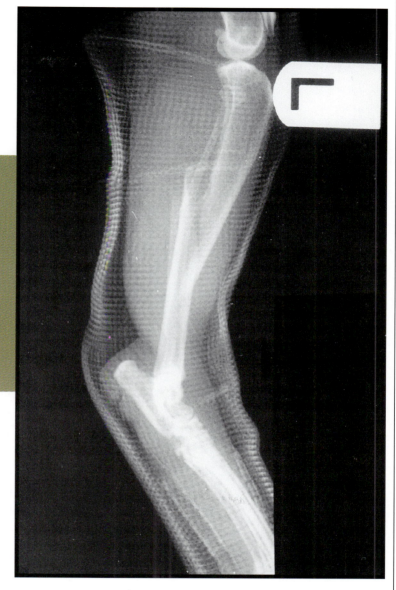

Radiograph of a fractured tibia managed with a fiberglass cast. Note the overriding ends of the fracture fragments due to the cast's inability to neutralize compressive forces.

Non-Infectious Inflammatory Diseases

Non-infectious inflammatory diseases tend to be immune-mediated, auto- or self-destructive processes. They also tend to be more generalized in their effects on the musculoskeletal system or the body as a whole. Because of their complexity and variability, they can be frustrating and challenging to diagnose and treat. Many of the tests used to diagnose these diseases are prone to false negatives; therefore, negative results are rather meaningless. Positive results are much more reliable.

In cats, the non-infectious inflammatory diseases of the musculoskeletal system are most often diseases of the joints. The diseases that we will discuss are chronic progressive polyarthritis, systemic lupus erythematosus (SLE), and polyarteritis nodosa.

CAT HEALTH ENCYCLOPEDIA

CHRONIC PROGRESSIVE POLYARTHRITIS

The most common disease in this group of immune-mediated diseases is chronic progressive polyarthritis. This disease is almost entirely limited to male cats. All breeds are at risk, and young adult cats are most often affected.

Although the cause of chronic progressive polyarthritis is not completely understood, it is thought that it is an immune-mediated disease. Most cats with chronic progressive polyarthritis also test positive for feline syncytium-forming virus (FeSFV). Nearly seventy percent of the cats in one study also tested positive for FeLV. Although cats do not get chronic progressive polyarthritis by simply being infected with FeLV or FeSFV, there is a statistical connection. Evidence indicates that the development of the disease is immune mediated.

Diagnosis is based on clinical signs, history, radiographic evaluation, and clinicopathologic data. The history of an adult male cat from one to five years old with polyarthritis strongly suggests the possibility of chronic progressive polyarthritis. Clinically affected cats show signs of generalized discomfort in most, if not all, of their joints. Radiographically, there are two presentations, or types, of this disease. First, there is the proliferative form. The proliferative form of chronic progressive polyarthritis is characterized early in the process by swelling of the periarticular soft tissues. As the disease progresses, periosteal new bone is formed, especially near the attachments of joint-related soft tissue. The bones of the lower legs, both front and back, are most commonly affected. More advanced cases may demonstrate lytic lesions in the same areas. The second form of the disease is referred to as the deforming type of polyarthritis. These cats show considerable destruction and deformation of the joints in the lower legs. If they become severe enough, they may result in dislocations.

Laboratory analysis of the synovial fluid from multiple joints will demonstrate an elevated cell count, decreased viscosity, and yellow-tinged synovial fluid. The joints are often distended with excess joint fluid. Culture and/or microscopic evaluation should confirm the absence of bacteria or other microorganisms.

Effective treatment of chronic progressive polyarthritis depends on control or suppression of the immune system. Prednisone and other glucocorticoids at fairly high doses are used alone or in conjunction with other immune-suppressive or cytotoxic drugs such as azathioprine (Imuran®) and cyclophosphamide (Cytoxan®). These drugs suppress the immune system, thereby limiting the disease process.

The long term prognosis for cats with chronic progressive polyarthritis is fairly guarded. Most cats will respond to prednisone and/or other immune-suppressive drugs. Some cases will achieve a complete remission. However, this disease tends to be progressive in nature. Most cats with this disease continue to suffer from the disease to a lesser degree. The clinical and radiographic signs will still progress at a slower rate. Some cats with this disease will respond to one or a combination of drugs when they do not respond to others, so it may be advantageous to try a variety of drugs singly or in combination.

SYSTEMIC LUPUS ERYTHEMATOSUS

Systemic lupus erythematosus (SLE) is an autoimmune disease

DISORDERS OF THE MUSCULOSKELETAL SYSTEM

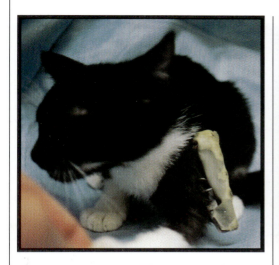

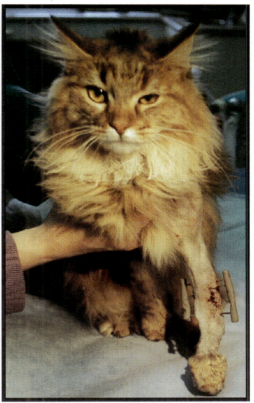

There are many possible configurations in designing external fixation devices. Here are examples of a few: *Above:* unilateral external fixator with acrylic molded connecting bar; *Right:* bilateral external fixator with acrylic connecting bar; *Below:* radiograph of a fractured tibia with a bilateral external fixator with metal connecting bars and metal clamps.

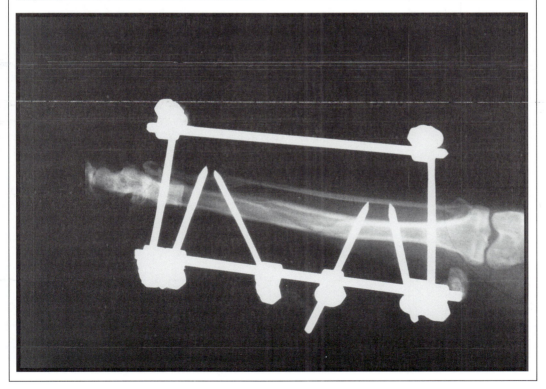

57

characterized by the immune system's forming antibodies against certain normal proteins in the patient's own body. SLE arthritis is only one small part of a generalized disease that may affect many organ systems of the body. The disease is characterized by immune complexes (antigen-antibody complexes) being deposited in various areas of the body. When they are deposited in the synovial membrane (joint lining), they initiate a potent inflammatory reaction. This inflammatory reaction causes the arthritis.

Diagnosis is based on the presence of multiple painful, swollen, inflamed joints in conjunction with disease signs in multiple other organ systems. Laboratory tests are essential in the diagnosis of SLE. Positive ANA (antinuclear antibody) tests are essential for a reliable diagnosis. ANA tests are often falsely negative; therefore, a negative ANA test does not conclusively mean that the cat does not have lupus. False-positive ANA tests are also common in cats with cholangiohepatitis and FeLV infections. Affected cats often have low white blood cell counts and high levels of complement in the blood. Histopathologic and immunopathologic analyses of tissue samples from other organs or skin that show characteristic features of lupus and/or deposition of immune complexes in the basement membranes may also be helpful in diagnosing SLE.

Treatment and prognosis for SLE is much the same as for chronic progressive polyarthritis. Prednisone or other immune-suppressive drugs are used individually or in concert to achieve control or at least suppression of the disease. Relapse is common and, in most cases, affected cats eventually succumb to the disease.

POLYARTERITIS NODOSA-ASSOCIATED ARTHRITIS

Polyarteritis nodosa is a rare disease in cats that can affect the joints as well as other systems of the body. It is caused by the inflammation and damage of the arteries by deposition of immune complexes and activation of complement. The vasculitis associated with feline infectious peritonitis can be very similar to polyarteritis nodosa and may lead to misdiagnosis. Palliative treatment is often effective using corticosteroids and/or cytotoxic drugs.

TRAUMATIC DISEASE

In spite of their agile, cautious, and athletic nature, cats are frequently involved in traumatic accidents. Automobiles, garage doors, large dogs, boots, bicycles, and firearms are but a few of the many objects that cats confront resulting in traumatic injury. As in most diseases, the environment plays an important part in the distribution and occurrence of various types of trauma and should be considered when evaluating each case. Preventive medicine and client education are extremely important concepts for the veterinarian and cat enthusiast to consider in dealing with cases of trauma or potential trauma. Prevention is much more important than good therapy.

The evaluation and therapeutic plan must be carefully developed and evaluated for each patient. Once a patient is stabilized from the initial injury, a thorough treatment plan must be made, taking into account each system involved in the injury. Care must be taken not to miss injuries that are not obvious. Less obvious injuries such as ruptured bladders, diaphragmatic hernias, and collapsed lungs due to pneumothorax or hemothorax are frequently

DISORDERS OF THE MUSCULOSKELETAL SYSTEM

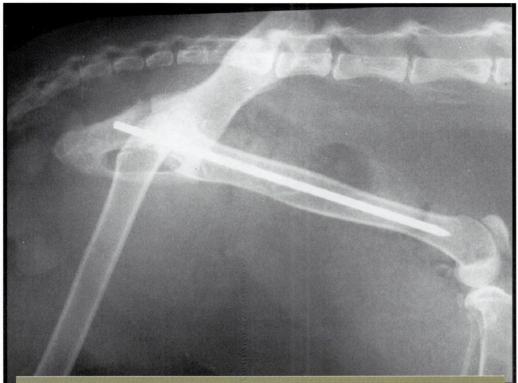

Fracture of the femur stabilized with an intramedullary pin. This fracture has healed well in spite of the relatively small size of the pin.

overlooked due to the dramatic nature of orthopedic injuries and the cat's ability to tolerate and compensate for serious injuries. Each problem must be assessed and prioritized, then treated accordingly.

Long Bone Fractures

For the purposes of this description, long bone fractures will be defined as fractures of the forelimbs to the level of the shoulder joint and hind limbs to the level of the hip joint. In order to maintain an effective scaffold for the body and a fulcrum for muscle contraction, bones must be able to neutralize the forces of bending, rotation, and compression (shortening). The veterinarian must consider each of these three forces and select a method of fixation that will effectively neutralize each of them, if fracture healing is to be achieved. Rather than discussing each individual bone fracture, we intend to summarize the various options for treating long bone fractures, i.e.: external coaptation (casts, splints, and braces), intramedullary pinning, interfragmentary fixation (screws and wires), external skeletal fixation (K-E fixators, ring fixators), and bone plating.

External coaptation is the method of fracture fixation that utilizes such devices as casts, support bandages, and splints to provide support and immobilization of the joint above and below the fracture site for a sufficient amount of time to allow fracture healing. Coaptation can effectively neutralize bending forces and in

CAT HEALTH ENCYCLOPEDIA

some instances rotational forces, but cannot neutralize compressive forces.

Unfortunately, due to perceived or real cost concerns, coaptation is often used to treat fractures for which it was not intended, frequently with poor results. The use of coaptation should be limited to:

- Fractures distal (below or closer to the foot) to the mid-shaft of the radius and tibia.
- Simple, closed, short oblique, or transverse fractures that are relatively stable with respect to compression and rotation.

Fractures proximal (above or closer to the body) to the mid-shaft of the radius and tibia are poor candidates for coaptation because of the difficulty in immobilizing the elbow and stifle (knee), leading to fracture instability and nonunion.

Open fractures, and fractures in which there is extensive soft tissue damage, are poor candidates for coaptation because of the risk of infection due to trapping contamination in the wound and the potential of creating a tourniquet effect on the limb from severe swelling occurring under the coaptation device. Comminuted (fragmented) or long oblique fractures tend to collapse and shorten due to the inability of coaptation to neutralize compression.

In our experience, long oblique fractures, open or contaminated fractures, comminuted fractures, and fractures proximal to the middle of the radius and tibia are excellent fractures for external fixators. There are many types of and modifications to external fixation devices, but the common characteristics of all external skeletal fixation devices are that a minimum of two pins will be placed in the fracture fragment that includes the joint above the fracture and that another two pins will be

placed in the fragment that includes the joint below the fracture. The pins will be placed through the skin, trapping as little muscle, tendon, and other soft tissue as possible, and into both the near and far cortex of the bone. The pin placement can stop at the far cortex of the bone or extend through the soft tissue and skin on the far side of the limb so that a second connecting bar can be applied. The exposed ends of the pins are then connected using clamps and bars, rings, or acrylic cements to form a rigid external column that transfers force from the upper joint through the column to the lower joint without placing stress on and movement of the healing fracture. Advantages of this type of fixator include:

- The ability to achieve very rigid fixation. External fixators can neutralize bending compression and rotational forces.
- Minimal equipment and expense required.
- Immediate weight bearing is possible.
- Pins can be placed to avoid infected or contaminated fracture sites and wounds can be left open for debridement and drainage.
- Injury to joint cartilage and interference with joint mobility are alleviated.
- Less risk of osteomyelitis or infection at the fracture site.

For tibial and radial fractures, external fixation is the authors' method of choice. The large muscle mass and inability to place pins and connecting bars on the medial side of the bone make other techniques preferable to external fixators for repairing fractures of the humerus and femur.

Intramedullary (IM) pins can work well in fractures of the humerus, femur, elbow, metacarpal,

Disorders of the Musculoskeletal System

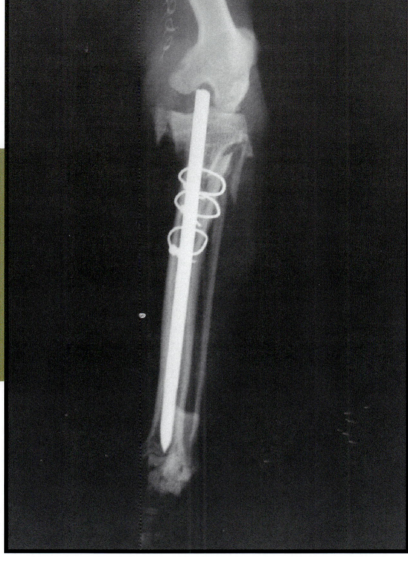

Collapse of fracture fragments around an IM pin allowing the pin to be forced up into the stifle joint damaging vital joint components.

metatarsal, and occasionally the phalanges. In large bones, they can be used alone or multiple pins can be placed in a "stack pin" fashion. Intramedullary pins, if placed properly, can neutralize bending and compression in simple fractures but do not neutralize rotation. Stack pinning (using multiple IM pins side by side) can contribute greatly to rotational stability. In comminuted fractures, IM pinning will not effectively neutralize compression.

IM pinning, as with external fixators, is relatively inexpensive and easy to apply. IM pins also avoid the concern of entrapping large amounts of soft tissue, which is a major concern in using external fixators on upper limb fractures. Disadvantages of IM pins are their relatively inferior ability to neutralize rotation and compression as compared to external fixation or bone plating.

Bone plating is the most expensive and technically demanding of long—

CAT HEALTH ENCYCLOPEDIA

bone fracture repair techniques. Plating, done properly, will (like external fixation) neutralize all three distraction forces. Generally, plating will provide the most rigid, stable repair of all of the fracture fixation techniques. Plating, like IM pinning, will avoid entrapping soft tissue. Disadvantages of plating include:

- Expense of equipment.
- Placement of large amounts of foreign material into contaminated or infected fracture sites can lead to chronic bone infection with eventual loosening of the plate and failure to heal. Therefore, if plating is selected, judicious treatment of open fractures and infected wounds must be part of the case management.
- Skin closure can be difficult when bone plating is used on fractures of the lower limb.

Cerclage wiring involves, as the name implies, placing wires around the fractured bone fragments to hold them in opposition. In the cat, cerclage wire fixation can rarely be used as a primary means of fixation, and its use is generally limited to augmentation of other repair techniques. Cerclage wiring can effectively neutralize rotation forces and, as such, complements IM pinning nicely in fractures where it is applicable. Cerclage wire technique mandates that a minimum of three wires be placed around the fracture at a minimum spacing of 1/2 centimeter. Failure to adhere to proper technique leads to force concentration around the wire, and often subsequent wire loosening and instability. This technique is limited to long oblique fractures.

Interfragmentary screws and wires are used to hold fragments of bone together. As with cerclage wires, interfragmentary techniques are most commonly used to augment the stability of IM pins, external fixators, or bone plates.

Pelvic Fractures

Pelvic fractures are second in frequency to femoral fractures. Pelvic fractures are usually the result of a severe blunt trauma or crushing injury such as a confrontation with an automobile. Other organs in close proximity to the pelvis must be carefully evaluated for injury. Organs such as the urinary bladder, urethra, rectum, and major nerves are vulnerable to injury either from the initiating injury or secondary to the sharp bone fragments associated with pelvic fractures. Diagnosis of pelvic fractures is based upon:

1) palpation of crepitation or grating between bone fragments.

2) palpably abnormal shape of the pelvis, and, most importantly.

3) radiographs. Cats with suspected pelvic trauma should be radiographed.

As a general rule, fractures cranial to or in front of the hip joint are more unstable and require fixation or stabilization to heal properly. The most common method of stabilizing pelvic fractures is the use of bone plates and screws. However, pins and cerclage wires can be used with good success. Fractures caudal to or behind the hip joint are considered non-weight bearing and will generally heal with strict confinement in four to six weeks.

Fractures involving the hip joint ideally require meticulous reduction and rigid fixation if they are to heal properly. If pelvic fractures cannot be stabilized surgically due to cost or other factors, they will often heal with satisfactory results with strict rest and cage confinement. However, when choosing to treat pelvic fractures non-surgically, the possibility of further complications

Disorders of the Musculoskeletal System

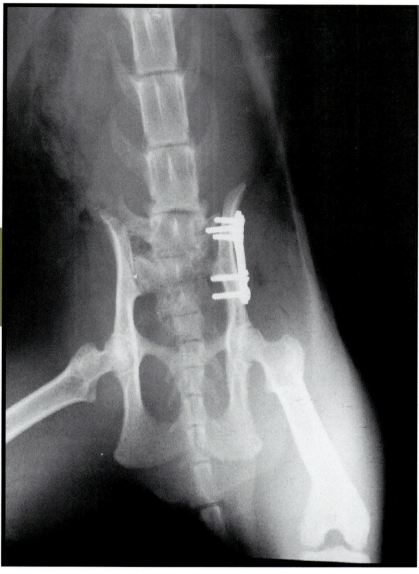

Bone plate applied to a pelvic fracture.

must be considered. Collapse of the pelvic canal due to bony callus formation or bone displacement can lead to constipation, bowel dysfunction, and further surgery to correct the blockage.

Fractures of the neck of the femur or head of the femur are most common in cats less than one year of age. Small divergent pins, with or without a bone screw, are effective in maintaining proper alignment while healing takes place. If pins or screws are not available or reduction is not possible for acetabular fractures or femoral head and neck fractures, an excision arthroplasty (removal of the femoral head and neck) is an effective method of treatment.

Fractures of The Spine

Vertebral fractures are occasionally seen in cats with severe trauma. The vertebrae are most prone to dislocation at intervertebral disk spaces with accompanying fractures involving fragments of the vertebral bodies or articular facets. In any traumatized cat, spinal fractures should be considered until proven otherwise. Neurologic exams, careful palpation, and radiographs are all valuable in diagnosing vertebral fractures or dislocations. Careful evaluation is essential to determine if surgery is warranted. With spinal cord compression, time is crucial in regard to decompressing the cord. The effects of spinal cord injury may be temporary or permanent, making it difficult to determine an appropriate course of action at the time of injury. Spinal fractures can be reduced and stabilized with plastic plates, small bone plates, or pins placed in the vertebra body and connected with bone cement. Due to the delicate nature of the spinal cord and spinal nerves, all spinal fractures must have a guarded-to-grave prognosis depending on neuromuscular evaluation. As a general rule, the closer to the tail, the better the prognosis for spinal cord injuries.

Fractures of the Maxilla and Mandible

Fractures of the maxilla and mandible, or upper and lower jaw, are frequently seen in injured cats. Maxillary (upper jaw) fractures are most often seen in cats from urban areas, where they fall from tall buildings. Mandibular (lower jaw) fractures are frequently a result of blunt trauma to the head and are one of the three most common fractures seen in cats.

The relatively thin soft tissue covering the bones of the skull facilitates digital palpation as an accurate aid to diagnosing fractures. Radiology is again an important part of the diagnostic workup. Once an accurate assessment of the injuries has been made, a careful therapeutic plan should be constructed. Care must be taken to pay close attention to factors such as dental occlusion, stability of the fractures, loss of teeth, maintenance of a free airway, and allowing for adequate nutritional support.

The use of pins, wires, dental acrylic external fixators, and bone

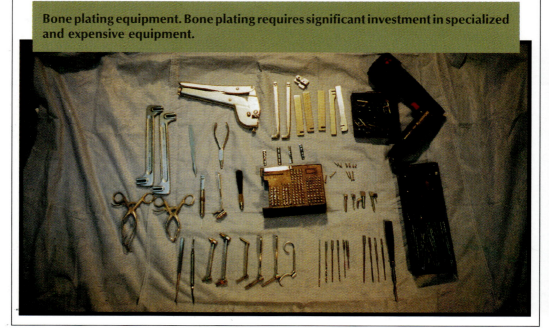

Bone plating equipment. Bone plating requires significant investment in specialized and expensive equipment.

Disorders of the Musculoskeletal System

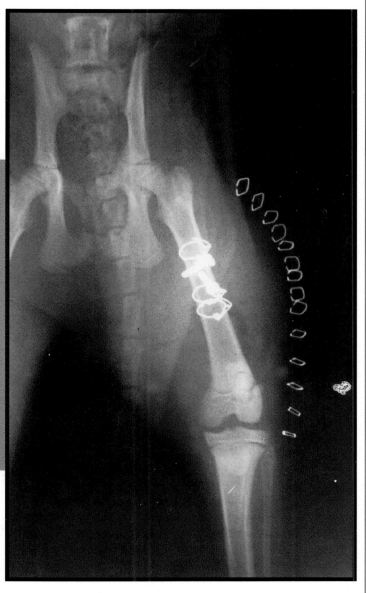

Interfragmentary screws used with cerclage wire to stabilize a long oblique fracture in a young cat. These two techniques are generally used to help maintain reduction with more stable forms of fixation. They are not usually used as pictured here by themselves or together as the sole form of stabilization.

plates, in combination or separately, can all be used to reconstruct and stabilize the bones, allowing them to heal. The prognosis is generally very good, providing that the same basic orthopedic principles as applied to any other fractures are applied to the mandibular or maxillary fractures.

Lower Leg Fractures

Lower leg fractures or fractures of lower legs and feet up to the level of the carpus and hock are common in cats. Once diagnosed, these fractures will often heal with manual reduction and splinting or bandaging. More severe fractures of the lower leg bones may require pinning, wiring, or occasionally external fixation. Prognosis for these fractures is generally quite good in spite of the complexity and involvment of the bone and joint structures in the lower legs.

Cat Health Encyclopedia

Fractures of The Scapula And Ribs

Rib and scapular (shoulder blade) fractures are uncommon in the cat. When they do occur, they rarely require surgical stabilization. Fractures of the scapula in or near the shoulder joint may require stabilization. The prognosis is very good for rib and scapular fractures with time and strict rest.

Joint Dislocation And Ligamentous Injuries

Dislocation of the joints of the cat's skeletal system requires immediate attention. Early diagnosis and reduction of dislocations help prevent further soft tissue damage and provides a more rapid return to function and a better prognosis. Once the dislocated joint is reduced, it must be stabilized long enough for the soft tissue elements that stabilize the joint to heal and scar in. The more stable joints such as the elbow and hip require less support than do joints like the stifle, which require substantial stability and support to heal. Surgical options for severely traumatized dislocations include surgical repair and support of the ligaments, tendons, and joint capsules injured. Transarticular pinning may also provide an option in some badly traumatized joints, such as the stifle and hip.

Prognosis varies depending on the severity of soft tissue damage and the inherent stability in the dislocated joint. Stable joints with little soft tissue injury have an excellent prognosis. Unstable joints like the stifle have a poorer prognosis, especially with more severe soft tissue injuries.

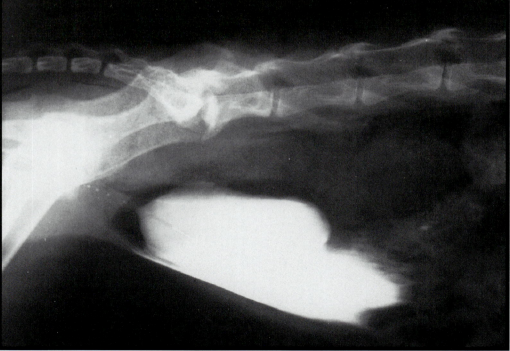

Ruptured bladder secondary to abdominal and pelvic trauma. Note the escape of radiopaque dye from the bladder into the abdomen.

Disorders of the Musculoskeletal System

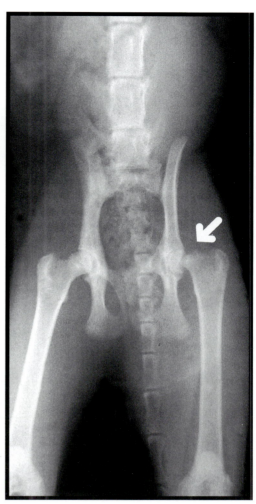

Right: Radiography of fractured femoral epiphysis (growth plate) in a young cat.

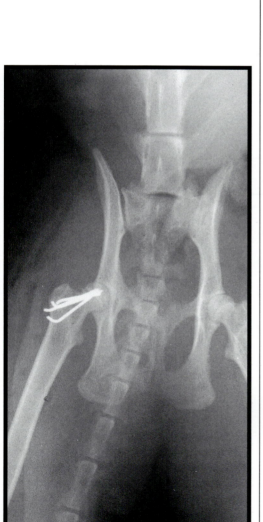

Left: Similar fracture repaired with multiple divergent pins.

Cat Health Encyclopedia

Cruciate Ligament Injury

Cruciate injuries in cats are fairly uncommon. When they are seen, they usually involve the anterior cruciate rather than the posterior cruciate. Ruptured or torn cruciates generally occur as a result of trauma and tend to cause moderate to severe lameness.

In the cat, cruciate injuries generally are accompanied by mild to marked lameness, which usually subsides and improves with time. Pain is usually present upon manipulation of the stifle (knee). Radiographs of the joint may show an effusion (excessive joint fluid). Anterior/posterior joint instability or anterior drawer motion is easily palpable in complete cruciate tears. In partial tears, the degree of laxity is less obvious, making a definitive diagnosis difficult.

If left untreated, cats with ruptured cruciate ligaments will generally improve. Their gait will usually improve four to five weeks after the injury. Treatment is necessary only in isolated cases and as a general rule is not recommended. Strict confinement is recommended for four to five weeks and weight loss is recommended in overweight cats. In those cats that do not respond to weight reduction and rest, surgery is indicated. Surgical stabilization of the stifle with imbrication of the joint capsule or other extracapsular stabilization techniques of the stifle may help some cats to return to full function. If surgical stabilization is necessary, the joint is usually stabilized by tightening the joint capsule and the placement of extracapsular sutures (large support sutures just outside the joint capsule).

INHERITED DISORDERS

The common domestic shorthair or domestic longhair cat is affected by very few inherited orthopedic-related problems. The popularity of the various breeds of purebred cat, on the other hand, has increased the numbers and variety of genetic disorders seen by veterinarians. Many of the inherited disorders we see are interestingly unique and actually the basis of some breeds. Other disorders are truly genetic defects and cause serious discomfort and suffering to those cats who are affected with them.

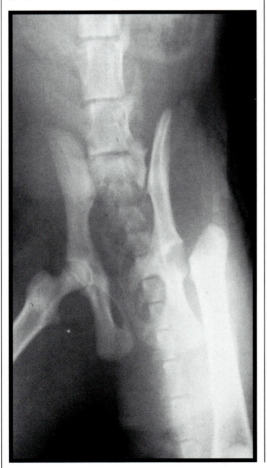

Post operative radiograph of a pelvis showing an excision arthroplasty. Note that the femoral neck has been removed at its base where it adjoins the femoral shaft.

Disorders of the Musculoskeletal System

Polydactyly

Polydactyly is a commonly inherited autosomal dominant condition in many domestic cats. Polydactyly is a condition whereby affected cats have more than the normal number of toes. It is most commonly observed in the front paws; however, it often involves all four feet. Polydactyly is generally harmless; however, in some cats the claws on the extra digit tend to grow and shed abnormally. Therefore the abnormal claws must be trimmed to prevent them from growing into the pads of the feet, causing discomfort and infection.

Taillessness

Taillessness is the result of a gene called the "Manx" gene. Affected cats are born without a tail. The gene responsible is a mutant dominant gene. This taillessness is the basis for the Manx breed, which was one of the earliest breeds of cat recognized and registered. The Manx gene is often associated with the development of spina bifida, a birth defect of the spine discussed within the next section. Taillessness is also caused by another mutation found in the Japanese Bobtail breed. This particular gene causes a short stubby tail. It is not the same as the Manx gene. The Bobtail gene is a recessive gene and is not associated with an increased incidence of spina bifida.

Spina Bifida

Spina bifida is a malformation of the neural tube or vertebrae. The vertebral arches, which form the spinal canal, do not completely form over the top of the spinal canal. This deformity usually occurs in the vertebrae of the lower spine. Herniation and deformity of the

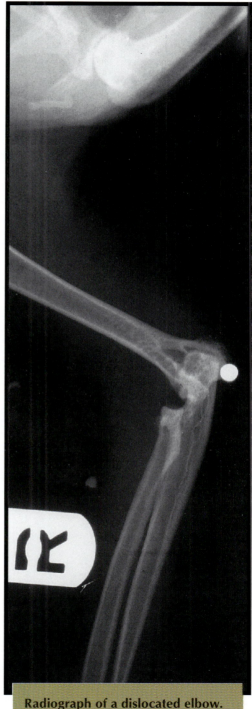

Radiograph of a dislocated elbow.

Cat Health Encyclopedia

spinal cord may also occur, leading to neurologic deficits such as hind limb weakness or incoordination, fecal or urinary incontinence, and/or reoccurring constipation. Medical or surgical therapy is rarely effective in treatment of these cats.

Pectus Excavation

Pectus excavation is a defect of the rib cage, causing a flattening of the chest in newborn kittens. It is rarely seen; however, when it is seen, it is more common in Maine Coon cats and Norwegian Forest cats. The severity can vary from case to case.

Mucopolysaccharidosis I & VI

Both MPS I and MPS VI are inherited diseases in cats. They are both autosomal recessive and are most commonly seen in Siamese, Siamese crosses, and Siamese-related breeds.

Achondroplasia

Achondroplasia, or dwarfism, is a condition that affects the cartilaginous development in the growth plates of the long bones and other areas such as the spinal vertebrae and bones of the skull.

There are two forms of this condition. The first form of achondroplasia is often associated with organ malfunctions of the liver, splenic-lymphatic systems, and neurologic systems. It is passed genetically in an autosomal recessive gene, and affected kittens usually do not survive past one to four months of age. This form of the disease is not always apparent until the kittens begin to grow. The second form of this condition has recently been recognized and used as the basis for forming the Munchkin breed. Munchkin cats have the characteristic appearance of the achondroplastic dwarf, with short legs in proportion to their body. However they do not have the other organ problems and lethal problems associated with the first form of achondroplasia. The Munchkin breed has just recently been recognized as a breed. The breed originated from a female feral cat found by Sandra Hochenedel. The cat had the short legs and normal body size. The cat produced 50 percent short-legged cats. Dr. Solveig M. V. Pflueger, a geneticist, became involved along with Lorie Bobskill and others and developed the breed. The short-legged gene appears to be an autosomal dominant gene.

Ear Cartilage Anomalies

There are two genetic anomalies that affect the cartilage in the ears of cats. Both have become the basis for separate breeds. We are not referring to these conditions as defects or disease but as anomalies of cats. One is the Scottish Fold breed; the other is the American Curl.

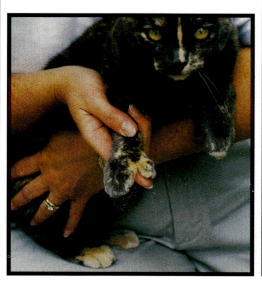

Polydactyly of the front feet of a domestic short hair cat.

Disorders of the Musculoskeletal System

The Scottish Fold gene is an incomplete dominant gene. When it is in the heterozygous (one fold gene and one non-fold gene) state, you get the desired folded ears. When the kittens are homozygous (two fold genes), they experience deformities in coccygeal (tail) vertebrae, shortening in the bones of the back, irregular convolutions of the cartilage in the nasal septum causing partial nasal obstruction, and periarticular exostosis joint fusion and osteodystrophy.

It is reported that the thickening of the tail base is often the first clinically observed sign of this disease, and some cats will not exhibit clinical or radiographic signs until later in life. Affected individuals will show lameness associated with decreased ability of the lower limbs to support weight, shortening of the metacarpal, metatarsal, and phalangeal bones, and overgrown nails. Radiographic evidence of proliferative new bones (exostosis) on the planter surface of the metatarsus and palmar surface of the metacarpus with thickened phalanges are indicative of Scottish Fold osteodystrophy. There is no known cure for this problem, but a recent report indicated that resolution of hind limb lameness associated with Scottish Fold osteodystrophy was achieved by pantarsal arthrodesis.

Because of the problems associated with homozygous Scottish Fold kittens, breeders should never breed two folded parents. Fold parents should always be bred to non-folded mates. When this is done, statistically the breeder should get one half heterozygous folded kittens and one half non-folded kittens.

The American Curl is a relatively new breed developed in the United States in the 1980s. The ear cartilage curls in a concave upright position. Genetically the curl gene is a dominant gene that resulted from a spontaneous mutation in 1981. There are no other known musculoskeletal problems associated with the curl gene.

Taillessness in a Manx cat.

Kinked Tail

The kinked tail gene is an autosomal recessive trait in cats, leading to a kinked or angular deviation of the tail. This deformity usually occurs near the tip of the tail and is not associated with any other harmful characteristics.

Ectrodactyly

The fusion of one or more of the digits is known as ectrodactyly. Ectrodactyly is a rare, inherited defect controlled by an autosomal dominant gene with variable expression in cats. It is usually only present in the front feet.

Hereditary Myopathy in Devon Rex Cats

Some bloodlines of Devon Rex cats have been reported to have a

Cat Health Encyclopedia

congenital myopathy (muscle disease), similar to some forms of muscular dystrophy seen in people. This disease seems to affect all of the striated muscles, including the skeletal muscles and the esophageal muscles.

Affected kittens are usually first noticed when they start to ambulate on their own. The affected kittens usually show severe exercise intolerance and weakness. They often have difficulty holding their heads up and appear to be flexing their neck with their chin against their chest. This "ventroflexion" is caused by the weakness in the muscles on the back of the neck. Often these cats will learn to sit up in a begging-type stance, enabling them to visualize their environment more easily. Kittens with this problem will often have difficulty supporting themselves during normal activities such as eating or using the litter box, collapsing on their abdomens on the floor or into the kitty litter.

Diagnosis is based on clinical signs, history, including pedigree, and radiographic barium studies of the esophagus. Clinical signs may appear as early as three weeks or as late as two years. Barium studies characteristically show a dilated or megaesophagus, or a hypomotile esophagus. Laboratory findings are generally normal, helping to rule out diseases such as hypokalemia, which may also be present with muscle weakness and ventroflexion of the head. Other diseases, such as myasthenia gravis, must be ruled out with skeletal muscle pathology and anticholinesterase drug tests.

Supportive care and patience are the only effective methods or means for treatment of these cats. Feeding liquid food on an elevated platform may help avoid some of the problems associated with the megaesophagus. The severity of the myopathy, especially the extent to which it affects the laryngo-pharynx, often determines the long-term prognosis for the cat. Most cats succumb to this disease as a result of laryngospasm from ingesta or aspiration.

Treatment and prevention for most of the inherited diseases must be based on a clear understanding of the nature of these diseases and a commitment to genetically select away from these problems. Treatment of individual cases is usually based on symptomatic evaluation and treatment.

MUSCULOSKELETAL CANCER

Neoplasia, or cancer, of the musculoskeletal system is a problem for cats just as it is in most species. However, like most diseases of the

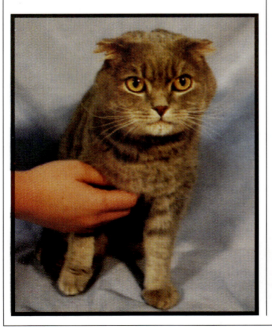

Scottish Fold cat. The ears are permanently folded down and forward due to anomalies that affect the ear cartilage.

DISORDERS OF THE MUSCULOSKELETAL SYSTEM

musculoskeletal system in cats, musculoskeletal neoplasia in cats is not as common nor is it as aggressive as it is in dogs. In general, neoplastic tumors of the bone, cartilage, and muscle in cats tend to be slower growing and not as likely to metastasize to other areas of the body as do similar tumors in dogs.

Musculoskeletal neoplasia is usually recognized in the cat by a swelling or growth, or by lameness caused by pain or mechanical interference of a tumor. A thorough physical examination must be done to rule out other possible causes such as abscesses, infections, trauma, neoplasia of other systems, and metabolic/nutritional disease. Radiographs are essential in localizing and determining the extent of tumors. Cytology (the examination of cells aspirated from masses) is often helpful in diagnosing these as well as many other cancers. The definitive diagnosis of musculoskeletal neoplasia rests with biopsies for histopathologic assessment. Histopathology is the examination of stained tissue sections by a qualified pathologist, and it is essential in achieving a proper diagnosis. Without such a diagnosis, prognosis and therapy are simply speculations. Tumor biopsies suitable for histopathology can be obtained from complete excision of the mass when possible, or from partial excisions such as wedge biopsies, core biopsies of bone and hard tissue, or small core biopsies taken by specially designed needles. Once a proper histopathologic diagnosis is obtained, a therapeutic plan can be made and a prognosis can be given to the owner. The following are some of the types of cancer that affect the feline musculoskeletal system.

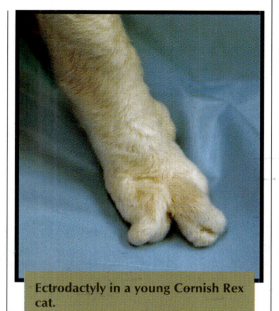

Ectrodactyly in a young Cornish Rex cat.

Osteosarcoma

Feline osteosarcoma is the most common bone cancer in the cat. Osteosarcoma is generally a disease most often seen in older cats and affects the long bones of the legs, although it can affect any bone in the body. Feline osteosarcoma can be either osteolytic (bone dissolving) or osteoblastic (bone forming). Osteolytic osteosarcoma is more prevalent in the long bones of the appendicular skeleton, whereas osteoblastic osteosarcoma is more common in the other bones of the body. Unlike dogs, osteosarcoma in cats does not metastasize quickly and excision of the tumor can be quite rewarding. Less than 10 percent of the osteosarcomas in cats have metastasized at the time of diagnosis. Amputation of the affected leg or removal of the tumor with adequate margins often leads to a "cure." Clinical cases of osteosarcoma are usually first recognized by either firm swelling or lameness. The tumors are usually not painful on palpation. Occasionally, pathologic fractures

Cat Health Encyclopedia

(fractures caused secondary to weakening of the bone due to the erosion of the bone from the cancer) may be present upon presentation. Any patient with a fracture that is more severe than one would expect from the severity of the injury suggests the possibility of a pathologic fracture. Careful examination of radiographs and a thorough physical exam should be done looking for the possibility of a bone-eroding cancer.

With timely diagnosis and adequate surgical care, cats with osteosarcoma have a fair prognosis. Long-term prognosis for tumors located in the skull, pelvis, or vertebra is poor due to their surgical inaccessibility. Osteosarcoma in the long bones of the legs offers a favorable prognosis with amputation. One study found long-term average survival times of four to five years in cats with osteosarcoma in the appendicular skeleton treated with amputation.

Juxtacortical Osteosarcoma

Juxtacortical osteosarcomas in cats act similarly to osteosarcoma in their initial presentation and locations; however, they are much less common. They most often affect the ends of long bones of the legs and the surfaces of the bones of the skull. Although uncommon in the cat, when diagnosed they are most commonly seen in older cats and are usually, but not always, slow-growing masses. Juxtacortical osteosarcomas are osteoblastic (bone forming) tumors and usually start on the periosteum, or outer surfaces, of the bones.

Diagnosis is usually made based on physical exam, radiographic findings, and histopathologic examination of biopsy samples. The most effective treatment for cats affected with juxtacortical osteosarcoma is amputation whenever possible. The prognosis seems to be good with amputation or wide excision, but there have not been enough cases reported to gain

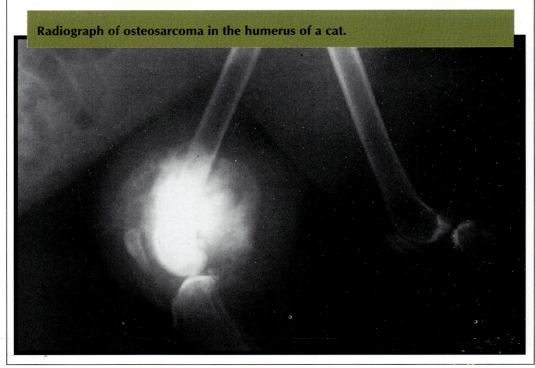

Radiograph of osteosarcoma in the humerus of a cat.

Disorders of the Musculoskeletal System

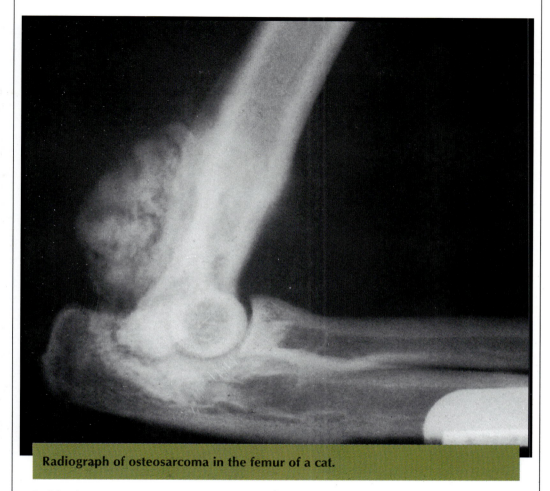

Radiograph of osteosarcoma in the femur of a cat.

reliable data to accurately give definitive prognostic guidelines.

Solitary Osteocartilaginous Exostosis

Solitary osteocartilaginous exostosis is characterized as a proliferation of bony tissue usually near the physis (growth plate) of the bone. Radiographically they appear to be masses of cancellous bone attached to the periosteum of the bones. These lesions form by ossification (bone formation) of a cartilaginous growth thought to arise from remnants of the growth plates. Diagnosis is usually determined by physical exam, history, radiology, and histopathologic biopsy. Solitary osteocartilaginous exostosis usually presents a history of a slowly progressive lameness.

Surgical excision of osteocartilaginous exostosis is the most effective method of treatment. The mass is usually more easily removed than radiographs might indicate. The masses most often have a relatively small base of attachment to the periosteal bone, making excision possible even on large exostosis. Prognosis is good with complete excision. Solitary exostosis do not metastasize but may regrow locally. When regrowth does occur, it may take several months. Malignant transformation to osteosarcoma has been reported. If malignant transformation or recurrent regrowth does occur, amputation or wide resection is necessary.

Feline Osteochondromatosis

Feline osteochondromatosis, or multiple osteocartilaginous exostosis, resembles solitary osteochondromatosis in that they both form from a cartilaginous cap that undergoes endochondral ossification as the cartilage cap grows. Osteochondromatosis appears in multiple locations; and as it matures, it more closely resembles a sarcoma rather than osteochondroma. Feline osteochondromatosis has been linked to a retro virus and many affected cats test positive for FeLV. The tendency for feline osteochondromatosis may be inherited as are similar conditions in dogs, horses, and man, but the most current indications are that osteochondromatosis in cats is virus induced.

Clinical signs are associated with the growth of the masses, including the visible and palpable masses and discomfort or lameness associated with the mechanical interference and pressure of the masses. Radiographically, the masses are found on the surfaces of the flat bones of the body, such as the ribs, scapula, vertebra, skull, and pelvis. The lesions resemble those seen with solitary osteocartilaginous exostosis; however, they rarely affect the long bones of the legs.

There is no known treatment. The prognosis of cats with feline osteochondromatosis is grave. The mortality of cats reported with confirmed osteochondromatosis was 100 percent within one year.

Chondrosarcoma

Chondrosarcoma is uncommon in cats. It is a malignant tumor of cartilaginous tissue and is found most often in older cats. Cats with

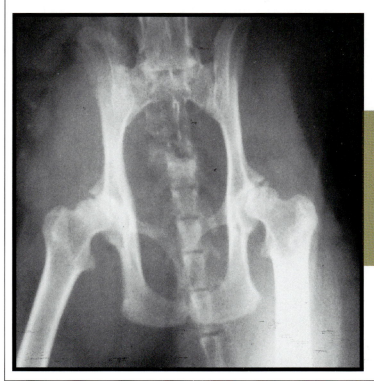

Radiograph of a two-year-old Maine Coon cat with hip dysplasia. Note the shallowness of the hip sockets and reactive bone deposits around the hip joints.

Disorders of the Musculoskeletal System

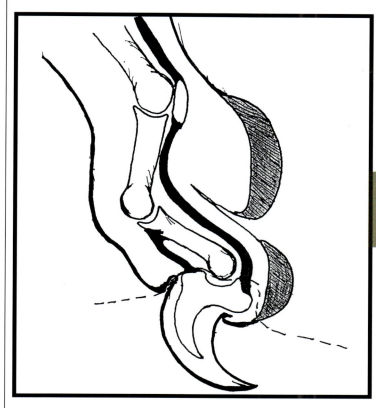

Diagram of a cat's toe showing line of excision for declaw.

chondrosarcoma usually present a progressive lameness and/or palpable or visibly enlarged masses.

Radiographically, chondrosarcomas have an osteoproductive core fading in diffused patterns into a soft tissue cortex. The scapula is the most commonly involved bone; however, they can affect the bones of the skull, long bones of the legs, ribs, or pelvis. Definitive diagnosis requires histopathologic evaluation. Effective treatment requires widespread surgical excision or amputation. Metastasis to the lungs has been reported, and local recurrence is to be expected if the tumor is not completely removed.

Fibrosarcoma

Fibrosarcoma is the most common feline musculoskeletal cancer. Feline fibrosarcoma generally affects the bones of the skull and the long bones of the legs with about equal frequency. Fibrosarcoma is found mostly in older cats and must be differentiated from the viral-induced sarcomas found in younger to middle-aged cats. Cats with fibrosarcoma of the skeletal system usually present first with a noticeable mass. They are usually not lame or painful on palpation until they are quite advanced. Radiographically, they appear to have a large soft tissue mass and are osteolytic (bone dissolving) where they affect the bone. Fibrosarcomas can cause pathologic fractures by weakening the bone; however, they are more difficult to appreciate since they are not osteoproductive and fractures may appear to be primary rather than secondary (pathologic) fractures. Metastasis is uncommon but does occur.

Surgical excision with wide margins, or amputation of affected limbs, is the most effective approach to treatment. Fibrosarcomas of the skull, vertebrae, or pelvis are difficult to treat surgically due to the invasive nature of the tumors into the bone. Radiation does offer some hope in prolonging the survivability of cats with fibrosarcoma. Chemotherapy, on the other hand, offers very little benefit.

Squamous-Cell Carcinoma

Squamous-cell carcinoma is a malignant soft tissue cancer that commonly affects cats around the ears, nose, mouth, digits, and other sparsely haired or lightly pigmented areas of the body. Light-colored cats are more prone to squamous-cell carcinoma. It is the most common malignant tumor that affects the mouth of a cat and frequently invades the bones of the maxilla and mandible. Once these tumors invade the bones of the mouth, the prognosis becomes very poor due to the difficulty of getting adequate cancer-free margins. Squamous-cell carcinomas are very aggressive locally and are osteolytic when affecting the bone. Radiographically, the bone may appear pitted or eroded from the cancer.

METABOLIC AND NUTRITIONAL MUSCULOSKELETAL DISEASES

Primary metabolic diseases are rare and for the purposes of this article will be limited to a description of feline mucopolysaccaridosis (MDS). Secondary metabolic bone diseases are more common and are related to nutritional imbalances or kidney disease.

Mucopolysaccharidosis

Mucopolysaccharidosis is a genetic disorder that is caused by the failure of the patient to produce appropriate enzymes to metabolize mucopolysaccharides. Mucopolysaccharides are the very large molecules that form the ground substance for connective tissue. Without the ability to degrade and metabolize these large molecules, they begin to accumulate in the body, causing disease. In humans, there are many forms of mucopolysaccharidosis. In the cat, only two of these have been reported. They are MPS Type I and MPS Type VI.

Affected cats can have a variety of clinical signs including:

- Broad, poorly developed faces
- Cloudy eyes with chronic mucoid discharge
- Stiff gait with paraparesis and abnormal spinal reflexes
- Widespread central neurologic abnormalities
- Flattening of the chest
- Renal failure

Chronic diarrhea is also seen in some patients. Radiographs commonly show hip dislocation and fusion of the vertebrae of the neck. Definitive diagnosis is made by isolating high levels of mucopolysaccharides in the urine. The prognosis for affected cats is poor, and there is no known treatment.

Nutritional Secondary Hyperparathyroidism

Nutritional secondary hyperparathyroidism can easily occur in kittens fed all-meat or fad diets containing an imbalance of calcium and phosphorous. This disorder has also been called juvenile osteoporosis, feline osteodystrophy, and paper-bone disease. High-meat diets that contain less than 10mg of calcium per 100 grams of diet and that have a calcium : phosphorous ratio of 1 : 20

DISORDERS OF THE MUSCULOSKELETAL SYSTEM

or greater are often fed to promote rapid growth. These diets have been implicated in this disease. A growing cat needs 200mg to 400mg of calcium and 150mg to 400mg of phosphorus per day or a ratio of calcium to phosphorus of 1:1. Excess levels of phosphorus stimulate the parathyroid gland to release parathormone, which stimulates release of calcium from bones to try to correct the body's calcium : phosphorous ratio. As a result of calcium depletion in the bones, the kittens become osteoporotic. Clinical signs include lethargy, wobbly gait, bow-legged stance, and frequently fractured limbs with no history of trauma or injury (pathologic fracture). Radiographs show generalized osteoporosis with severe demineralization of the skull and other large relatively flat bones.

Treatment is directed at correcting the dietary imbalances. If pathologic fractures are present and minimally displaced, they often heal rapidly with no fixation. If fixation is necessary, it should be as lightweight as possible to prevent pathologic fractures of adjacent bones or opposite limbs from the increased weight applied by the fixation device.

Calcium supplementation is rarely necessary and should under no circumstances be undertaken until phosphorus levels are brought back to normal. Calcium supplementation in the face of excessive phosphorus levels can result in soft tissue calcification.

Renal Secondary Hyperparathyroidism

Renal secondary hyperparathyroidism can occur in kidney failure patients. These patients are often aged, or have a history of toxin ingestion (antifreeze), drug therapy with aminoglycoside antibiotics, or systemic antifungal drugs. These patients are often quite ill and present dehydration, lethargy, vomiting, and reluctance to eat. They will have high blood levels of urea nitrogen, creatinine, and phosphorus, along with normal or dilute urine. The high blood levels of phosphorus lead to a similar osteoporotic condition as that described for nutritional secondary hyperparathyroidism. Treatment is again directed at resolving the underlying renal failure by fluid diuresis, administration of phosphate binders orally, and offering a high carbohydrate/low protein diet.

In acute kidney failure, the kidneys can compensate and prognosis can be fair to good if they survive the initial crises. Prognosis for patients with chronic renal failure is guarded to poor.

Hypervitaminosis A

Excessive vitamin A supplementation is another nutritional disorder that can cause skeletal deformities. Hypervitaminosis A can be induced by feeding high levels of liver and milk over several months or by oversupplementing vitamin A. It has not been reported when cats are fed commercial diets. Affected cats often start to show lameness and pain on palpation of the neck or back. Chronic cases can show fusion of vertebrae and exostosis (excessive bone proliferation), particularly around joints and tendon insertions. Unfortunately, even after the vitamin A levels are corrected, the bony lesions persist.

MISCELLANEOUS DISEASES

Hip Dysplasia

Hip dysplasia is a chronic form of degenerative arthritis caused by instability, laxity, and shallowness of the hip joint.

CAT HEALTH ENCYCLOPEDIA

Unlike dogs, in which the disease is a serious problem, cats are usually not affected clinically. When cats are affected, they show stiffness and soreness in the hip joints. They may be reluctant to jump, or go up stairs and may be intermittently lame.

Most often, cats are inadvertently diagnosed with hip dysplasia when radiographing the lower abdomen or pelvis for other unrelated problems. Occasionally, cats will be diagnosed by suggestive clinical signs, a thorough physical exam and radiography. Radiographically, affected cats show looseness or subluxation (partial dislocation), shallowness of the hip socket, flattening of the femoral head (ball of the hip joint) and presence of bony deposits (osteophytes) around the hip joint. Hip dysplasia is more common in Maine Coon cats than in other breeds.

Due to the infrequency of hip dysplasia, treatment is rarely necessary. When treatment is necessary, the choice of a therapeutic approach should be carefully weighed depending on the severity of the symptoms. Weight loss in obese cats, medical therapy, and surgery are all options in treating hip dysplasia. Since cats are generally intolerant of many non-steroidal anti-inflammatory medications such as ibuprofen and acetaminophen, medical management is limited to steroidal drugs, aspirin (in small doses), and some supplements that contain glycosaminoglycans (which are not proven for efficacy in the cat). Aspirin can be used sparingly in cats at a dose of 10mg. per kg. of body weight every 48 to 72 hours. Corticosteroids often offer fast effective relief; however, their long-term side effects may make them unacceptable solutions. Aspirin can be effectively used in cats but must be used with extreme caution.

Surgical approaches to the treatment of hip dysplasia include pectineal myectomy (where the pectineus muscle is removed) and excision arthroplasty, whereby the femoral head and neck are removed, allowing a fibrous "scar tissue"-type joint to form, replacing the original ball and socket joint.

Patellar Luxation

Patellar luxation is a condition in which the patella, or knee cap, displaces to the inside (medial) or outside (lateral) of the stifle joint.

Patellar luxation is not as common in cats as it is in dogs. It is, however, a fairly common problem. Medial patellar luxation is more common than lateral patellar luxation. Traumatic luxations tend to be unilateral whereas congenital luxations tend to be bilateral. Congenital patellar luxations tend to be found more commonly in purebred cats, especially Devon Rex and Abyssinian cats, although it has been reported in other breeds and mixed breed cats. Congenital patellar luxations have been found to be inherited in some breeds of dog; however, it has not yet been proven to be an inherited problem in cats. The severity of the luxation can be graded, as in dogs, with the scheme of grades I through IV.

GRADATION OF PATELLAR LUXATION

Grade I: Patella easily luxates with manual pressure with the joint in extension but quickly returns to the trochlear groove when the joint is flexed and extended.

Grade II: The patella luxates most of the time. It luxates on flexion of the joint and remains luxated until it is reduced to its normal position manually.

Disorders of the Musculoskeletal System

Grade III: The patella is permanently luxated. It can be manually reduced with the stifle joint in extension, but it quickly reluxates when it is released.

Grade IV: The patella is permanently luxated outside the trochlear groove and cannot be reduced into the trochlear groove without surgery.

Traumatic patellar luxations are generally acutely painful and are often associated with other injuries. Careful palpation will often reveal a rent or tear in the tendons and muscle fascia on the opposite side of the joint from the luxation. These cats will frequently improve with time and many will walk fairly normally. In traumatic luxation, the trochlear groove, the groove the patella rests in, is usually normal. Surgical repair is recommended with grade III or higher luxation to prevent chronic abnormal wear and degenerative joint disease over a prolonged period of time.

Congenital bilateral patellar luxation is usually a result of abnormal bone development causing a bow-string effect, pulling the patella one way or the other, usually medially. The trochlear groove is usually shallow and often slopes toward the side of the luxation. Cats with medial patellar luxation will often walk with a bowlegged gait and tend to arch their back and have a hopping type gait in an effort to avoid flexing and extending their stifles.

Definitive diagnosis requires the demonstration of the luxated patella. This can be seen radiographically on either an anterior poster view, or a skyline view. The skyline view often gives more information regarding the depth of the trochlear groove, which is necessary when contemplating surgery. Palpation also is essential in diagnosing and grading the severity of the luxating patella. Grades I and

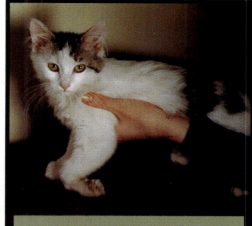

Kitten with radial nerve paralysis secondary to tourniquet placement for declawing.

II are occasionally clinical, but more often they are incidental findings. Grades III and IV are usually easy to diagnose and frequently result in clinical disease. Palpation of the luxated patella is easily performed by an experienced surgeon. This is done by straightening the stifle, allowing the extensor apparatus to loosen and the patella to be easily manipulated to one side or the other. The joint can be gently put through a range of motion to determine the grade of severity of the luxated patella.

The treatment of choice for luxated patella depends on the cause and severity of the luxation. The patient should be thoroughly evaluated to determine exactly what problems resulted in the luxation. Traumatic luxation may have predisposing problems, such as a shallow trochlear groove predisposing the joint to injury. Therefore, before making a surgical plan, the surgeon must evaluate the following:

- The strength and ability of the joint capsule and muscle fascia medial or lateral to the patella must be strong enough to support the stresses required to hold the patella in place during and after healing.

- The depth and shape of the trochlear groove must be such that it will hold the patella in place.
- What are the overall mechanical forces on the patella? If the overall direction of pull on the patella is not in the plane it needs to be, the repeated pull of the muscles and tendons will eventually overcome the lateral or medial tension and, again, predispose the patella to luxation.

The surgical techniques necessary to relocate and stabilize the patella coincide with the points listed above.

- Lateral or medial imbrication of the joint capsule, tendons and muscle fascia to repair torn or stretched structures which allow the patella to luxate in the opposite direction.
- Trochleoplasty: Deepening and/ or widening the trochlear groove to accommodate the smooth movement of the patella within the trochlear groove.
- Tibial crest transposition: moving the attachment of the patella to align the pull of the muscles and tendons in the same plane with the trochlear groove and patella, eliminating the bow-string effect and preventing recurring problems.

Myositis Ossificans

Myositis ossificans is characterized by a formation of non-neoplastic bone in a single muscle or group of muscles. This bone formation is not associated with the normal skeletal bones. This disease is rare and is most frequent in young adult cats. Treatment consists of removal of the affected muscle bone tissue. The prognosis is generally good with return to normal function. Recurrence is unlikely in most cases.

Hypertrophic Osteopathy

Hypertrophic osteopathy is a disease seen in dogs and rarely in cats. In dogs, it has been referred to as hypertrophic pulmonary osteoarthropathy and hypertrophic osteoarthropathy. The disease is characterized clinically and radiographically by widespread periosteal and soft tissue reactions developing into new bone growth and reaction around the bones of the legs. In most cases it is associated with intrathoracic disease such as thoracic tumors or pulmonary tuberculosis. The exact cause of this disease is not understood; however, current thoughts are that increased blood flow to the legs may play an important part. Prognosis is difficult to determine based on such a small number of cases in cats. However, treatment should center around curing the underlying thoracic pathology if possible.

Feline Onychectomy (Declawing)

Declawing is a somewhat controversial procedure in which the claw, including the third phalanx (last bone of the toe) of the front feet, is surgically removed. This procedure is practiced to prevent household destruction by cats as they attempt to sharpen their front claws.

With declawing, there are many possible long-term problems resulting in post-operative pain. Some of these problems are as follows:

- Neuroma formation: The nerves of the toes, when severed, can develop neuromas, causing painful sensation or phantom pains in the affected toes.
- Alteration in the weight-bearing distribution in the toe pads. Removing the third phalanx

Disorders of the Musculoskeletal System

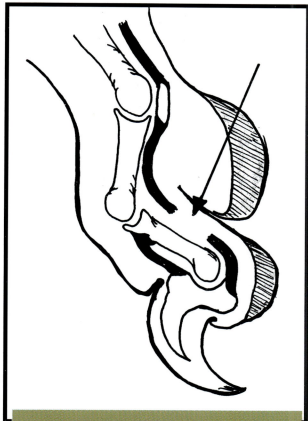

Diagram of cat's toe showing location of flexor tendon transection.

if this surgery is performed.
• Nerve damage secondary to placement of a tourniquet to control surgical hemorrhage.

Other objections to declawing center around the cat's ability to defend itself and climb or ambulate normally. Many people currently feel that declawing is not in the cat's best interest in light of the potential complications. On the other hand, others feel that if the procedure allows for a cat to have a quality life in a good home, it is a worthwhile procedure. However, alternatives should always be explored first. Training and behavioral modification can be very effective at curbing undesirable behaviors but require intensive owner involvement. Nail caps are simple devices that fit over the claws and prevent damage. Ask your veterinarian for more details.

Tenectomy

Tenectomy is a surgical procedure in which the flexor tendon to the third phalanx is severed, allowing the elastic ligament of the paw to permanently retract the claw. This disables the cat's ability to extend its claws. The advantage of this procedure over onychectomy is that there is very little immediate or chronic discomfort to the cat. The major disadvantage is that the cat cannot keep its own claws sharpened or worn off by scratching, so they must be trimmed on a regular basis or they will grow around and into the

removes much of the bone over the toe pad, concentrating the pressure on the end of the second phalanx, resulting in possible sensitivity and damage to the soft tissue.
• Other surgical complications associated with declawing are a result of not completely removing the germinal tissue of the nail bed, resulting in ongoing growth of the claws under the skin and subcutaneous tissue of the toes leading to chronic infections, granulomas, and sterile abscesses. The nail bed must be meticulously removed when and

Cat Health Encyclopedia

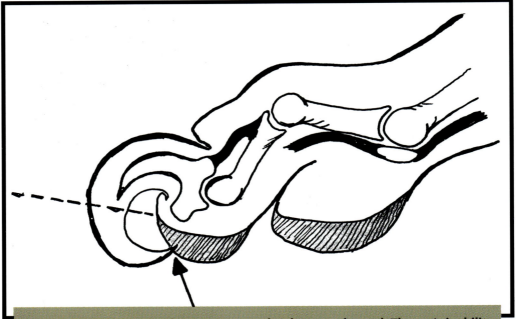

Diagram of a cat's paw after a tenectomy has been performed. The cat's inability to wear off excess calw has resulted in the claws growing into the pads. Also showing the line at which the claw should be trimmed.

toe pad, causing infection and discomfort. This could be a very serious problem if a cat were lost or abandoned, making it unlikely that someone would maintain and trim the claws.

REFERENCES AND RECOMMENDED READING

Schrader, SC; Sherding, RG: Disorders of the skeletal system. p.1247. *The Cat: Diseases and Clinical Management.* RG Sherding, Ed. First edition. Churchill Livingston Inc., New York, 1989.

Macy, DW; Small, E: Deep mycotic diseases. p.237. *Textbook of Veterinary Internal Medicine.* SJ Ettinger, Ed. New edition: *Diseases of the Dog and Cat.* Second edition. WB Saunders, Philadelphia, 1983.

Carro T: Polyarthritis in cats, *Compendium on Continuing Education for the Practicing Veterinarian* 16:57. 1994.

Pedersen, NC; Wind, A; Morgan, JP; Pool, RR: Joint diseases of dogs and cats. p.2329. *Textbook of Veterinary Internal Medicine.* SJ Ettinger, Ed. Third edition. WB Saunders, Philadelphia, 1989.

Gorman, NT; Werner, LL: Immune-mediated diseases. p.54. *The Cat: Diseases and Clinical Management.* RG Sherding, Ed. First edition. Churchill Livingston Inc., New York, 1989.

Smith, GK: Biomechanics pertinent to fracture etiology, reduction, and fixation. p.195. *Textbook of Small Animal Orthopaedics.* CD Newton, DM Nunamaker, Eds. JB Lippincott Co., Philadelphia, 1985.

DeCamp, CE: External coaptation. p.1661. *Textbook of Small Animal Surgery.* D Slatter, Ed. Second edition. WB Saunders, Philadelphia, 1993.

DISORDERS OF THE MUSCULOSKELETAL SYSTEM

Nunamaker, DM: Methods of internal fixation. p. 261. *Textbook of Small Animal Orthopaedics.* CD Newton, DM Nunamaker, Eds. B Lippincott Co., Philadelphia, 1985.

DeYoung, DJ; Probst, CW: Methods of internal fracture fixation. p. 1610. *Textbook of Small Animal Surgery.* D Slatter, Ed. Second edition. WB Saunders Co., Philadelphia, 1993.

Schrader, SC: Orthopedic surgery. p.1293. *The Cat: Diseases and Clinical Management.* RG Sherding, Ed. First Ed. Churchill Livingston Inc., New York, 1989.

Leighton, RL; Gordon WR: Orthopedic surgery. p.100. *Diseases of the Cat.* J. Holzworth, Ed. WB Saunders Co., Philadelphia, 1987.

Umphlet, RC: Feline stifle disease. *The Veterinary Clinics of North America-Small Animal Practice.* 23(4): p.897. 1976.

Clark, DR: *Medical, Genetic, and Behavioral Aspects of Purebred Cats.* Forum Publications, Inc. St. Simons Island,GA. 1992.

Pool, RR: Osteochondromatosis. p.641. *Pathophysiology in Small Animal Surgery.* MJ Bonjab, Ed. Lea and Febiger, Philadelphia, 1981.

Rowland, GN; Fetter, AW: Nutritional secondary hyperparathyroidism. p.677. *Pathophysiology in Small Animal Surgery.* Lea and Febiger, Philadelphia, 1981.

Armstrong, PJ; Hand, MS: Nutritional disorders. p. 141. *The Cat: Diseases and Clinical Management.* RG Sherding, Ed. Churchill Livingston, New York 1989.

Werner, BE; Taboda, J: Use of analgesics in feline medicine. *Compendium on Continuing Education for the Practicing Veterinarian,* 16(4): p.493 1994.

Holland, M; Chastain, CB: Uses and misuses of aspirin. p.70. *Kirk's Current Veterinary Therapy XII.* JD Bonagura, Ed. W.B. Saunders Co. Philadelphia, 1995.

Bennett, D: Treatment of the immune-based inflammatory arthropathies of the dog and cat. p.1188. *Kirk's Current Veterinary Therapy XII.* JD Bonagura, Ed. W.B. Saunders Co. Philadelphia, 1995.

Couto, CG: Oncology. p.589. *The Cat: Diseases and Clinical Management.* RG Sherding, Ed. First edition. Churchill Livingston, Inc. New York, 1989.

Ogilvie, GK; Moore, AS: Bone tumors. *Managing the Veterinary Cancer Patient.* p.451. Veterinary Learning Systems Co. Trenton, NJ, 1995.

Wastlhuber, J: History of domestic cats and cat breeds. *Feline Husbandry: Diseases and Management in the Multiple-cat Environment.* PW Pratt, Ed. American Veterinary Publications, Inc. 1991:12-4.

Jackson, OF: Congenital bone lesions in cats with folded ears. *Bulletin of The Feline Advisory Bureau* 1975:14 (4); 2-4.

Malik, R.; Mepstead, K; Yang F; Harper C: Hereditary myopathy of Devon Rex cats. *Journal of Small Animal Practice.* 34, p.539. 1993.

Mathews, Kyle: Resolution of lameness associated with Scottish Fold osteodystrophy following bilateral ostectomies and pantarsal arthrodesis. *Journal of the American Animal Hospital Association,* Volume 31, July-August 1995. 280-288.

Dr. Charles L. Martin

Dr. Martin is a charter Diplomate of the American College of Veterinary Ophthalmologists (ACVO) and has served as president of the ACVO as well as the American Association of Veterinary Ophthalmology. He has taught at the veterinary colleges of the University of Pennsylvania, Ohio State University, Western College of Veterinary Medicine, Kansas State University, and University of Georgia. He has authored over 125 journal articles and book chapters and written one textbook on veterinary ophthalmology.

THE FELINE EYE IN HEALTH AND DISEASE

By Charles L. Martin, DVM, MS, Diplomate, ACVO
Professor, Department of Small Animal Medicine

College of Veterinary Medicine
University of Georgia
Athens, GA 30602

THE FUNCTION AND ANATOMY OF THE NORMAL CAT EYE

The cat's eyes have fascinated man throughout time, as evidenced by prose and drawings. The cat eye represents a visual system that has been modified for both day and night hunting. While the cat's vision exceeds man's ability to discriminate in the dark by a factor of about 5, their visual discrimination in daylight is from 5 to 10 times less than man's (Duke-Elder, 1958; Wassle, 1971; Blake et al, 1974; Bonds, 1974) . The eyes of the cat are more frontally placed than are the dog's, which results in a greater degree of overlap of each visual field or a binocular visual field of 120° and a total field of 280° (Duke-Elder, 1958). This serves the hunter by producing better depth perception. As the cat cannot discriminate or perceive form as well as man, it relies on movement for visual clues that subserve its predatory nature.

Various modifications of the cat eye allow for vision under nocturnal conditions and make it distinctive in appearance. One of the more externally obvious modifications is the large size of the cat eye in relation to its body size.

Weight of the Eyes in Relation to the Body Weight

Animal	Average body weight in Kilograms	Weight of eyes in grams	Ratio
Horse	500	101	1:4960
Cow	400-500	65	1:6923
Sheep	85	23	1:3648
Pig	75	19	1:3947
Dog (large)	37	14	1:2574
Dog (small)	4.7	9	1:545
Cat	3	11	1:267

Translated and adapted from J. Bayer, *Augenheilkunde*, Braumueller, Vienna, 1914.

CAT HEALTH ENCYCLOPEDIA

The large eye and cornea and a pupil that widely dilates allow the maximum amount of light to be gathered under nocturnal conditions. Internally, the lens in the cat eye is large and is situated relatively deep in the eye, which produces a small, but concentrated, image on the retina. The back of the eye, or ocular fundus, has a mirror-like structure, the tapetum, behind the retina, or film, of this camera system. The tapetum produces the glow that you see at night when a light is directed into the eye. The retina is a transparent tissue that contains specialized cells, photoreceptors, that are stimulated by light as it passes through. In eyes with a tapetum, light is reflected back into the retina to enhance this stimulation. The tapetum of the cat is approximately 40 percent effective in reflecting; thus the effect of small amounts of light on the retinal photoreceptors is enhanced (Weale, 1953). The yellow color of the tapetum has been attributed to riboflavin, which has been found in high concentrations in the cat eye (Pirie, 1966). As in man, the cat retina contains photoreceptors of two types: rods and cones. The photoreceptors in the cat retina are predominantly rods for night vision, and to a lesser extent cones for color and day vision (Steinberg, et al, 1973). The rods enhance night vision because their neural network in the retina and brain is summated, such that many rods converge on a single cell higher in the network. Thus the impulse from faint light that stimulates many rods, will be multiplied by converging on a single higher cell to excite it to send an impulse to the brain.

Many of the previously described anatomic features in the cat eye that aid vision in dim light also hinder sharp visual acuity. The optics of the cat eye result in a small image; the tapetum reflecting the light back onto the retina probably blurs the image as does a large pupil and the predominance of rods in the retina. With the presence of cones in the cat retina, it would be anticipated that the cat has some color vision. Behavioral studies testing for color vision over the years have given conflicting results, but more recent studies indicate that cats have some color perception but cannot distinguish yellow versus green. The consensus seems to be that while cats may have some color vision, color does not play an important role in their visual clues (Duke-Elder, 1958; Jacobs, 1981).

EXAMINATION OF THE CAT EYE

History

Pertinent histories tend to range into the two extremes of very detailed (the cat kept exclusively indoors) or none available (free-roaming outdoor cats). When considering the history of ocular diseases, it is important to consider the rapidity of onset, course since detection of the problem, age of the patient, and concurrent general (systemic) problems, if any. Very rapid onset may indicate traumatic origin of a disease; whereas a slow, deliberate course may indicate neoplastic (cancerous) diseases, chronic infectious disease, or failing metabolism. The risk of most neoplasms increases with age, as do most organ failures such as kidney and liver failure. Many of the ocular diseases in cats are part of a systemic or general disease, and thus the total animal must always be considered and examined.

Opposite: **Diagram of cat's eye.**

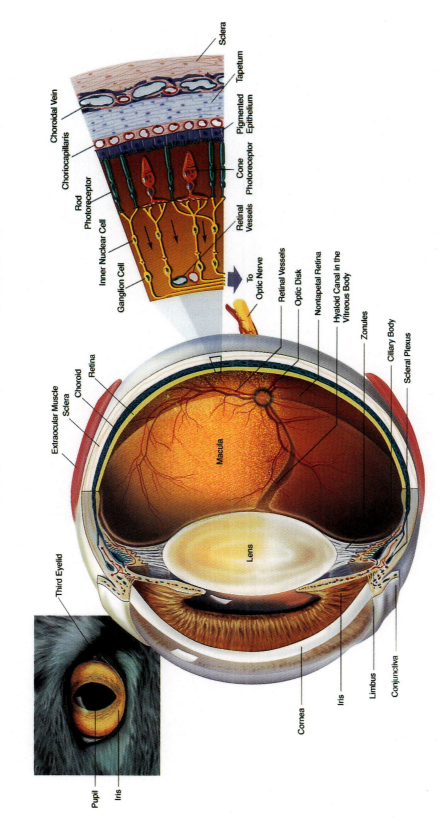

Cat Health Encyclopedia

Restraint

As one might expect, examination of the cat eye poses certain challenges due to the unique personality of the cat. In general, cats are not tolerant of examination with a bright light (remember their nocturnal nature) or manipulative procedures that might be uncomfortable or require some patience. They have a very mobile third eyelid (membrana nictitans) that often quickly covers part or all of the cornea, obscuring examination of underlying structures. If any discomfort is present from the ocular problem, the third eyelid's protective function is initiated, hampering examination of deeper structures without manipulation.

If the cat is fractious, impatient, or in pain, restraint may be necessary to complete an examination. The handler can protect himself by wrapping the body of the cat in a large heavy towel or using restraint bags specifically designed for this task. Most pet cats do not require these precautions if one recognizes and modifies techniques to respond to the unique personality of the cat. The experienced observer may overcome an uncooperative patient by decreasing the intensity of the examination light and performing multiple short examinations. Short examination bursts, combined with keeping the cat alert by changing head positions and keeping the patient off balance, may keep the third eyelid retracted enough to see deeper structures. In completely uncooperative cats and if the examination is critical to the diagnostic process, sedation with ketamine (Ketaset, Fort Dodge Laboratories Inc., Fort Dodge, IA 50501) allows examination as the eyes remain straight, the third eyelid is retracted, and the pupils are dilated.

Examination

OWNER EXAMINATION

Utilizing a penlight, an owner can often make some preliminary observations regarding diseases of the front of the eye. The following problems can be evaluated on a preliminary basis by an owner, but should always be confirmed by a veterinarian.

1. Asymmetry of structures
2. Ocular discharge
3. Ocular pain
4. Ocular redness
5. Opacities of the eye
6. Pupil size and similarity
7. Color changes in the eye
8. Vision loss

Frontal view of cat eye illustrating the vertical slit pupil, tight lid-globe conformation, and slightly oval cornea.

The Feline Eye in Health and Disease

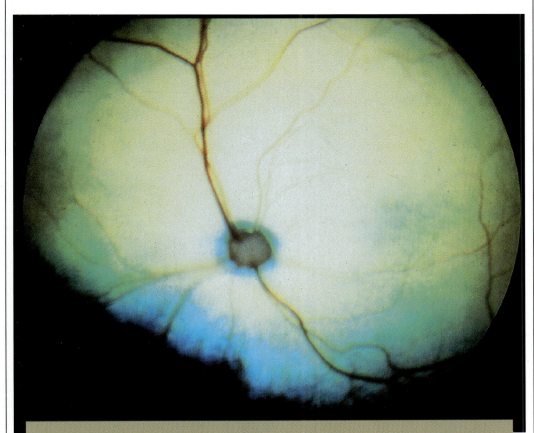

Normal cat ocular fundus with the bright colored tapetum. The vessels are originating from the round optic nerve that transmits the signals from the eye to the brain.

Symmetry

In general, the examiner should always try to evaluate facial and ocular symmetry, or making sure that both sides look similar. Asymmetrical facial swellings should be evaluated for size, tenderness, and rapidity of onset. Trauma from car accidents and infections from fighting will typically be rapid in onset and tender, whereas tumors will typically be slow and nonpainful. The eyelids and openings (palpebral fissures), position of the third eyelid, and the pupil size should be evaluated for symmetry. The presence of asymmetry helps the examiner to localize the source of the problem.

Discharge

The presence of ocular discharge, type of discharge, unilateral vs bilateral nature, season, source of a recently acquired cat, and housing conditions may be clues as to the origin of a discharge problem. Thick yellow discharge is indicative of bacterial involvement, whereas watery discharge may indicate irritation, viral infection, or obstruction of the outflow ducts (lacrimal openings). Free-roaming cats and multiple-cat households have an increased exposure risk to infectious diseases. Infectious diseases in cats may produce either bilateral or unilateral ocular discharge.

Cat Health Encyclopedia

Pain

Even with relatively minor irritation, cats frequently guard their eyes, evidencing a partial closure of the eyelids known as blepharospasm (*blepharo* refers to lid), so asymmetry of the lid openings should be evaluated. Prolapse of the third eyelid is usually found concurrently with blepharospasm. Unlike dogs, cats will develop blepharospasm even with minor conjunctival or surface irritation. The cornea is one of the most sensitive areas of the body, and, thus, breaks in the surface or ulcerations are a common and very important source of ocular pain. Whenever ocular pain is manifest, the cornea should be considered as a possible source of the pain. Your veterinarian will do this by staining the surface with fluorescein to detect ulcers or breaks in the surface of the cornea. The feline herpesvirus, which produces an upper respiratory infection, frequently produces very small defects in the corneal surface, and these may be difficult to see even with fluorescein. Larger ulcers may be detected as irregularities or craters on the surface of the cornea. When ulcers are suspected, your veterinarian should confirm as soon as possible, as ulcers always have the potential to worsen. Acute diseases inside the eye may produce outward pain, but the more common, insidious intraocular problems produce a radiating discomfort that is more akin to a headache. Thus, with conditions such as chronic inflammation inside the eye (uveitis) or glaucoma (increased pressure), the cat may hold the eyes open because the discomfort is not localized to the eye. Ocular pain should always be considered a serious sign until proven otherwise.

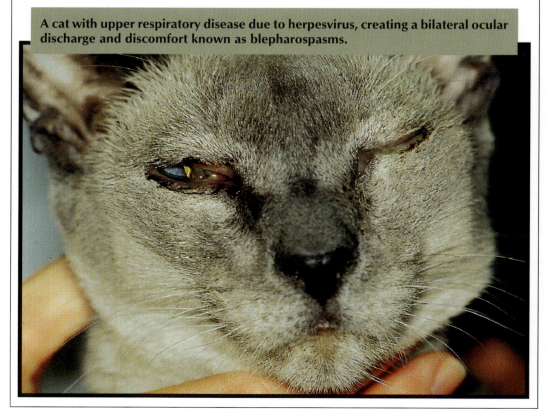

A cat with upper respiratory disease due to herpesvirus, creating a bilateral ocular discharge and discomfort known as blepharospasms.

THE FELINE EYE IN HEALTH AND DISEASE

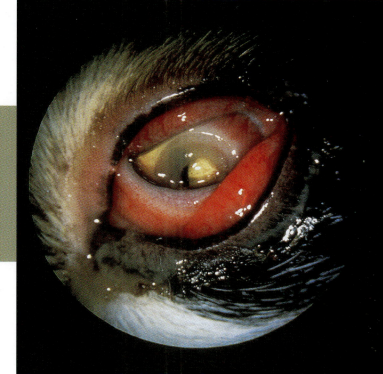

A very deep central corneal ulcer. The conjunctiva is very red and swollen and this was probably a complication of the herpes virus.

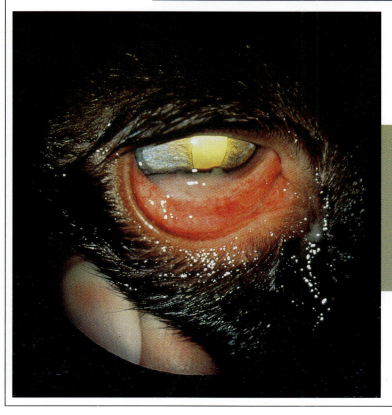

The lower lid is pulled down to expose the red, swollen conjunctiva that in this case was due to chlamydia infection. Note the ocular discharge.

CAT HEALTH ENCYCLOPEDIA

OCULAR REDNESS

Ocular redness usually refers to the increased redness of the mucous membranes or conjunctiva surrounding the cornea and lining the lids. Unless swollen and protruding from under the lids, redness may not be obvious in the cat because it has little exposed "white of the eye" due to a small fissure and tight eyelid conformation. Everting or pulling out the upper or lower lid may expose more of the conjunctiva to evaluate for redness and swelling (edema). Redness of the conjunctiva may indicate conjunctivitis (surface inflammation) or conjunctival hemorrhage, which is not serious, or intraocular disease, which may be blinding. Only a thorough examination by your veterinarian can differentiate the cause of the redness. Inflammation of the cornea eventually results in new blood vessels growing into the surface; and if numerous, they can be very red or mimic hemorrhage. Intraocular hemorrhage into the front of the eye is easily seen in most instances and can be localized internally versus the surface redness of the conjunctiva. Intraocular redness or hemorrhage always has serious implications and may indicate trauma, inflammation, hypertension (high blood pressure), or neoplasia.

OPACITIES TO THE EYE

Any opacity or clouding of the eye should be considered serious. A common concern of owners is the opacification due to prolapse or protrusion of the third eyelid over the globe. If owners have not observed this phenomenon, it is often misinterpreted as the eye having rolled back into the "head," because only part of the cornea is visible. This form of opacity is, of course, completely reversible in most cases. True opacities on the surface or in the eye are serious signs that require professional evaluation. Increased water (edema) in the cornea produces a bluish-white surface opacity that can be produced from a variety of causes. When accompanied by pain, corneal ulcerations should be suspected. Opacities deeper in the eye than the surface can be seen with a penlight and may occur from inflammation or cataracts. Cataracts are relatively infrequent in the cat whereas inflammation (uveitis) is quite common. If opacities are partial or involve one eye, vision problems will not be noted.

PUPIL SIZE

The cat's pupils are very distinctive and relatively easy to access as their irises are usually light in color and the dark pupil stands out in contrast. The pupils should be equal in size; and when examined in bright light or when directing a light into the eye, the pupils should briskly constrict (unless the cat is very frightened). Because of crossing fibers in the higher nervous pathways, both pupils should constrict equally when light is only shone into either one of them. Unequal pupils, dilated pupils that don't constrict, or constricted pupils that don't dilate in dim light are all abnormal findings. A professional examination will be needed to localize and find the cause for the abnormality. The most common cause for pupil abnormalities is intraocular disease and not a brain tumor.

COLOR CHANGES WITHIN THE EYE

The eye color inside the eye is imparted by the iris. While it can be

94

The Feline Eye in Health and Disease

normal to have a cat with two different colored irises or have one iris with more than one color (usually blue + another color), if it is normal, it will have been present since the cat was a kitten. Acquired changes in color in the interior of the eye should always be considered abnormal (although old cats may have senile darkening). The iris color may darken diffusely or in small areas and occur suddenly or very insidiously. Inflammation of the iris (iritis or anterior uveitis) is the most common cause of iris color change and is most dramatic in lightly pigmented and blue irises where they darken. If the condition is unilateral, the difference is often striking. Tumors invading the iris must also be considered but are slow and insidious in their course. Hemorrhage into the interior of the eye will change the eye color and obscure the iris. Hemorrhage, whether bright red or, if chronic, black, is usually easily distinguished, although the cause may not be obvious.

Vision loss

Evaluation of vision is often more accurately performed while watching the cat in an unknown environment. If vision has been insidiously lost, the patient in its own home will often accommodate without the owners being aware. Evaluation of vision in the cat is more difficult than in the dog because of their adaptive habits (tactile clues from whiskers) and because they often do not move around quickly and thus collide with objects. It is often unknown whether they are immobilized due to loss of vision or just not interested in exploring the environment. Animals can adjust to visual clues until almost all their vision is lost; and thus if blindness is obvious, they have probably lost a profound amount, or 90 percent, of their vision in both eyes. Owners frequently ask what percentage of vision their cat may have with a disease, but any answer is simply a guess and probably not a very accurate one at that.

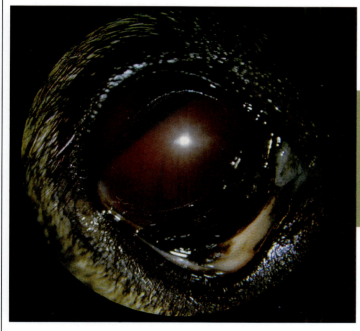

A cat that has the interior of the eye about half full of blood (hyphema) due to malicious BB injuries. Note the ocular discharge.

Cat Health Encyclopedia

OCULAR DISEASES

The emphasis on types of ocular diseases in the cat is quite different from that in the dog. While both species can get most of the same types of diseases, the frequency in which they are observed is quite different. The cat's head conformation has not been manipulated as much as in the dog (except for the Persian and Himalayan), and line breeding is not as widespread. Thus, conformational defects and genetic ocular defects are not observed with the same frequency. Excluding traumatic disease, the cat has few primary ocular problems, but many ocular syndromes associated with systemic diseases. Diseases will be discussed from the front to the back of the eye, and we will attempt to cover the unique and/or important diseases of feline ophthalmology.

Diseases of the Eyelid

NEONATAL CONJUNCTIVITIS

Everyone is aware that the eyelids of a kitten are fused at birth and do not separate until about ten days of age. Occasionally, the lids will open prematurely; but if tear production is adequate, usually there are no detrimental effects. If the closed lids should appear to bulge or a drop of discharge is seen at the inner corner of the eyelids, it might indicate an infection or conjunctivitis. The danger in the neonate is that the discharge can not drain and is retained against the cornea. Secondary ulceration and even perforation of the globe may occur before the owner realizes a problem exists. If the condition is suspected, your veterinarian can improve the condition by forcing the lids open, rinsing and treating with

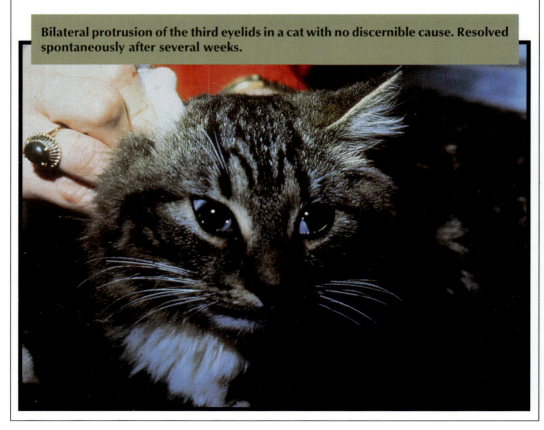

Bilateral protrusion of the third eyelids in a cat with no discernible cause. Resolved spontaneously after several weeks.

The Feline Eye in Health and Disease

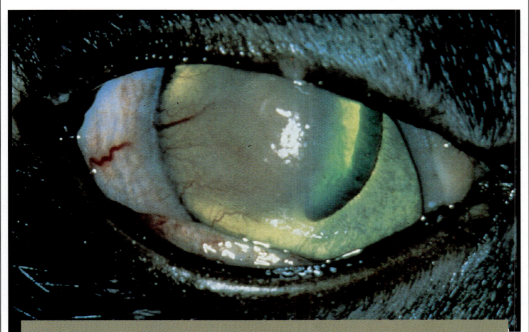

Proliferative lesion on the cornea of a cat that is typical of eosinophilic keratitis. Diagnosed by appearance and scraping of the surface to look for eosinophils.

topical antibiotics. One of the causes of this syndrome is the herpesvirus, but a variety of bacterial agents may be isolated. If the cornea is not ulcerated, the prognosis is usually good.

Agenesis of the Upper Eyelid

This is a relatively rare, but unique, disease of cats in which both of the upper lateral (outer portion) eyelids have not developed, leaving a large defect in the lid margin. Because the normal lid margin is missing, facial hairs are frequently misdirected against the cornea, producing pain and scarring of the surface. The condition may be isolated to an individual kitten, or varying degrees of the problem may be present in an entire litter. It has not been reported as an inherited condition. The dilemma is correcting the condition before it produces significant scarring, but having a patient of sufficient size to make the surgery safe and practical. The ocular pain is most noticeable in the young kitten and attenuates with age, and the scarring is not blinding so usually it is prudent to wait for growth to occur. Cryotherapy, or freezing the hair follicles, is an easy way to provide at least a temporary if not a permanent improvement. Severe forms may require extensive plastic surgery to reconstruct the upper eyelid. Additional anomalies may be present within the eye, so your veterinarian should examine the eye to determine the prognosis for vision.

Entropion

Entropion, or a rolling inward of the eyelid so that facial hairs are rubbing on the cornea, is usually secondary to sustained ocular pain in the average cat. The exception is the shortfaced Persian, in which the nasal side of the lids may roll inward because of crowding of tissue in this area. Entropion in the average cat involves the lower outer lid and can be secondary to prolonged discomfort from conjunctivitis or corneal ulcers. Once the facial hairs are rubbing on the cornea, a cycle of increased pain producing more spasms of the lids is established that must be broken to maintain normal conformation. Since the entropion in these cases is secondary, it is possible (if recognized early) to avoid entropion surgery if the primary problem can be treated and the pain relieved. Most cases are recognized at a later state, and the entropion is well established. In these instances, the entropion must be corrected, usually by skin excision and the primary problem that created the pain must also be treated if it is still present. Entropion surgery in the cat usually gives excellent results. The minor entropion seen medially in Persian cats is usually not treated surgically because the signs are mild, and there is not a good procedure for operating in this region.

BLEPHARITIS

Blepharitis, or inflammation of the eyelids, can occur from a variety of causes and may be part of a more generalized dermatitis. Causes may be trauma, mites, ringworm, solar radiation, immune-mediated skin diseases, and bacterial infections. Infections from fight wounds are the most common syndrome in male cats. They manifest as a tender swelling, usually over the eye. They may drain spontaneously outwardly or inwardly into the conjunctival sac. The abscess must heal from the inside out, and premature closure of the opening often results in

Heterochromia in a white cat that was deaf.

The Feline Eye in Health and Disease

A Siamese cat that had a unilateral anterior uveitis (iritis) that caused the iris to turn brown.

recurrence. Chronic blepharitis requires systematic diagnostic testing by your veterinarian. Testing may include skin scrapings, fluorescent light examination, cultures for bacteria and fungi, and skin biopsies to detect the cause. Testing for viral agents that produce immune suppression such as feline immunodeficiency virus (FIV) may also be indicated for chronic or relapsing abscesses and mange. Any attempt at home remedies should consider that the medications should be safe and nonirritating for the eye, as they are likely to contact the cornea.

Eyelid Neoplasms (Tumors)

In general, neoplasms in the cat are not as frequent as in the dog; but when they occur, they are almost always more malignant. This is evidenced in the cat by the most common lid tumor being a squamous-cell carcinoma (SCC). It is typically found in lightly pigmented or white cats. It is related to chronic exposure to sunlight (ultraviolet radiation) and may accompany changes to the tips of the ears, lips, or nostrils. The condition increases with age and typically appears as an erosive, raw granulating lesion on the lid margin. While locally invasive, they usually do not spread to distant organs until late in the course of the disease. Immune suppression from FIV may have a modulating influence on the spread of the tumor. Confirmation of the clinical impression is by biopsy, either by excising a piece, fine needle aspiration, or by exfoliative cytology (scraping cells off of the surface). In general, the larger the piece of tissue examined the more accurate the diagnosis. Many therapies have been successful in treating SCC, and the choice will vary as to the location, invasiveness, availability of equipment, and risk to the patient. Early detection may be treated with simple excision, freezing (cryotherapy), heat (hyperthermy), radiation, and intralesional chemotherapy. Early detection with regular rechecks is the key to successful therapy, combined with minimizing ongoing ultraviolet radiation exposure. As these cats are predisposed, other sites of involvement may develop and thus monitoring is a critical element (Rogers, 1994).

Conjunctival Diseases

CONJUNCTIVITIS

Conjunctivitis, or inflammation of the conjunctiva, is a common disease in cats and usually is due to an infectious agent. Because of the tight lid-globe conformation and little exposed conjunctiva to the environment, the normal cat does not have the high percentage of resident bacterial flora that is found in the dog (34 percent. vs. 91 percent (Campbell et al, 1973).

The signs of conjunctivitis are varying degrees and type of ocular discharge. Despite the systemic infectious origin, the condition may be unilateral; and after seven to ten days, may or may not become bilateral. With inflammation, the conjunctiva becomes red or hyperemic and swollen or edematous (chemosis). Unless the swelling causes protrusion of the conjunctiva from under the lids, the latter signs may not be noted. Conjunctivitis in man is often described as producing a sensation like having sand in your eye. Cats with conjunctivitis often manifest with some degree of ocular discomfort, namely third eyelid protrusion and narrowing of the palpebral fissure. Systemic signs or the history may provide clues to the cause, as many cases are associated with respiratory viruses and exposure to new ("carrier") cats. The appearance of the signs of conjunctivitis is not enough to make a definitive diagnosis as to the cause. Practical diagnostic techniques include taking scrapings from the conjunctival surface to look for cell types and infectious agents. Similar slides can often be sent to special laboratories for immunoflorescent staining to detect herpesviruses and chlamydial organisms. Viral culturing is generally expensive and not

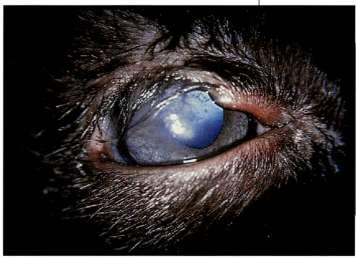

Agenesis of the upper eyelid that creates a large defect in the margin of the lid and the facial hairs are rubbing the cornea, producing scarring and discomfort.

The Feline Eye in Health and Disease

practical in most situations. Infectious agents are most likely to be detected early in the course of the disease. Even with systematic and extensive diagnostics, the cause of chronic conjunctivitis in the cat is often not determined (Nasisse et al, 1993).

Three infectious syndromes have been described with feline conjunctivitis. In order of decreasing frequency they are: feline herpesvirus, *Chlamydia*, and *Mycoplasma*. Only the chlamydial agent has been documented to produce conjunctivitis in man, the feline herpes agent being specific for the cat. Despite this, because the cause of conjunctivitis may not be definitively diagnosed, it is prudent to wash one's hands after handling a cat with conjunctivitis to minimize self-inoculation.

Feline herpesvirus: The herpesvirus is one of the main agents responsible for upper respiratory disease in cats and in most studies is the most common cause of conjunctivitis in the cat. It is a ubiquitous virus that virtually all cats become exposed to and most (80 + percent) become chronic carriers. Cats that are carriers are carriers for life, but only intermittently shed the virus. When they are not shedding the virus, there is no practical way to isolate the agent, as they become sequestered in the nerve cells of certain ganglia in the brain. Shedding is precipitated by stress, which can come from many sources, i.e. other diseases, surgery, boarding, corticosteroids. The virus is usually spread by direct contact and aerosolization for 3 to 4 feet. The virus survives a day in the environment and is killed by most disinfectants (Gaskell, 1984, Nasisse et al, 1992).

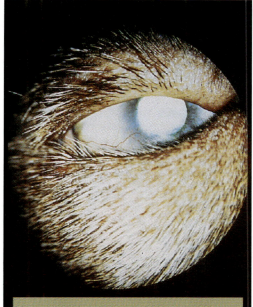

Entropion of the lower lid with the facial hairs rubbing on the cornea.

A squamous cell carcinoma on the lower lid of a white cat. This is the most common cancer of the eyelid of the cat and is related to ultraviolet light exposure.

Cat Health Encyclopedia

The manifestations of disease vary and depend on the interaction of the individual cat's immunity and the particular strain of the virus. Cats that are immune compromised, such as those with feline leukemia virus (FeLV) or feline immunodeficiency virus (FIV), are more susceptible to manifestations as are those individuals that respond with excessive inflammation. In general, the very young will have the most severe manifestations of either ocular or respiratory signs. In most individuals, the manifestations of herpes are mild and self-limiting; and it is only a small group of individuals that have either severe or persistent manifestations that are of therapeutic concern. Although the latter are a small group, they are a very frustrating group to manage in many instances.

Herpes conjunctivitis is usually, but not invariably, bilateral. The signs may be present with obvious respiratory involvement in the young kitten; but in older cats, the latter may not be noted. The conjunctival signs begin with watery (serous) discharge that usually becomes mucoid to mucopurulent or yellow with chronicity. The young kitten may develop raw surfaces that result in varying degrees of adhesions of the conjunctiva (symblepharon) to adjacent surfaces. The cornea may be involved with varying degrees of ulceration or inflammation and if present helps to differentiate herpes from the other infectious causes. The most practical diagnostic test is fluorescent antibody staining of conjunctival scrapings to look for virus. Because of the carrier state, negative results do not preclude the diagnosis; and response to specific antiviral therapy may be suggestive. Unfortunately, the various antiviral preparations are expensive, require frequent therapy for a period of time, and not all herpes strains will respond to a given antiviral preparation. The available antivirals were developed for human ocular use. In limited testing of the available preparations with the feline herpesvirus, the relative potency was triflurothymidine (Viroptic, Burroughs Wellcome Co., Cornwallis Rd., Research Triangle Park, NC 27707), idoxuridine (Stoxil, Smith Kline & French Lab., 1500 Spring Garden St., PO Box 7929, Philadelphia, PA 19101), adenine arabinoside (Vira-A, Parke-Davis Division of Warner-Lambert Co., Morris Plains, NJ 07950), and acyclovir, which is not available as an ophthalmic preparation in the US (Nasisse et al, 1989). If the signs are unremitting or relapses are common, additional immunostimulants such as topical interferon and utilizing vaccine virus to stimulate immunity might be attempted. The latter forms

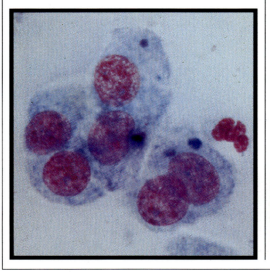

Conjunctival cells that contain small blue inclusion bodies of *Chlamydia psittaci* from a case on conjunctivitis.

THE FELINE EYE IN HEALTH AND DISEASE

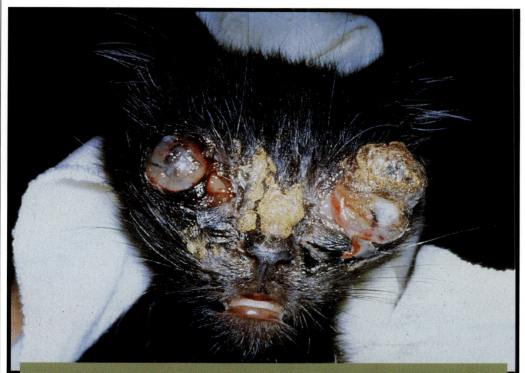

A kitten with dramatic ocular complications of herpes infection. One globe is ruptured from a perforated corneal ulcer and the other cornea is scarred and covered with crusted exudate. This severity is unusual and most likely to occur in the young.

of therapy have mainly anecdotal evidence as to their effectiveness.

It is questionable what role vaccination has in modulating or preventing ocular signs of herpes. In catteries with outbreaks, increasing the ventilation, diluting the concentration of cats, washing and disinfecting hands between handling cats, separating pregnant queens, and vaccination and isolation of obviously sick animals should be performed to stop the outbreak (Ford, 1991, Dawson et al, 1993).

Chlamydial conjunctivitis: This is another infectious disease that is spread via the respiratory system. It is caused by *Chlamydia psittaci*, and the signs are almost exclusively a conjunctivitis, although young cats may develop some respiratory signs.

The signs typically start in one eye and spread to the second eye in seven to ten days. Untreated, the signs persist for months and perhaps years. Coinfection with the feline immunodeficiency virus prolongs the carrier state (O' Dair, et al, 1994). With chronicity, the conjunctiva becomes very thickened and the discharge decreases. Ocular discomfort is often marked. If the patient is presented early enough, conjunctival scrapings often have inclusion bodies in the epithelial cells which are diagnostic, but with chronicity they are unlikely to be found. Therapy is a topical tetracycline ointment, which is required for at least two weeks beyond remission of signs to minimize a relapse (Cello, 1967,

Martin, 1989). Vaccines are available to prevent this syndrome (Gill et al, 1987). The agent is short lived in the environment and most disinfectants are effective.

Mycoplasma felis: This is the least common form of infectious conjunctivitis and recent surveys would suggest it is of minimal importance. The diagnosis is made by conjunctival scrapings and finding the organism on the cells. A variety of antibiotics are effective (Campbell et al, 1973).

Third Eyelid, or Haw

The third eyelid, or haw, of the cat is a mobile structure that functions to protect the eye, contains lymphoid follicles used in local immunity, and has one of the two lacrimal glands that produce tears. It has a supporting structure of cartilage that is covered with conjunctiva; thus it is usually involved with most cases of conjunctivitis. The movement of the third eyelid across the globe is produced by a muscle that pulls it across and by retraction of the globe into the orbit that pushes it across by pressing on a fat pad at its base. A smooth muscle helps to keep it retracted. It is necessary to understand these various mechanisms to determine the cause of protrusion or prolapse. Any condition that either increases or decreases the mass in the bony orbit can cause protrusion. The latter conditions may range from inflammation, neoplasia, hemorrhage, dehydration, emaciation, to muscle atrophy. Pain is a major cause of protrusion where it is acting in a protective manner. Nerve dysfunction, usually with an accompanying decrease in pupil size, may produce protrusion, as may toxins that affect muscles or nerves. A syndrome of bilateral protrusion of the third eyelid is known in the cat where there are no obvious causes for

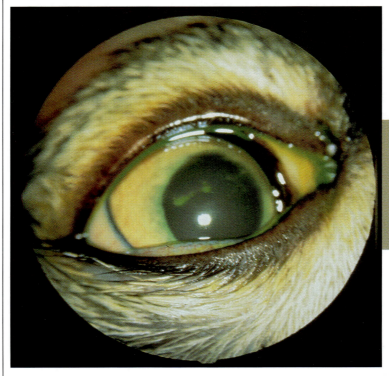

A linear ulcer stained with fluorescein that is indicative of herpes infection in the corneal epithelium.

The Feline Eye in Health and Disease

Performing a Schirmer tear test in a cat to determine the volume of tear production.

the protrusion. The cats are systemically healthy, and there is no evidence of orbital or ocular diseases. Many veterinarians have reported vague signs of digestive upset, malaise, internal parasitism, and claimed improvement with deworming. The course of the protrusion is usually about four to eight weeks. A study in England reported finding a torovirus in many cats with third eyelid protrusion and diarrhea (Muir et al, 1990). As this form of protrusion is self-limiting, it is usually not treated, although some owners feel the protrusion is so severe that the animal can not see well. Topical drops that stimulate the smooth muscle will temporarily produce retraction but must be continued until spontaneous improvement occurs.

Lacerations of the third eyelid: Fighting cats frequently suffer wounds to the third eyelid. Defects in the leading edge rarely heal without suturing. While small defects are only of esthetic significance, if appearances are important they should be sutured to promote healing.

Lacrimal (Tear) system

The lacrimal system consists of two lacrimal glands and the collecting ducts for the tears. One lacrimal gland is located under the upper outside (lateral) rim of the orbit, and the second is located at the base of the third eyelid. Tears serve several functions and are a surprisingly important component of the ocular surface, i.e. cornea, conjunctiva. Tears supply nutrition, oxygen, and infection-fighting substances to the cornea and conjunctiva. They wash out and dilute noxious or irritating substances from the surface, and they fill in any small optical imperfections to the corneal surface. Tears are what are responsible for the luster one is used to observing from the ocular surface. In broad terms, diseases of the lacrimal system are manifested usually as either a deficiency or an excess of tears.

Keratoconjunctivitis sicca (KCS) is a deficiency of tears and is not nearly as common in the cat as in the dog. Cats also seem to tolerate a decreased tear production without developing the profound lesions that are usually found in the dog. The diagnosis is made by measuring the tear production with small strips of filter paper (Schirmer tear test) placed in the conjunctival sac for 1 minute. Normal for the cat is 17 mm/minute wetting; but the production of tears is very labile in the cat, and multiple tests should be taken to make the diagnosis. The causes of KCS in cats are not well clarified, but known causes are: herpesvirus infection, trauma, and congenital (Burmese) (Whitley et al, 1993). Herpes and trauma-induced KCS may be transient, and artificial tears should be administered until recovery. The use of cyclosporine to treat herpes KCS is unresolved as cyclosporine is known to potentiate herpes infections. Congenital KCS will not respond to stimulation with drugs, and transplanting a salivary duct (parotid duct transplant) may be the only means of improving the surface lubrication. The latter is a difficult surgery in the cat.

Epiphora is an overflowing of tears onto the face due to an obstruction of the outflow ducts as opposed to lacrimation, which is an increased production of tears that then overflow onto the face. Obstruction of the outflow ductal openings may occur in kittens with severe herpes conjunctivitis and the formation of secondary adhesions. Persian and Himalayans may have malpositioning of the ductal openings because the lower lid is rolling in (entropion). These breeds may also have a congenital lack of development of either the orifice or the ducts. Differentiation as to the cause requires lacrimal duct flushing, which in the cat usually necessitates general anesthesia. In addition, conjunctivitis, with its attendant increased lacrimation, is not managed as well in the short-nosed cats. Treatment and emphasis on

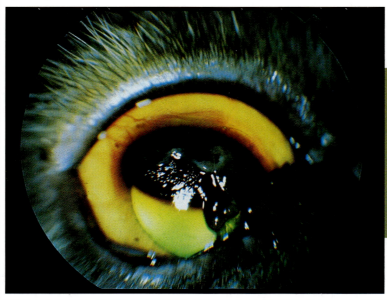

A corneal sequestrum or nigrum that is characterized by a black plaque on the surface of the cornea. A brown mucous is also accumulated on the lower lid.

The Feline Eye in Health and Disease

Multifocal flat pigment patches that have slowly developed in the iris. Once they are of this magnitude the diagnosis of iris melanoma is quite obvious.

diagnostics will depend on the history, involvement of one or both eyes, severity, and breed. When multiple contributing factors are present in an individual, usually the easiest things are treated first to determine the degree of improvement.

Cornea

The cornea, or anterior window into the eye of the cat, is large, transparent, and normally has a healthy luster imparted by the tear film on the surface. The cat cornea can sustain considerable damage and heal amazingly well.

Trauma

Fight wound lacerations and punctures are common in fighting males. The history will usually be sudden, and the accompanying changes will be increased tears, blepharospasm (blinking), third eyelid protrusion, and swollen conjunctiva. If the cornea can be examined, a wound of varying length and depth may be seen. Penetrating wounds may have the iris protruding out to plug or fill the defect, smaller wounds may be penetrating but be self-sealing, and partially thick wounds may exhibit gaping edges. Professional help will be required because anesthesia will be necessary both to fully evaluate and to treat. Infection should be assumed to be present and treated intensively with antibiotics that may be delivered by multiple routes (topical, intraocular and oral). The type of surgical correction will vary with the severity. While the prognosis must be guarded for any perforating injury into the inside of the globe, prompt therapy may save many of these eyes for function and esthetics.

Keratitis

Inflammation of the cornea is termed keratitis and may be ulcerative or proliferative in nature.

The cause of inflammation is quite variable, and inflammation is not synonymous with infection. Keratitis is usually accompanied by pain, watery discharge, conjunctivitis, third eyelid prolapse, corneal opacity/irregularities, and blood vessel ingrowth.

The causes of keratitis vary from mechanical causes (i.e., hair, foreign bodies, and trauma), tear deficiencies, nerve deficits, infections, immune-mediated (allergy?), chemicals, and irradiation. Viral infection with or without an interaction with the host immune response is thought to be responsible for the majority of ulcerative and non-ulcerative keratitis syndromes in cats. The major agent is once again the ubiquitous feline herpesvirus. The most characteristic corneal change occurs in the initial primary infection stage, where it produces an unusual linear or branching ulcer that is superficial in the epithelium (Bistner et al, 1971). These changes require fluorescein staining and often special blue lights to visualize. They are usually self-limiting, although topical antiviral drugs will shorten the course. On occasion, the ulcer may become larger in size and depth. Progression in depth may occur from bacterial contamination or sterile enzymatic digestion of the cornea. Persistence of the virus in the cornea, specific strains of the virus, and the host response to the virus may all interplay to produce more complex and devastating inflammatory changes that result in scarring and vascularization (Nasisse et al, 1995). The diagnosis of this syndrome is often by presumption, as the virus may not be isolated or demonstrable. Therapy is more controversial, as both antiviral therapy and anti-inflammatory therapy may be needed.

CORNEAL SEQUESTRUM

Corneal sequestrum, or nigrum, refers to a unique syndrome in which a black-to-brown plaque develops within the cornea, starting from the surface and spreading in size and depth. The predisposing factor appears to be a chronic break in the surface of the cornea. Among the cat breeds, the Persian and the Himalayan are predisposed, so other as-of-yet undefined factors also need to be considered. The cause for the slow-healing ulcer that allows the process to get started can probably be anything that produces an ulcer, but once again the main cause appears to be the herpesvirus and has been experimentally produced (Nasisse et al, 1989). The syndrome can progress very rapidly up to a point, remain static, and then some individuals will spontaneously slough the plaque from the cornea. Most cats experience pain and the sloughing is unpredictable, so surgical excision is a more rapid and predictable resolution. Simple excision may result in a reoccurrence in the surgical area, so most surgeons will do ancillary procedures to cover the surgically created ulcer (Whitley et al, 1993).

EOSINOPHILIC KERATITIS

Eosinophilic keratitis is a bilateral proliferative change in the cornea that is characterized by the unique finding of numerous eosinophils (blood cells associated with allergy and parasitism) on corneal scrapings. The condition is diagnosed by the typical appearance and the presence of eosinophils on corneal scrapings. The process can cover significant amounts of the corneal surface, and the patient is usually in pain. The cause is unknown, although the cellular reaction would indicate an immune reaction or allergy. Many clinicians feel that the herpesvirus is involved with this syndrome and treat with antivirals in addition to drugs to control inflammation. Relapses may occur if chronic low-level therapy is not maintained (Whitley et al, 1993).

CORNEAL DYSTROPHIES AND DEGENERATIONS

Noninflammatory corneal opacities are relatively rarely observed in the cat compared to the dog. These opacities may result from calcium, various kinds of fats, water (edema), or other metabolic products that are not degraded because of an enzyme deficiency. The latter conditions are termed lysosomal storage diseases and result from an inherited deficiency in a cellular enzyme. In addition, those cats with enzyme deficiencies often have skeletal and neurologic abnormalities. While they are of interest as animal models of human diseases, they are very rare.

In Florida, dogs and cats frequently develop white spots 1 to 3mm in size that are white and hazy. An animal may develop several spots, but blindness does not occur. Inflammation does not develop, and they do not seem to be responsive to any medications used; and thus most veterinarians have given up trying to treat them. The cause is unknown, but an acid-fast bacillus (bacteria) has been demonstrated on biopsy material (Fischer et al, 1987).

Diseases of the Iris

A blue iris in either both eyes, one eye or part of one eye (heterochromia) is normal for animals that have an albino gene. The dominant gene for white fur in cats allows the expression of the gene for blue eye; but it is incompletely dominant, so all white-furred cats do not have blue eyes. White-furred cats with blue irises may also be deaf due to defective development in the internal ear. The genes for eye color in the white-furred cat are independent of the coat color, but the blue eye color is expressed only in the presence of the gene for white fur. Small pigmented spots on the head of white-furred cats decrease the likelihood of deafness (Bergsma et al, 1971).

The Siamese cat is a partial albino and while it does not have hearing problems, a misrouting of nerve fibers from the eye to the brain may result in "crossed eyes," or esotropia. The inward deviation of the eyes develops in the first six months of life and is thought to be a compensatory mechanism to the abnormal nerve projections from the retina to the brain (Creel, 1971, Hubel et al, 1971). A fine pendular nystagmus, or fine rapid eye movements, may also be noted.

The most common disease of the iris is inflammation and is termed anterior uveitis, iritis, or iridocyclitis (usually the ciliary body is also inflamed). Uveitis is potentially very serious because of the potential to blind the cat through sequelae of cataracts, glaucoma, pupillary membranes, or involvement of the back of the eye. The condition may be unilateral or bilateral, depending on the cause. While external blunt or penetrating trauma may produce uveitis, the most common cause appears to be systemic viral or protozoal infections. Fungal infections, neoplasia, and hypertension may also produce uveitis syndromes. The last decade has brought great progress in elucidating the various causes of uveitis in the cat with the availability of several diagnostic tests for the infectious agents. Various serologic surveys (an animal's antibody response) and series of pathologic

CAT HEALTH ENCYCLOPEDIA

cases have given conflicting evidence that, to date, remains to be clarified.

The signs of anterior uveitis are more dramatic when unilateral and the normal eye is compared to the abnormal. Typically, minimal pain is evidenced, the conjunctiva is red, the cornea may have a hazy appearance, and some degree of a fibrin clot admixed with blood may be seen in the anterior chamber of the most severe cases. The iris color darkens and the pupil may be smaller than normal, but more frequently adhesions develop that create an irregular contour to the pupil and limits mobility.

The relative importance of the various causes of anterior uveitis based on serologic surveys were: *Toxoplasma gondii* (toxoplasmosis, caused by a protozoan parasite) was associated with 79 percent, feline immunodeficiency virus (FIV) with 23 percent, feline leukemia virus (FeLV) with 6 percent, feline infectious peritonitis (FIP) with 27 percent, and 10 percent were negative for all agents tested (Chavkin, et al, 1992). Some pitfalls with interpretation are:

- a negative FeLV test does mean that the cat does not absolutely have FeLV because only 70 percent with the ocular form of lymphoma are positive;
- FIP titers are of little value in diagnosing disease as they cross react with more benign forms of the virus and only measure exposure;
- while serology links *Toxoplasma* with anterior uveitis in the majority of cases, histopathology of uveitis cases enucleated because of glaucoma complications has failed to demonstrate the organism in the eye (Peiffer et al, 1991). Thus it is either in very low numbers or the uveitis is perhaps immune-

mediated. Despite the lack of visible organisms in the tissues, cats treated with an antibiotic effective against toxoplasmosis have a better response than those treated with anti-inflammatory drugs used alone.

Therapy of anterior uveitis should include atropine to dilate the pupil and a topical corticosteroid to suppress inflammation unless the cause is known to be a bacterium or fungal agent. Topical corticosteroids are utilized with good ocular responses against the viral-associated uveitis but are only palliative because of the primary systemic disease. The intraocular pressures should be monitored in these eyes, as glaucoma or increased intraocular pressure is a common complication.

HEMORRHAGE IN THE EYE (HYPHEMA)

Blood may be visualized in the anterior chamber or interior of the eye in front of the iris. Bleeding is usually recognized by the bright red color; but, if old, the hemorrhage changes to a black color. Hemorrhage may occur secondary to blunt or perforating injuries, bleeding disorders, diseases of the blood vessels, tumors in the eye, hypertension (high blood pressure,) and various leukemias. If the bleeding is only in one eye and blood obscures the examination, ultrasound is often invaluable to detect a tumor or foreign body. All old cats with hemorrhage should have their blood pressure checked, as hypertension is quite common. If possible, therapy is directed at the primary problem; and in most cases the blood will spontaneously escape from the eye unless it is clotted.

NEOPLASIA OF THE IRIS

The most common primary tumor arising from the iris is a melanoma,

The Feline Eye in Health and Disease

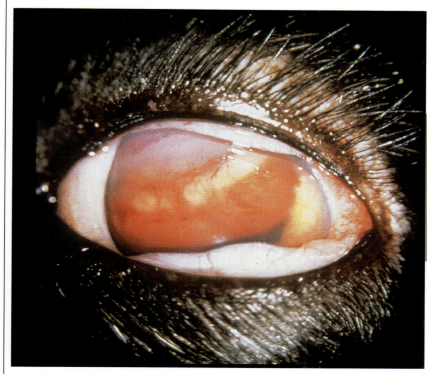

A large mass in the eye that is arising from the iris and associated with lymphosarcoma.

or a tumor derived from pigment. It manifests as a pigment patch that slowly enlarges and usually is diffuse, rather than nodular. The course may be rapid or slow but eventually, thickening of the iris leads to glaucoma due to obstruction of fluid leaving the eye. In the early stages these can be difficult to differentiate from senile benign pigmented spots on the iris. As with most tumors in cats, these are reported to metastasize to internal organs in about 60 percent of the cases (Patnaik et al, 1988). Because these eyes are quite functional until late complications occur, there is great owner resistance for enucleation (removal of the eye). Intuitively, one would say that this delay increases the chance for spread, but this has not been confirmed. Enucleation is the treatment of choice as the lesion in most cases is diffuse.

Lymphosarcoma, which in the cat is caused by the feline leukemia virus (FeLV), is the most common secondary tumor and typically involves both eyes. It may appear as a solid tumor or be associated with anterior uveitis. Significant palliative effects can be obtained with the eye lesions with topical or systemic corticosteroid therapy. Despite the ocular improvement, the prognosis is guarded for the life of the cat.

Glaucoma

Glaucoma is an elevation of the intraocular pressure, which in turn destroys function in the back of the eye (retina and optic nerve), thus resulting in blindness. In the cat, glaucoma is usually secondary to other diseases that interfere with the normal circulation of fluid in the anterior chamber. Aqueous, or the fluid filling the front of the eye, is continuously produced by the ciliary process, circulates through the pupil into the anterior chamber, and then escapes through small vascular channels in the periphery of the anterior chamber (this region is termed the "angle," or iridocorneal angle). Any process that obstructs the flow of the aqueous may produce glaucoma. Those obstructions are usually produced by anterior uveitis or, less commonly, neoplasia (Peiffer et al, 1991). On rare occasions, no obstructive or inflammatory phenomena are present, in which case, the condition is termed a primary glaucoma.

The signs of glaucoma in the cat are often subtle until late, and most cases of feline glaucoma are recognized quite late in the course. Injection of the large conjunctival vessels, enlargement of the globe, corneal haziness, and a dilated pupil are the signs most likely to be seen with glaucoma. If the condition is bilateral and advanced, blindness will be noted. Early detection relies on a means to measure the intraocular pressure, and this instrument is called a tonometer. Two tonometers are in common usage in veterinary medicine. They are the Schiotz tonometer, which the general practitioner is likely to have, and a Tono-Pen tonometer, which the specialists use. The latter is more versatile but is quite expensive. The high normal intraocular pressure is about 25mm Hg.

Glaucoma is a frustrating disease to treat because it is often presented too late and because it is often difficult to keep the pressure low no matter what therapy is employed. If vision is present and the intraocular pressures are intermediate in range (25-40), the pressure may be controlled with one or more medications. Medications used to treat glaucoma range from diuretics that decrease aqueous production, to topical drops that either increase the outflow capabilities or decrease the aqueous production. Pilocarpine-like drugs improve the outflow capabilities while beta-blockers such as timolol maleate decrease aqueous production. Because the continuous therapy often becomes erratic and the disease waxes and wanes, good consistent control is often difficult with medical therapy. Surgical alternatives for sighted eyes usually try to destroy the secretory capacity of the ciliary body utilizing either freezing (cryo) or heat (laser) applied to the surface of the eye. The pressures may drift upward over time and reapplication of the cryogen or laser may be necessary. Surgery is often combined with medications to achieve control of difficult cases.

Eyes that are blind but have elevated pressures should either be enucleated (removal of the eye) or have an evisceration with an ocular prosthesis placed. Enucleation is the only alternative if neoplasia is causing the glaucoma; but in most glaucomas, secondary to uveitis, evisceration offers a cosmetic alternative to enucleation.

Evisceration is a procedure that salvages the outer layer of the globe but removes all the internal tissue and replaces it with a black silicone ball. Postoperatively, a globe still remains, although the cornea has various degrees of opacification.

Diseases of the Lens

The lens continues to grow throughout most of the animal's life and is composed of a series of concentric fibers that meet opposing fibers at junctions that are called sutures. New lens fibers develop from cells on the surface so that the oldest portion of the lens, like the tree, is in the center, or nucleus. The newest portion is termed the cortex. The lens is encapsulated in an "elastic"

The Feline Eye in Health and Disease

An older cat that has glaucoma and a cataractous lens that is displaced forward. The dilated pupil is the glaucomatous eye. Both conditions are associated with anterior uveitis and toxoplasmosis is one of the underlying causes.

capsule and held in place by ligaments called zonules. The lens is unique in its transparency, and the most common disease is a loss of this transparency, or a cataract.

Cataracts

A cataract is any opacity of the lens or its capsule, and the definition does not imply that they are blinding. Cataracts are much less common in the cat than in the dog. Only a few instances of inherited cataracts have been noted, and they have usually been in Persian or Persian crosses. The cat is very resistant to cataracts secondary to diabetes mellitus, which is another common cause in the dog. Cataracts, when observed in the cat, are usually secondary to the effects of intraocular inflammation, trauma, feeding a queen's milk replacer, or secondary to toxic effects of drugs (often transient).

The pupil must be dilated fully to evaluate for the presence and extent of cataracts. Cataracts are often classified as to their stage of development. A minimal cataract, which an owner would not see, is called an incipient cataract. If a cataract is complete and in the swollen stage, it is called mature; and the owner would see this in the pupil. Cataracts that have become long-standing lose some of their water content and undergo varying degrees of shrinkage and reabsorbtion. Such cataracts are termed hypermature. Classification can also be based on age of onset (congenital, juvenile, senile), location in the lens (capsular, cortical, or nuclear), and by their cause (inherited, metabolic, toxic, radiation).

Other than very early cataracts due to toxicity, the vast majority of opacities once formed are permanent. If a cataract is complete, the only curative therapy would be surgical removal. There is no medical cure for cataracts despite many claims of a cure over the years. If the cataract is associated with inflammation, the prognosis for good surgical results is reduced because of the exaggerated postoperative inflammation and the possibility of additional lesions in the back of the eye. Focal cataracts usually require no therapy but should be monitored for progression.

DISPLACED LENS

The lens is held in place by a series of "ligaments," or zonules, and when these are congenitally defective, destroyed by inflammation, or torn with trauma, the lens may become displaced to varying degrees. Complete displacement (luxation) may occur either forward or backward, with the former more likely to be noted by the owner. Partial displacement (subluxation) will not be detected by the owner. Lens luxation is most common in older Siamese cats and may be bilateral in 21 percent of the cases. Uveitis is present with about two-thirds of the cases and has been serologically linked to FIV and toxoplasmosis (Olivero et al, 1991). Lens luxation may precipitate glaucoma. If the eyes are blind and the pressure is normal, no therapy is indicated. Elevated intraocular pressure and / or still visually functional eyes should have the lenses surgically removed. Removal of the lenses may not be completely curative for glaucoma if it is present.

Retinal Disease/Fundus Diseases

Because lesions of the back of the eye cannot be detected by the owner, they are usually noted because they are producing profound signs (i.e., blindness, dilated pupils), found incidentally on physical examination by the veterinarian, or the eye is being examined in searching for diagnostic clues for a systemic disease. All of the agents discussed in anterior uveitis may be responsible for posterior lesions as well. Lesions may be focal, multifocal, or diffuse. It is usually only the diffuse lesions that produce outward signs of blindness; and the mechanism is usually by either creating a retinal detachment, retinal degeneration/atrophy, creating an opacity in front of the retina, or extending to the optic nerve (transmits message from retina to brain). Blindness associated with inflammatory lesions produced by infectious agents usually is due to detachment of the retina. Genetic defects, increased intraocular pressure, nutritional deficiencies, and toxins produce retinal degeneration; and inflammatory lesions and glaucoma may affect the optic nerve.

Chorioretinitis is a term used to describe inflammation of the retina and the underlying choroid (vascular layer). In the cat, chorioretinitis is often due to an infectious agent, examples of which are feline leukemia virus, feline infectious peritonitis, feline immunodeficiency virus, toxoplasmosis, systemic fungal infections, migrating fly larvae, and, rarely, systemic bacterial infections. Kittens exposed *in utero* (during development in the mother) to viral panleukopenia may have residual focal scars in the retina and retinal dysplasia (malformed retina).

Retinal degeneration and cardiomyopathy (heart muscle degeneration) may be produced by a deficiency of taurine, which is a required amino acid in the cat. Most animals can manufacture taurine

The Feline Eye in Health and Disease

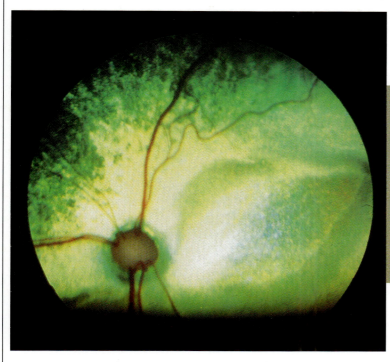

The football-shaped lesion in the tapetum was produced by a taurine deficiency in this cat. While quite large, cats with this degree of involvement do not usually have any vision problems.

from other sulfur-containing amino acids, but the cat can not and must get it from its diet. Cow milk and vegetable products are low in taurine, whereas meat and seafood are high. Cat food produced by reputable manufacturers now is routinely supplemented with taurine. The deficiency must be long standing to produce lesions. In young kittens, it took 10-45 weeks to produce retinal lesions; and in cats over 6 months of age, it required 11 months of a deficient diet. Dog foods have been deficient in taurine and when fed to cats for reasons of economy have been responsible for producing ocular lesions. Initial lesions are focal and do not produce symptoms if the deficiency is transient. Chronic deficiency results in diffuse retinal degeneration, which is irreversible. The incidence of the disease has significantly decreased over the last several years (Da Costa et al, 1990; Aguirre, 1978; Ricketts 1983, Hayes et al, 1975).

Inherited retinal degeneration (including progressive retinal atrophy, or PRA) in the Abyssinian has been reported from England, Europe, and the United States. The syndrome in the United States appears to be rare, judging from the few reports and clinical experience. In the Abyssinian, two forms have been described based on the age of onset: early onset, with lesions present at 1.5 to 2 years; and a late onset, with lesions at 6 years. Progressive retinal atrophy is a disease of the retinal photoreceptors, which prematurely die; and eventually the entire retinal architecture is disrupted. As the name implies, it is progressive to blindness and in almost all cases studied in the dog and cat has had a recessive mode of inheritance. The early-onset disease has photoreceptors that are abnormal from the beginning of birth and then start to degenerate over the ensuing months. Later onset disease has photoreceptors that are initially normal but undergo early cell death. The result is an insidious progressive disease that results in blindness. The young onset disease progresses more quickly than the older onset disease. Both eyes are identical in their appearance and are typified by having an increased tapetal sheen and a decrease in size and number of retinal vessels until they are almost completely lost (similar to advanced taurine deficiency). No therapy is available, and the condition is inherited as a simple recessive trait (Narfstrom et al, 1986; Barnett, 1982).

A variety of systemic infections, metabolic, and toxic diseases may manifest lesions in the retina and may or may not produce outward signs. Knowledge of these changes allows the veterinarian to use the eye as a window into the body for diagnostic clues. One of these diseases that is often "silent" until it affects the eye is hypertension, or high blood pressure. This is usually a disease of old cats, and the most common outward manifestations are ocular. The most typical lesions are multiple hemorrhages in the back of the eye and retinal detachments. Some of these patients will present with anterior ocular hemorrhages as discussed under hyphema. While other causes of bleeding disorders should be considered, if doppler equipment for measuring blood pressure is available, it can be easily diagnosed with a consistent systolic blood pressure over 160mm Hg. The causes of hypertension may be more difficult to detect, but the most common is chronic renal disease. Other causes of hypertension are hyperthyroidism, hyperadrenalcorticism, and, rarely, a tumor of the adrenal gland called pheochromocytoma. Essential hypertension is diagnosed when no predisposing diseases can be found for producing hypertension. Hypertensive therapy is still in its infancy in cats and often requires a trial of various drugs, drug combinations, and dosages. As frequent monitoring of the blood pressure is necessary, many of these patients pose logistical problems. Retinal detachments will reattach with normalization of the blood pressure; but most of the retinas evidence atrophy, and it is unusual to have vision return once the patient is blind (Morgan, 1986, Stiles, 1994).

Globe and Orbit

The orbit is the encasement for the globe in the skull and in the cat and dog is not completely enclosed by bone. Orbital disease usually produces signs referable to changes in volume that either make the eye more prominent (exophthalmos) or sunken (enophthalmos). Concurrent with the change in globe position is a protrusion of the third eyelid. Inflammation, with its attendant swelling, produces exophthalmos and pain on opening the mouth. In most instances, this develops over a short period of time. The source of the infection may be from a tooth root, salivary gland, or foreign body migration from the mouth. Neoplasia from structures in the orbit, adjacent to the orbit (such as the mouth, sinuses, nose and bone), or from a multicentric neoplasia such as lymphosarcoma are typically slow and progressive in development without the acute pain. In the cat, neoplasia may have the paradoxical effect of producing marked enophthalmos. Treatment of orbital infections is systemic antibiotics that may have to be injected because of the inability to administer oral medications with the pain on

The Feline Eye in Health and Disease

Advanced taurine deficiency in which all of the retinal blood vessels have disappeared and the tapetum is very bright. Cats with this degree of involvement are irreversibly blind.

opening the jaw. Removal of the source of the infections, e.g. tooth, is desirable but often not possible. Orbital neoplasia is most easily diagnosed with the newer imaging modalities such as CT (computed tomography) scanning and MRI (magnetic resonance imaging). The prognosis for orbital neoplasia is poor, with radiation therapy being the most promising palliative therapy.

Trauma to the orbit is common with car accidents and often results in proptosis of the globe or forward displacement of the eye out of the orbit. The amount of trauma to produce this in the cat is so great that frequently the globe is ruptured and massive internal damage to the globe has occurred. The condition is obviously an emergency, but even prompt therapy will not save those globes that have had severe injuries. While your veterinarian can readily replace the globe in the orbit and temporarily suture the lids closed to protect the globe, visual function will probably be lost (Gilger et al, 1995). If the globe has suffered severe internal damage, it is preferable to remove the eye, as it will usually shrink in size (phthisis bulbi), be blind, and have problems with discharge and lid conformation.

Traumatized eyes that become blind and have opaque media, so that your veterinarian can not visualize the entire eye, should be enucleated because of the risk of a tumor developing within the eye and spreading to the brain. Many of these eyes are also shrunken (phthisis bulbi). Undifferentiated sarcomas (connective tissue tumor) may develop from the injured lens, and the tumor has a tendency to travel up the optic nerve to the brain. If the media is opaque and the eye is nonvisual, this development occurs without the owner having any forewarning (Dubeilzig et al, 1994).

Congenitally small eye(s), or microphthalmos, may be observed in kittens. Depending on the severity, the eyes may or may not be visual. Genetic causes have not been established.

CAT OWNERSHIP BY IMMUNE-COMPROMISED INDIVIDUALS

Immune-compromised individuals should use some common sense and relatively simple precautions when owning pets such as cats. A wide variety of diseases may produce a suppressed immune system as may various therapies for cancer, organ transplant patients, and autoimmune diseases. While diseases as common as diabetes mellitus and chronic renal failure may reduce immunity, infection with the HIV (Human Immunodeficiency Virus) is one of the most catastrophic of the known syndromes.

Zoonotic diseases are those transmitted from animals to man and should be of concern to immunocompromised individuals. If such individuals are pet owners, they should share this concern with their veterinarian. While there are many zoonotic diseases, evidence to date indicates that the immunocompromised individual has a low risk with pet ownership. Zoonotic diseases that the cat may carry are: *Toxoplasma gondii*, *Salmonella* sp., *Chlamydia psittaci*, *Campylobacter* sp., *Bartonella* spp., *Rochalimaea henselae* (the agent causing cat scratch disease), and *Mycobacterium* sp.

General preventive measures should include feeding only quality

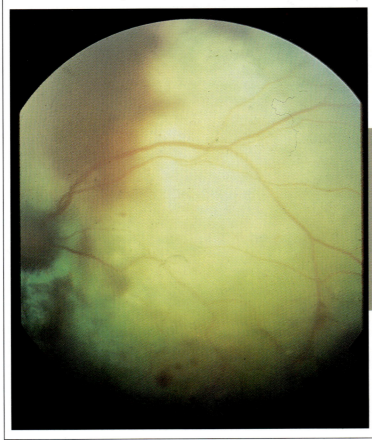

Retinal and subretinal hemorrhages associated with hypertension (high blood pressure) in an old cat. The retina is also detached. This is one of the most common causes of blindness in old cats.

THE FELINE EYE IN HEALTH AND DISEASE

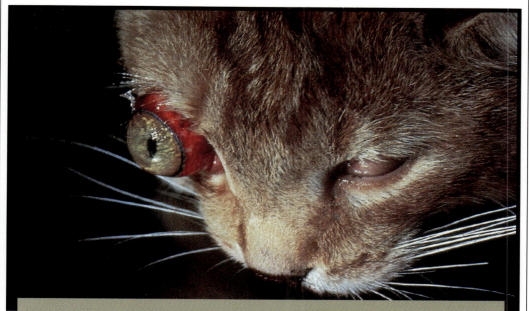

Proptosis of the globe. The lids become trapped behind the globe keeping the eye proptosed. As a rule the eye will be blind because of the magnitude of the trauma that is needed to do this in the cat.

commercial pet food, or cook thoroughly any supplemented food. Pets should not be allowed to drink from the toilet, scavenge garbage, or hunt. Litter boxes should be cleaned daily, preferably by a nonimmunocompromised individual; and the box should not be in the kitchen or dining areas. Disposable gloves should be worn if it is necessary to clean the litter box and hands should always be washed after handling the pet and especially before eating. Cats should be kept indoors to limit exposure and hunting. The immunocompromised person should avoid rough playing or restraint of the pet to minimize bites and scratches. If bitten or scratched, prompt thorough washing should be performed. Declawing or claw covers may be an option in an individual problem pet (Angulo et al, 1994).

Prompt veterinary attention should be sought for cases of diarrhea or any evidence of infections in the pet.

Obtaining young kittens from humane societies or pet stores should be discouraged because of the risk factors regarding age and source. Good preventive care for the pet should be maintained, including routine fecal examinations.

Additional information on pet ownership by immunocompromised owners may be obtained from Pets Are Wonderful Support (PAWS), 1278 University Ave, San Diego, CA 92103.

REFERENCES AND RECOMMENDED READING

Barnett, K: Progressive retinal atrophy in the Abyssinian cat. *Journal of Small Animal Practice.* 1982; 23: 763-766.

Bergsma, D; Brown, K: White fur, blue eyes, and deafness in the domestic cat. *Journal of Heredity.* 1971; 62: 171-185.

Bistner, SI; Carlson, JH; Shiveley, JN, et al: Ocular manifestations of feline herpesvirus infection. *JAVMA.* 1971; 159; 1223-1237.

Blake, R; Cool, SJ; Crawford, MLJ: Visual resolution in the cat. *Vision Res.* 1974; 14: 1211-1217.

Bonds, AB; Optical quality of the living cat eye. *Journal of Physiology.* 1974; 243: 777-795.

Campbell, LH; Fox, JG; Snyder, SB: Ocular bacteria and mycoplasma of the clinically normal cat. *Feline Practice.* 1973; Nov\Dec: 10-12.

Campbell, LH; Snyder, SB: Reed, C; Gox, JG: Mycoplasma felis-associated conjunctivitis in cats. *Journal of the American Veterinary Medical Association.* 1973; 163(8): 991-995.

Cello, RM: Ocular infections with PLT (bedsonia) group agents. *American Journal of Ophthalmology.* 1967; 63: 244-248.

Chavkin, MJ; Lappin, MR; Powell, CC; Roberts, SM; et al: Seroepidemiologic and clinical observations of 93 cases of uveitis in cats. *Prog Vet & Comp Ophthalmology,* 1992; 2: 29-36.

Creel, D: Visual system anomaly associated with albinism in the cat. *Nature,* 1971; 231: 465-466.

Da Costa, P; Hoskins, J: The role of taurine in cats: current concepts. *Compendium on Continuing Education for the Practicing Veterinarian.* 1990; 12: 1235-1240.

Dawson, S; Gaskell, RM: Problems with respiratory virus vaccination in cats. *Compendium on Continuing Education for the Practicing Veterinarian.* 1993; 15(1) 1347-1369.

Dubeilzig, RR; Hawkins, KL; Toy, KA; Rosebury, WS; Mazur, M; Jasper, TG: Morphologic features of feline ocular sarcomas in 10 cats: light microscopy, ultrastructure, and immunohistochemistry. *Prog. Vet & Comp Ophthalmology,* 1994; 4(1), 7-12.

Duke-Elder, S.: The vision of vertebrates. *System of Ophthalmology,* Vol. 1: *The Eye in Evolution.* C.V. Mosby Company, St. Louis, Missouri, 1958, 597-707.

Fischer, CA; Peiffer, RL: Acid-fast organisms associated with corneal opacities in a dog. *Trans Am College Vet Ophthalmology,* 1987; 18: 241.

Ford, RB: Viral upper respiratory infection in cats. *Compendium on Continuing Education for the Practicing Veterinarian.* 1991, 13(4): 593-602.

Gaskell, RM: The natural history of the major feline viral diseases. *Journal of Small Animal Practice.* 1984; 25: 159-172.

Gilger, BC; Hamilton, HL; Wilkie, DA; van der Woerdt, A; McLaughlin, SA; Whitley, RD: Traumatic ocular proptoses in dogs and cats: 84 cases. (1980-1993). *JAVMA.* 1995; 206(8): 1186-1190.

Gill, MA; Beckenhauer, WH; Thurber, ET: Immunogenicity and efficacy of a modified live feline *chlamydia* vaccine. *Norden News,* Summer 1987; 26-30.

Hayes, K; Carey, R; Schmidt, S: Retinal degeneration associated with taurine deficiency in the cat. *Science,* 1975; 188: 949-951.

Hubel, D; Wiesel, T: Aberrant visual projections in the Siamese cat. *Journal of Physiology.* 1971; 218: 33-62.

Jacobs, GH: Comparative color vision. Academic Press, San Francisco, CA, 1981, 129-131.

Martin, CL: Feline ophthalmology. 13th Kal Kan Symposium. 1989; 61-72.

Morgan, R: Systemic hypertension in four cats: ocular and medical findings. *Journal of the American Animal Hospital* Association. 1986; 22: 615-621.

Muir, P; Harbour, DA; Gruffydd-Jones, TJ; Howard, PE; Hopper, CD; Broadhead, HM; Clarke, CM; Jones, ME: A clinical and microbiological study of cats with protruding nictitating membanes and diarrhoea: isolation of a novel virus. *Veterinary Record.* 1990; 127: 324-330.

Narfstrom, K; Nilsson, S: Progressive retinal atrophy in the Abyssinian cat. *Invest. Ophthalmology Vis. Sci.* 1986; 27: 1569-1576.

Nasisse, MP; Davis, BJ; Guy, JS; Davidson, MG; Sussman, W: Isolation of feline herpesvirus 1 from the trigeminal ganglia of acutely and chronically infected cats. *Journal of Veterinary Internal Medicine.* 1992; 6(2): 102-103.

Nasisse, MP; English, RV, PhD; Tompkins, MB; Guy, JS; Sussman, W: Immunologic, histologic, and virologic features of herpesvirus-induced stromal keratitis in cats. *American Journal of Veterinary Res.,* 1995; 56(1): 51-55.

Nasisse, MP; Guy, JS PhD; Stevens, JB; English, RV; Davidson, MG: Clinical and laboratory findings in chronic conjunctivitis in cats: 91 cases (1983-1991). *JAVMA.* 1993; 203(6): 834-837.

Nasisse, MP; Guy, JS; Davidson, MG; Sussman, W; De Clercq, E: *In vitro* susceptibility of feline herpesvirus-1 to vidarabine, idoxuridine, trifluridine, acyclovir, or bromovinyldeoxyuridine. *American Journal of Veterinary Res.* 1989: 50(1): 158-160.

O'Dair, HA; Hopper, CD; Gruffydd-Jones, TJ; Harbour, DA; Waters, L: Clinical aspects of *chlamydia psittaci* infection in cats infected with feline immunodeficiency virus. *Veterinary Record,* 1994; 134: 365-368.

Olivero, D; Riis, R; Dutton, A. et al: Feline lens displacement: a retrospective analysis of 345 cases. *Prog. Vet. & Comp. Ophthalmology,* 1991; 1:485-491.

Patnaik, AK; Mooney, S: Feline melanoma: a comparative study of ocular, oral, and dermal neoplasms. *Veterinary Pathology.* 1988; 25: 105-112.

Peiffer, R; Wilcock, B: Histopathologic study of uveitis in cats: 139 cases. *Journal of the American Veterinary Medical Association.* (1978-1988)., 1991; 198: 135-138.

Pirie, A: The chemistry and structure of the tapetum lucidum in animals. *Aspects of Comparative Ophthalmology.* O. Graham-Jones, Ed. Pergamon Press Ltd., Great Britain, 1966, pp. 57-68

Ricketts, J: Feline central retinal degeneration in the domestic cat. *Journal of Small Animal Practice.* 1983;24: 221-227.

Rogers, KS: Feline cutaneous squamous cell carcinoma. *Feline Practice.* 1994; 22(5): 7-9.

Steinberg, RH; Reid, M; Lacy, PL: The distribution of rods and cones in the retina of the cat. *Journal Comp Neur.* 1973; 148(4): 229-248.

Stiles, J; Polzin, DJ; Bistner, SI: The prevalence of retinopathy in cats with systemic hypertension and chronic renal failure or hyperthyroidism. *Journal of the American Animal Hospital Association.* 1994; 30: 564-572.

Wassle, H; Optical quality of the cat eye. *Vision Res.* 1971; 11: 995-1006.

Whitley, DR; Gilger, BC; Whitley, EM; McLaughlin, SA: Diseases of the orbit, globe, eyelids, and lacrimal system in the cat. *Veterinary Medicine.* Dec. 1993; 1150-1162.

Whitley, DR; Whitley, EM; McLaughlin, SA: Diagnosing and treating disorders of the feline conjunctiva and cornea. *Veterinary Medicine.* Dec. 1993; 1138-1148.

Dr. Deborah Hadlock

Dr. Deborah Hadlock grew up in Maine and spent her senior year of high school as an AFS exchange student in Germany. She received her Bachelor of Science degree from the University of Illinois at Champaign-Urbana and Doctor of Veterinary Medicine (DVM) from the University of Pennsylvania. She completed an internship in small animal medicine and surgery at the prestigious Animal Medical Center (AMC) in New York City. After leaving the AMC, she entered private practice at Gramercy Park Animal Clinic in Manhattan. After several years in private practice, she joined the staff of Cardiopet full time as a consultant specializing in cardiology. Dr. Hadlock is a Diplomate of the American Board of Veterinary Practitioners, canine and feline specialty. She has contributed articles to several publications and has lectured internationally. She is better known as "Dr. Debbie."

CARDIOVASCULAR DISORDERS

Debbie Hadlock, DVM, Diplomate, ABVP

Cardiopet
48 Notch Road
Little Falls, NJ 07424

INTRODUCTION

At the center of the circulatory system lies the heart, a hollow, muscular, contractile organ serving as a pump to provide oxygenated blood to the peripheral circulation. It is composed of three layers: The outer (epicardium); the middle (myocardium), composed of cardiac muscle; and the inner (endocardium). The heart is enclosed in a fibrous sac (pericardium). Normally, there is a small space (pericardial cavity) between this sac and the outer layers of the heart.

The heart is divided into four cavities. Each lower cavity is the ventricle, right and left; each upper one the atrium, also right and left. The right side normally has no communication with the left. The atria are thin walled and serve as receiving chambers. The ventricles are thick walled and serve as pumping chambers. Valves between each atrium and ventricle (mitral valve on the left side, tricuspid valve on the right), as well as between each ventricle and outflow tract (aortic valve on the left side, pulmonary valve on the right) help regulate blood flow through the heart.

Contraction of the heart is called systole; relaxation when the heart fills and dilates is called diastole. Deoxygenated blood from body tissues enters the right heart, which pumps it to the lungs where blood is oxygenated. The left heart receives oxygenated blood from the lungs and pumps it to the tissues.

Heart disease includes numerous anatomic and physiologic abnormalities of various causes or unknown causes, which may result in or may never cause clinical consequences. Often shrouded in mystique, cardiac disease is, however, a logical sequence of events following biological rules that are becoming more understood with time, thanks to extensive research efforts and technical innovations. Great strides have taken place over the past few decades in the understanding of feline heart disease. Many voids continue to exist, however, with much work to be done in the future. Sophistication of cardiac diagnosis has improved dramatically in the last decade, although thorough clinical examination and assessment remains the cornerstone of accurate diagnosis.

While it is not the intention of the author to review in depth the complex pathophysiology of heart disease, the purpose of this chapter is to give the reader an up-to-date resource on common cardiovascular diseases of the cat, including diagnostic and treatment modalities.

OVERVIEW

Congenital Heart Problems

Congenital heart defects, generally recognized in the young animal, are

CAT HEALTH ENCYCLOPEDIA

due to anomalies that may be hereditary and that occurred during fetal development (gestation). Congenital heart defects are less common in the cat than in the dog. The incidence appears to approximate 2 percent based on post-mortem examination, while prevalence of acquired heart disease ranges from 8-15 percent. Familial patterns have been reported in many breeds, although there is no consistent breed predilection. Genetic transmission has been demonstrated only in the Burmese breed for endocardial fibroelastosis. The most common defects are ventricular septal defect (VSD) and atrioventricular valve (mitral, tricuspid) malformations.

Congenital lesions may be lethal within the first few days or months of life; or, less severely affected cats may live to adulthood or old age. Many cats show no signs, and a cardiac defect is often first detected by auscultation (listening with a stethoscope) of a murmur at time of initial vaccination or neutering. Since cardiomyopathy can affect cats as young as five months of age, myocardial disorders must be differentiated from congenital heart disease, which often can present a diagnostic challenge to the clinician. Also, not all young cats with heart murmurs have congenital or acquired disease. Some present to the veterinarian with innocent murmurs that usually disappear by six months of age.

ACQUIRED HEART PROBLEMS

Acquired heart disease in the cat includes cardiomyopathy, which may be primary or secondary, heartworm disease, and cardiac disease that develops secondary to other organ system diseases (systemic and metabolic). The heart can also be affected secondary to pericardial disease, which may be acquired or congenital. Pericardial disease is uncommon in the cat.

Cardiomyopathies

Cardiomyopathies represent the majority of feline cardiovascular diseases. The clinical incidence has been estimated at 12-15 percent when both primary and secondary cardiomyopathies are considered. Primary cardiomyopathy has been defined by the World Health Organization as "a primary disease process of heart muscle in absence of a known cause." A secondary cardiomyopathy may be caused by an infectious, toxic, metabolic, or other disease process that affects the myocardium.

Primary cardiomyopathies are classified according to their structural (morphologic) appearance as hypertrophic, dilated, or unclassified (restrictive or intermediate). Strict categorization is not always possible. Until relatively recently, dilated cardiomyopathy was commonly diagnosed. In 1987, it was established that many cats with dilated cardiomyopathy were taurine deficient and that supplementation with taurine (an amino acid) would reverse myocardial failure. Since that time, widespread supplementation of commercial foods with taurine has greatly reduced the incidence of dilated cardiomyopathy. Now, the most commonly diagnosed forms are hypertrophic and unclassified cardiomyopathies, although idiopathic dilated cardiomyopathy still occurs. The cause for hypertrophic cardiomyopathy is at this time unknown, although it has been hypothesized that a genetic predisposition to abnormal myocardial protein synthesis may be involved.

Cardiovascular Disorders

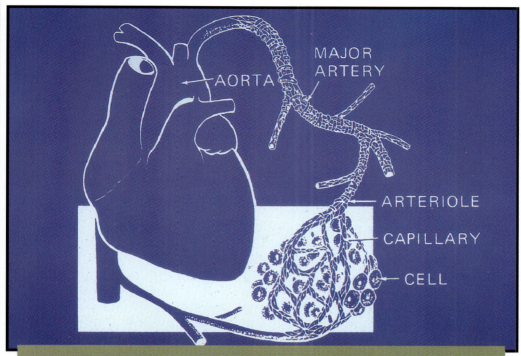

Schematic of the heart and its relationship to the peripheral circulation.

Secondary causes of cardiomyopathy in the cat include nutritional (taurine deficiency), metabolic or endocrine (hyperthyroidism), infiltrative (neoplasia), inflammatory (infectious), and toxic. Taurine is an essential amino acid in the cat. It is not produced by the body and must be provided entirely from food. Its deficiency is believed to be an inadequacy of taurine in the diet. Interestingly, not all taurine-deficient cats develop heart failure. Other factors have been proposed that may contribute to development of heart failure. Hyperthyroid heart disease is the most common endocrine-related cardiac disorder in the cat. It is diagnosed in middle-aged to geriatric cats (to 22 years) and is generally caused by a benign growth on the thyroid gland (thyroid adenoma). If uncontrolled, heart disease potentially leading to heart failure in some cats may develop as a result of elevations of circulating thyroid hormone. Heart disease as a result of hyperthyroidism is often confused with hypertrophic cardiomyopathy. Hyperthyroidism does not cause hypertrophic cardiomyopathy. Neoplasia of the heart in cats is rare, lymphosarcoma being reported as the most common.

Currently, hypertrophic cardiomyopathy is very common and represents the largest percent of primary myocardial disease diagnosed in the cat. It is also the most overdiagnosed cardiac disease. Of the secondary cardiomyopathies, taurine-responsive cardiomyopathy and hyperthyroid heart disease are diagnosed with the most frequency.

Vascular Problems

Numerous disorders can affect the arteries and veins of animals. Thrombosis refers to the presence of a formed clot in a blood vessel. It may obstruct blood flow. Thromboembolism refers to sudden obstruction of an artery by a thrombus (clot) carried from one site to another in the circulation. In the cat, this disease is strongly associated with thrombus formation in the left atrium, usually a result of cardiomyopathy and associated cardiac chamber enlargement. Ninety percent of cats with thromboembolic disease embolize (lodge in) the aorta, where it divides into the femoral arteries supplying blood to the hind limbs. Other reported sites include the forelimbs, kidneys, and brain. These patients present with acute pain, often dragging one or both hind limbs. Femoral pulses are often absent. Signs of heart failure may or may not be present. Clinical signs related to the arterial occlusion are due to loss of blood supply (ischemia), as well as release of chemicals by the thrombus, which inhibits collateral circulation. These cases should be treated as a cardiovascular emergency.

Hypertension (Elevated Blood Pressure)

An elevation in systemic arterial blood pressure is termed systemic hypertension. Blood pressure (BP) can be measured by direct arterial puncture or indirectly by blood flow probes or arterial wall motion detection. Indirect measurement is generally used by the veterinarian, as it is less painful. Repeat indirect measurements of systolic BP greater than 180mm Hg and diastolic greater than 145mm Hg is considered suggestive of hypertension. Hypertension secondary to kidney disease and hyperthyroidism is common in the cat. Hypertension has been reported in 60 percent of cats with chronic kidney (renal) failure and up to 75 percent with hyperthyroidism.

Heartworm Infection

Heartworm infection (dirofilariasis) is being recognized more frequently in cats. It is caused by the parasite *Dirofilaria immitis*. It undergoes an indirect life cycle involving many species of mosquito. The total life cycle takes about 200 days to complete, with the first 15-20 days spent within a mosquito. The parasite enters the cat via a mosquito bite wound. After six months, microscopic offspring (microfilaria) may uncommonly be found in the blood. Only about 20 percent of infected cats will have microfilaria in the blood, due to a typical low worm burden. Cats are relatively resistant to infection compared to the dog. The disease, however, seems to be more pathogenic, i.e., if it develops, it is more exaggerated in the cat than in the dog. Infections in some cats may be self limiting. Adult worms have a shorter life span (two to three years) in cats compared to dogs. If clinical signs develop, they are generally respiratory signs such as a cough, rather than cardiac. Maturing worms and adults residing in the pulmonary arteries are responsible for causing pulmonary injury and clinical signs. The incidence of sudden respiratory and neurologic complications, including sudden death, is higher in the cat than in the dog.

Feline Urologic Syndrome

Feline urologic syndrome is likely familiar to many cat owners. Urinary retention occurs due to a blockage of the urinary outflow tract (urethra). If left untreated, these patients become critically ill and will frequently die. Accumulation of metabolic waste products occurs due to the blockage and inability of the kidneys to excrete these. Death is due to the effects of high serum potassium (hyperkalemia) on the heart. As serum potassium

CARDIOVASCULAR DISORDERS

Schematic representations of a normal cat heart compared to different forms of cardiomyopathy.

DILATED (CONGESTIVE) CARDIOMYOPATHY

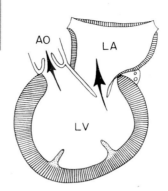

RESTRICTIVE CARDIOMYOPATHY

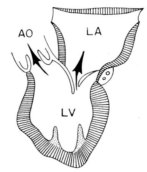

HYPERTROPHIC CARDIOMYOPATHY
(Symmetric)
(Asymmetric)

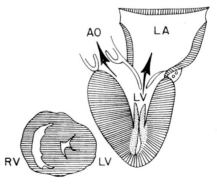

NORMAL

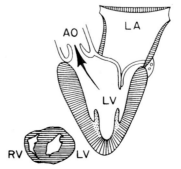

rises, its effect on the heart can be seen as electrocardiographic abnormalities. Life threatening cardiac arrhythmias (abnormal heart rhythms) can ensue. This should be treated as a medical emergency and prompt treatment undertaken.

HISTORY AND PHYSICAL EXAMINATION

History

A complete history and physical examination are paramount in establishing a correct diagnosis and guiding appropriate therapy. The purpose of the history is to collect medical information from the pet owner, while establishing a doctor-client relationship. The history should include the age of the animal, breed, sex, weight, and utilization of the animal (example: Is it used for breeding?). Other things that should be included in the history are duration of signs, attitude and behavior of the patient, appetite, diet, and respiratory patterns. The owner should be asked if any episodes of collapse or lameness have been observed.

Early signs of cardiovascular disease may be masked by the sedentary indoor existence of many cats or may go unnoticed in a cat allowed outdoors. Signs can often be subtle and non-specific. Cardiovascular disease in the cat is often detected as an incidental finding when a cardiac murmur, abnormal heart sound or rhythm, is detected by auscultation. At the other extreme, cats in congestive heart failure may present in severe respiratory distress secondary to development of fluid in the lungs (pulmonary edema) or within the chest cavity (pleural effusion). If thromboembolism occurs, the patient may present with acute onset of hind limb dysfunction. Cough is uncommon unless associated with heartworm disease or other pulmonary diseases such as asthma.

If cardiac arrhythmias (abnormal heart rhythms) occur, a patient may present with a history of sudden weakness or collapse (syncope). It is often preceded by a period of excitement, accompanied by crying. The duration of collapse is often only a few seconds but may last as long as a few minutes. In addition to cardiac arrhythmias, hypertrophic cardiomyopathy as well as cardiac conduction disturbances are the most common causes of syncope in the cat. It is often difficult to differentiate cardiovascular syncope from disease of the central nervous system, as well as various metabolic disorders.

Weight loss, loss of appetite (anorexia), vomiting, and acute blindness may be associated with hypertensive heart disease. In general, the most common symptoms associated with cardiovascular disease in the cat include accumulation of fluid in the lungs and less commonly in the abdomen, tiring on exercise, fainting or syncopal episodes, dyspnea or difficulty breathing, and hind limb dysfunction or paralysis. Other less common symptoms include change in urinary habits, vomiting, and diarrhea.

Physical Examination

Early asymptomatic disease can frequently be detected by routine physical examination. Abnormalities detected by auscultation may precede development of clinical signs by days, months, or even years. General observations should be made regarding the general condition of the animal and any gross abnormalities. Posture, rate, and rhythm of respiration should be noted. Refusal to lie down, standing with elbows out,

Cardiovascular Disorders

Not every patient is cooperative when it comes to the physical examination!

head extended, and open mouth breathing are indications of severe respiratory distress. Fluid in the abdomen (ascites) may develop in some cats with right heart failure, although much less commonly than in the dog. Elevated temperatures (greater than 102.5° F) can be seen with infectious disease and bacterial endocarditis (inflammation of the valves generally caused by invasion of microorganisms). The color of the mucous membranes should be assessed. Pale mucous membranes may indicate anemia or poor perfusion. Reddened mucous membranes may indicate increased red cell content secondary to a congenital cardiovascular shunt. The jugular vein should be assessed for distention, which may indicate congestive heart failure, pericardial disease, or an obstructive mass (e.g., heart base tumor). Normally, the jugular vein is not observed.

Arterial pulses represent the peripheral indicators of circulation. Femoral pulses are commonly assessed. These can often be difficult to feel in a normal cat, and care should be taken not to interpret this as absence of pulses due to thromboembolism. Normal pulse rate in the cat approximates 160-240 beats per minute. Pulse deficits are noted with arrhythmias.

Palpation should be performed. The hands of the examiner are placed over the sides of the cat's chest. The point of maximal intensity of the heartbeat is felt and assessed to be normal or not. Cardiac enlargement or shifting of the heart in the chest due to fluid or a mass can cause alterations. Loud cardiac murmurs (grade IV/VI or more) may be felt as thrills. An increase in the force of the heartbeat may be noted with heart failure, shock, and severe anemia. The abdomen should be palpated for presence of fluid secondary to right heart failure. The neck is palpated for evidence of a thyroid mass.

Auscultation (listening with a stethoscope) can be the most helpful part of the cardiac examination. Heart murmurs are the most common auscultatory abnormality found on physical examination in cats with acquired or congenital heart disease. Heart murmurs are caused by turbulent blood flow often by passage of blood in an abnormal direction. They are generally described by their intensity (grades one through six), duration, timing during the cardiac cycle, quality and position of maximal intensity. A quiet environment and cooperative patient are necessary for good auscultation. Purring is often a hindrance to successful auscultation. The heart and lungs should be auscultated separately.

The first heart sound is due to closure of the mitral and tricuspid valves. The second heart sound is produced by closure of the aortic and pulmonic valves. Most murmurs heard in the cat occur between the first and second heart sounds (systolic) and are found on the left side. They occur, generally, secondary to myocardial disease with secondary valve dysfunction. Primary disease of the valve apparatus (e.g. bacterial endocarditis and endocardiosis) is uncommon in the cat, unlike the dog. Significant anemia and fever can also cause soft murmurs in the cat. Gallop rhythms are other common abnormal sounds in cats. Here, three heart sounds occur, mimicking the sound of a galloping horse. The extra heart sound(s), S3 and/or S4, occur as a result of heart dilation generally secondary to cardiomyopathy.

A fundoscopic examination is evaluation of the posterior inner part of the eye. This should be part of the exam, as it may reveal changes in the retina associated with taurine deficiency or systemic hypertension.

DIAGNOSTIC TESTING
Appropriate diagnostic tests are chosen to investigate clinical signs. The radiographic examination plays an important role in the evaluation of the cardiovascular system, providing information on the size of the heart and, if present, on the degree of heart failure. Two views are necessary to properly assess the heart and lung fields. If indicated, the patient's degree of respiratory compromise should be assessed and stabilized prior to positioning for radiography. If pleural effusion is present, fluid drainage (thoracocentesis) is preferred prior to radiography. The patient is positioned on its side for a lateral projection, and then on its chest for a dorsoventral projection. In addition to changes in heart size, there may be evidence of lung disease, pleural effusion, or masses. If left heart failure is present, pulmonary edema will be seen as well as pulmonary venous enlargement. Unlike in the dog, pulmonary edema is often unevenly distributed and patchy. Pleural effusion, if present, collects between the lung lobes and thoracic wall.

Heart failure represents circulatory imbalance as a result of decreased cardiac output into the vascular systems or decreased filling of blood by a thickened (hypertrophied) ventricle. Blood is shifted from the systemic to the pulmonary circulation in left heart failure, while in right heart failure, the shift occurs from the pulmonary to the systemic circulation. These changes are seen radiographically as pulmonary edema and congestion of the pulmonary veins with left heart failure, and enlargement of the liver, fluid in the abdomen (ascites), and pleural effusion with right heart failure.

Cardiovascular Disorders

Careful auscultation can provide much information about the state of the heart. A quiet environment is necessary.

The electrocardiogram is a well-established, non-invasive, inexpensive technique for assessing the heart and diagnosing cardiac arrhythmias. The ECG is a graphic recording of the electrical impulses produced by the heart muscle during different phases of the cardiac cycle. Each portion of the ECG arises from a specific anatomic area of the heart. The ECG waveforms include the P wave, QRS complex, and T wave, all of which arise from specific areas of the heart in sequential fashion. An abnormality of the ECG indicates an abnormality of the corresponding portion of the heart. The heart rate and rhythm are assessed from the ECG. An arrhythmia is any disturbance in the normal rhythm of the heart. The most common arrhythmias noted in the cat are atrial premature complexes, ventricular premature complexes, and atrial fibrillation. As electrocardio-graphy can often be complicated and challenging, transtelephonic electrocardiography has become well established in veterinary medicine. Here, a small portable battery-powered preamplifier is used by the veterinarian to convert ECG signals into tones that can be transmitted over the telephone line to an expert for interpretation.

Echocardiography is the use of ultrasonic technique to produce a photograph of the echo resultant from sound waves reflected from tissues of different density. Three modalities, M-mode, 2-D, and Doppler, provide different types of information regarding anatomy and function. As it is often impossible to determine what type of heart disease is present from the physical examination and radiographs alone, echocardiography provides a non-invasive means to identify specific cardiac disease. It is especially useful when radiographs show no evidence

CAT HEALTH ENCYCLOPEDIA

of heart enlargement, or the cardiac silhouette is obscured by pleural effusion. Cardiac ultrasound has been used clinically in veterinary medicine for approximately 15 years. It remains, generally, a referral procedure due to the expense of equipment and expertise required for the procedure and interpretation (generally done by a board-certified cardiologist or other specialist in cardiology). Prior to the availability of this procedure, angiocardiography was employed. Here, following injection of an opaque contrast medium, radiographs were made enabling visualization of flow of opacified blood through the heart valves, chambers, and vessels.

Echocardiography is extremely useful in differentiating idiopathic hypertrophic cardiomyopathy, hyperthyroid heart disease, and hypertensive heart disease, all of which can mimic each other. Generally, dilated cardiomyopathy can be easily recognized by dilation of all four heart chambers and decreased contractility. A clot (thrombus) in the left atrium may be visualized in some cats with cardiomyopathy. Cats with heartworm disease may have evidence of right ventricular enlargement. Worms may actually be visualized in the right ventricle and pulmonary outflow tract. Accurate identification of the underlying abnormality with echocardiography is often essential to determine correct medical therapy.

Measurement of systemic arterial blood pressure should be employed in any cat diagnosed with kidney disease or hyperthyroidism. As cardiac disease may result in or be secondary to disease of other organ systems, it is important to review blood work and a urinalysis. Elevations in liver values may be noted with hyperthyroidism and heart failure. Abnormal clotting parameters and muscle enzymes may be seen with arterial thromboembolism. Any cat with pale mucous membranes should have a total red cell count (hematocrit) evaluated to assess for presence of anemia. Assessment for circulating microfilaria (baby heartworm) is generally not performed in the cat, unlike the dog, due to presence of small numbers if infection is present. Currently, an enzyme-linked immunosorbent assay (ELISA) is used to detect female adult heartworm antigen (a substance that induces formation of antibodies). This can be done in the veterinary office. False negatives do occur, often due to the typical low worm burden in feline cases.

Although serum thyroxine (T4) concentrations are increased in most cats with hyperthyroidism, borderline results may be misleading. Often times, the T4 is rechecked one to two weeks later in borderline cases. Other tests, including a free T4 and triiodothyronine (T3) suppression test may be performed in questionable cases. If available, nuclear scintigraphy (scanning organs by photographing emissions of radioactive substances injected into the body) of the thyroid gland may establish a diagnosis of hyperthyroidism.

In cases of feline dilated cardiomyopathy, measurement of plasma concentrations of taurine can be helpful to exclude taurine deficiency. A plasma concentration of less than 20 nmol/ml is indicative of taurine deficiency. Evaluating thoracic effusions for cell content, protein content, and specific gravity (weight of a substance compared with an equal volume of water) may help to determine if the cause is cardiac or non-cardiac.

Cardiovascular Disorders

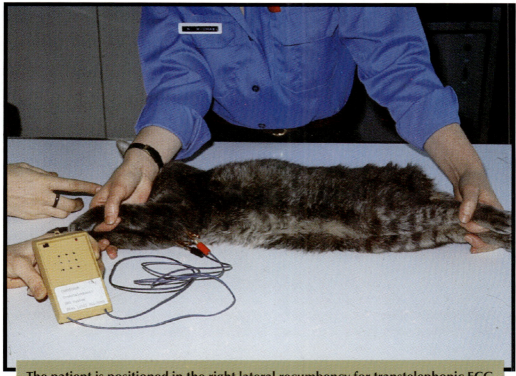

The patient is positioned in the right lateral recumbency for transtelephonic ECG monitoring.

THERAPY FOR SPECIFIC CARDIOVASCULAR DISEASES

Therapy should be based on a final diagnosis and guided by severity of signs. Often with cardiovascular disease, lifelong therapy is necessary. Success of therapy is dependent on the severity of disease, the cat's response to treatment, and owner's compliance.

Disorders of cardiac function can be broken down into those resulting in systolic and diastolic dysfunction. Diastolic dysfunction means that a disease has resulted in an inability of the heart to fill properly during diastole. Simplistically, systolic dysfunction includes a number of problems, such as decreased myocardial contractility, volume overload, and pressure overload. Another important point is that the cardiovascular system compensates for a decreased amount of blood ejected by the left ventricle (stroke volume) by increasing heart rate and salt and water retention by the kidneys. With these concepts in mind, some basic therapeutic strategies for managing feline cardiovascular disease will be discussed.

Cats presenting with fulminant pulmonary edema require emergency medical therapy. Administration of furosemide, a diuretic that hastens removal of pulmonary edema, may be life saving. Oxygen therapy may be required. A venodilator such as two percent nitroglycerin ointment applied topically may be employed to reduce pulmonary congestion. In cases of severe pleural effusion, bilateral thoracocentesis may be required.

CAT HEALTH ENCYCLOPEDIA

Cats with hypertrophic cardiomyopathy have impaired diastolic function. Long-term treatment goals are to improve filling of the ventricles. This is accomplished by improving myocardial relaxation and reduction of the heart rate. Diltiazem, a calcium channel blocker, accomplishes this as well as improves coronary arterial blood flow. A long-acting form of diltiazem (Cardizem CD or Dilacor) may be administered once a day. Digoxin, a cardiac glycoside, is most often used in cats with dilated cardiomyopathy. It helps to improve contractility, slows the heart rate, and is effective in managing atrial arrhythmias. Serum digoxin levels can be assessed if toxicity is suspect.

The beta-adrenergic blocking agents, propranolol and atenolol, are often used to control inappropriate rapid heart rates often seen with hyperthyroidism and to treat atrial tachyarrhythmias (fast heart rhythms) in cats. Management of ventricular tachycardia if life threatening may indicate the need for lidocaine therapy. Cats are sensitive to this drug; therefore, it is given at a low dose (25 percent of the dog dose) with careful electrocardiographic monitoring. Beta-adrenergic blockers or procainamide may be used as long-term oral therapy for ventricular arrhythmias.

Cats with systemic hypertension due to renal failure or hyperthyroidism seem best treated with the long-acting calcium channel blocker amlodipine besylate.

Treatment of thromboembolic episodes involves disintegration of the clot when applicable, therapy to prevent further thrombosis, management of the underlying disorder, and supportive care. A specialist should be consulted prior to the use of thrombolytic therapy,

such as streptokinase, as treatment is often associated with high morbidity and mortality. Anticoagulation with heparin to prevent further thrombosis is a more conservative approach, but its efficacy is questionable. Low-dose aspirin therapy is the most commonly employed prophylaxis. There is, however, no objective evidence for its efficacy; and recurrence of thromboembolism has been reported as high as 75 percent in cats receiving prophylactic aspirin. Warfarin may be considered as an alternative prophylactic anticoagulant. This alternative should be considered only for indoor cats that can be monitored frequently due to the high risk of bleeding complications.

Various modalities are available for treating feline hyperthyroidism, including medical, surgical thyroidectomy (surgical removal of the thyroid gland), as well as radioactive iodine therapy. Methimazole is the most commonly used drug to control hyperthyroidism. Although fewer side effects have been seen with this drug than with other previous therapies, blood counts should be routinely performed to rule out any hematological or biochemical abnormalities. Beta-adrenergic blocking drugs may be indicated to control tachycardia and block increased thyroid hormone effects on the heart until the cat develops normal thyroid levels. Radioactive iodine therapy, although seemingly expensive, is a one-time treatment with few potential side effects, eliminating the need for daily medication and frequent blood monitoring.

Therapy for cats with dirofilariasis (heartworm) is undertaken infrequently, as cats are very sensitive to the drugs (adulticides:

134

Cardiovascular Disorders

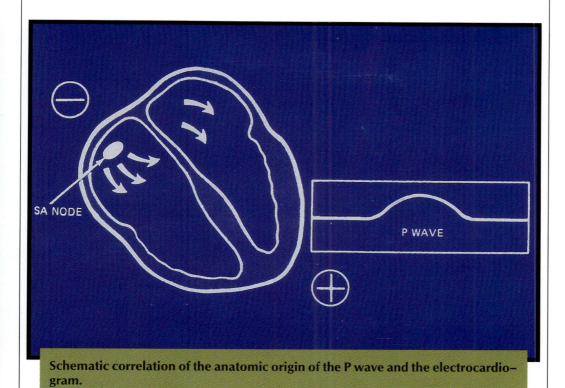

Schematic correlation of the anatomic origin of the P wave and the electrocardiogram.

caparsolate and melarsamine) used to kill the worms. If treatment is performed, death is not uncommon due to embolization of the pulmonary arteries. Preventative heartworm therapy such as milbemycin and ivermectin may be effective in ridding immature worms. Symptomatic cats may benefit from 12-14 months of therapy at preventative dosages. Clinical signs of vomiting and coughing in infected cats may respond in part to glucocorticoids (steroids). Although not licensed for use in cats, preventative heartworm therapy is probably advisable for outdoor cats in areas with a high incidence of heartworm disease.

Sodium restriction is a generally recognized part of managing heart disease. Many special prescription diets are available that have been specially formulated with reduced sodium content. As an alternative, homemade diets can be substituted. All good-quality commercial foods at this time are appropriately supplemented with taurine. If a patient's diet is in question, a good-quality diet with known taurine supplementation should be provided. In cats with dilated cardiomyopathy, if plasma taurine levels have not been established, taurine supplementation should be tried at 250-500mg twice daily orally.

As congenital diseases of the feline heart are much less frequently encountered than acquired diseases, only a few salient points of management will be mentioned here. A ventricular septal defect (VSD) is a hole or communication between the ventricles, usually high in the wall (septum) that separates the ventricles. This allows blood to be shunted from the left to the right ventricle causing pulmonary overcirculation and volume overload of the left heart. It is often associated

Cat Health Encyclopedia

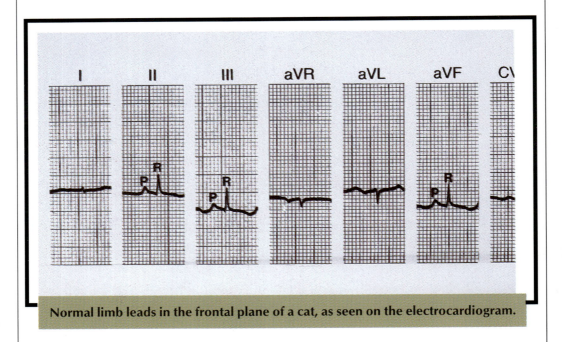

Normal limb leads in the frontal plane of a cat, as seen on the electrocardiogram.

An ECG from a cat with ventricular premature complexes.

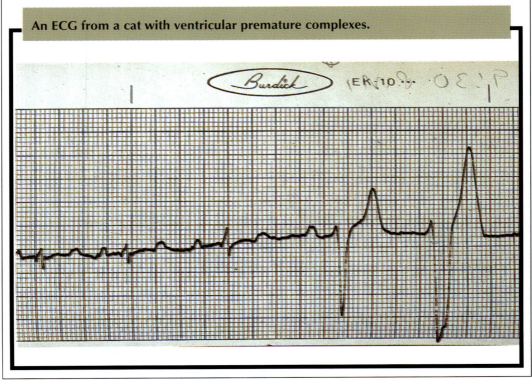

Cardiovascular Disorders

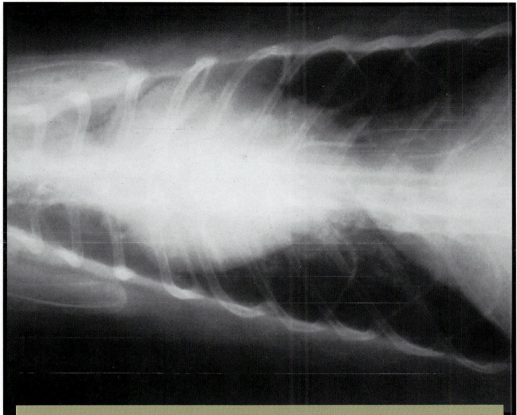

Dorsoventral radiograph of a cat with hypertrophic cardiomyopathy. Note the classic "valentine-shaped" heart.

with other cardiac anomalies. If clinical signs develop, treatment is individualized depending on the type of heart failure (left or right sided) and severity. Small ventricular septal defects are well tolerated, with some cats living symptom free well into adulthood. Spontaneous closure has been reported.

Anomalies of the mitral and tricuspid valves, as a group, exceed the incidence of ventricular septal defects. Affected cats may have a heart murmur associated with the affected valve(s). Mildly affected cases may never show signs of heart failure. Severe lesions will cause volume overload of associated chamber(s) with resultant left- or right- sided heart failure, or both.

Death may occur as early as six months of age. Standard therapy for congestive heart failure, if it develops, is followed.

In humans and dogs, patent ductus arteriosus (PDA) is an inherited trait, but in cats only a familial tendency has been reported. Here, a remnant of the fetal circulation persists. Blood is shunted from the aorta to the pulmonary artery instead of into the peripheral circulation. Early diagnosis is important, as it is often a surgically correctable defect.

No discussion of cardiovascular therapy would be complete without mention of cardiopulmonary resuscitation (CPR). Cardiopulmonary arrest is a sudden cessation of

Cat Health Encyclopedia

ventilation and effective circulation. Signs of cardiopulmonary arrest must be recognized immediately. Typical signs include loss of consciousness, gasping or absence of respiration, absence of heartbeats and pulses, fixed dilated pupils, and electrocardiographic evidence of a fatal arrhythmia (for example, ventricular fibrillation) or lack of electrical activity. Once the presence of cardiopulmonary arrest has been established, the A B C's of CPR are followed. An open airway is generally established by placing a tube in the trachea (orotracheal intubation). If spontaneous breathing is not noted, artificial ventilation is initiated. The rate of ventilation should approximately be 12 to 16 ventilations per minute. Manual compression of the chest is undertaken to restore circulation, although at best this will provide only 30 percent of normal cardiac output. Massage should compress the chest approximately 20 to 30 percent and should be done 60-80 times per minute. After establishing an intravenous line, drug therapy is begun. An electrocardiogram should be evaluated as a guide to therapy. When applicable and if available, electrical defibrillation is employed to restore normal cardiac rhythm. Signs of successful resuscitation include: return of heartbeats and pulses, improved mucous membrane color, pupillary constriction, and voluntary respiration. A total failure of responsiveness after ten minutes of CPR is generally grounds for discontinuing life support.

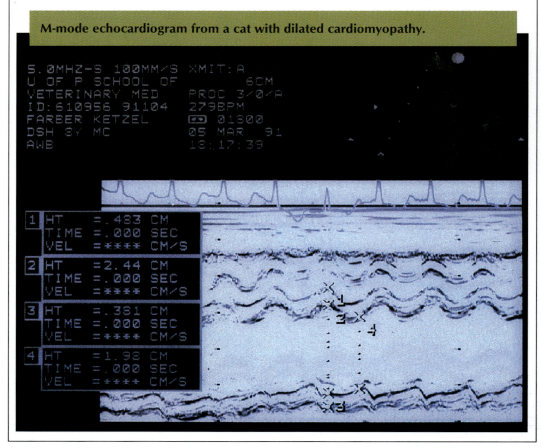

M-mode echocardiogram from a cat with dilated cardiomyopathy.

Cardiovascular Disorders

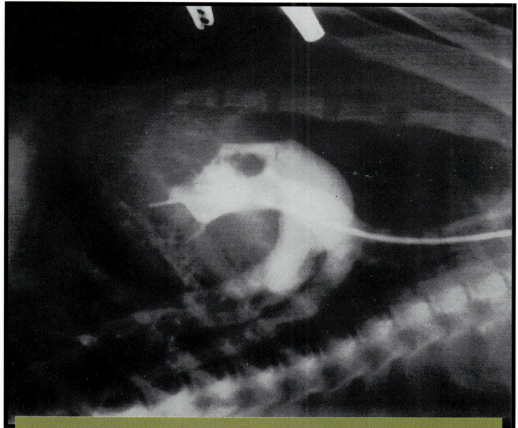

Angiogram of a three-month-old cat with a ventricular septal defect.

SUMMARY

Close owner observation of his pet is important for early detection of signs of common heart diseases. Good detective work may be life saving for a pet. Pets are living longer now, so heart disease is more commonly detected. It is important to know the general signs of heart disease. A veterinarian should be contacted when signs of weakness, vomiting, diarrhea, persistent lethargy, inappetence, or a significant increase or decrease in the heart rate is observed. Immediate professional attention should be sought if signs of collapse, seizures, refusal to lie down, head extended, or open-mouth breathing are noted. Owners should be aware that self-medicating their pet may prove fatal. The cat is a different biological animal from man and the dog. Metabolism of drugs is often different from other species. Administration of Tylenol® (acetaminophen) is contraindicated in cats at any dosage because it is extremely toxic to felines. Aspirin must be used cautiously in cats. Symptoms of toxicity such as vomiting, anorexia, and increased respiratory rate may occur if dosed recklessly. Highly trained veterinary specialists with specialized skills and equipment are available to properly assess, diagnose, and treat the cardiac patient appropriately.

Great strides have been made in the understanding, diagnosis, and treatment of feline cardiovascular disease in the past twenty years. Many exciting avenues of research are currently being pursued, constantly expanding our knowledge and horizons in the field of feline heart disease. Recently, a family of Maine Coon cats was identified with hypertrophic cardiomyopathy, the first clue that this disease in cats may be genetically transmitted. Studies are underway on the effects of growth hormone in cats with heart disease, as well as the efficacy of warfarin therapy as anticoagulant treatment for thromboembolism.

Veterinary knowledge is expanding exponentially, with opinions and techniques constantly changing. Sophisticated methods of diagnosis such as echocardiography, endomyocardial biopsy, and radionuclide imaging are now available. The number of veterinarians pursuing post-graduate education has grown rapidly over the past few years. Board-certified cardiologists and other specialists with advanced training in cardiology can now be more easily accessed by the pet owner outside the veterinary school environment.

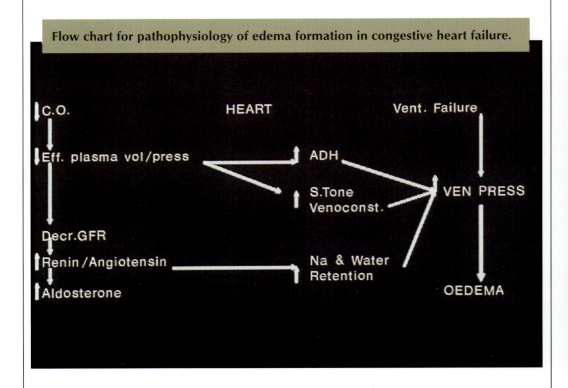

Flow chart for pathophysiology of edema formation in congestive heart failure.

Cardiovascular Disorders

Just as in humans, most heart disease in pets can be controlled through proper treatment and care.

GLOSSARY

Acquired valvular disease—disease of the heart valves resulting in incompetence.

Amino acid—organic compounds necessary for metabolism or growth. Some are supplied by food, and the others can be produced by the body. The ones provided by food are called essential.

Anorexia—loss of appetite.

Arrhythmia—irregular heart beat caused by physiologic or pathologic disturbances in discharge or conduction of impulses through conductile tissue of the heart.

Ascites—excessive accumulation of pale straw-colored fluid in the abdominal cavity.

Auscultation—listening for sounds of the lung and heart with a stethoscope.

Bacterial endocarditis—inflammation due to invasion of microorganisms of the inner membrane of the heart, usually confined to the external lining of the valve.

Benign—not recurrent or progressive; opposed to malignant.

Beta-adrenergic blocker—drugs that block receptors responsible for sympathetic tone (increase in heart rate, etc.).

Blood pressure—the pressure exerted by blood on the wall of a vessel functionally related to cardiac output and systemic vascular resistance.

Calcium channel blocker—drug that inhibits entry of calcium into cells. Calcium plays a major role in regulating electrical and mechanical activity of cardiac and vascular tissues.

Cardiac ultrasound (echocardiography)—non-invasive evaluation of cardiac anatomy and function via reflection of sound waves from tissues of different density.

Cardiomyopathy—disease of the heart muscle generally of unknown cause, however, hereditary and nutritional components may be a factor in certain cases.

Dyspnea—difficult, labored or painful breathing.

Electrocardiogram—a graph of the heart's electrical activity plotted over time.

Endocrine—pertaining to hormones secreted by glands into the blood or lymph; may have a specific effect on an organ or a general effect on the entire body.

Enzyme—complex proteins capable of inducing chemical changes in other substances without being changed themselves.

Feline hyperthyroidism—disease of middle-aged to geriatric cats generally caused by a benign growth of the thyroid gland (adenoma) with excessive secretion of thyroid hormone. This results in multisystemic disturbances including cardiac, with possible cardiac failure as a sequela.

Heart failure—inability of the heart to provide adequate circulation to meet the body's needs.

Heart murmur—caused by turbulence of blood flow through the heart.

Heart sounds—caused by acceleration or deceleration of blood; first sound is due to closure of the mitral and tricuspid valves; the second to closure of the aortic and pulmonic valves.

Heartworm disease—a parasitic infection transmitted by the bite of a mosquito; the parasite undergoes several changes in form leading to development of adult worms that live in the right side of the heart. Heart failure can occur if left untreated.

Ischemia—local loss of blood due to obstruction of circulation to a part.

Lesion—a circumscribed area of pathologically altered tissue.

Neoplasia—new, abnormal tissue formation, as a tumor or growth.

Palpation—examining by application of the hands to the external surface of the body to detect evidence of disease in various organs.

Pathogenic—capable of producing disease.

Pericardial disease—disease involving the membranous sac enclosing the heart; most commonly an abnormal accumulation of fluid in the sac.

Pleural effusion—fluid accumulation in the space surrounding the lungs.

Pulmonary edema—fluid accumulation within the lungs generally secondary to back up of the blood within the veins and capillaries from heart failure.

Retina—the innermost light-sensitive structure of the eye, which receives images formed by the lens.

Serum—the watery portion of the blood after coagulation.

Syncope—transient loss of consciousness due to inadequate blood flow to the brain.

Thoracocentesis—surgical puncture of the chest wall for removal of fluids.

Thrill—abnormal tremor accompanying a cardiac murmur felt on palpation.

Thromboembolism—a blood clot that has become detached from its site of formation resulting in obstruction of a blood vessel.

Ventricular fibrillation—rapid, ineffectual contractions of the ventricles.

CARDIOVASCULAR DISORDERS

RECOMMENDED READING

Atkins, CD; Galto, AM; Kurzman, ID, et al: Risk factors, clinical signs, and survival in cats with a clinical diagnosis of idiopathic hypertrophic cardiomyopathy: 74 cases. (1985-1989). *JAVMA* 1992; 201:613-18.

Bonagura, JD: Cardiovascular diseases. 1995. *The Cat: Diseases and Clinical Management.* Sherding, RG; Ed. WB Saunders, Philadelphia. 819-946.

Bonagura, JD, Ed.: *Kirk's Current Veterinary Therapy XII.* Philadelphia, WB Saunders, 1995. 771-927.

Darke, PG; Bonagura, JD; Kelly, DF: *Color Atlas of Veterinary Cardiology.* London, Mosby-Wolfe, 1996.

Ettinger, SJ; Feldman, EC: *Textbook of Veterinary Internal Medicine.* Philadelphia, WB Saunders, 1995. 884-1068.

Fox, PR, Ed.: *Canine and Feline Cardiology.* New York, Churchill Livingstone, 1988.

Hadlock, DJ: Nutritional concerns in cardiology. *Veterinary Forum,* 1993, 8:48-49.

Hadlock, DJ: Selected topics in electrocardiography. *The Five Minute Consult.* Tilley, LP; Smith, FW, Eds. Williams and Wilkins, Philadelphia, 1996.

Miller, MS; Tilley, LP Eds.: *Manual of Canine and Feline Cardiology* Second edition. Philadelphia, *WB* Saunders, 1995.

Opie, LH: *Drugs for the Heart.* Fourth edition. Philadelphia, WB Saunders, 1995.

Pion, PD; Kittleson, MD; Thomas, WP et al: Clinical findings in cats with dilated cardiomyopathy and relationship of findings to taurine deficiency. *JAVMA.* 1992; 201:267-74.

Snyder, PS: Feline cardiovascular disease. *Waltham Focus.* 1995; 5:9-17.

Suter, PF; Lord, PF: Cardiac diseases. *Thoracic Radiography of the Dog and Cat.* 1984. Published by the author (Peter F. Suter), Wettsurl, Switzerland. 351-516.

Tilley LP, ed.: Feline cardiology. *The Veterinary Clinics of North America.* 1977; 7:225-430.

Tilley, LP: *Essentials of Canine and Feline Electrocardiography.* Third edition. Philadelphia, Lea & Febiger, 1992.

Dr. W. Jean Dodds

Dr. W. Jean Dodds graduated from the Ontario Veterinary College, and thereafter spent 25 years in research and clinical hematology with an emphasis on bleeding diseases. She is nationally and internationally recognized as an authority in hematology, immunology and blood banking, and more recently has developed interests in endocrinology, nutrition, and alternative veterinary medicine. Dr. Dodds is President and Director of Hemopet, a non-profit national animal blood bank servicing North America with canine transfusion products and supplies. She also provides consultations to veterinarians and animal breeders in her areas of expertise and lectures widely on these subjects.

BLOOD DISORDERS

By W. Jean Dodds, DVM

Hemopet
938 Stanford Street
Santa Monica, CA 90403

OVERVIEW OF THE BLOOD ELEMENTS

The blood elements primarily include the circulating blood and bone marrow but can also be extended to include all hematopoeitic (blood-forming) organs and tissues (i.e., thymus, lymph nodes and follicles, spleen, reticuloendothelial system (RES), liver, stomach and intestines, and kidneys).

PERIPHERAL BLOOD

The circulating blood consists of the cellular elements (red and white blood cells, and platelets) and plasma proteins (albumin and globulins including coagulation factors, transport proteins, immunoglobulins, and complement components). The red blood cells of healthy animals are mature biconcave discs, and very few immature, nucleated or reticulum-containing cells (reticulocytes) are present in the circulation. The function of red blood cells is to carry oxygen to the tissues.

White blood cells of granulocytic and lymphocytic origin are found in the circulation. These cells are known specifically as neutrophils, basophils, eosinophils and lymphocytes. Collectively, those leukocytes (white blood cells) function to fight infection, attract and engulf (phagocytize) foreign particles and microorganisms, elicit cellular immune responses, and release chemical messengers. Platelets, derived from their megakaryocytic precursors in the bone marrow and other tissues, are also present in the blood. Their function is to promote hemostasis, the arrest of bleeding, and to act as a specialized inflammatory mediator.

BONE MARROW

This tissue is the major focus of hematopoiesis (blood formation) in the body and consists of (pluripotent) stem cells that differentiate into the myeloid and lymphoid stem cells, which in turn mature into the precursor cell lines of the peripheral blood elements. For example, in the myeloid stem cell line, megakaryoblasts produce platelets, rubriblasts produce erythocytes (red blood cells), and myeloblasts produce monocytes and macrophages (mononuclear cells), and neutrophils, eosinophils and basophils (granulocytes, implying the presence of "granules" in the cytoplasm). In the lymphoid stem cell line, lymphoblasts produce T- and B-lymphocytes and plasma cells. The myeloid:erythroid (M:E) ratio of the bone marrow is the ratio of the number of nucleated erythroid precursors to the number of granulocytic precursors present. In the cat, the normal M:E ratio ranges from 1.2-2.2, with a mean of 1.63. This is higher than that of most domestic animal species except for the pig. In addition to hematopoiesis, the bone marrow stores iron.

Cat Health Encyclopedia

OTHER HEMATOPOIETIC TISSUES/ORGANS

The primary functions of these elements are summarized as follows:

- Thymus—central lymphoid organ that differentiates bone marrow-derived precursor cells into T-lymphocytes, and is involved in cellular immunity and production of lymphokines (special chemical messengers important in immune regulation);
- Lymph nodes and follicles—produce lymphocytes and plasma cells, and are involved in antibody synthesis;
- Spleen—same as lymph nodes but also acts as a reservoir for erythrocytes and platelets, stores iron, destroys aged (senescent) and abnormal erythrocytes, degrades hemoglobin, and retains embryonic potential for hematopoiesis;
- Reticuloendothelial System (RES) aka Mononuclear-Phagocyte System—acts as the major phagocytic system of the body in cellular defense of microbial infection, destroys various blood cells, stores iron, degrades hemoglobin, and secretes various chemical mediators and macromolecules;
- Liver—stores vitamin B_{12}, folate, and iron; produces most of the coagulation factors, albumin and some globulins, conjugates free bilirubin for excretion into bile, produces erythropoietin precursor, and retains embryonic potential for hematopoiesis;
- Stomach and intestines—produce factors necessary for absorption of vitamin B_{12}, iron, and folates and the release of iron; and
- Kidneys—produce erythropoietin and thrombopoietin, the

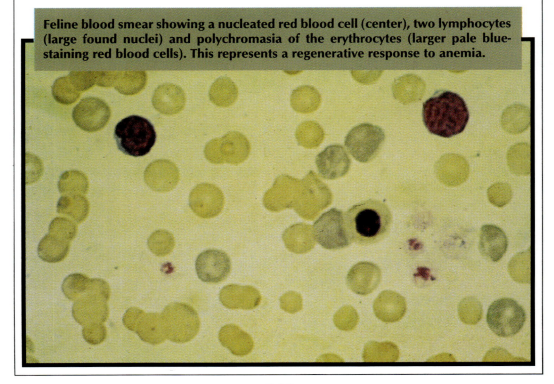

Feline blood smear showing a nucleated red blood cell (center), two lymphocytes (large found nuclei) and polychromasia of the erythrocytes (larger pale blue-staining red blood cells). This represents a regenerative response to anemia.

Blood Disorders

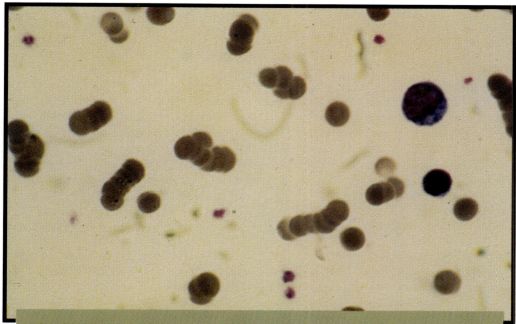

Feline blood smear showing rouleaux formation, a normal phenomenon where the red blood cells form short chains.

hormones that stimulate production of red cells and platelets, respectively, and degrade iron and bilirubin for excretion into urine.

ANEMIA

Anemia is the reduction below normal levels of the red blood cell (RBC) count, hemoglobin, or packed cell volume (PCV). General causes of anemia are one or more of: hemorrhage, hemolysis (RBC destruction), and bone marrow suppression. Anemias are classified as regenerative or nonregenerative (depending on whether the body can compensate by increasing production) and can be mild, moderate, or severe. Regenerative anemias can be further classified as being of adequate or inadequate degree.

Regenerative anemia is demonstrated by finding elevated numbers of reticulocytes or more immature nucleated RBCs in the peripheral blood. Hemorrhage typically presents as a regenerative anemia and low plasma protein level. Hemolysis (blood breakdown), on the other hand, can be associated with the presence of spherocytes (rounding up of the red blood cells) and autoagglutination (usually of autoimmune or immune-mediated cause), Heinz bodies, intracellular red cell parasites such as *Hemobartonella felis*, and RBC fragmentation as seen in vasculitis or thrombosis.

Nonregenerative anemia has a variety of causes including iron deficiency; chronic kidney disease; being secondary to inflammatory disease; retroviral infection with feline leukemia virus (FeLV) and/or feline immunodeficiency virus (FIV); autoimmune or immune-mediated hemolytic disease; bone marrow suppression with aplastic anemia; and following use of chloramphenicol

Cat Health Encyclopedia

and chemotherapeutic drugs to treat sick cats. The nonregenerative anemia seen in FeLV infection results from bone marrow suppression by the virus.

Diagnosis of the cause of anemia requires careful evaluation of the various RBC parameters and precursors in the blood and bone marrow. Treatment may require blood transfusions (whole blood or packed red blood cells), which must always be cross-matched for blood type A and B compatibility, iron, trace vitamins, and supportive care.

FELINE INFECTIOUS ANEMIA (FIA)

This disease occurs in acute, subacute, chronic, and latent forms in cats. It is caused by a microscopic parasite, *Hemobartonella felis*, that infects red blood cells resulting in their removal and destruction by the spleen and certain other tissues. The precise mode of transmission of the parasite has not been determined; fleas and other biting or sucking insects might act as mechanical carriers of the parasite. Infected queens can transmit the disease to their unborn kittens, and transfusion of blood from infected cats will transfer the parasite to the recipient. Clinical signs are more likely to be exhibited by cats with underlying disease.

The disease runs a cyclic course. With appropriate treatment, most cats will recover from the acute phase of FIA but will remain carriers of the parasite. The use of antibiotics, such as tetracycline, is usually successful if the anemia has not advanced too far. In view of the possibility of transmission of the parasite by fleas or other insects, it is important for owners to control fleas on the cat and in the cat's environment.

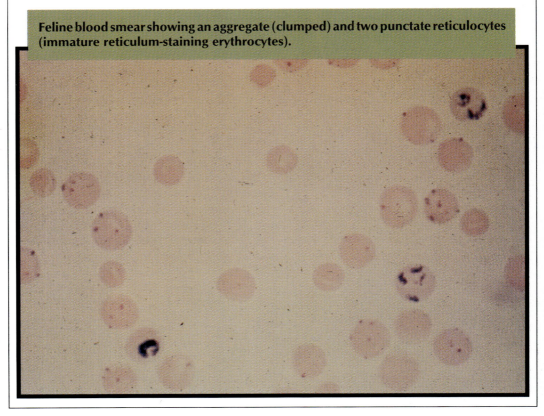

Feline blood smear showing an aggregate (clumped) and two punctate reticulocytes (immature reticulum-staining erythrocytes).

BLOOD DISORDERS

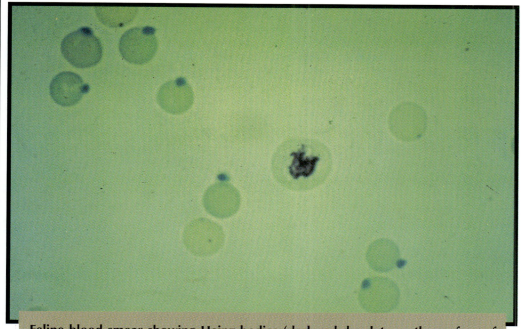

Feline blood smear showing Heinz bodies (dark red droplets on the surface of erythrocytes) and a reticulocyte with aggregated central reticulum.

OTHER BLOOD ELEMENTS

Neutropenia (low circulating neutrophil count) occurs quite often in cats, especially in association with viral diseases.

Eosinophilia (high circulating eosinophil count) is commonly seen with a variety of feline diseases. Examples are feline asthma and allergic bronchitis; infectious parasites such as fleas and tapeworms; neoplasia, especially of the lymphoid system (lymphosarcoma); dermatitis especially from flea allergy, adverse food reactions, or autoimmune skin disease; and immune-mediated inflammatory bowel disease.

Lymphocytosis (high circulating lymphocyte count) is a unique physiologic response of cats to stress.

BACTEREMIA AND TOXEMIA

The presence in the blood of bacteria (bacteremia) or toxins (toxemia) typically results in a reduction of white blood cells, especially neutrophils, which engulf or phagocytize the bacterial or toxic particles. The resultant neutropenia leaves the affected cats more prone to infections. Chemotherapeutic drugs can cause low white blood cell counts (leukopenia) in cats, and chloramphenicol has been reported to cause reversible changes in the bone marrow. Antithyroid medication used to treat feline hyperthyroidism can produce anemia and low platelet counts (thrombocytopenia).

BLEEDING DISORDERS

In normal situations, very little blood leaks out of blood vessels because of a special mechanism of hemostasis that rapidly seals damaged areas and arrests bleeding. When the hemostatic process becomes overactive, however, thrombosis occurs and clots form that block blood flow and cause tissue death. Thrombosis is also called intravascular coagulation and can be localized or generalized (i.e., disseminated intravascular coagulation, DIC).

Normal hemostasis involves three steps: local constriction of the damaged blood vessel, activation and adhesion of blood platelets to the injured site, and blood coagulation that forms a fibrin clot to plug and seal the hole. This process is followed by a mechanism called fibrinolysis, which dissolves the clot and reestablishes the normal surface (endothelium) and patency of the blood vessel. Actually, the entire response is likened to that of wound healing following an injury.

Blood coagulation is achieved when a series of plasma clotting factors are sequentially activated by exposure to the tissue juice and platelet constituents that are released following tissue injury. Bleeding disorders arise when the hemostatic process, outlined above, is impaired. These can be inherited or acquired. The typical clinical signs of bleeding can be quite variable. For example, pinpoint hemorrhages (petechiae) of the skin and mucous membranes usually indicate low numbers of platelets or platelet dysfunction. Bleeding from the nose, mouth, rectum, or into the urine may be seen, joints may be swollen, and large bruises or blood-filled lumps (hematomas) can appear on the body surface. Occasionally, severe or even fatal bleeding can occur into the chest, abdomen, or bowel.

Diagnosis requires a careful medical and family history and physical examination, followed by

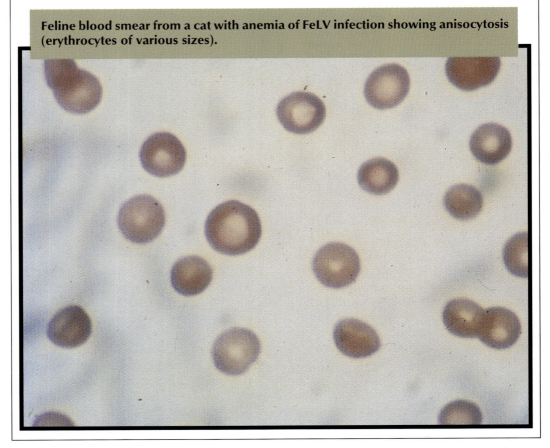

Feline blood smear from a cat with anemia of FeLV infection showing anisocytosis (erythrocytes of various sizes).

BLOOD DISORDERS

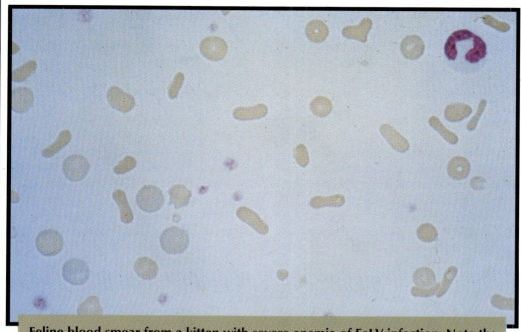

Feline blood smear from a kitten with severe anemia of FeLV infection. Note the very pale-staining erythrocytes (hypochromasia) and poikilocytosis (erythrocytes with abnormal pointed shapes).

screening and/or specific blood coagulation and platelet testing as needed for the particular case. Cats mildly to moderately affected with a bleeding disease or carrying an inherited disorder, like hemophilia, will usually not be identified by routine blood screening tests of hemostasis. Quantitative specific assays for the individual clotting factors are required, and blood specimens for those tests need special preparation and shipment to the testing laboratory. Only a few laboratories specializing in animal coagulation testing offer this service in North America.

Treatment of bleeding diseases includes fresh blood-type compatible transfusion(s) to supply platelets and clotting factors and correct anemia, supportive care and treatment of any underlying illnesses, and removal of offending drugs or toxins. Stored blood components can also be used, but they do not supply platelets. It is imperative that the blood donor and recipient patient be cross-matched beforehand because incompatibility of the A and B blood group system, if the patient has blood type B, can be instantly fatal.

INHERITED BLEEDING DISEASES

In cats, the recognized inherited bleeding disorders are hemophilia A (factor VIII deficiency), hemophilia B (factor IX deficiency), von Willebrand's disease (vWD), platelet dysfunction, and factor XII deficiency. The latter defect typically does not express a bleeding tendency. It is usually discovered accidentally when routine blood coagulation testing reveals a very long activated partial thromboplastin time (APTT) in an otherwise healthy or only mildly bleeding cat. All of these disorders are rare.

Cat Health Encyclopedia

The hemophilias (A and B) are X-chromosome-linked recessive traits in cats, as they are in other species. Affected cats are males born to obligatory carrier females. Hemophilia A is more common than hemophilia B and has been recognized in several purebred cat families as well as mixed breeds. Hemophilia B was first seen in a family of British Shorthairs but has since been diagnosed in Siamese and mixed breeds. Within inbred cat families, the frequency of these serious life-threatening diseases can be quite high unless vigorous genetic screening and counseling are applied. The typical presenting history involves a young male kitten bleeding after castration or declawing operations. Blood transfusion(s) are necessary to contain the bleeding in these cases and will be needed periodically throughout life to control spontaneous or traumatic bleeding episodes. Owners need to be aware of this medical and financial commitment if they elect to keep a hemophilic cat as a pet. Immediate relatives should be screened for carrier/affected status, and those testing abnormal are removed from the breeding population. An alternative to testing is to refrain from breeding any close relatives, especially siblings and cats on the dam's side of the pedigree.

Von Willebrand's disease (vWD) is generally a much more common bleeding disorder than hemophilia, tends to be less severe, and is inherited by both sexes. Affected cats of either sex typically exhibit excessive bleeding from mucosal surfaces (bowel, urinary tract, nose, and mouth) or after surgical procedures. The Himalayan was the first cat breed recognized to have severe vWD. Although vWD is the most common inherited bleeding disease of humans and dogs, it is only rarely diagnosed in cats. This may reflect the fact that few cats are actually tested for vWD with the

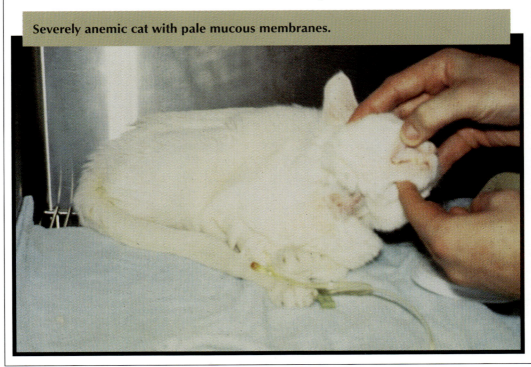

Severely anemic cat with pale mucous membranes.

BLOOD DISORDERS

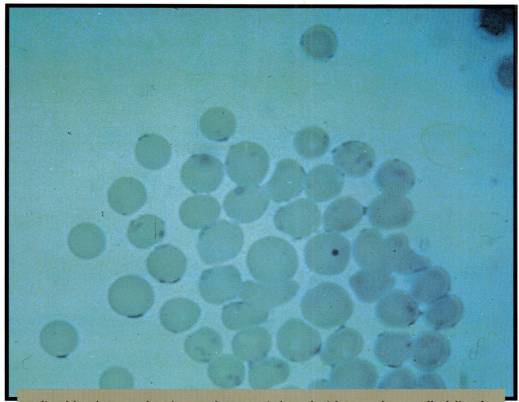

Feline blood smear showing erythrocytes infected with Hemobartonella felis. The organisms appear as dark-staining bodies on the erythrocyte surfaces.

required specific von Willebrand factor assay.

Platelet dysfunction can be an inherited or familial trait in cats. Affected animals of either sex usually are of breeds showing coat color dilution (e.g., white, silver, blue and cream) and also can have the Chediak-Higashi (CH) syndrome. In CH disease, the platelets of affected cats contain abnormal lysosomal storage granules that render the cells dysfunctional. The resulting bleeding tendency is clinically similar to vWD.

ACQUIRED BLEEDING DISEASES

Bleeding animals are more likely to have acquired the problem, as a result of some trauma, underlying disease, drug, or toxic exposure, or response to vaccination. The most common of these acquired conditions affects the numbers and/or function of blood platelets. A low circulating platelet count (thrombocytopenia) causes the pinpoint hemorrhages mentioned above. The problem can be an acute, single event following viral infection, vaccination, toxic exposure or use of certain drugs, or it can be chronic and recurrent. In the latter case, the disease is usually immune-mediated as discussed earlier. Platelet dysfunction (thrombopathia), in addition to being of the rare inherited form, can be acquired from the use of a wide array of drugs. Common examples are aspirin, phenylbutazone, and the glycosaminoglycan "nutraceuticals"

Cat Health Encyclopedia

used to treat arthritic diseases. Use of these drugs would be contraindicated in cats with inherited bleeding diseases.

Vitamin K deficiency states can be acquired from the accidental or therapeutic ingestion of anticoagulant rodenticides (e.g., warfarin or the newer, more potent toxins used for rodent control). As these compounds interfere with vitamin K-dependent synthesis of clotting factors in the liver, the antidote is to give vitamin K. Treatment may be needed for up to four to six weeks, if the more potent toxins were involved. Occasionally, prolonged use of oral antibiotics can sterilize the normal bacterial flora of the bowel and induce a vitamin K deficiency.

Disseminated intravascular coagulation (DIC) or thrombosis occurs when the body's hemostatic system becomes hyperresponsive to an inciting condition. It is always the result of an underlying problem, and the more common examples in cats are obstetrical complications, the "saddle" embolism seen at the terminal aorta in cats with cardiomyopathy or other heart defects, heat stroke, shock, cancer, and snake bites. This is a life-threatening disease that requires prompt diagnostic testing, alleviation of the underlying cause (if possible), and treatment with anticoagulants such as warfarin or heparin and/or antiplatelet drugs such as aspirin or nonsteroidal anti-inflammatory agents. The prognosis is usually guarded.

Other causes of bleeding tendencies in cats include liver disease, because the liver is the major source of coagulation factor production; and kidney disease, because platelet function is impaired in kidney failure. As older cats often have progressive kidney disease, a bleeding tendency may be an associated clinical sign.

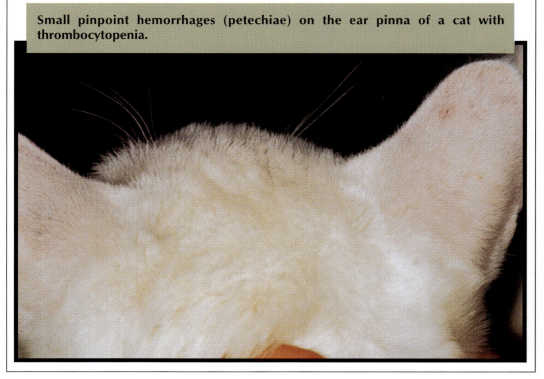

Small pinpoint hemorrhages (petechiae) on the ear pinna of a cat with thrombocytopenia.

BLOOD DISORDERS

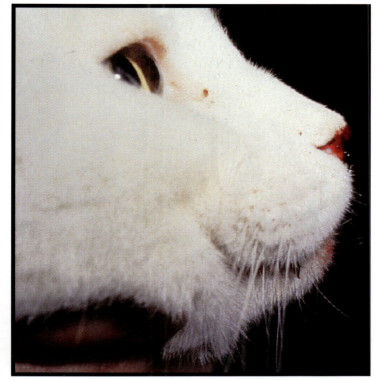

Right: Cat with a nosebleed (epistaxis), a relatively rarely encountered sign of bleeding disorders.

Below: Cat showing diffuse abdominal wall hemorrhage and bruising (ecchymoses).

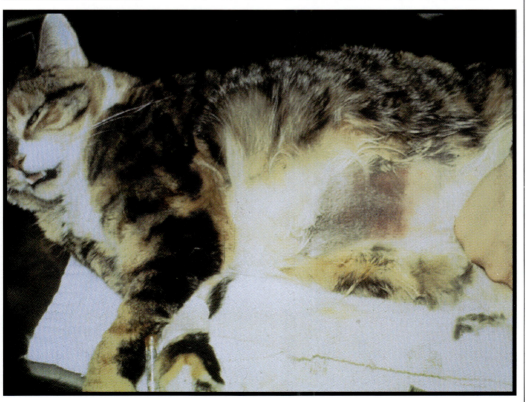

Cat Health Encyclopedia

AUTOIMMUNE BLOOD DISEASES

The classic autoimmune or immune-mediated hematologic diseases are autoimmune/immune-mediated hemolytic anemia (AIHA/IMHA) and idiopathic thrombocytopenic purpura (ITP).

Autoimmune or immune-mediated hemolytic anemia (AIHA,IMHA) is less common in cats than dogs. Affected cats are usually middle aged, and males may be more predisposed; this apparent male sex predilection is the opposite to that seen in humans and dogs. Diagnosis is confirmed by finding a positive Coombs' antiglobulin test or the presence of autoagglutinated RBCs in an anemic, jaundiced cat. Spherocytes may also be present on the blood smear, but this is a less reliable indicator of AIHA in cats than in dogs. While the anemia is typically described as regenerative, nonregenerative anemia has been a frequent finding in recent years. Some affected cats also have thrombocytopenia, which produces the combination known as Evan's syndrome. Contributing factors that apparently trigger the immunologic destruction of RBCs include viral diseases such as FeLV or FIV; adverse reactions to feline vaccines; hemobartonellosis; and hemolytic disease of newborn kittens receiving colostrum from a blood type B queen that was mated with a type A tom. Exposure to drugs and toxins are also potential underlying causes. Treatment requires immunosuppressive drugs (corticosteroids, cyclophosphamide,

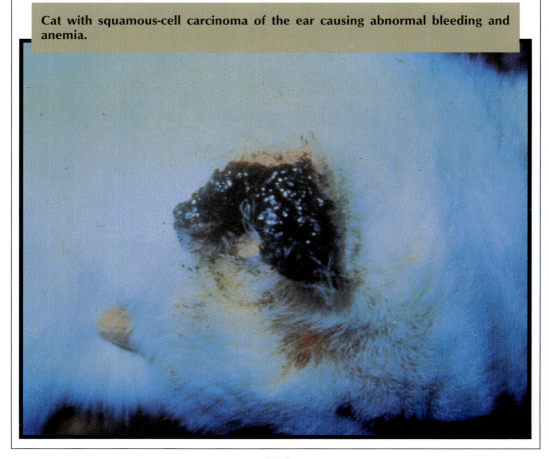

Cat with squamous-cell carcinoma of the ear causing abnormal bleeding and anemia.

BLOOD DISORDERS

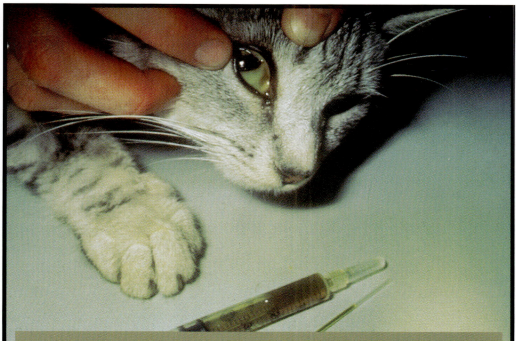

Cat with severe icterus associated with autoimmune hemolytic anemia. There was also severe bilirubinuria (loss of bilirubin into the urine).

Feline blood smear showing severe thrombocytopenia.

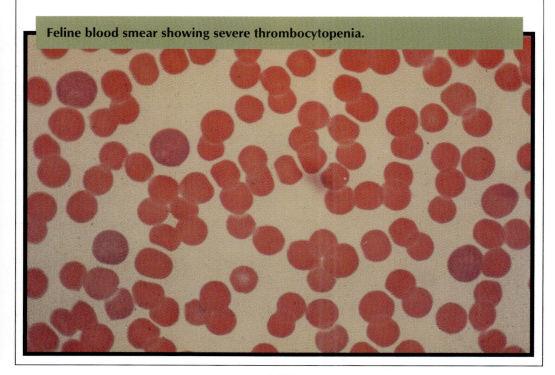

CAT HEALTH ENCYCLOPEDIA

azathioprine, or cyclosporine), transfusion with blood-type compatible whole blood or packed red blood cells to control the anemia, hematinics, and supportive care.

Idiopathic thrombocytopenic purpura (ITP) or immune-mediated thrombocytopenia (IMP). The lowered platelet count of affected cats causes the pinpoint hemorrhages and mucosal surface bleeding mentioned earlier. Nearly all cases are secondary to an underlying cause or trigger rather than a true primary or idiopathic event. Identifying an offending infectious agent, especially viruses like FeLV and FIV, vaccine, toxin, drug or hormonal change is an important part of diagnosis and case management. Platelets damaged by immunologic attack tend to be predominantly small on the blood smear or count (microthrombocytosis). Specialized antiplatelet antibody tests may be available at reference laboratories. Treatment consists of the immunosuppressive drugs listed above for AIHA, and transfusions of fresh compatible whole blood or platelet-rich concentrates if bleeding is severe enough to be life threatening.

LEUKEMIA AND LYMPHOSARCOMA

Leukemia, the presence of neoplastic leukocytes in the blood, occurs as a consequence of feline lymphosarcoma, which is caused by the FeLV. This retrovirus infects normal lymphocytes and transforms them into malignant lymphomatous cells. The FIV has also been implicated as a cause of lymphomas in the nose and pharynx of cats. In one study, cats infected with both FeLV and FIV had a 77 times higher risk of developing leukemia/ lymphoma than those with FIV or

FeLV alone (five to six and 62 times, respectively). However, not all cats that develop leukemia/lymphoma are FeLV and/or FIV infected. Lymphosarcoma in cats most commonly occurs in the gastrointestinal tract, liver, kidney, and nasal cavity. More generalized lymph node enlargement (lymphodenopathy) throughout the body can also be seen.

HYPERLIPIDEMIA

An increased level of lipids (fats) in the blood is called hyperlipidemia. Both triglyceride and cholesterol levels can be elevated and contribute to the high blood lipid concentration. The most common cause of hyperlipidemia is from a recent meal (postprandial) and so cats need to be fasted for 12-24 hours to elevate true metabolic lipid levels. Secondary hyperlipidemia occurs most often in cats with diabetes mellitus, but it also can be seen with hyperadrenocorticism (Cushing's syndrome), liver disease with bile stasis, nephrotic syndrome, and drugs such as megestrol acetate, and corticosteroids.

A genetic form of juvenile hyperchylomicronemia has been recognized in sibling kittens. In these cases the blood appears like a thick, creamy red-tinged "soup". Therapy requires a low-fat diet and lipid-lowering drugs for the long term, and control of any underlying metabolic disorder.

RECOMMENDED READING

Cowell, RL; Tyler, RD: Diagnosis of anemia. *Consultations in Feline Internal Medicine*. JR August, Ed. WB Saunders, Philadelphia, 1991, pp. 335-342.

Dodds, WJ: Bleeding disorders. *Consultations in Feline Internal Medicine*. JR August, Ed. WB

Saunders, Philadelphia, 1991, pp. 383-388.

Dodds, WJ: Bleeding disorders. *Handbook of Small Animal Practice*. RV Morgan, Ed. Churchill Livingstone, New York, 1992, pp. 765-777.

Hall, RL; Giger, U: Disorders of red blood cells. *Handbook of Small Animal Practice*. RV Morgan, Ed. Churchill Livingstone, New York, 1992, pp. 715-733.

Jain, NC: *Essentials of Veterinary Hematology*. Lea & Febiger, Philadelphia, 1993, 417 pp.

Knoll, JS: Disorders of white blood cells. *Handbook of Small Animal Practice*. RV Morgan, Ed. Churchill Livingstone, New York, 1992, pp. 735-749.

Dr. Gary D. Norsworthy

Dr. Gary D. Norsworthy is a private practitioner whose specialty is feline medicine. He has spoken to veterinarians throughout the United States and Canada about feline diseases and has written numerous papers and book chapters on feline diseases. He is the editor and major author of Feline Practice, *a textbook for veterinarians about feline diseases. He was recognized by the Texas Veterinary Medical Association as the 1992 Companion Animal Practitioner of the Year and is a Charter Diplomate of the Feline Specialty of the American Board of Veterinary Practitioners.*

DISEASES OF THE RESPIRATORY SYSTEM

Gary D. Norsworthy, DVM
Diplomate, American Board of Veterinary Practitioners,
Feline Practice Specialty

Acres North Animal Hospital
16302 San Pedro Avenue
San Antonio, TX 78232

INTRODUCTION

The respiratory system delivers oxygen to the cat's lungs and removes the waste product, carbon dioxide. Air enters the nose, goes down the trachea (windpipe), and reaches the tiny alveoli (air-exchanging sacs) deep in the lungs. All of these structures are part of the respiratory system. This system also includes several other organs and structures necessary to facilitate oxygen delivery and carbon dioxide removal. These include the diaphragm and the muscles and ribs forming the chest cavity.

Diseases of the Nose

The first organ of the respiratory system is the nose. It includes the external nares, the nasal planum, the nasal cavity, and the turbinates. The latter are thin, scroll-like bones within the nasal cavity that warm incoming air and filter out dust and other foreign material.

CLINICAL SIGNS

Diseases of the nose result in sneezing, abnormal sounds, or fluid discharge from the nose. Sneezing usually signals that something is irritating the front part of the nose. Sneezing may be caused by infection, foreign material, or a mass within the nasal cavity. Abnormal sounds, usually called stertor, signal the presence of a partial obstruction of the air passageways within the nose.

Fluid discharge occurs when infection, foreign material, or a mass has been present for several days or more. A nasal discharge is considered chronic if it has been present for more than one month. It may be described as purulent (pus), sanguinous (bloody), serous (thin, watery fluid), or a combination of the three.

The presence of nasal discharge for more than one month is cause for concern because it means that a disease process is present that will probably not resolve without aggressive medical treatment or surgery. The most common causes are chronic bacterial, viral, or fungal infections, nasal tumors (usually malignant), inflammatory polyps, and foreign bodies.

DIAGNOSIS

Several tests are necessary to diagnose the cause of chronic nasal discharge. Radiographs (x-rays) should be taken of the skull with the cat placed in special positions on the radiographic table so the nasal cavity and frontal sinuses can be seen clearly. Some veterinarians are equipped to view the inside of the nasal cavity with a tiny, flexible

Cat Health Encyclopedia

instrument called an endoscope. It is often helpful to perform a microscopic study of the cells and debris within the nose. Specimens are collected through a catheter that is inserted deep within the nasal cavity while the cat is under anesthesia. If the diagnosis has not been determined with these procedures, the nose can be opened surgically so that biopsy samples can be taken. All of these procedures require anesthesia.

MANAGEMENT

Some of these conditions can be treated successfully, and some cannot. Removal of a foreign body will generally produce good results. The presence of chronic infection often requires extensive surgery or long-term medical therapy. Even then, the result may not be a permanent cure. Nasal inflammatory polyps and nasal tumors are difficult or impossible to treat successfully even with extensive surgery.

Upper Respiratory Infections

The upper respiratory tract includes the nose, the nasal sinuses, the pharynx (back of the mouth), and the larynx (voice box). Diseases in these locations are generally caused by viruses, bacteria, or bacteria-like organisms. They are collectively referred to as upper respiratory infections (URI).

About 90 percent of viral URIs are caused by the feline herpesvirus, also called the rhinotracheitis virus, and the feline calicivirus. The other ten

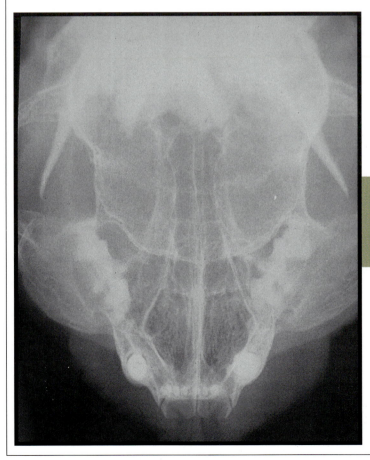

This view of the cat's skull allows the veterinarian to view the nasal cavity.

Diseases of the Respiratory System

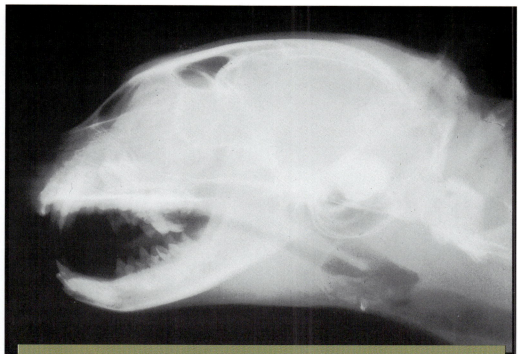

This is a view of the skull made from the side. It is called a lateral view. It shows the frontal sinuses. When normal, they are filled with air so they are black.

percent are due to the feline reovirus and *Chlamydia psittaci*. The disease caused by *C. psittaci* is commonly called pneumonitis.

Clinical Signs

The primary clinical signs of all viral URIs are sneezing and a serous (watery) nasal discharge. Conjunctivitis (inflammation of the outer part of the eyes) and ulcers of the tongue are also common with some of these infections. The feline herpesvirus can cause deep ulcers in the corneas, and the feline calicivirus can cause pneumonia (infection within the lungs). Most cats have fever and refuse to eat; dehydration often follows.

Diagnosis

Most viral URIs are diagnosed based on the clinical signs and known exposure to other cats, especially sneezing cats. It is possible to firmly diagnose the specific disease with a viral culture. However, culturing is generally not necessary since treatment for all of these infections is essentially the same.

Management

There are no drugs that kill the viruses; they must, and will, run their course in a few days. If pneumonitis is suspected, tetracycline may be used because it is effective against this bacteria-like organism. Most cats with viral URIs have secondary bacterial infections that make the viral infections much worse; therefore, antibiotics are given orally or by injection. Antibiotics are also used topically in the eyes if conjunctivitis or corneal ulcers are present. Fluids are needed, intravenously or subcutaneously (under the skin), to correct

CAT HEALTH ENCYCLOPEDIA

dehydration. Food is essential; it may be fed by hand or through a stomach feeding tube.

The respiratory viruses and *Chlamydia* run their course in a few days. If proper antibiotics are given, secondary bacterial infections can be controlled. If this is done and if dehydration and malnutrition are corrected or prevented, the prognosis is very good. However, if these cats remain dehydrated and do not receive nutritional support, many will die.

Many cats that are infected with the feline herpesvirus will remain chronically infected for life. They will shed the virus to other cats and develop new symptoms of the disease when they are stressed. Many cats infected with the calicivirus also become chronically infected; however, their infection is generally not life-long. It lasts for weeks or months. These cats continuously shed the virus so they are a threat to non-vaccinated cats.

PREVENTION

Cats should be vaccinated against the feline herpesvirus, the feline calicivirus, and *Chlamydia*. A series of injections are given to kittens; adults should be boostered each year.

Cats with viral URI should be isolated from non-infected cats because these infections are very

The frontal sinuses are seen at the top of the skull. The one on the left is normal, air-filled, and black. The one on the right is abnormal, filled with purulent material (pus), and white.

Diseases of the Respiratory System

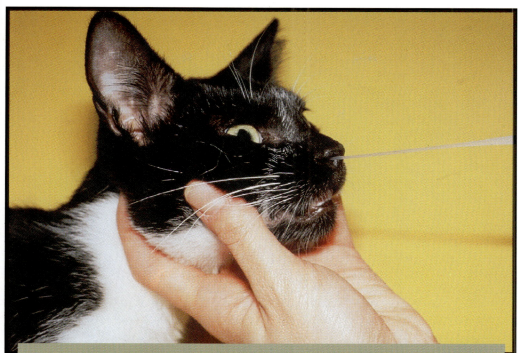

A diagnostic nasal flush is performed by passing a tiny catheter (tube) deep into the anesthetized cat's nasal passages. Fluid is flushed through the catheter and aspirated back into the syringe. The tissue recovered is observed under the microscope for signs of infection and cancer.

contagious. Since the organisms are readily transmitted to kittens, cats about five-six weeks of age should be removed from the environment of any sneezing or chronically infected cat, including their mother.

Stricture of the Trachea

The trachea is also known as the windpipe. It begins at the larynx and ends as it bifurcates (splits) in the chest. Its round shape is maintained by a series of cartilage rings that go from the two o'clock to the ten o'clock positions. A rubbery ligament stretches across the top of the trachea between the ends of the rings. Tracheal diseases are not common in cats, but a few notable situations do arise.

The normal round shape of the trachea permits rapid flow of air.

Any narrowing of the trachea reduces airflow and creates serious breathing difficulty. A collapsing trachea is one in which the tracheal rings do not maintain their normal, round shape. They will flatten, as viewed from top to bottom, stretching the tracheal ligament. This is common in small breeds of dog, but it also occasionally occurs in cats. Strictures may also be caused by masses within the trachea. These masses are usually benign or malignant tumors. A third cause of tracheal stricture is an impinging mass that is adjacent to the trachea, often in the chest cavity.

CLINICAL SIGNS

Cats with tracheal stricture have difficulty breathing, especially after

CAT HEALTH ENCYCLOPEDIA

exercise. To prevent respiratory distress, they often severely limit their activity. They may develop a chronic or recurring cough. If a growing mass is present, air passage will become so restricted that open mouth breathing will occur. At that point, the tongue may become cyanotic (blue).

DIAGNOSIS

Radiographs (x-rays) of the trachea will usually identify a tracheal stricture. Masses within or adjacent to the trachea may be seen. A collapsing trachea may require more than one radiograph for confirmation since the trachea often collapses only during inspiration or only during expiration, depending upon which segment of the trachea is abnormal.

MANAGEMENT

Masses within or adjacent to the trachea are usually very difficult for the surgeon to reach, especially if the segment of trachea within the chest cavity is involved. However, some masses in the neck region can be managed surgically. A collapsing trachea can be reshaped by surgically placing artificial rings on the outside of the trachea. This is possible in the neck region but difficult or impossible within the chest cavity.

A cat with a mass restricting air passage has a good prognosis if the mass can be removed. However, many of these masses are within the chest cavity, so they are often not operable. Lymphosarcoma (LSA), caused by the feline leukemia virus (FeLV), is a common malignant tumor within the chest cavity that will compress the trachea. Cats with LSA generally have a poor prognosis. Tracheal collapse has a good prognosis if it can be successfully corrected surgically.

Tracheal Foreign Body

The normal playing habits of cats often result in them getting small objects within their mouths. These are usually spit out or swallowed; however, occasionally a small object will be inhaled into the trachea. Coughing will occur immediately in an attempt to expel the foreign body. However, the foreign body may lodge in the trachea if it is sharp pointed or if it becomes entrapped within tracheal mucus.

CLINICAL SIGNS

A tracheal foreign body causes immediate, violent coughing as the cat attempts to expel the object. Coughing will not stop until the object is removed. If the foreign body is large enough to obstruct air passage, open mouth breathing and cyanosis of the tongue will occur. Many of these cats will assume a characteristic body position with the head extended upward.

DIAGNOSIS

Radiographs (x-rays) may identify a tracheal foreign body if it is composed of bone or metal or if it is quite large. However, many things that cats inhale are not visible on a radiograph. A small endoscope may be used to visualize the foreign body, but this procedure requires anesthesia, and a mucus-covered object may not be discernible with an endoscope. Therefore, the diagnosis is usually presumptive based on a sudden onset of the described clinical signs.

MANAGEMENT

Treatment is often not rewarding if the cat is unable to cough out the object. The size of the trachea makes surgical removal of any foreign body very difficult or impossible because few veterinarians have the tiny instruments required.

166

DISEASES OF THE RESPIRATORY SYSTEM

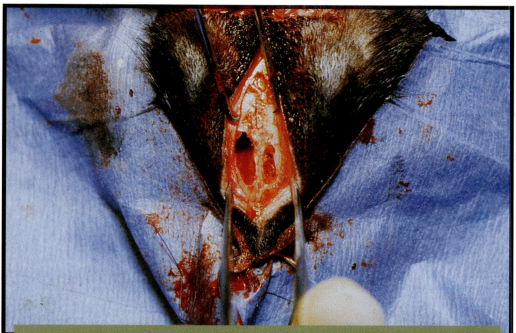

Biopsy samples can be taken through a surgically-created slot made in the bone over the nasal cavity.

A surgical opening has been made in the bone over the nasal cavity exposing an inflammatory polyp.

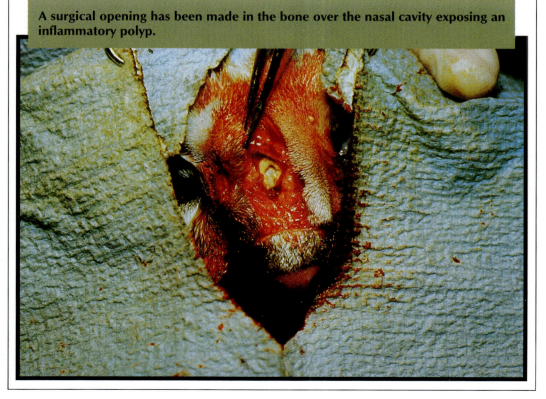

CAT HEALTH ENCYCLOPEDIA

Asthma

Feline asthma is a term that describes a common respiratory disease of cats. It is also known as allergic bronchitis, allergic pneumonitis, and eosinophilic pneumonitis. Each of these terms describes a feature of the disease. The basis of the disease is an irritant or allergic reaction within the bronchi and lungs. Sometimes, the offending agent can be identified; however, despite extensive research, the cause of most cases of feline asthma is unknown.

An irritant reaction is not the same as an allergic reaction. Some agents cause irritation to the bronchi and lungs without causing the abnormal response from the immune system known as allergy. Although they are technically different, the effects on the cat are essentially the same.

CLINICAL SIGNS

Cats with feline asthma have a characteristic dry cough. The cat often assumes a characteristic crouched position with its neck extended. There will be episodes of coughing that will last a few minutes, then the cat will be normal. This may occur a few times each week to several times each day.

In advanced stages of asthma, lung changes may occur that will result in difficulty exhaling. This can result in open-mouth breathing, cyanosis, and a frantic demeanor that reveals the cat's state of panic. Cats with terminal disease may hysterically claw at their face.

DIAGNOSIS

Because feline asthma is the leading cause of coughing in cats, any coughing cat should be suspected of having it, especially if the cat assumes the characteristic crouched position during the coughing episodes. Confirmation of asthma can usually be made with a chest radiograph (x-ray); characteristic lung changes will usually be found on the radiographs. Most of these cats have an increase in eosinophils in the blood so a complete blood count (CBC) can be helpful. A tracheal wash can also be diagnostic. This is a procedure in which a catheter is passed to the end of the trachea, and a small volume of saline is injected. Immediately, the saline is aspirated back into the syringe. The fluid's sediment is studied under a microscope to determine if an abnormal number of eosinophils is present. Because many of these cats have a bacterial infection accompanying asthma, the fluid may also be cultured.

Since asthma is often an allergic reaction, identifying the allergen is the most desirable first step in treatment. However, this is often not possible. In addition, even if the allergen can be identified, the cat cannot always be removed from it. Commonly suspected respiratory allergens or irritants include dusty cat litter, cigarette or cigar smoke, fumes from new carpet, perfumes, and tree and grass pollens.

MANAGEMENT

If it is not possible to remove the respiratory allergen or irritant from the cat's environment, the cat is treated with various drugs to block the reaction and to improve breathing. Corticosteroids (cortisone compounds) are very effective in most cats, and various bronchodilators may also be very effective. Since infections commonly occur in the lungs during an asthmatic episode, a broad-spectrum antibiotic is often given for one to two weeks.

If the offending agent can be identified and removed from the cat's

DISEASES OF THE RESPIRATORY SYSTEM

Cats with upper respiratory infections are usually sneezing and have serous (watery) discharge from the eyes.

Ulcers on the tongue are common in cats with upper respiratory infections.

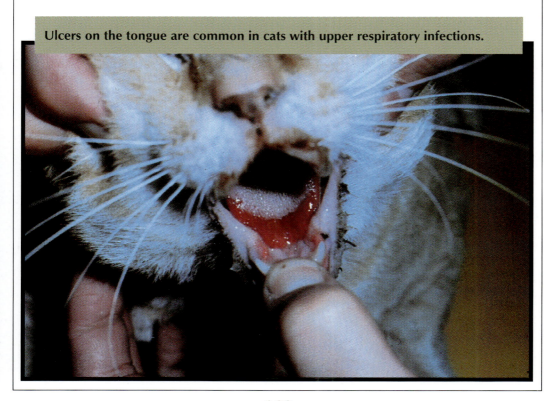

Cat Health Encyclopedia

environment, the prognosis is excellent. However, this is usually not possible, making medical management necessary.

Most cats respond very favorably to treatment. Their coughing stops, and their breathing returns to normal. If the allergen or irritant is in the cat's environment seasonally, periodic treatment will be necessary; but it is generally successful each time. However, cats that are constantly exposed to the offending agent have chronic asthmatic episodes. Many of these cats become resistant to treatment and develop chronic lung scarring. At that point, the prognosis is very guarded.

Pneumonia

Pneumonia is an inflammation of the lung tissue. It is commonly caused by infection, but it may be caused by other entities that inflame the lungs. The most common types of pneumonia in cats are fungal, bacterial, and foreign body.

Mineral oil pneumonia is a notable disease in cats. Mineral oil has little taste and does not elicit a good swallowing reflex in cats. If it is given orally (for hairballs, etc.), it may easily go into the trachea and lungs. Food may also be a cause of foreign body pneumonia. The most common cause of food inhalation occurs when a cat vomits. If the vomited food remains in the mouth when the cat inhales, it is likely to go down the trachea and into the lungs.

Clinical Signs

Coughing is not a common response of the cat to lung

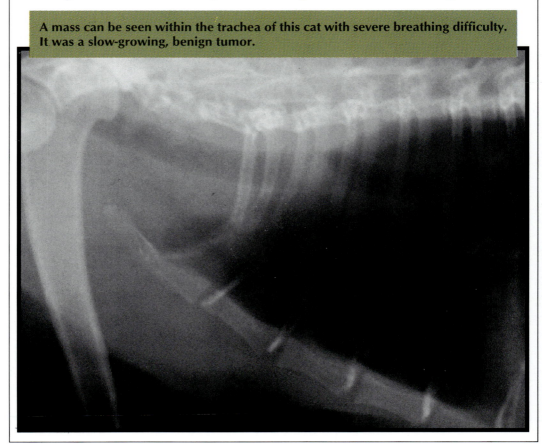

A mass can be seen within the trachea of this cat with severe breathing difficulty. It was a slow-growing, benign tumor.

DISEASES OF THE RESPIRATORY SYSTEM

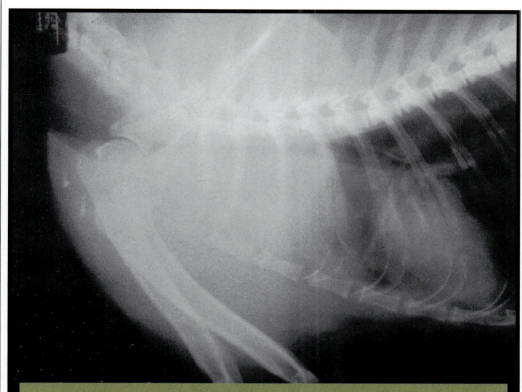

A cancerous mass within the chest cavity is putting pressure on the trachea resulting in difficulty breathing.

inflammation, as it is in dogs and people. Most infectious forms of pneumonia do not cause coughing. However, pneumonia caused by the presence of a foreign substance in the lungs is more likely to do so.

Cats with foreign body pneumonia are very susceptible to secondary infections. Therefore, any form of pneumonia is likely to be or become complicated by infection. Any infection in the lung, whether primary or secondary, is likely to cause generalized signs of illness. These include fever, weight loss, poor appetite, unkempt hair coat, and lethargy.

Diagnosis

Cats with the listed clinical signs are suspected of having pneumonia. Auscultation (listening with a stethoscope) of the lungs will reveal increased, harsh lung sounds. A radiograph (x-ray) of the chest is the most specific diagnostic test and is easily performed. A tracheal wash can be performed, but it requires anesthesia, which is not desirable for cats with pneumonia. Lung aspiration is another test that can be very helpful. A tiny needle is passed through the chest wall into the lungs. Very quickly, some lung cells are aspirated into the syringe. They are placed on a microscope slide and studied for cell type and the presence of infectious organisms.

Management

Foreign body pneumonia is difficult to treat because it is usually not possible to remove the offending

Cat Health Encyclopedia

substance from the lungs. These cats are treated with antibiotics for the secondary infections and with bronchodilators. They should receive good supportive care, such as fluids and adequate nutrition. Good nursing care is important, as well as isolation from further stress, especially any situation that might require increased respiration.

Bacterial pneumonia is treated with antibiotics. If a sample of lung fluid can be obtained, a culture can be performed allowing identification of the appropriate antibiotic to use. If a culture is not feasible, a broad spectrum antibiotic is used. Good supportive care is important, as is minimizing stress.

There are several fungi that cause pneumonia; these are called systemic fungi. The common feline fungal pneumonias in the United States are histoplasmosis, blastomycosis, coccidioidomycosis, and cryptococcosis. These are all very serious infections that are treated with specific antifungal drugs. Many respond to treatment, but treatment should last at least six months.

The prognosis for foreign body pneumonia is always guarded. If the body can mobilize the foreign material and expel it, and if bacterial infections can be controlled, there is hope for good recovery. However, even if this happens, many cats sustain permanent scarring of the

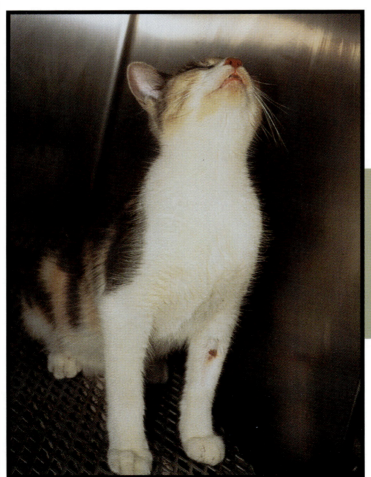

The position assumed by this cat is typical for cats with tracheal foreign bodies. A small piece of an acorn shell was aspirated and lodged deep in the trachea.

Diseases of the Respiratory System

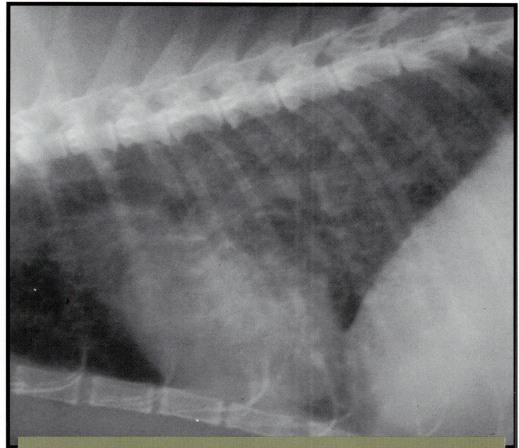

Increased density of the lungs makes them look white. This is due to the inflammation caused by feline asthma.

lungs resulting in chronic breathing difficulty and reduced activity.

Bacterial pneumonia is usually curable. If the appropriate antibiotics are started promptly and continued long enough, the cat should recover completely.

Fungal pneumonia is difficult to treat successfully. Prolonged treatment is necessary, sometimes lasting six to nine months. However, even then, relapse is possible when medication is discontinued. Even though the drugs that are now available are much less toxic and much more effective than older drugs, the prognosis is always guarded.

Lung Cancer

Cancer frequently occurs in the lungs of cats. A primary pulmonary tumor begins in the lungs. A metastatic pulmonary tumor arises in another organ and spreads to the lungs. Metastasis (spreading of a tumor) generally occurs when cancer cells get into the blood stream and lodge in other organs. Since the lungs have millions of tiny capillaries, it is easy for cancer cells to be filtered out there. Cancer cells multiply rapidly, creating masses in the lungs.

Breast cancer is common in cats, especially cats that have not been spayed. It has also been associated with the administration of megestrol acetate, a drug used for estrus (heat) control and for its anti-inflammatory properties. As in women, this form of cancer spreads rapidly; it has often already metastasized by the time the breast mass is found. This is the main type of metastatic lung cancer in cats.

Lung cancer is also common in cats with masses on one or more toes. The tumor on the toe may drain fluid and be mistaken for an infection or bite wound. These are usually squamous-cell carcinomas that metastasize readily to the lungs.

Clinical Signs

Cats with early lung cancer usually do not show any signs of illness. However, as the tumors grow, respiration becomes affected. Cats have the unfortunate ability to hide many diseases until they become very severe. This is often the case with lung cancer. Rapid shallow breathing is the first respiratory sign. It may be missed by the owner until it becomes pronounced.

Many cats with lung cancer will have signs of systemic illness. Gradual weight loss, poor appetite, lethargy, and an unkempt hair coat are common. If the primary tumor is elsewhere, there may be signs related to failure of the other affected organ, or a mass may be found if the organ is superficial.

Diagnosis

A radiograph (x-ray) of the chest will generally identify a lung tumor. However, if it is less than 2 mm in

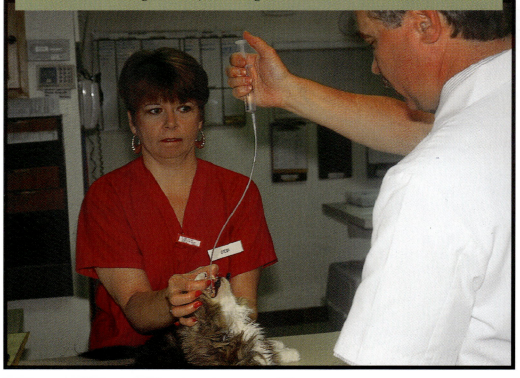

A tracheal wash is performed by passing a catheter into the trachea of an anesthetized cat, injecting fluid (saline solution) into the lungs, and aspirating the fluid back into the syringe. The fluid is analyzed in an attempt to determine the cause of various lung diseases, including feline asthma.

DISEASES OF THE RESPIRATORY SYSTEM

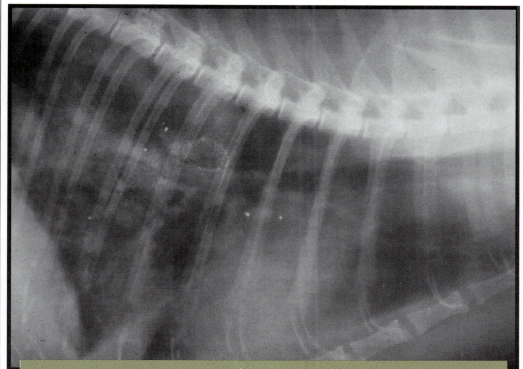

The increased density of the lung field is due to mineral oil that was given to this cat for hairballs. Mineral oil causes the cat to not swallow properly so it may easily go into the lungs causing foreign body pneumonia.

diameter, it may not be visible. Lung aspiration is another meaningful test. However, this procedure is meaningful only if the needle gets into the tumor. A lung biopsy may be needed to firmly identify lung cancer, but this requires major surgery into the chest. Some forms of lung cancer are confirmed at necropsy (autopsy on an animal).

Management

The most desirable treatment is to completely remove the tumor surgically. Chemotherapy is another form of treatment that has been used in some cats.

The prognosis is generally grave since few lung tumors are successfully treated. However, some lung tumors grow rather slowly. If a lung tumor is diagnosed serendipitously from a chest radiograph and clinical signs are not present, it may be prudent to do nothing. Many cats will still have many months of quality life.

Pulmonary Edema

Pulmonary edema is a collection of fluid within the lungs. Since the lungs are responsible for oxygen and carbon dioxide transport, the presence of fluid in the airways can be life threatening.

There are two ways that pulmonary edema forms. It may occur secondary to heart failure, which results in poor movement of blood through the millions of capillaries in the lungs. As blood flow slows, fluid leaks out of the vessels into the airways. It may also occur due to an allergic-type reaction within the lungs. This is most likely due to a drug reaction or to transfusion of incompatible blood.

CLINICAL SIGNS

Cats with pulmonary edema have great difficulty breathing. They attempt to remove the fluid by coughing or gagging. The respiration rate increases, and open mouth breathing often occurs. Severe pulmonary edema prevents proper movement of oxygen into the blood so the cat becomes cyanotic, most often seen in the tongue. The signs of respiratory distress may begin very suddenly if a drug or blood transfusion reaction occurs. Its onset may take several hours or days if it is due to heart failure. But because the cat is able to conceal breathing difficulties until they are severe, the onset may seem more acute than it really was.

DIAGNOSIS

A chest radiograph (x-ray) shows a collection of fluid within the lung field. However, the radiographic findings may be similar to other lung diseases. If there is doubt, a diuretic may be administered, and the chest radiographed again a few hours later. If pulmonary edema is present, the lungs will be more normal in the second set of radiographs.

MANAGEMENT

Immediate treatment is the administration of a diuretic intravenously. This is a drug that stimulates the kidneys to remove fluid from the body. Edematous fluid in the lungs is some of the first fluid to be removed, so improvement usually occurs within a matter of minutes.

The next step is to determine the cause of the fluid collection in the

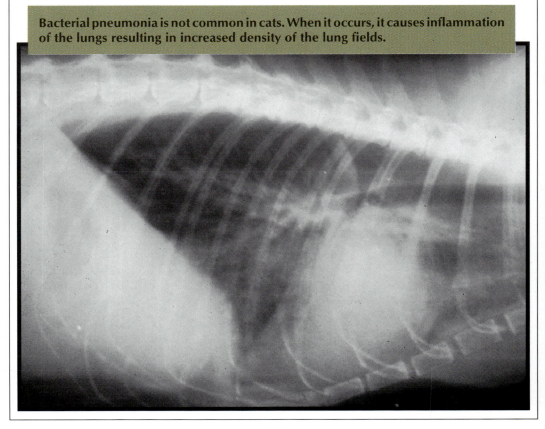

Bacterial pneumonia is not common in cats. When it occurs, it causes inflammation of the lungs resulting in increased density of the lung fields.

DISEASES OF THE RESPIRATORY SYSTEM

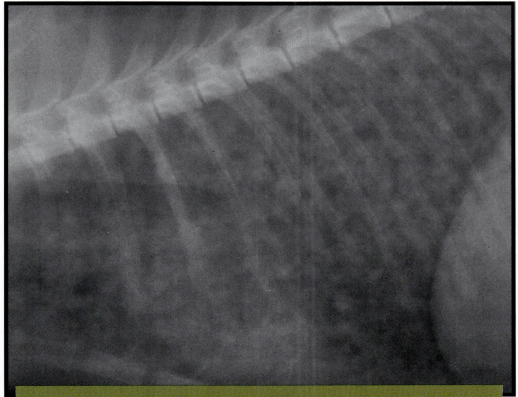

This cat has a fungal pneumonia caused by Histoplasma capsulatum. The severe density of these lungs is typical of fungal-induced disease.

lungs. Reviewing the cat's history for drug and blood administration may reveal the answer. Making radiographs after diuretic administration permits better visualization of the heart, making a determination of heart disease more reliable. An ultrasound examination of the heart is also very helpful in identifying heart abnormalities consistent with heart failure. An electrocardiogram (ECG) will reveal other information about heart function.

The use of diuretics can usually clear the lungs of pulmonary edema. However, preventing it from recurring depends upon one's ability to determine and treat the cause. Drug and blood transfusion reactions require anti-inflammatory treatment with corticosteroids (cortisone) until the offending substance is out of the body. This may take several hours, during which time further treatment with diuretics may be necessary. At that point, the prognosis is very good. If heart failure is present, the prognosis depends on one's ability to control it. Some heart diseases are very responsive to treatment and carry a good prognosis. Others do not respond to treatment, and the prognosis is grave.

Pleural Effusion

The pleural cavity is the space between the lungs and the chest wall. In a normal cat, this space is essentially non-existent since the lungs should remain in contact with the chest wall. However, certain diseases cause formation of an effusion (fluid) that collects in the pleural space. This results in compression of the lungs and difficulty breathing. There are several diseases that may cause pleural effusion. The four most common ones will be discussed.

Pleural Effusion Due to Lymphosarcoma

Lymphosarcoma (LSA) is a malignancy of lymphoid tissue. There are many sites of lymphoid tissue, including lymph nodes and the tonsils. Malignancy of the lymph node in the anterior (front) part of the chest cavity causes enlargement of that lymph node and the production of effusive fluid within the pleural space. This disease is caused by the feline leukemia virus (FeLV).

Clinical Signs

The clinical signs of pleural effusion relate to its effect on the lungs. Because the lungs are located in a space of relatively fixed size, they become compressed by the fluid. This creates breathing difficulty. Cats with mild pleural effusion have an increase in their respiration rate. It is normally about 30 breaths per minute and may increase to 100 breaths per minute when pleural effusion is present. As the amount of fluid increases, respiration is impaired even more. The cat assumes an upright position because lying on its side makes breathing more difficult. Some cats will sleep in this position. Further fluid accumulation causes open mouth breathing and cyanosis of the tongue.

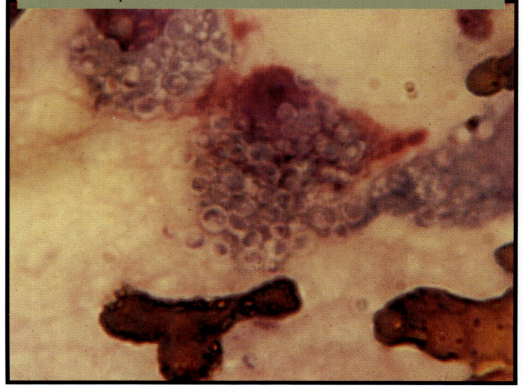

A lung aspiration recovers cells from the lungs that help to determine the cause of pneumonia and other lung diseases. This lung aspirate contains hundreds of fungi that cause histoplasmosis.

Diseases of the Respiratory System

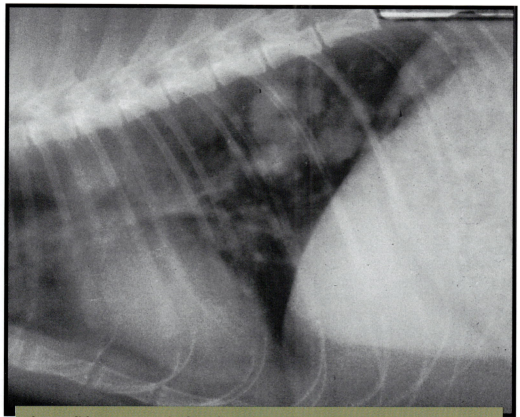

These solid masses seen in these lungs are malignant tumors (cancer).

LSA usually has adverse effects on the bone marrow, resulting in anemia (decreased number of red blood cells). The combination of anemia and pleural effusion causes the cat to be very weak and listless and depresses the appetite. If the lymph node in the chest enlarges greatly, it may compress the esophagus (food tube to the stomach) and cause vomiting immediately after eating. It may also compress the trachea as described in the section on tracheal structure. Dehydration occurs very soon due to lack of fluid intake.

Diagnosis

Pleural effusion is best diagnosed with a chest radiograph. Fluid in the pleural space has the same radiographic density as the heart, so the heart's visibility becomes lost in the fluid. The lungs are compressed as evidenced by reduced air density within the chest. A needle and syringe are used to aspirate some of the fluid from the chest cavity, confirming the presence of pleural effusion and providing a sample for analysis.

The fluid of LSA contains large numbers of malignant lymphoblasts (immature cells from lymph nodes). Their presence confirms the diagnosis. Further tests for LSA include a blood count for anemia and a test for the presence of the FeLV.

Management

Removing the fluid from the pleural space will result in improved

CAT HEALTH ENCYCLOPEDIA

respiration. This can be done with a syringe and needle. However, if LSA is present, the fluid will reform within a few days.

Treatment for LSA is generally not rewarding. Although some cats will have marked reduction in fluid formation and lymph node size due to chemotherapy, the treatment does nothing to kill the FeLV.

The prognosis for LSA is grave in most cases. Even with good response, the disease will recur within a few weeks to months, and the cat remains contagious to other cats. Most owners elect euthanasia.

PREVENTION

Cats can, and should, be vaccinated against the FeLV. The vaccine is reliable for 90+ percent of cats with occasional exposure to the FeLV. Cats with constant exposure have a lower protection rate.

Pleural Effusion due to Feline Infectious Peritonitis

Feline infectious peritonitis (FIP) is a disease caused by the FIP virus (FIPV). It occurs in the non-effusive ("dry") and effusive ("wet") forms. The effusive form causes an accumulation of fluid within the abdominal cavity and/or the chest cavity. The latter is a form of pleural effusion.

CLINICAL SIGNS

The signs of pleural effusion due to FIP are the same as any pleural effusion, as discussed above. FIP is a chronic, wasting disease. It causes progressive weight loss, a declining appetite, and increasing lethargy. Most cats have a high fever (104-107° F). These signs usually precede the respiratory distress caused by the pleural effusion.

Fluid is removed from the pleural space and analyzed. There are some characteristics that are typical for FIP, but other diseases can cause the production of fluid with similar characteristics. There are also some abnormalities in blood tests that are typical for FIP; however, these are also not limited to this disease. The only way to confirm FIP is with a biopsy of an affected organ. In the case of wet FIP in the chest, the lung or lining of the chest wall must be biopsied. This is difficult because it requires major surgery on a very debilitated cat. In most cases, several pieces of information are assembled that result in a strong, but still presumptive, diagnosis of FIP. The diagnosis is usually confirmed by a pathologist's study of tissues taken at necropsy (autopsy on an animal).

MANAGEMENT

There is no known successful treatment for FIP. A few cats have recovered, even without treatment, but they are exceptional cases. Therefore, the prognosis for FIP is grave. Euthanasia is the most commonly chosen route once the diagnosis is reasonably sure.

PREVENTION

Cats may be vaccinated for FIP. The vaccine is effective in only about 70-80 percent of cats, but this is the only effective means of prevention available other than preventing exposure to cats shedding the virus.

Pleural Effusion due to Chylothorax

Chylothorax is a collection of chyle-containing fluid in the pleural space. Chyle is the fluid made by the lymph nodes and is part of the body's immune system. It is channeled through tiny ducts from one lymph node to another into the thoracic duct near the heart. The thoracic duct empties into the vena cava, the large blood-carrying vein that enters the heart.

DISEASES OF THE RESPIRATORY SYSTEM

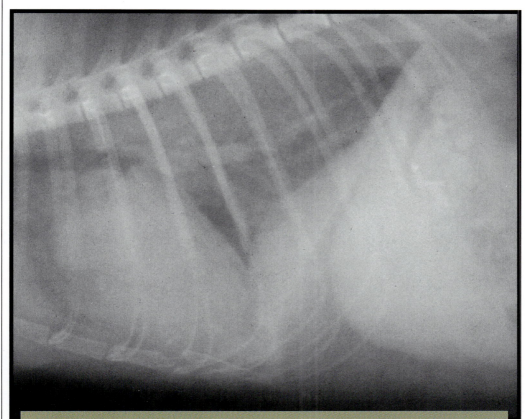

The increased whiteness of these lungs is due to a collection of fluid within the lungs and is called pulmonary edema.

Chylothorax may occur secondary to trauma that causes rupture of the thoracic duct. More often, it occurs when the thoracic duct becomes partially obstructed or when pressure within the vena cava increases. This usually occurs secondary to a mass in the chest or secondary to heart disease (especially cardiomyopathy or heartworm disease). Some cases of chylothorax have no definable cause so they are considered idiopathic or primary chylothorax.

Clinical Signs

The signs of pleural effusion due to chylothorax are the same as any pleural effusion, as discussed above. Many cats with chylothorax have a history of coughing, which is unusual for most feline diseases. The other signs are typical of a cat with a serious systemic disease. They include weight loss, lethargy, and appetite depression.

Diagnosis

Recovery of fluid from the pleural space permits analysis. Chylothorax produces a characteristic fluid that is milky white in color. It contains a predominance of very small, mature lymphocytes. These are cells from the lymph nodes. LSA fluid also contains a large number of lymphocytes, but they are very immature, blastic forms (lymphoblasts). Measuring the amounts of cholesterol and triglycerides and comparing them to similar levels in the cat's blood is a

CAT HEALTH ENCYCLOPEDIA

reliable means of confirming that the fluid is truly chylous.

Once it is confirmed that chylous effusion is present, the underlying cause is sought. Radiographs are repeated after the fluid has been removed from the chest; they are looking for the presence of a mass within the chest and looking for evidence of heart disease. A blood test should be performed for heartworms. An ultrasound examination of the heart is also indicated to assess heart size and function and to look for heartworms.

If all of these tests do not reveal a cause for chylothorax, a diagnosis of idiopathic chylothorax is made. However, if response to treatment is not satisfactory, repetition of radiographs and the ultrasound examination should be considered, as some conditions may progress and be better detected at a later time.

MANAGEMENT

The first priority for treatment is to relieve the respiratory distress. The effusive fluid is removed from the chest with a syringe and needle. This may be repeated once or twice daily, but it is a painful procedure that requires sedation. The preferred approach is to surgically place a chest drain tube so the veterinarian can drain the chest as often as needed without inducing further stress. If a cause of chylothorax can be determined, it must be treated, if possible.

If chest drainage does not cause resolution within a couple of weeks, some veterinary surgeons will enter the chest cavity and ligate (tie off) the thoracic duct. This is more successful in dogs with chylothorax than in affected cats, but it can be successful in some cats.

The idiopathic form of chylothorax generally has a good prognosis. Fluid production generally stops within a few days to a couple of weeks, at which time the drain tube can be removed. However, there is always the possibility that an undetected, underlying disease was not found, and the disease will recur.

If chylothorax is caused by trauma, the duct will generally heal during the time the chest tube is in place. If not, successful surgery will permit a good prognosis. If heartworms are the cause, they can often be treated successfully. Some forms of heart disease are very treatable, and other forms are not. The presence of a malignant mass in the chest justifies a grave prognosis. If a benign mass is present and can be successfully removed, the prognosis is good.

Pleural Effusion due to Pyothorax

Pyothorax is a collection of pus in the pleural space. It is caused by a bacterial infection. It is postulated that the infection gets in the pleural space either by a penetrating wound or bite through the chest wall or through the blood stream. Some cases are known to be caused by a foreign body, such as a splinter or grass awn, that enters the plural space through the chest wall. However, in most cases the actual source of the infection is not identified, and no foreign body is present.

When pyothorax has been present for several weeks, adhesions form between the lungs, the pericardium, and the body wall. This condition is called fibrosing pleuritis.

CLINICAL SIGNS

The signs of pleural effusion due to pyothorax are the same as any pleural effusion, as discussed above. Because infection is present, cats with pyothorax often, but not always, have fever and do not eat. There will

Diseases of the Respiratory System

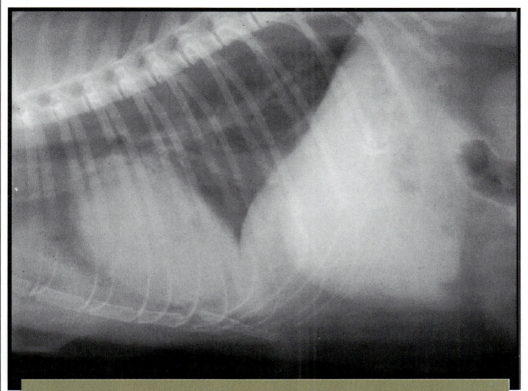

When a diuretic is given to a cat with pulmonary edema, the fluid is removed by the kidneys, and the lungs clear. The cat's breathing improves quickly.

have been a gradual decline in their activity level over the last several days to weeks. They are very lethargic and usually very dehydrated when presented for treatment. Many of these cats have a low grade anemia (low red blood cell count) and a high white blood cell count.

Diagnosis

Respiratory difficulty is the basis for making a chest radiograph that can confirm the presence of pleural effusion. Fluid is recovered from the pleural space as for all cats with pleural effusion and analyzed. This fluid is very thick and creamy with a foul odor. When examined under a microscope, large numbers of bacteria and inflammatory cells are seen. This is confirmatory evidence of pyothorax.

If fibrosing pleuritis is present, the lung lobes will have a rounded appearance on radiographs due to the adhesions.

Management

The first priority, as with all cases of pleural effusion, is to restore normal respiration. Fluid is removed from the chest as soon as possible. Repeated fluid aspiration can be done, but surgical placement of a drain tube permits more complete and comfortable fluid removal, which is necessary for five to ten days.

A culture is performed on the pleural fluid for both aerobic (grows in the presence of oxygen) and anaerobic (grows in the absence of oxygen) bacteria. It is very important that these cultures be performed so that the correct antibiotics can be chosen. Antibiotics should be given for three to six weeks to rid the cat of the infection.

Cats with pyothorax should respond to chest drainage and antibiotic therapy within seven to ten days, at which time the drain tube is removed. However, if pus is still forming after ten days, surgical exploration of the chest should be considered to look for a foreign body that is perpetuating the disease.

Cats treated with the appropriate antibiotic and proper chest drainage have a good prognosis, if fibrosing pleuritis is not present. However, marked improvement should occur within seven to ten days. If not, the prognosis is downgraded to poor unless surgery is successful in removing the causative agent from the chest.

The presence of fibrosing pleuritis is a poor prognostic sign. Even if the infection is treated successfully, the lungs will not reinflate so respiration will always be impaired.

Pneumothorax

Pneumothorax is the presence of air in the pleural space. Air should be confined to the inside of the lungs; the pleural space should contain a vacuum that helps to keep the lungs inflated. When air escapes into the pleural space, the vacuum is lost, and the lungs collapse.

Pneumothorax occurs when there is a puncture into the respiratory airways. If the puncture occurs in the cervical (neck) trachea, air can migrate along the outside of the trachea into the chest cavity. If it occurs in the thoracic (chest) trachea, air leaks directly into the pleural space. A puncture in the lung or in the chest wall can also cause pneumothorax. Trauma is the most common cause of pneumothorax, but spontaneous pneumothorax, usually

This cat's unusual sleeping position occurs because its lungs are surrounded by fluid (pleural effusion). The cat breathes easiest when in an upright position.

Diseases of the Respiratory System

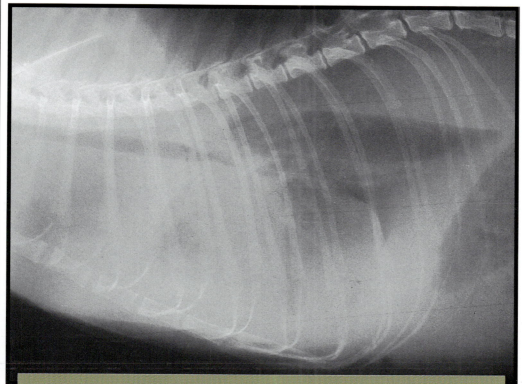

Pleural effusion compresses the lungs so their capacity is very limited. On a radiograph, the fluid and the heart have the same density, making the heart no longer definable.

due to cancer or chronic asthma, has been documented. Tension pneumothorax is a special form of pneumothorax. It is present when air is continuing to leak into the pleural space.

Clinical Signs

Because one or more lobes of the lungs collapses during pneumothorax, respiration is very compromised. The cat has rapid, shallow breathing, often with an open mouth. It is reluctant to lie on its side or back, and often becomes frantic trying to breathe.

Pneumothorax is suspected for any cat with a very acute onset of breathing difficulty, especially if it has been hit by a car or sustained a significant fall. Signs of trauma may be seen. These include tire marks on the hair coat, abrasions on the skin, and frayed toenails.

Diagnosis

A chest radiograph demonstrates the classic signs of pneumothorax. On the lateral (side) view, the heart appears to be elevated from the sternum (breast bone). Collapsed lobes of lung do not contain air. The stomach is often filled with air, due to swallowing of air while desperately trying to inhale.

The diagnosis is confirmed when air can be aspirated freely from the pleural space with a syringe and needle. Tension pneumothorax is diagnosed when air is removed from the pleural space and then is present there again within minutes.

CAT HEALTH ENCYCLOPEDIA

MANAGEMENT

The first priority is to reestablish normal respiration. This is accomplished by aspirating air out of the pleural space with a syringe and needle. As much as 200 ml of air may be removed from some cats. If the leak has sealed, this procedure is curative. However, if tension pneumothorax is present, repeated aspiration is necessary. The veterinarian must make a judgment call on the necessity of surgery to repair the leak since cats with tension pneumothorax are very poor surgical risks.

Simple pneumothorax has a good prognosis. One or two aspirations of air are usually curative. However, tension pneumothorax is usually fatal if the hole in the trachea or lungs is not repaired very quickly.

Diaphragmatic Hernia

The diaphragm is a thin sheet of muscle that separates the chest from the abdomen. Without it, the organs in the abdomen would move forward, compress the lungs, and greatly impair respiration. The diaphragm also is important in inhalation and exhalation of air.

A diaphragmatic hernia (DH) is a tear in the diaphragm. It usually occurs due to trauma, especially when a cat is hit by a car. The liver lies immediately caudal to (behind) the diaphragm, so it is usually one of the first organs to move into the chest. The small intestines are very mobile within the abdomen, so they, too, often migrate through a hole in the diaphragm.

There is also a congenital form of DH in which a hole is present at birth. This type of DH has an opening at the center and base of the diaphragm, connecting the abdominal cavity to the pericardium (the sac that surrounds the heart).

Generally, the hole is too small for the liver to go through so the typical occurrence is for a segment of the small intestines to enter the pericardium. Pressure is placed on the heart by the intestines; however, the pericardium stretches enough so that cardiac compression is not significant. However, the pericardium will enlarge to the point that there will be some compression of the lungs.

Clinical Signs

Cats with a traumatically induced DH will have difficulty breathing, due to compression of the lungs. At first, only a single lobe of the liver may enter the chest, causing only mild respiratory impairment. However, over the next few hours or days, more of the liver and other abdominal organs may enter the chest, creating greater difficulties for the cat. Many of these cats will be reluctant to lie on their sides, and many will have open mouth breathing. They will often limit their activity greatly because exercise and movement will increase their respiratory difficulty.

If the tear in the diaphragm is fairly small, few abdominal organs will enter the chest. This may create mild respiratory distress that has little effect on the cat. By restricting strenuous activity, the cat may function rather normally for many months or years. This becomes a chronic DH.

Cats with congenital DHs usually have few signs of respiratory distress. The condition is often diagnosed serendipitously when the chest is radiographed (x-rayed) for other reasons.

Diagnosis

Most DHs can be diagnosed with a chest radiograph. There will be a break in the normal diaphragmatic

DISEASES OF THE RESPIRATORY SYSTEM

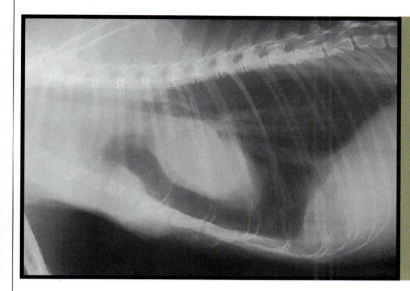

Pneumothorax occurs when air surrounds the lungs. The lungs appear darker than normal, and the heart appears to rise off of the sternum (breast bone). This air must be removed for the cat to breathe normally.

line, and there will be abdominal organs where the lung field should be. However, some cases are not as obvious; they require special radiographic studies using contrast materials. Barium is placed in the stomach. As it passes down the intestinal tract, a radiograph is made. If barium is seen in the chest, it will be obvious that the intestines are misplaced. A second approach, a celiogram, begins with an injection of a contrast material into the abdominal cavity. The cat's rear quarters are gently elevated, causing the contrast material to move forward toward the diaphragm. If a DH is present, a radiograph will reveal the contrast material in the chest cavity. Another way to diagnose DH is with an ultrasound examination of the chest. This will usually be able to verify that liver or intestinal tissue is present in the chest.

MANAGEMENT

Relieving respiratory distress is the immediate goal of therapy. This may be achieved by placing the cat in an oxygen cage. The restriction of movement induced by the cage and the high oxygen levels will stabilize most cats. However, at some point surgery must be done to replace the abdominal organs in their correct positions and to repair the tear in the diaphragm. Ideally, surgery should be delayed until the cat is stable; however, if a cat will not stabilize in an oxygen cage, surgery must be done immediately.

The surgery is always risky and difficult. However, a skilled surgeon is usually able to repair the damage and return the cat to normal.

Chronic DHs are always more difficult to repair because the abdominal organs have generally adhered to the lungs and pericardium. Conversely, a congenital DH is usually relatively easy to repair because the hole in the diaphragm is smaller and only the small intestines are involved.

If surgery is performed successfully, the prognosis is generally very good. The exception is the cat with a chronic DH in which the lungs do not reinflate normally because of long-standing adhesions. However, even in that circumstance, the cat's overall respiratory condition will be greatly improved.

Dr. Kenneth Lyon is a board-certified veterinary dentist, and a Diplomate of the American Veterinary Dental College. He is also the President-Elect of the Academy of Veterinary Dentistry. He is the past editor of the Journal of Veterinary Dentistry and a world-renowned expert on feline dentistry. Dr. Lyon is head of the Department of Veterinary Dentistry at Mesa Veterinary Hospital in Mesa, Arizona.

Dr. Kenneth Lyon

Dr. Gregg DuPont is a board-certified veterinary dentist, a Diplomate of the American Veterinary Dental College, and the President of the Academy of Veterinary Dentistry. Dr. DuPont is the Director of Shoreline Veterinary Dental Clinic, a division of Halecrest Veterinary Hospital in Seattle, Washington.

Dr. Gregg DuPont

DENTAL PROBLEMS AND CARE

By Kenneth Lyon, DVM
Diplomate, American Veterinary Dental College

Mesa Veterinary Hospital, Ltd.
858 N. Country Club Drive
Mesa, AZ 85201

and Gregg DuPont, DVM
Diplomate, American Veterinary Dental College

Fellow, Academy of Veterinary Dentistry
Shoreline Veterinary Dental Clinic
16037 Aurora Ave. N.
Seattle, WA 98133-5653

INTRODUCTION

It is only relatively recently that cat owners are becoming increasingly aware of the proper means of caring for their pets' teeth. Poor oral health will directly affect a cat's overall health, both by extension of disease and by interfering with the cat's ability to take in adequate nutrition. When a kitten is born, all the teeth are still under the gums waiting to erupt. Within a few weeks the baby teeth, or deciduous teeth, (also called primary teeth) begin to break through the gingiva. The adult, or secondary, teeth erupt toward the oral cavity under or adjacent to their primary counterparts. The root of the deciduous tooth is resorbed (removed by the body) as the crown of the underlying new tooth places pressure against it, activating the resorption process. Eventually the primary tooth has almost no root left, and the remaining crown remnant exfoliates. A cat's owner will frequently not be aware of the loss of these primary tooth caps, as they are lost in the environment or sometimes swallowed by the cat. When all the adult teeth are in place, a normal cat will have a set of 30 teeth. This is in contrast to 32 teeth in humans and 42 teeth in dogs. Cats rarely experience problems related to the process of tooth eruption and replacement, although some will develop a transient gingivitis, or inflammation, during this period.

TOOTH ANATOMY

The structure of cats' teeth is very similar to that of our own. They have one, two, or three roots supported in the socket by a specialized joint with a periodontal ligament. This ligament holds the tooth firmly in place but also acts as a shock absorber to dampen and distribute the biting forces placed on the tooth. Other structures in the mouth, such as the gingiva and the supporting bone, contribute as functional units of the periodontal support apparatus. The crown of the tooth is the part that is visible above the gumline. Although

CAT HEALTH ENCYCLOPEDIA

the layer of enamel that covers its surface is the hardest substance in the cat's body, the enamel of a cat is weaker and thinner than that of either a human or a dog. This exposed crown is the part of the tooth that the cat's owner can clean at home. The enamel protects the underlying "dentin." The dentin is also quite hard, although not as hard as the enamel. It comprises the bulk of the tooth in a mature cat and contains cell processes that allow the tooth to sense heat, cold, and pressure changes if damage or loss of the protective enamel covering exposes it to the oral environment. The dental pulp is located in a channel that extends through the center of the crown and of the root. The nerves and blood vessels in the pulp enter the tooth through its apex, bringing nutrients to the tooth and carrying sensory information from the tooth.

COMMON DENTAL PROBLEMS

External Odontoclastic Resorptions

Also known as resorptive lesions, neck lesions, root resorptions, cervical line lesions, and invasive resorptions, these painful lesions are one of the most common problems affecting cats' teeth today. They were first described in 1976 and have steadily increased in prevalence. Although recognized for 20 years, their exact cause or causes remain undetermined. There are many theories about their etiology, and many veterinary dentists feel that there are most likely a number of different processes that all result in a similar clinical problem. Some of the more popular theories include: 1) abnormal forces directed to the teeth due to the texture of cat foods. These forces can cause "abfraction" from stresses directed to the base of the

crown with resulting loss of tooth structure, 2) inflammation from poor dental hygiene, 3) infectious agents, 4) immune system disorders, and 5) the mineral content and balance of cats' diets.

Clinical signs: The facial (outside, or "buccal") surface of the lower premolars are often the first teeth affected. When a lesion begins under the gingival margin in the "furcation area" (where the tooth's two roots meet to form the crown), it may first present as an area of very localized gingivitis. Reflecting the gingival margin with an instrument or a gentle flow of air exposes the lesion. Frequently the gingiva will grow into and fill the defect, giving the appearance of the gingiva growing up onto the surface of the tooth. Less commonly, a lesion may occur above the gingival margin on the crown of the tooth. When a lesion has progressed to its final stages with complete destruction of the crown, it may appear as a raised bump of gingiva with no tooth structure remaining above the gums. Cats may show signs of excess salivation, inappetence, depression or lethargy, and lower jaw spasms or tremors when biting on hard food. Some cats may lose weight, while others may gain weight. Some people have surmised that this latter group of cats may eat more in an effort to "scratch" the "itch" on the affected tooth.

DIAGNOSIS

Invasive resorption lesions are diagnosed by direct visual observation or by probing with a dental probe. If an owner were to gently touch a tooth in an affected area with a finger nail, the cat would react with an immediate jaw movement and a pain response. This is not recommended, as a painful cat

Dental Problems and Care

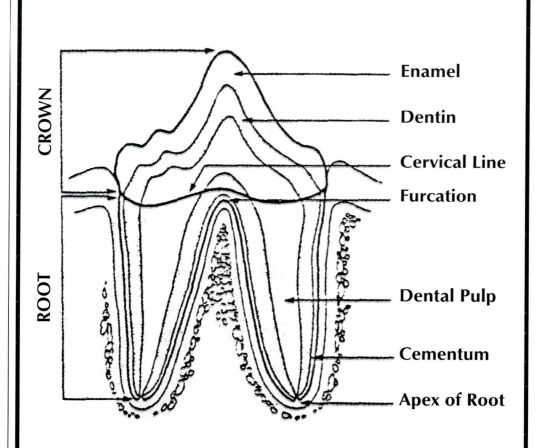

(Reprinted with permission from Tholen, M: *The Role of the Technician in Veterinary Medicine. 1. Dental Anatomy and Pathology, Veterinary Technician* 1984, 5:286-291).

Anatomy of the tooth.

may hurt the owner in an attempt to protect itself. General anesthesia, removing any accumulation of calculus covering the area, and oral examination may be necessary to know whether a lesion is present and to determine its severity. Some lesions may be completely subgingival and found only on deep subgingival probing or on radiographs. A lesion that appears relatively small clinically may actually have extensive resorption of the roots visible in a radiograph.

TREATMENT

The current most popular recommendation for treatment is to treat very early lesions with a fluoride varnish or a dental sealant. Lesions that are larger and deeper may be filled with a restorative if a radiograph demonstrates healthy roots. Once it has invaded the pulp cavity or destroyed a large amount of the tooth's crown, it is generally recommended to remove the painful and poorly functional tooth.

PREVENTION

Until we know the cause or causes, prevention will be difficult. Regular dental cleaning and home care will minimize gingivitis and inflammation, which is suspected to contribute to their progression. In individuals predisposed to the lesions (i.e., that have had one or more previously diagnosed), semi-weekly home fluoride treatments may be helpful to slow their progression and desensitize any affected areas, although this has not been proven.

Gingivitis and Periodontitis

Young cats from three to seven months old commonly experience a transient juvenile gingivitis. Local tissue trauma from tooth eruption may cause many of these, and they will resolve after the secondary teeth have erupted. Abyssinian cats, and less commonly Persians and Himalayans, are predisposed to a moderate to severe hyperplastic gingivitis at an early age.

Up to 40 percent of adult cats from one to four years of age suffer from adult-onset gingivitis. This adult form of gingivitis is caused by plaque, which is the sticky tan substance found accumulating on the tooth surface. Plaque consists almost entirely of bacteria, creating a constant challenge to the natural defense mechanisms in the mouth.

When gingivitis progresses to involve the supporting periodontal ligament, then it becomes periodontitis or periodontal disease. If this process is allowed to continue, the tooth will become mobile and eventually will exfoliate.

CLINICAL SIGNS

The first sign of gingivitis is a reddened area of gingiva, usually at the margin next to a tooth. Cats most commonly show no other clinical signs with either gingivitis or periodontitis. They generally are not painful until a tooth becomes quite loose in its alveolus. A malodorous breath may be the only observable clinical sign.

DIAGNOSIS

Gingivitis and periodontitis are diagnosed by visual signs and periodontal probing; red and swollen gingiva is evidence of gingivitis, and periodontal pocket formation indicates periodontal disease. Affected cats are frequently otherwise healthy animals, although those with unusually severe disease should be tested for retroviral infection, metabolic diseases, or other possible contributing factors.

Dental Problems and Care

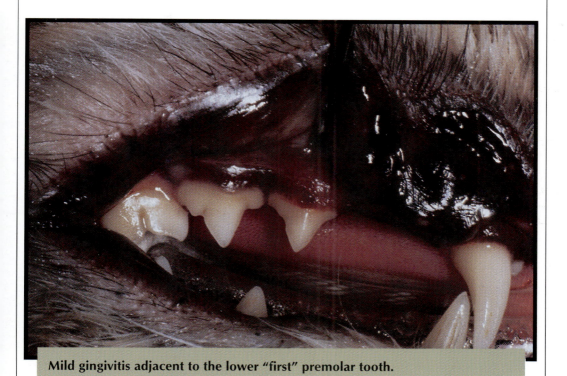

Mild gingivitis adjacent to the lower "first" premolar tooth.

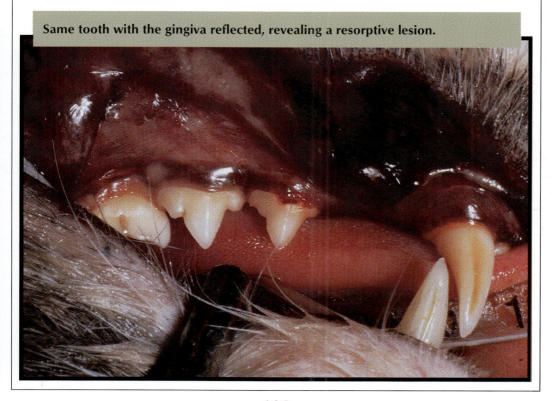

Same tooth with the gingiva reflected, revealing a resorptive lesion.

CAT HEALTH ENCYCLOPEDIA

TREATMENT

Dental and periodontal cleaning are indicated when gingivitis or periodontal disease is present. Local oral antiseptics, such as chlorhexidine solution (CHX, Nolvadent), or solutions of vitamin C and zinc (MaxiGuard) may be helpful. Active periodontitis may also require systemic antibiotics, such as clindamycin, amoxicillin with clavulanic acid, or tetracycline.

PREVENTION

Brushing the teeth daily with a soft-bristle pediatric or feline toothbrush prevents plaque accumulation. Eliminating plaque will prevent gingivitis and periodontititis in the majority of cases.

Feline Tooth Super-Eruption Syndrome

Sometimes referred to as "cuspid extrusion syndrome," super eruption of teeth can occur when periodontal disease extends to the surrounding alveolar bone. It most commonly affects the canine teeth, although others have been reported to be affected as well. The cat's defense mechanisms treat the tooth as a foreign body, and the tooth is slowly extruded from its alveolus.

CLINICAL SIGNS

The canine teeth (one or more) may appear abnormally long. It may look as though the gingiva has receded as the cemento-enamel junction or "neck" of the tooth (where the gingiva normally attaches) moves further away from the gingival margin. When the tooth finally becomes loose, the cat may show discomfort by pawing at the mouth or licking excessively. The tip of the root may keep a firm attachment, resulting in root tip fractures as the poorly supported tooth moves from normal forces.

DIAGNOSIS

Visual observation of the teeth reveals progressive lengthening of affected teeth.

TREATMENT

The process is difficult to stop once it has begun. Antibiotics, periodontal cleaning and root planing, and good oral hygiene by the owner may slow the progression. Current research in human dentistry using antibiotic-impregnated periodontal inserts to treat active periodontal infections may show some use in the future for this syndrome.

PREVENTION

Routine dental cleaning and regular toothbrushing prevent the periodontal disease from becoming established.

Stomatitis

Stomatitis is an inflammation of the entire mouth. It may be caused by oral irritants, some viruses, immunodeficiency diseases, metabolic diseases, drug reactions, or fungal infections. The term stomatitis is often used to describe a very painful and severe syndrome of cats more properly called ulceroproliferative faucitis.

CLINICAL SIGNS

Stomatitis causes the gingiva, mucosa, and sometimes the lips and tongue, to be red and painful. Ulceroproliferative faucitis most commonly begins in the fauces, which is the area in the back of the mouth where the lower jaw meets the upper jaw. The fauces becomes red, swollen, and ulcerated, causing pain when a cat opens its mouth or eats. Affected cats become very "moody" and irritable. They will stop eating entirely when the syndrome becomes severe.

DENTAL PROBLEMS AND CARE

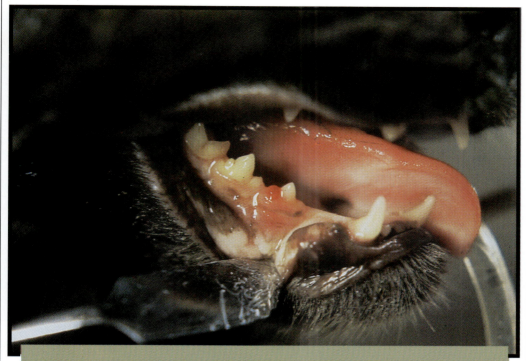

Gingiva extending onto the surface of a tooth and can indicate an underlying lesion.

DIAGNOSIS

Stomatitis is diagnosed by the characteristic appearance of the affected tissues. Histopathologic examination (biopsy) of affected tissue helps to determine whether it was caused by an agent that may be directly treatable and also rules out other diseases that can look similar. Samples from ulceroproliferative faucitis/stomatitis will be reported as having a dense infiltrate of plasmacytes and lymphocytes (hence the old name "lymphocytic/plasmacytic stomatitis"). Retroviral tests also help to rule out a patient predisposed to this problem due to leukemia or immunodeficiency viruses.

TREATMENT

If the cause can be identified (i.e., foreign body, virus, renal failure, malocclusion, poor oral hygiene), then specific therapy aimed at the cause is indicated. For ulceroproliferative faucitis/stomatitis, strict plaque control and frequent professional cleanings are necessary. Oral antibiotics such as clindamycin, amoxicillin/clavulinic acid, and metronidazole should be rotated, and topical treatment with chlorhexidine and zinc ascorbate solutions should be administered. Anti-inflammatory agents are often used due to their dramatic but temporary relief, but they should probably be reserved for those cases that need it for survival, and then for only very short-term therapy. In resistant cases, a cat sometimes needs to have all its teeth extracted and the empty sockets debrided before healing can occur.

PREVENTION

Again, routine oral hygiene is the best method of prevention. Protection from infection by retroviruses will eliminate them as a predisposing factor.

Endodontic Disease

Endodontic disease occurs when the pulp becomes irreversibly inflamed. This inevitably leads to death of the pulp. In the cat, endodontic disease is most commonly caused by dental trauma. In rare cases, the tooth may die from an extension of periodontal disease. In very rare cases it may be caused by progression of resorptive lesions. Cats' maxillary (upper) canine teeth are particularly predisposed to trauma since they protrude out of the mouth and are positioned on each side of the chin. When a cat's chin strikes the ground, their canine tooth is often the first structure to make contact. When a tooth fracture exposes the pulp chamber, bacteria present in the oral cavity invade the pulp and eventually kill the tooth. This infection extends up the canal and causes disease at the apex (tip) of the root.

CLINICAL SIGNS

When a pulp is first exposed, the tooth is painful. In chronic exposure with tooth death, there may be no pain at all, or possibly a dull ache when pressure is applied to the tooth. Some tooth root abscesses may open to the outside as a draining tract, or "fistula," or cause swelling of the mouth.

DIAGNOSIS

Evidence of an open hole in a fractured tooth, a draining tract

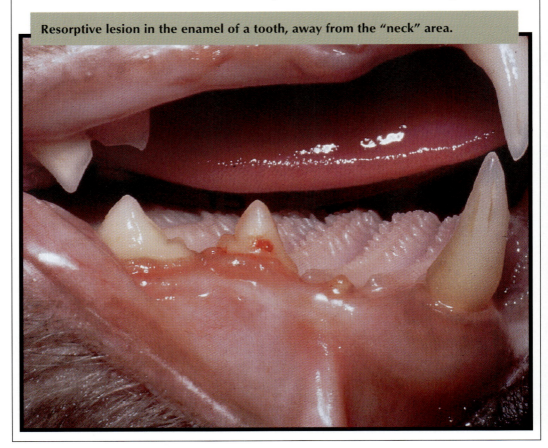

Resorptive lesion in the enamel of a tooth, away from the "neck" area.

DENTAL PROBLEMS AND CARE

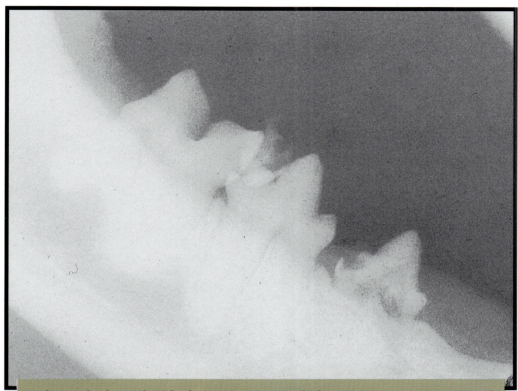

Radiograph of a tooth with a lesion showing very little remaining root structure and internal damage to the tooth. A tooth like this may not show severe damage from the surface.

associated with a fractured tooth, or a brown or dark colored tooth indicates endodontic disease. Radiographs will reveal a dark radiolucent lesion around the apex of chronically involved teeth. In cats, the root tip often resorbs and appears blunted. On upper canine teeth, a small red spot may appear, marking the opening of a draining tract from the lesion. On lower canine teeth, the lesion may drain from under the jaw and can exhibit swelling.

Treatment

Endodontically involved teeth should have endodontic treatment (a "root canal") or be extracted. Without one or the other of these treatments, the infection can not be resolved. Endodontic treatment allows the cat to keep the tooth as a functional unit. The upper teeth are important in maintaining facial contour and to hold the upper lip away from the lower canine tooth. With an upper tooth missing, some cats will entrap the upper lip on the lower tooth. This can be esthetically displeasing, but, more importantly, it can cause chronic lip irritation and scarring and may be uncomfortable.

Prevention

Protection from trauma provides the only means of prevention.

Jaw Fractures

Fractures of the jaw occur from trauma caused by automobile injuries, falls from high places, and occasionally from fights with other animals. The mandibular symphysis, the fibrous joint in the center where the two halves of the lower jaw join, is the most common site of injury. The body of the mandible, the condyles that form the mandibular side of the temporo-mandibular joint, and the upper jaws also can suffer fracture injuries.

CLINICAL SIGNS

Blood from the mouth, misaligned teeth, and an inability to close the mouth frequently indicate jaw fractures.

DIAGNOSIS

Palpation and radiographs confirm the diagnosis.

TREATMENT

Surgical stabilization of the fragments allows the bones to mend. Antibiotics and oral cleansing agents may also be indicated. Repairs can be made with wires, acrylic splints, interdental wiring, and rarely with bone plates. Caution and careful planning will allow a repair without damaging the roots of the teeth. Sometimes extractions or root canals may be necessary.

PREVENTION

Again, protection from trauma is the only means of prevention.

Viral infections

Both symptomatic and asymptomatic (apparently healthy but infected) cats can shed FeLV (feline leukemia), FIV (feline immunodeficiency virus), and FeSFV (feline syncytium-forming virus) retroviruses in their saliva. Although they do not directly cause oral pathology, the retroviruses predispose a patient to moderate-to-severe gingivitis during immunosuppressive episodes. The compromised immune system allows opportunistic pathogens normally found in the oral cavity to cause inflammation and disease. FHV-1 (feline herpesvirus, type 1) can be isolated in the saliva from cats during the active stage of a primary infection. Panleukopenia virus, which causes feline distemper, usually results in primarily gastrointestinal symptoms, but oral lesions of ulceration and sloughing of the tongue, gingiva, and soft palate have also been reported. FCV (feline calici virus) is frequently found in the saliva of healthy cats. The role of calici virus in disease is difficult to determine since it is found in many healthy cats as well as those with stomatitis.

CLINICAL SIGNS

Cats infected with retroviruses may show an excessive gingivitis in the face of only moderate amounts of plaque and calculus. Active calicivirus infection will frequently cause lingual ulcers as well as upper respiratory disease and fever. FHV-1 commonly causes upper respiratory disease, rhinitis, and conjunctivitis.

DIAGNOSIS

Specific retroviral tests are available for FeLV and FIV. FCV and FHV-1 can be diagnosed by virus isolation but are frequently presumptively diagnosed based on clinical signs.

TREATMENT

Nutritional support and antibiotics to treat and prevent secondary bacterial infections are indicated.

PREVENTION

Obtaining a cat from a known virus-free cattery, then keeping it indoors will help to ensure that it isn't infected when acquired and doesn't become infected. For

Dental Problems and Care

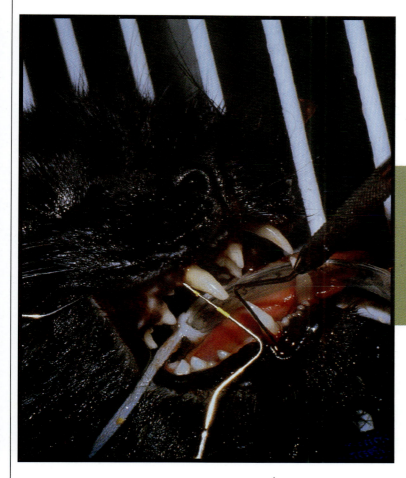

Periodontal probe measuring pocket depth and attachment loss on an upper canine tooth.

catteries, new additions should be isolated until they are tested negative and have shown no signs of illness for at least two weeks.

Eosinophilic Granuloma Complex

The eosinophilic granuloma complex is a common group of skin disorders in cats. They are characterized by localized lesions of ulceration or irritation. They often manifest themselves cyclically with flare-ups and remissions.

Clinical signs

There are three forms of the disease, all of which are found anywhere on the skin and in and around the mouth. The first, called indolent ulcer or eosinophilic ulcer, is an ulceroproliferative cheilitis (lip inflammation) that can be quite dramatic. It can also be found on the skin, but 80 percent are oral. It frequently affects the upper lip adjacent to the canine teeth and can involve the entire rostral lip and philtrum. Indolent ulcers are sometimes called "rodent ulcers," a descriptive term referring to the deforming nature of the lesion, which can make a cat's mouth look like that of a rodent. They can be premalignant and can transform into squamous cell carcinoma. This form is three times more frequent in females than in males. The second type, the eosinophilic plaque, is a well circumscribed, raised, ulcerated, bright red, circular lesion that can affect almost any tissue inside the mouth but is most common on the abdomen or inner thighs. The third is the linear granuloma. In the mouth, this one can appear as a proliferative, ulceroproliferative, or plaque-like lesion. It is typically a firm, raised, gray-pink lesion with a pattern of white streaks or spots on its surface. It can also appear as a swollen chin, frequently called "chin edema."

Diagnosis

Definitive diagnosis can be made only through biopsy, as these lesions often look like neoplastic disease. Histologically, they appear as an eosinophilic infiltrate. Linear granulomas, including chin edema, also exhibit a central area of collagen necrosis.

Treatment

Early and aggressive use of corticosteroids. Methylprednisolone acetate can be given subcutaneously every two weeks until the lesion resolves. In some cats, the lesion may recur. If this happens, long-term therapy may be needed to keep it in remission. Methylprednisolone acetate injections at three-month intervals, or oral prednisone or prednisolone on alternate evenings may be necessary. In refractory cases, surgery, radiation, or cryotherapy may be helpful.

Prevention

In those cases with an underlying cause of hypersensitivity, such as flea saliva allergy, inhalant allergy, or

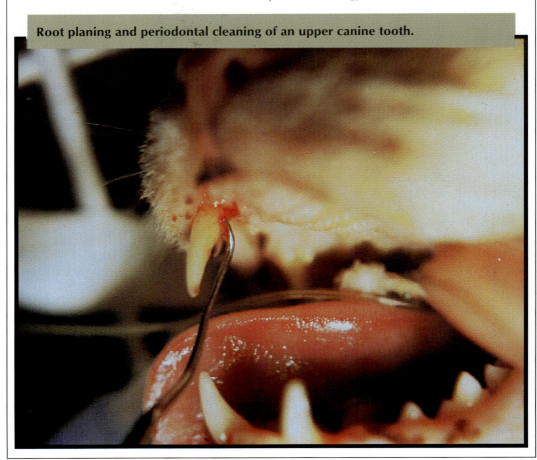

Root planing and periodontal cleaning of an upper canine tooth.

Dental Problems and Care

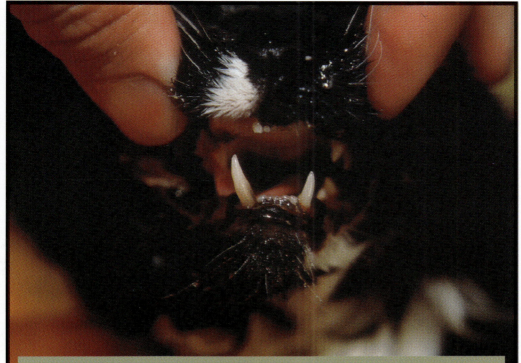

One lower canine tooth appears longer than the other. The longer tooth is being extruded.

food allergy, identification and elimination or desensitization to the allergens can produce dramatic results and prevent recurrences.

Environmental Conditions

Cats are naturally curious and inquisitive. Their environment affords many opportunities for oral injuries. Biting through electrical cords and licking caustic chemicals that may have spilled on their coats are the two most frequently seen.

Clinical signs

Biting through an electrical cord can complete the circuit through the oral cavity. The resultant electrical burn can cause necrosis of the lip, gingiva, and palate in that area. Molar and premolar teeth can become devitalized, evidenced by a gray discoloration of the tooth's crown.

Grooming caustic chemicals from the coat can cause a linear ulcer on the tongue and on the adjacent hard or soft palate.

Diagnosis

Clinical signs along with an appropriate history of exposure to these hazards.

Treatment

For electrical burns, surgical debridement and repair of burned tissue may be indicated as well as antibiotic therapy to prevent infection in the damaged tissues. Devitalized teeth need root canal treatment or extraction. Exposure to toxic or caustic chemicals should be handled by first bathing any remaining chemicals from the fur with a mild shampoo to prevent further injury, and oral antiseptics such as dilute

CAT HEALTH ENCYCLOPEDIA

chlorhexidine solution to assist local immune mechanisms.

PREVENTION

Behavior modification should be implemented to train cats not to play with electrical cords. Homes should be "cat-proofed" to eliminate the possibility of exposure to caustic chemicals.

Oral Tumors

Tumors in cats' mouths are very frequently malignant. The most common tumor found in a cat's mouth is squamous cell carcinoma. The next most common is fibrosarcoma. Cats can also develop mast cell tumors, lymphosarcomas, malignant melanomas, epulides, ameloblastomas, and other carcinomas and sarcomas. Not all swellings or mass lesions are tumors; cats can also suffer from foreign body granulomas, eosinophilic granulomas, fungal infections, nasopharyngeal polyps, and infections such as osteomyelitis, which can all mimic malignant tumors. A nasopharyngeal polyp is a non-malignant mass that appears to be peculiar to cats.

CLINICAL SIGNS

Squamous cell carcinoma appears as a red ulcerated swelling with an irregular surface. They most commonly affect the gingiva, tongue, and the tissues beneath the tongue. Due to their vascular nature, they bleed easily. They are very locally aggressive, invading surrounding tissues and bone. Fibrosarcomas appear more smooth on the surface. They are much more firm, less vascular, and more firmly attached to underlying tissues. Nasopharyngeal polyps arise from the nasal or pharyngeal epithelium or from the lining of the Eustachian tube or

bullae. They appear as pink, firm, spherical masses on a long pedunculated base. Since they are found behind the soft palate (or occasionally deep in the ear canal), they are not visible on routine oral examination. An affected cat or kitten will show signs of dyspnea, upper respiratory obstruction or stridor, and sometimes voice changes or difficulty swallowing.

DIAGNOSIS

Any oral mass or lesion, with the possible exception of obvious nasopharyngeal polyps, should be biopsied. Radiographs will help to determine the extent of local bone involvement.

TREATMENT

Surgical excision with wide margins is the treatment of choice. Tongue lesions are difficult to treat while maintaining function. Mandibular or maxillary SCC may metastasize to regional lymph nodes or lungs. If it has not yet spread, the best treatment for mandibular neoplasia is removal of the entire half of the affected jaw. Maxillectomy is more difficult in the cat but may be considered for maxillary neoplasia.

PREVENTION

Neoplastic lesions should be diagnosed and treated as early as possible. Regular oral examinations will help to prevent extensive disease progression before treatment. Early diagnosis and prevention of oronasal inflammatory conditions may help prevent polyps.

Malocclusion

Cats, unlike dogs or humans, are true carnivores. They have teeth designed for cutting their food. Even their molars and premolars have no flat table surfaces for

Dental Problems and Care

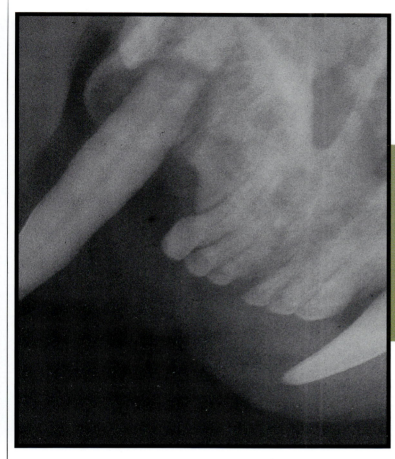

Radiograph of hyper-erupted tooth with expanded alveolus from periodontal disease. Tip of root has fractured and will need surgical removal.

grinding or chewing food the way humans and dogs do. Although cats will often bite or chew a few times while eating, for the most part they just move the food back in their mouths and swallow it without chewing. The classification of their teeth parallels our own. The very small teeth in front are the incisors. The large pointed canine tooth is next, followed by the premolars and then the molars. There are twelve incisors with six on top and six on the bottom. These teeth normally come together with the upper teeth meeting almost directly over the lower teeth. In the normal pattern, all the remaining teeth have a scissors-type relationship with the upper teeth: meeting just to the outside of the lower teeth. Cats generally have very few malocclusion problems in which the upper and lower sets of teeth don't come together properly. The exceptions are those breeds that have been bred for a retrusive (squashed) mid-face, such as the Persians. These cats often appear to have undershot jaws (mandibular prognathism), and there is often insufficient space to fit the premolar and molar teeth in their normal position. The resultant rotation and crowding of these teeth creates periodontal and cleaning difficulties.

Clinical signs

Oral discomfort may not be apparent until late in the course. Many cats will not show any clinical signs.

DIAGNOSIS

Teeth protruding from the mouth, erupting at abnormal angles, or contacting other teeth or soft tissues indicate a malocclusion and are readily identified by oral examination.

TREATMENT

Orthodontic tooth movement, tooth shortening procedures performed with endodontic health in mind, and selective tooth extractions can resolve most malocclusions.

PREVENTION

Knowledge of genetics and careful breeding programs are the best preventive measures.

Foreign Bodies

Oral foreign bodies are not extremely common, but they can be dangerous. One of the most common offenders is string. Cats love to play with it. Generally, this causes no problems. However, a cat will sometimes swallow a long piece of string in a way that catches the string under the tongue while both ends go down the throat. The string can cut deeply into the tissues under the tongue before the problem is identified. Be careful when sewing as well. It is not unusual for cats to swallow needles or for them to pierce the palate or throat. Other foreign bodies, such as plant materials or feathers, can cause granulomas under the tongue, causing discomfort and difficulty eating.

CLINICAL SIGNS

Excess salivation, a swollen tongue, interest in food but reluctance to eat, or an oral malodor may be observed in affected cats.

DIAGNOSIS

Pushing up on the soft tissue between a cat's mandibles while opening the mouth and looking under the tongue will reveal the string or the severe trauma that it has caused.

TREATMENT

Cutting the string to relieve the "anchor" effect of the tongue may resolve the problem, but the patient should be monitored to be sure no further problems develop.

PREVENTION

Although cats love playing with long strings, there are safer "toys."

Oral Manifestations of Systemic Diseases

Kidney failure, leptospirosis, neutropenias, malnutrition, bleeding disorders, toxicity, epidermal necrolysis caused by a drug reaction, and autoimmune diseases are some of the systemic illnesses which can manifest in oral lesions. Any process that causes vasculitis, or that interferes with the immune system, can result in oral ulcerations, inflammation, and mucosal lesions.

CLINICAL SIGNS

Each of these diseases has, in addition to oral lesions, more characteristic systemic manifestations. In the mouth, renal failure causes oral ulcerations and uremic stomatitis, especially on the lateral margins of the tongue. Malnutrition can affect epidermal and mucosal surfaces in different ways. Thrombocytopenia, von Willebrand's disease, or other bleeding disorders can cause gingival or mucosal hemorrhages or outright bleeding from the gingival margins.

DIAGNOSIS

Specific laboratory tests along with an appropriate history and clinical signs.

DENTAL PROBLEMS AND CARE

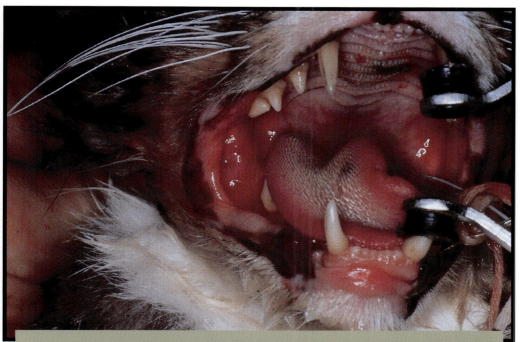

Severe inflammation in the back of the mouth can cause a cat to stop eating due to the discomfort.

TREATMENT

Treatments vary with the causes, severity, and syndrome.

PREVENTION

In the cat, ingestion of ethylene glycol (antifreeze) is the most common cause of acute renal failure. Indoor cats are not at risk. Post-renal acute renal failure is most commonly caused by urethral obstruction. Identification of male cats with feline urologic syndrome and feeding those cats an acidifying diet low in magnesium is preventive. Chronic renal failure is frequently diagnosed with no known inciting cause. Cats can be affected with a variety of serotypes of leptospirosis, but they rarely develop clinical leptospirosis. Protecting cats from exposure to infected animals and objects prevents infection. The most common diseases that result in neutropenia are the viral diseases. Many are preventable through vaccination regimens (feline distemper, feline leukemia).

ORAL MANIFESTATIONS OF AUTOIMMUNE DISEASES

The immune system of the cat is responsible for protecting against bacterial, viral, and fungal pathogens. The reactivity of the host's antibodies and white blood cells (both polymorphonuclear leukocytes and lymphocytes) can be beneficial in this function. It can also, however, be harmful when it acts against the cat's own body tissues, causes excessive complement activation, results in allergic reactions, or interferes with the ability to recognize bacteria by blocking receptor sites. Autoimmune diseases occur when a cat's body produces autoantibodies against its own tissues. Many systemic diseases resulting from either inappropriate or overactivity of the immune system have oral manifestations. Oral lesions are sometimes the most prominent or

CAT HEALTH ENCYCLOPEDIA

the only lesions present. Some of these include systemic lupus erythematosus (SLE), the pemphigus diseases, and idiopathic vasculitis.

CLINICAL SIGNS

Oral ulcerations and crusts are most commonly found at mucogingival junctions but can also be found on the palate, tongue, lips, gingiva, and nasal philtrum.

DIAGNOSIS

Biopsy and histopathologic examination of active lesions. Ulcers due to pemphigus will show fluid-filled clefts or bullae within or under the epidermal cell layer, and lesions caused by SLE or vasculitis will show disruption of the local blood supply and deposits of immune complexes. Protein losing glomerulonephropathy, polyarthropathy, and hematologic disorders are associated with many of these.

TREATMENT

Various anti-inflammatory regimens specific for the disease. High doses of prednisone, sometimes in combination with Imuran, are often used to bring the disease under control. The drugs are then reduced to a maintenance level.

PREVENTION

There are no preventive measures for autoimmune diseases.

Hypersensitivity Reactions

Drug eruptions are the result of a hypersensitivity reaction. The most frequently implicated drugs are the antibiotics, but almost any drug or chemical can cause a drug reaction. One of the more severe reactions is toxic epidermal necrolysis. Hypersensitivity reactions in the mouth can also be caused by insect stings. Cats are great insect hunters,

but oral stings are generally short lived and mild.

CLINICAL SIGNS

Ulcerations and bleeding of the oral mucosa. Advanced cases lead to tissue necrosis. Cats affected with toxic epidermal necrolysis will also exhibit fever, inappetence, and depression.

DIAGNOSIS

Typical symptoms with a history of recent drug ingestion, followed by improvement after withdrawal of the drug.

TREATMENT

Removal of the drug or chemical that was responsible. Soft foods and flushing with 0.12 percent chlorhexidine may also be indicated.

PREVENTION

Although these reactions are uncommon, they cannot be predicted other than through prior episodes. Animals who have drug allergies must be protected from future exposures.

Fungal Infections

Candidiasis is a form of mycotic stomatitis caused by *Candida albicans*. It is most commonly a complication of immune suppression or prolonged antibiotic use. Pigeon and dove feces contain *Cryptococcus* organisms. Inhalation of the yeast form can cause cryptococcosis, which infects the lungs, nasal cavity, eyes, and central nervous system. This and other nasal fungal infections such as aspergillosis and penicillinosis can occasionally extend into the oral cavity. Systemic fungi, such as histoplasmosis or blastomycosis, can also sometimes invade oral tissues. On rare occasions, a soil fungus has been known to invade the oral cavity of cats to cause mycetomas.

Dental Problems and Care

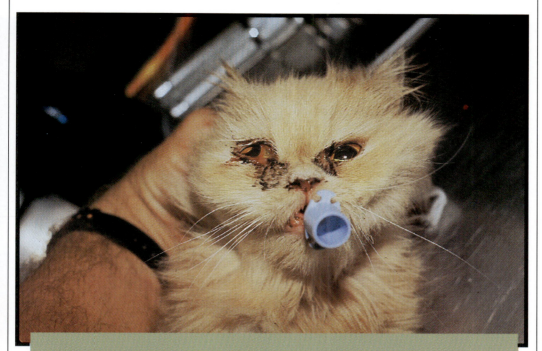

Right side of the face is swollen from infection caused by a fractured canine tooth.

Clinical signs

Lesions of candidiasis appear as white plaques with ulcerated bleeding surfaces. When mycotic nasal infections break into the oral cavity, they can cause lesions on the palate, gingiva, lips, or tongue. They can also cause redness or ulceration around the incisive papilla.

Diagnosis

Affected tissues examined with an India ink stain, or culture of the organism.

Treatment

Identification and treatment of the underlying cause, local antifungal topical agents such as chlorhexidine or nystatin, and systemic therapy such as ketoconazole.

Prevention

Avoidance of predisposing causes and exposures.

HOME CARE

Without regular brushing, a perfectly clean tooth will develop plaque within hours and calculus (tartar) deposits within a day. The calculus then facilitates more plaque accumulation by providing it with a rough surface for easier adhesion. Chronic plaque leads to inflammation and periodontal disease. Our pets' teeth are similar to ours anatomically, and they reside in an oral cavity that also has many similarities to our own. It therefore stands to reason that their teeth will need the same regular hygiene as ours if they are to remain healthy and functional. Self cleaning of the teeth in a healthy mouth helps to some degree. Because of this, cats that eat only hard or dry food tend to have cleaner teeth than those that eat soft or canned food. Very crunchy or hard snacks, such as uncooked pasta, may be helpful in removing some

CAT HEALTH ENCYCLOPEDIA

plaque. Cats do not naturally chew their food except to remove portions small enough to swallow. Many cats will even swallow dry food kibbles without biting them. Therefore, dry food alone is not enough to keep the teeth clean and healthy. There is no substitute for daily, or every other day, home brushing or rubbing the teeth for plaque removal.

Most cats do not like their mouths manipulated or their teeth brushed. You will need patience to train your cat to allow regular toothbrushing. Although it would be nice, it is not generally necessary to brush all surfaces of the teeth. If you are able to brush the outside surfaces (toward the cheeks and lips), then you can be successful in removing 80 percent of the problem-causing plaque. A cat's scissors-like occlusion helps keep the other surfaces clean. The inside surfaces of the upper teeth are cleaned by the outsides of the lower teeth. These in turn are cleaned by the inside of the uppers. The inner surface of the lower teeth is cleaned by the cat's tongue. It is the outside surface of the upper teeth that accumulates the most plaque and calculus, both due to the lack of opposing teeth and due to the saliva that is secreted in this area. The ideal method of cleaning the teeth is with a very soft-bristled toothbrush. Pediatric or small children's toothbrushes work well for this. There are also specialized small-headed brushes designed for cats. The bristles of a toothbrush mechanically remove plaque from the exposed tooth surface, plus they can splay out to clean under the gum margin. It may help to start brushing with a little tuna fish liquid on the brush as a flavoring agent so that your cat will enjoy the session. If this does not work, then you may have more luck with a finger brush. These are small rubber toothbrushes that fit snugly over your finger.

A toothbrush alone can be very effective in removing plaque. You may also want to use a toothpaste to enhance the effectiveness. Pets will sometimes tolerate a dentifrice made for them better than those made for humans, due to the flavorings that are added. When first starting your home hygiene program, do not begin too fast. Start slowly and gently to allow your pet to become accustomed to the new social interaction. Lift the lip, clean one tooth, and then stop for the day. You may want to start with a soft cloth rather than a toothbrush until the cat becomes accustomed to the handling. The goal is to avoid creating a situation in which home care becomes a battle. It should be at least tolerable, and ideally enjoyable. Each time you have a session, increase the number of teeth treated until eventually you are able to clean them all. Remember to be gentle to avoid damaging the gums, but be thorough. If all else fails and your cat will not allow any brushing, then a quick gentle wipe with a cloth or gauze pad is also helpful.

We learn early in life that we should brush our teeth at least twice a day. Imagine what your teeth would look like if you brushed them once a week, or once a month! Plaque begins forming immediately after brushing the teeth and continues to accumulate until it is again mechanically removed. Within only a few hours, a buildup is visible on the tooth's surface. If this remains, mineralization of the plaque begins forming a hard brown material called calculus, or tartar. Calculus adheres strongly to the surface and can not be brushed or rubbed from the tooth. It forms a roughened surface that helps the plaque to attach and accumulate more effectively, thus

208

DENTAL PROBLEMS AND CARE

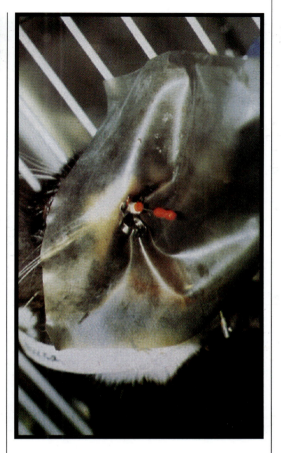

Root canal treatment of a fractured tooth in a cat.

accelerating the process. To be most effective in a home hygiene program, plaque removal must occur before it has time to mineralize. This means that the teeth should be cleaned daily. Every extra day delay between brushing allows a little more mineralized material to develop. The result is more material that cannot be removed with simple brushing.

Other home oral hygiene products are available in addition to toothbrushes, tooth paste, and gauze pads. There is a possibility that fluoride application may slow the development or progression of the resorptive lesions of which we spoke earlier. This has not yet been proven, but fluoride also acts to desensitize teeth. For these reasons, it is sometimes recommended for certain individuals to have regular fluoride treatments at home. Ideally, you should first discuss this with your veterinarian.

There are also chlorhexidine gels and solutions available that can inhibit bacteria and plaque in the mouth. Cats seem to object less to the gel than to the liquid flushes, plus it has a longer contact time. Other products include enzyme solutions, sprayed dentifrice, vitamin solutions, and mineral acetates.

VETERINARY CARE

Until only a few years ago, we did very little for our cats' teeth. If he or she lived long enough, they could spend their later years in discomfort or without any teeth. Cats often display no outward signs of these problems, and their owners frequently would not even be aware of them. More and more people have found the joy of sharing their homes with cats and accepting them as an important part of their lives. As we care for our pets better, they are living longer and healthier lives. They also have a longer time for dental and periodontal diseases to progress. Cats require and deserve regular veterinary dental care.

Periodontal disease and oral infections can drive bacteria into a cat's blood circulation. The immune system must continually work at clearing them from the blood. If the quantity of bacteria becomes overwhelming, it may contribute to damage of the heart valves, kidneys, and other areas of the body. Without regular dental cleaning and care, a cat can almost expect to develop gingival and periodontal problems. This is the bad news. The good news is that periodontal disease and infections are preventable. If your cat will not allow regular home care, it may need more frequent dental cleaning and prophylaxis performed by a veterinarian. Again the analogy to our own dental care holds true. Some people require professional cleaning of their teeth only every one or two years. Others, however, due to local factors in their mouths or to other complications, may need dental cleanings every three to six months. With cats, the most important determinant is often the disposition of your pet and how frequently you are able to clean its teeth at home. If frequent home care is not possible, then your cat may need professional cleaning annually.

Unlike our visits to the dental hygienist, the professional "prophy" for our pets requires the use of a general anesthesia. This is vital for adequate cleaning. Without this, only the crowns can be cleaned. This amounts to little more than breaking off the large pieces of calculus. This can make your cat "mouth shy," creating more difficulty with your home program. It also does not allow examination and cleaning of all surfaces, including under the gumline where it is most important.

Veterinary dentistry is now an approved specialty field that is recognized by the American Veterinary Medical Association. Dental care for your cat has progressed to the point where oral surgery (tumor removal, trauma repair, etc.), orthodontics (moving teeth), prosthodontics (crowns, etc.), endodontics (root canals), periodontal surgery (surgery on the tissues supporting the teeth), and restoratives (fillings and tooth structure replacement) are all available. Your regular veterinarian can perform many of these procedures. For some of the more advanced procedures, your primary care veterinarian may refer you to a veterinary specialist or to a veterinarian who has advanced training in veterinary dentistry.

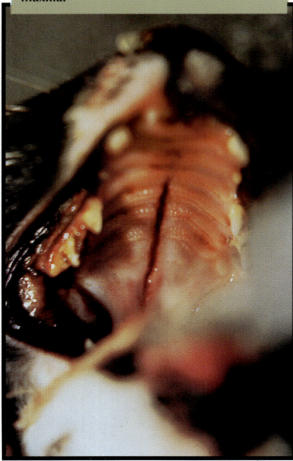

Split palate from a traumatic fracture of the maxilla.

DENTAL PROBLEMS AND CARE

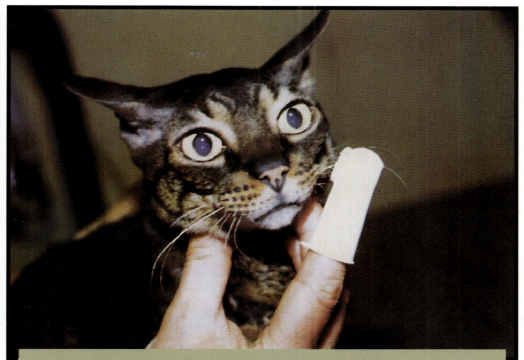

This cat is about to have its teeth cleaned with a finger toothbrush. Some cats prefer finger toothbrushes over regular toothbrushes with handles.

SUMMARY

Our cats are dependent upon us for all of their needs, including the health of their teeth and mouth. They are prone to many of the same types of problems that we are, plus they are subject to a number of additional syndromes peculiar to felines. It is our responsibility to be aware of these and to prevent or treat them whenever possible.

Brushing the teeth frequently and regular veterinary dental prophylaxis are the best methods of preventing many of these problems. Although they require a commitment of both time and money, they are the surest hope for keeping your pet's teeth healthy as she or he ages. There are a number of products available to assist us with their oral hygiene. If problems do arise, it then becomes important to identify them early so that treatment may be started immediately.

Veterinary dentists are available who have been trained in the more advanced procedures that may become necessary to keep your cat's mouth healthy, or to return it to health and function should the need develop.

ADDITIONAL READING

Bojrab, MJ; Tholen, M: *Small Animal Oral Medicine and Surgery.* Lea & Febiger. Philadelphia, 1990.

Harvey, C; Emily P: *Small Animal Dentistry.* Mosby, Philadelphia, 1993.

Holmstrom, S; Frost, P; Gammon, R.: *Veterinary Dental Techniques.* WB Saunders Co., Philadelphia, 1992.

Lyon, K; Ackerman, L: *Dog Owner's Guide to Proper Dental Care.* T.F.H. Publications, Neptune, NJ, 1993, 32pp.

Dr. Minta Keyes

Dr. Minta Keyes received her Bachelor of Arts degree from Linfield College in 1983 and her Doctor of Veterinary Medicine from Oregon State University in 1988. She completed her small animal and surgery internship at Coast Pet Clinic Animal Cancer Center, Hermosa Beach, California. She completed a small animal medicine residency at Tufts University and is now board certified in small animal internal medicine. She practices in Tucson, Arizona, and counts five cats as family members, along with her husband and daughter.

DIGESTIVE TRACT DISORDERS

By Minta Keyes, DVM, Diplomate, ACVIM

Mesa Veterinary Hospital, Ltd.
858 N. Country Club Drive
Mesa AZ 85201

and Cat Hospital of Tucson
7292 E. Broadway Blvd.
Tucson AZ 85710

INTRODUCTION

Gastrointestinal disease manifestations such as vomiting, regurgitation, diarrhea, weight loss, anorexia, and straining to eliminate account for a substantial number of veterinary visits. Because diseases of other body systems such as the urinary tract and thyroid gland, as well as systemic diseases such as feline leukemia and feline immunodeficiency viruses may also cause these signs, a complete patient assessment is needed. This includes a history, physical exam, and, in most instances, further diagnostic testing.

DISEASES OF THE ESOPHAGUS

The esophagus transports food, immediately after swallowing, into the stomach. Diseases of the esophagus are uncommon, but the primary clinical sign is regurgitation, the passive expulsion of undigested food. There is no heaving prior to the expulsion, or bile-staining, as is frequently seen with true vomiting. The more common diseases associated with regurgitation are esophagitis (inflammation of the esophagus), esophageal stricture (a narrowing of the esophagus) and neoplasia (cancer).

Esophagitis

Esophagitis is inflammation of the esophagus, usually as a result of gastric acid reflux. This can occur in animals that are vomiting from other disease processes or from diseases or irritations affecting the esophagus. It sometimes occurs when the sphincter between the stomach and esophagus relaxes under a general anesthesia. Diagnosis is made with chest radiographs (x-rays) and esophagoscopy (inspection of the esophagus with an endoscope). It is treated with sucralfate (Carafate®) to protect the irritated tissue, and acid blockers such as famotidine (Pepcid®) or cimetidine (Tagamet®) to decrease acid reflux from the stomach. The prognosis for recovery is excellent.

Esophageal Stricture

Esophageal stricture is narrowing of the esophagus by scarring that may occur from a number of causes, and in rare instances after esophagitis. The diagnosis is made with chest radiographs and esophagoscopy. Treatment varies depending on severity, but it may include balloon catheter dilation of the stricture area, placement of a feeding tube, use of the medications described for esophagitis, and the use

CAT HEALTH ENCYCLOPEDIA

of prednisone to prevent further scarring. The prognosis is highly dependent upon the degree of stricture formation present.

DISEASES OF THE STOMACH

The stomach produces a digestive enzyme, pepsin, and hydrochloric acid that breaks food down into fine particles. Gastric juices can damage the stomach itself, and this may lead to vomiting fresh blood or digested "coffee grounds"-appearing blood. Common presenting complaints with gastric disease are vomiting and decreased appetite.

Trichobezoars (Hairballs)

Hairballs are vomited when they cannot pass through the stomach into the intestine and then be otherwise eliminated. Intermittent use of a petrolatum-based over-the-counter product can aid in their passage, while frequent brushing of the coat to remove loose hair can also diminish their frequency. Cats with hairballs vomit hair and then resume acting normally. A cat that is acting sick, vomiting, and not bringing up hair should be seen promptly by a veterinarian.

Gastrointestinal Ulcers

Vomiting fresh or digested blood is the hallmark of gastrointestinal ulcers. Non-gastric causes can include liver disease, kidney disease, and intestinal disease. Gastric (stomach) causes can include *Helicobacter* infection, inflammatory gastritis, foreign bodies, and neoplasia. Each of these conditions may also cause vomiting without bringing up blood. A complete blood count (CBC), biochemical panel, and urinalysis to check for anemia, liver disease, and kidney disease are

Complete blood counts are useful to identify anemia associated with gastrointestinal disease.

Digestive Tract Disorders

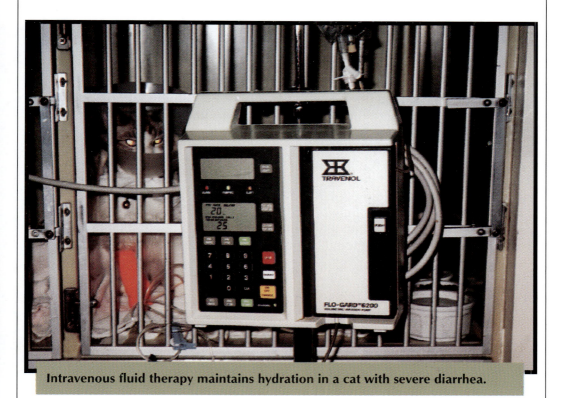

Intravenous fluid therapy maintains hydration in a cat with severe diarrhea.

performed to aid in diagnosis. Radiographs (x-rays) are used to help look for the presence of foreign bodies, for evidence of obstruction, and to assess liver and kidney size. Endoscopic examination allows biopsies to be collected to diagnose *Helicobacter* infection, inflammatory gastritis, and neoplasia. Symptomatic treatment of gastric ulceration includes the use of sucralfate and acid blockers as described for esophagitis.

Helicobacter Infection

Helicobacter sp. are spiral-shaped bacteria that can establish an infection in the stomach. The exact mode of transmission of the organism is unknown. There are currently no preventive recommendations. It is treated with a course of antibiotics, such as amoxicillin or doxycycline, and metronidazole and acid blockers. Many clinicians also will use bismuth subsalicylate (Pepto-Bismol®) or sucralfate. Most cats will be cured, but occasional cats will require additional antibiotic treatment. Because feline *Helicobacter* infections are potentially transmissible to humans, careful hygiene should always be employed when cleaning up feline vomitus.

Acute Gastritis

Acute, nonspecific gastritis (inflammation of the stomach) is the term used to describe vomiting of short duration to which no specific underlying cause is found. Generally, these patients have a normal physical exam, normal radiographs, a normal biochemical panel, and a history of being normal except for vomiting of a few hours' to a few days' duration. Symptomatic treatment with a 12-24 hour fast, followed by several days of a bland diet, such as boiled

CAT HEALTH ENCYCLOPEDIA

chicken or chicken baby food, is frequently employed. Clinical deterioration or a failure to improve are reasons to pursue a definitive diagnosis with further testing. An upper gastrointestinal series (radiographs taken after oral administration of a dye) or endoscopy with biopsy collection are generally performed.

DISEASES OF THE SMALL INTESTINE

The proximal (upper) small intestine, in concert with the pancreas, continues the process of digestion initiated in the stomach. Absorption of the digested food occurs in the remainder of the small intestine. Failure in either the digestive or absorptive functions may result in voluminous, watery diarrhea. Dehydration and weight loss may occur rapidly. Malabsorption (disturbed nutrient absorption) is the result of many common feline intestinal diseases including inflammatory enteritis, viral enteritis, bacterial enteritis, and neoplasia.

Inflammatory Enteritis / Inflammatory Bowel Disease

Inflammatory enteritis occurs when an increased population of inflammatory cells (lymphocytes and plasma cells or eosinophils) are present in the mucosa, the innermost layer of the small intestine. Lymphocytic-plasmacytic gastroenteritis is by far the most common form. It may represent a sensitivity to specific proteins (antigens) in the food. The most common clinical sign is chronic vomiting. Some cats will experience anorexia and diarrhea. Weight loss is rare. Endoscopic exam and biopsy are necessary to confirm the diagnosis. Most cats will have pathologic (disease) changes in both

the stomach and small intestines. Treatment may include dietary changes. Strategies employed are bland diets and hypoallergenic diets. Hypoallergenic diets utilize protein sources to which the cat has not previously been exposed. Metronidazole and tylosin, antibacterial agents with anti-inflammatory properties, may also be used. Frequently, prednisone (a form of cortisone) is required to control the inflammation. Because serious complications are related to prednisone use, including skin changes, joint weakness, kidney disease, and diabetes mellitus, it is desirable to restrict its use, if possible, to the first few months of therapy. The goal of therapy is to minimize clinical signs; intermittent relapses are expected as this is a chronic disease. Some cats will require intermittent or lifelong use of prednisone in order to control clinical signs.

Bacterial Enteritis

Salmonella and *Campylobacter* infections may cause fever, lethargy, vomiting, and diarrhea. Infection occurs when contaminated food, water, or other material is ingested. Other cats, dogs, and humans in the household are also at risk of infection, so caution must be exercised in the handling of fecal material from the infected cats. Diagnosis is made with fecal culture. Specific antibiotic treatment is directed by the results of the fecal culture. Commonly employed medications include enrofloxacin (Baytril®), furozolidine (Furoxone®), and erythromycin. Severely dehydrated cats require intravenous (IV) fluid treatment. Frequent small meals of a bland diet are employed until the diarrhea subsides. Most cats recover completely.

216

Digestive Tract Disorders

Left: Hairballs are an inevitable part of life with cats. Right: Proper carpet selection makes the affected area inconspicuous after cleaning.

Viral Enteritis

Multiple viruses may infect the gastrointestinal tract, including feline leukemia virus (FeLV), feline immunodeficiency virus (FIV), feline coronavirus, and feline panleukopenia virus. FeLV and FIV are covered elsewhere in this text.

Feline Coronaviruses

The feline coronaviruses include a large group of closely related viruses that may cause subclinical (no obvious signs) or clinical infections. Cats have a brief diarrheal illness that resolves completely without specific therapy other than employing a bland diet. There are no commercially available tests to definitively diagnose the infection. The most severe of these viruses are those that lead to the development of feline infectious peritonitis (FIP).

Feline Panleukopenia

This virus is spread by direct contact between cats as well as contact with objects previously used by infected cats. Cats most commonly develop lethargy, fever, vomiting, and diarrhea. Diagnosis is presumed based on very low white blood cell counts. Treatment requires IV fluid therapy, antibiotics for secondary bacterial infections occurring due to intestinal damage and low white blood cell counts, and other supportive care as appropriate. The prognosis is guarded. Kittens born to affected queens have a characteristic uncoordinated gait due to the neurologic damage caused *in utero* (before birth) by the virus.

Intestinal Parasites

An amazing variety of parasites can infect the gastrointestinal tract. These parasites were covered in great detail in *Owner's Guide to Cat Health*, and that information will not be repeated here. The more common ones, as well as those of human health concern, are discussed below. These infections are the result of oral ingestion of the immature parasite. The parasite matures and eggs are

CAT HEALTH ENCYCLOPEDIA

shed in the feces. The infection can then be generally diagnosed with a fecal floatation and microscopic exam for the eggs. Clinical signs may range from none to vomiting, diarrhea, unthriftiness, a pot-bellied appearance, and dehydration. The prognosis is generally excellent with treatment. Prevention includes cleaning the litter pan of fecal material daily, keeping cats indoors to avoid exposure to other cat's stools, discouraging predation, and avoiding flea infestation.

ROUNDWORMS

These parasites are common in kittens and may even be spread from the queen via her milk. They can also cause human infection. For these reasons, routine deworming of all kittens is recommended. Many agents are effective, including pyrantel pamoate (Nemex®, Strongid®), febantel/praziquantal (Vercom®) and piperazine.

HOOKWORMS

These parasites may lead to severe gastrointestinal blood loss and anemia, especially in kittens. Pyrantel pamoate is recommended for treatment of severe infections. Some kittens will require transfusion treatment of anemia. This parasite may cause skin infections in humans.

COCCIDIA

This parasite is also relatively common in kittens. Sulfa drugs (Albon®, Tribrissen®) are used to eradicate infection. Rarely, kittens will also require fluid rehydration treatment.

GIARDIASIS

This parasite is spread by many species of animals and birds. The *Giardia* parasite can be difficult to

find on fecal exam, so treatment may be prescribed empirically. Drugs that may be used include metronidazole (Flagyl®), furozolidine (Furoxone®), and febendazole (Panacur®). Dehydrated animals may require fluid therapy. *Giardia* organisms may cause disease in humans; proper sanitation should be used when cleaning the litter box.

TOXOPLASMOSIS

This gastrointestinal parasite only rarely causes signs of gastrointestinal illness in cats, even when present in their stool. However, it can cause serious neurological injury to the human fetus if a pregnant woman is exposed. The parasite can also occur in the muscle tissue (meat) of many species of animals. To prevent feline exposure to the parasite, cats should be kept strictly indoors, should not be allowed to hunt, and should not be allowed to eat raw meat. To prevent human fetal exposure, pregnant women should never clean litter pans, which should be cleaned daily by another person. Pregnant women should also wear gloves when gardening and be cautious in handling raw meats.

TAPEWORMS

Tapeworms are spread by ingestion of fleas or by eating raw meat (usually after hunting). Rice-sized tapeworm segments are seen surrounding the anus in affected cats. Many medications are effective in eliminating the infection, with praziquantel (Droncit®) and epsiprantel (Cestex®) being commonly employed. It is essential that flea infestation also be treated to prevent reinfection.

CRYPTOSPORIDIUM

This parasite is a rare cause of diarrhea in cats. There are no

DIGESTIVE TRACT DISORDERS

Cats will frequently vomit ingested plant material.

effective medications available for treatment. Cats infected with FIV or FeLV can become severely debilitated and die of this infection. Cats with a normal immune system will rid themselves of the infection over a couple of weeks. Humans are susceptible to cryptosporidiosis; immunocompromised people can die as a result of this infection.

Foreign Bodies

Cats eat a variety of objects that are indigestible and may lodge in various locations throughout the gastrointestinal tract. Objects that lodge in the esophagus or stomach may be retrieved endoscopically in many instances. Objects that cannot be retrieved endoscopically or that are lodged in the small intestine must be removed surgically.

Of particular concern to cat owners are linear foreign bodies. These can include thread, yarn, string, tinsel, ribbons, and other such objects. One end may be caught around the base of the tongue or in the stomach, while the rest of the object is propelled by normal intestinal activity further through the small intestine. The intestines then plicate or are gathered up. This may result in perforation of the intestines and fatal peritonitis (abdominal infection). Linear foreign bodies are treated by surgical removal. Any string small enough to be easily swallowed, including those on cat toys, can create problems. All should be eliminated from the cat's environment.

DISEASES OF THE LARGE INTESTINE

The large intestine removes water from the stool prior to elimination. Signs of large intestinal disease include diarrhea with mucus and fresh blood in the stool, and straining to eliminate. Because straining in the litter pan is seen more frequently with urethral obstruction in male cats, prompt veterinary assessment is essential to identify this life-threatening problem.

Lymphoplasmacytic Colitis

Lymphoplasmacytic inflammation is seen in the colon as well as the stomach and small intestine. Clinical signs include straining as well as bloody diarrhea or diarrhea with mucus. Physical examination will frequently demonstrate an empty colon or soft stool. Fecal examination is performed to rule out parasitic infection. The diagnosis is established with endoscopic exam and biopsies. Treatment with a hypoallergenic diet, high-fiber diet, or the addition of fiber to the diet in the form of psyllium is generally successful. Occasionally, animals require the use of prednisone to control signs.

Constipation/Obstipation

Constipation is straining to eliminate excessively hard or dry fecal material. Obstipation is excessive retention of hard fecal material causing enlargement of the colon. It is also accompanied by straining. On physical examination, the veterinarian will assess the cat's hydration and for any signs of neurologic, orthopedic, or other conditions that may be associated with discomfort while defecating. Some cats can have obstruction from foreign bodies or tumors preventing elimination. Diagnostic assessment includes blood chemistries and urinalysis to check for metabolic reasons for dehydration, such as kidney disease or diabetes mellitus. Radiographs (x-rays) are taken to assess the size of the colon and to evaluate for bony abnormalities of the lumbar spine and pelvis. Endoscopy and biopsy may be performed if neoplasia (cancer) is suspected.

Constipated cats respond well to rehydration, laxatives, and enemas. Obstipated cats will generally require manual removal of fecal material under general anesthesia. They are rehydrated with intravenous fluids prior to the procedure. Prevention of dehydration, a high-fiber diet, maintenance use of psyllium,

lactulose, or other laxatives may be used to prevent recurrence. Cisapride (Propulsid®) may be used to promote colonic motility. Over-the-counter phosphate enemas can cause seizures and death in cats and should never be used. Some cats with recurrent episodes of obstipation require surgical removal of the colon to prevent recurrence.

Gastrointestinal Neoplasia

Cancer of the gastrointestinal tract causes signs mimicking benign diseases; regurgitation, vomiting, diarrhea, straining to defecate, anorexia, and weight loss. In some cats, a mass will be found on physical examination; other cats may have intestinal thickening suggestive of cancer. A complete blood count, biochemical panel, FeLV/FIV testing , thyroid testing, and urinalysis are performed to assess the patient's general health. A needle aspirate or biopsy may be performed on any masses found. Ultrasound or endoscopy may be used to search for occult (hidden) cancers. Some cats require exploratory surgery to establish a definitive diagnosis.

Lymphosarcoma is the most common malignant tumor of cats. It is a malignancy of lymphocytes (cells of the immune system) that may occur in any tissue, including the gastrointestinal tract. Chemotherapy can be used in an effort to gain a remission, but lymphosarcoma is considered incurable. Chemotherapy protocols are tailored for the individual patient; a typical one uses vincristine, cyclophosphamide, and prednisone. Frequent veterinary monitoring is essential to assess the response to treatment and to identify any chemotherapy-related problems.

Carcinomas, adenocarcinomas, and various sarcomas also occur in the gastrointestinal tract of cats. With

DIGESTIVE TRACT DISORDERS

Children can become infected with roundworms, Giardia, and other parasites if allowed to handle feline fecal material.

the exception of mastocytoma, none are likely to respond to chemotherapy. Surgery can be curative in the early stages of disease. Unfortunately, most cats develop clinical signs after the disease has become extensive; hence the prognosis is poor.

DISEASES OF THE PERITONEUM

The peritoneum is the lining of the abdominal cavity. The main clinical sign associated with peritoneal disease is fluid distention of the abdomen. Diseases of the heart and liver can result in effusion (fluid accumulation). The most common disease causing peritoneal effusion in cats is feline infectious peritonitis (FIP), caused by coronaviruses that are indistinguishable from those causing enteritis. Besides fecal-oral exposure, cats may acquire the FIP virus by inhalation. In catteries and multiple-cat households, few cats will ever get the disease. It is believed that other factors besides viral exposure, such as immune competence of the cat and concurrent stress, also play a role. Two forms of the disease, effusive ("wet") and non-effusive ("dry") are described. In both, cats become lethargic, febrile, anorexic, and experience weight loss. The cats with effusive disease will have abdominal distention. Some cats will also have vomiting, diarrhea, breathing difficulties, and icterus (jaundice; yellow coloration of the gums, eyes, and skin) as well.

Diagnosis is made on the basis of clinical signs, results of CBC and biochemical panel tests, FIP serology (blood test), and, in the effusive form, fluid analysis. Because cats exposed to enteric coronaviruses will test positive on FIP serology, it is recommended that cats without clinical signs of illness never be euthanized on the basis of a positive

FIP test alone. A few cats, particularly those with non-effusive FIP, will require surgical exploration and biopsy to establish the diagnosis.

There are currently no treatments available to cure FIP. The prognosis is poor, and most affected cats die within weeks of diagnosis. Immunosuppressive treatment may be tried in an effort to decrease the cat's immune response to the virus, which is the cause of most of the organ damage. An intranasal FIP vaccine is available, which appears to offer some protection against the virus. Its use should be considered in catteries and households with indoor/outdoor cats. Because the virus may be passed to kittens in catteries prior to the kittens being old enough to start the vaccination series, it has been proposed that kittens in catteries affected with FIP be raised in isolation from the adult cats. Management of a cattery with FIP is problematic. It should always be done under the direction of a veterinarian.

DISEASES OF THE EXOCRINE PANCREAS

The pancreas produces bicarbonate and digestive enzymes that are released into the first portion of the small intestine to continue the digestive process. Signs of pancreatic disease in cats are non-specific: weight loss, anorexia, diarrhea, and, rarely, vomiting. Pancreatic disease may occur concurrently with liver disease and diabetes mellitus.

Cats are fond of ribbons, strings, tinsel, and other potential linear foreign bodies.

DIGESTIVE TRACT DISORDERS

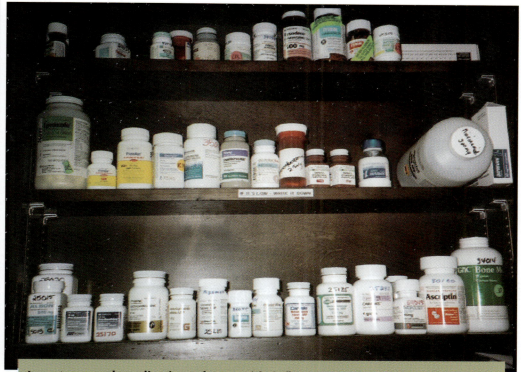

Long-term oral medication of cats with inflammatory bowel disease requires commitment and patience on the part of the owner.

Exocrine Pancreatic Insufficiency

When insufficient amounts of pancreatic enzymes are produced, which may occur after long-standing pancreatitis, digestion of food is incomplete. Many cats so affected will pass large amounts of pale, foul-smelling stools. As a result of incomplete assimilation of nutrients, most cats will have an increased appetite and weight loss. A CBC, biochemical panel, FeLV/FIV blood test, thyroid test, fecal flotations, and, possibly, fecal culture will be performed to consider other causes of diarrhea. Confirmation of pancreatic insufficiency requires a specialized test, trypsin-like immunoreactivity (TLI), that is currently offered by only a few laboratories. Alternatively, a check for the pancreatic enzyme activity of fresh stool may be performed.

Treatment is with the addition of pancreatic enzymes to the food. Almost all cats will then regain weight and lead a normal life. Because giardiasis is more common and causes similar clinical signs, especially in kittens, treatment for this parasite may be recommended empirically.

Pancreatitis

Pancreatitis is inflammation of the pancreas as a result of inappropriate activation of the digestive enzymes produced there. Clinical signs are often vague: anorexia, weight loss, liver disease, and poorly regulated diabetes mellitus. Only rarely is vomiting present. Routine biochemical analysis frequently is normal, even in cats with severe pancreatitis. The diagnosis may be established with abdominal ultrasonography or with the TLI blood test. Some cats may be diagnosed only by biopsy at exploratory surgery. There are currently no documented methods for treatment of feline pancreatitis. Fasting, intravenous fluids, and antibiotics are frequently employed with variable results. The prognosis is guarded, particularly for cats with concurrent diabetes mellitus or suppurative hepatitis.

DISEASES OF THE LIVER

The liver has many roles in metabolism. It produces the bile acids required for fat digestion. It receives the nutrients absorbed from the intestines. Glucose from the intestines is stored in the liver and used to regulate blood glucose. The liver processes amino acids, the products of protein digestion, into new proteins required by the body. Excessive proteins are processed into urea nitrogen for elimination through the kidneys. Clotting factors are manufactured in the liver. The liver is also responsible for the metabolism and elimination through the bile of many toxins and drugs.

Failure of any of these functions may result in signs of liver disease. The signs can include icterus (also known as jaundice), abdominal effusion, anorexia, weight loss, vomiting, mental dullness, and other neurologic signs including coma and seizures. Some cats will have increases in water consumption and urination or edema formation (fluid accumulation in the tissues). The initial evaluation of a cat with

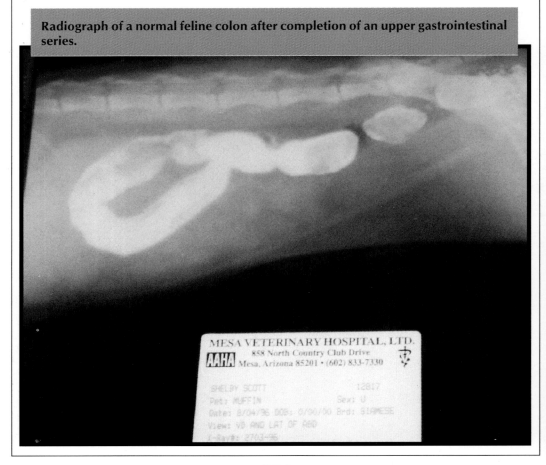

Radiograph of a normal feline colon after completion of an upper gastrointestinal series.

Digestive Tract Disorders

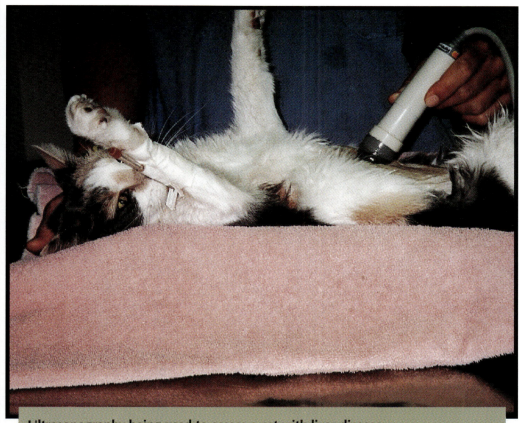

Ultrasonography being used to assess a cat with liver disease.

suspected liver disease includes performing a CBC, biochemical panel, thyroid testing, urinalysis, and, possibly, FeLV, FIV, and FIP testing. A fasting and postprandial (after eating) bile acids tolerance test may be performed to assess liver function. Abdominal radiographs are helpful in establishing the size of the liver. Ultrasonography (ultrasound examination) is performed to find discrete masses in the liver, changes in the appearance of the liver tissue as a whole, or changes in the gall bladder and biliary system. Discrete masses of the liver, gallstones, and biliary obstruction (blockage of the flow of bile from the liver) are uncommon findings that are addressed with exploratory surgery. Diseases causing diffuse changes throughout the liver may be identified with an ultrasound-guided needle biopsy under general anesthesia. A liver culture may be performed on tissue removed at that time. It is essential that blood clotting parameters be assessed prior to the procedure to minimize the risk of excessive bleeding.

Hepatic Lipidosis

In this condition, fat has been mobilized from body stores more rapidly than the liver can metabolize it. This may occur secondary to other metabolic diseases or may represent a primary disease state. Cats with primary hepatic lipidosis frequently have a history of being obese and of recently going off their food because of a recent stress. The stress can include a diet change (including being put on a reducing diet to lose weight), a recent move, or other change in the household (e.g., addition of a new cat or person). As the disease progresses, vomiting, icterus, and weight loss may occur. The diagnosis is confirmed with liver ultrasound and biopsy. Treatment requires meeting all caloric needs in the diet so that fat is no longer moved from peripheral stores to the liver. This generally requires placement of a feeding tube and feeding of a puréed diet through the tube to ensure adequate caloric intake. Antibiotics may also be employed. The prognosis for recovery is guarded. Some cats may require tube feeding for several months. Cats developing neurologic signs upon initiation of tube feeding have a poor prognosis. Frequent monitoring of weight and liver values on the biochemical profile during recovery is necessary.

Lymphocytic-Plasmacytic Cholangiohepatitis

Lymphocytes and plasma cells may infiltrate the liver as well as the gastrointestinal tract. The diagnosis is made with liver ultrasound and biopsy. Prednisone therapy tapered over a couple of months is used for treatment. Some clinicians will also prescribe an antibiotic. If anorexia has been a clinical problem, placement of a feeding tube to prevent lipidosis may be recommended. The prognosis for recovery is fair to guarded. Frequent rechecks to monitor weight and biochemical parameters will be required.

Suppurative Cholangiohepatitis

In suppurative cholangiohepatitis, inflammatory cells called neutrophils are found in increased number on liver biopsy. A liver culture may be negative, but, because neutrophils are generally associated with

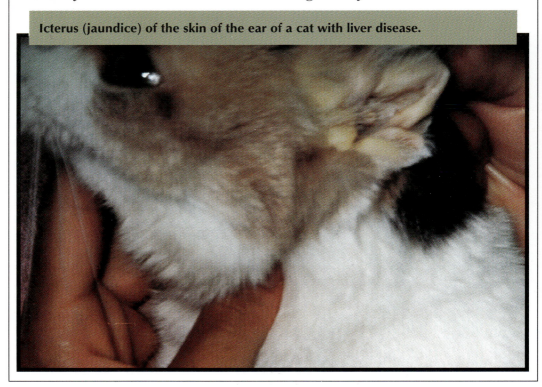

Icterus (jaundice) of the skin of the ear of a cat with liver disease.

DIGESTIVE TRACT DISORDERS

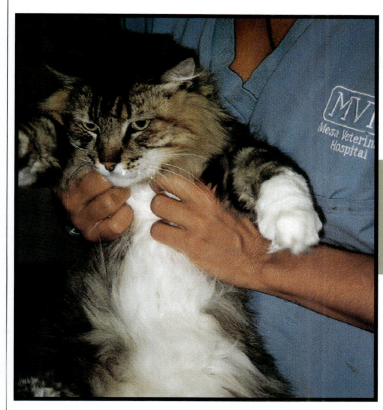

Obesity predisposes cats to the development of hepatic lipidosis.

bacterial infection, antibiotics are prescribed. Amoxicillin, amoxicillin-clavulanate (Clavamox®), cephalexin, or metronidazole may be used. Because liver inflammation can result in fibrosis, prednisone is frequently prescribed. As with the other conditions discussed above, nutritional support is vital, and placement of a feeding tube may be required. Frequent weight and biochemical monitoring is again required. Suppurative cholangiohepatitis may occur with pancreatitis or inflammatory bowel disease.

Hepatic Fibrosis

Fibrosis is the end result of an inflammatory process in the liver. If left unchecked, fibrosis can progress to cirrhosis, or end-stage liver scarring. Some cats will develop clinical signs very late in the course of liver disease, after extensive fibrosis has occurred. The liver is small on physical examination, radiographs, and ultrasound. Liver biopsy is more dangerous when the liver is small. It is less likely to yield information as to why the fibrosis has occurred and therefore is not routinely performed. Fibrosis is irreversible. Prednisone is often prescribed to prevent further fibrosis from occurring. The prognosis for cats with fibrosis severe enough to cause decreased liver size is poor.

Hepatic Encephalopathy

When the liver cannot process the byproducts of protein digestion and metabolism, these byproducts affect the brain and cause neurologic signs such as mental dullness, confusion, head-pressing, coma, and seizures. This occurs when very little liver function is remaining as a result of any underlying liver disease or when blood from the digestive tract bypasses the liver. Because retention of stool can contribute ammonia from protein metabolism by intestinal bacteria, enemas are frequently employed as part of treatment. Lactulose is a laxative that also has a primary effect preventing ammonia formation. It can be used orally, or it can be given rectally in comatose animals. Metronidazole is used to decrease the number of ammonia-forming bacteria. H-2 blockers may be used if gastric ulcers are suspected or prophylactically to try and prevent their occurrence. Gastrointestinal bleeding contributes to the protein load of the gastrointestinal tract and may worsen signs of encephalopathy. A low-protein diet is prescribed as part of treatment. The development of severe signs of hepatic encephalopathy, regardless of the underlying condition, portends a poor prognosis.

Congenital Portosystemic Shunt

A congenital portosystemic shunt is caused by abnormal development of the blood vessels draining the gastrointestinal tract *in utero* (before birth). Instead of going from the intestines to the liver, the liver is bypassed and is therefore unable to perform many of its normal metabolic functions. Clinical signs include drooling, incoordination, mental dullness, seizures, and stunted growth. Some cats may also be presented for blindness. Physical examination may reveal other congenital anomalies. Diagnostic assessment includes performing a complete blood count, biochemical panel, urinalysis, and serum bile acids. The abdominal radiographs (x-rays) and ultrasound show a small liver. Ultrasonography may reveal the anomalous blood vessel. Surgical exploration with a special dye study (mesenteric portogram) may be required to identify the shunt.

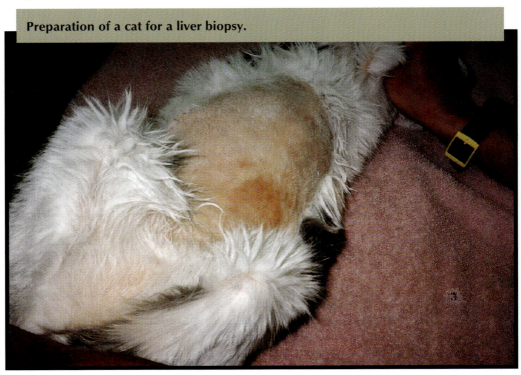

Preparation of a cat for a liver biopsy.

Definitive treatment is surgical ligation (tying off to stop blood flow) of the shunt. In some cats, the vessel can only be partially ligated or not ligated at all. Preoperative and postoperative medical management for hepatic encephalopathy is generally needed. The prognosis is favorable for cats that are able to have complete shunt ligation, guarded with partial ligation, and poor in long-standing cases or those unable to have the shunt ligated.

RECOMMENDED READING

Barlough, JE; Stodart, CA: Feline coronaviral infections. *Infectious Diseases of the Dog and Cat*, C E Greene, Ed. WB Saunders Co., Philadelphia, PA, 1990, pp. 300-312.

DeNovo, RC; Dright, RM: Chronic feline constipation/obstipation. *Kirk's Current Veterinary Therapy XI Small Animal Practice*, RW Kirk and JD Bonagura, Eds. WB Saunders Co., Philadelphia, PA, 1992, pp.619-625.

DeNovo, RC; Magne, ML: Current concepts in the management of *Helicobacter*-associated gastritis. *Proceedings of the 13th Annual Veterinary Medical Forum*, 1995, pp. 57-61.

Dimski, DS: Therapy of inflammatory bowel disease. *Kirk's Current Veterinary Therapy XII Small Animal Practice*, JD Bonagura, Ed. WB Saunders Co., Philadelphia, PA, 1995, pp. 723-727.

Greene, CE; Scott, FW: Feline panleukopenia. *Infectious Diseases of the Dog and Cat*, CE Greene, Ed. WB Saunders Co., Philadelphia, PA, 1990, pp. 291-299.

Guilford, WG: Diagnostic and therapeutic approach to the cat with chronic diarrhea. *Proceedings of the 14th Annual Veterinary Medical Forum*, 1996, pp. 143-145.

Hall, JA: The need for definitive diagnosis in the chronic vomiting cat. *Proceedings of the 14th Annual Veterinary Medical Forum*, 1996, pp. 135-137.

Hardy, RM: Diseases of the liver and their treatment. *Textbook of Veterinary Internal Medicine.* Third edition. ST Ettinger, Ed. WB Saunders Co., Philadelphia, PA, 1989, pp. 1497-1527.

Legendre, AM: Feline infectious peritonitis: what is new? *Proceedings of the 14th Annual Veterinary Medical Forum*, 1996, pp. 603-604.

Mahoney, OM; Moore, AS; Cotter, SM, et al: Alimentary lymphoma in cats: 28 cases (1988-1993). *JAVMA*, 1995;207(12):1593-1598.

Steiner, JM; Williams, DA: Feline trypsin-like immunoreactivity in feline exocrine pancreatic disease. *Compendium on Continuing Education for the Practicing Veterinarian*, 1996: 18(5):543-547.

Weiss, DJ; Gange, JM; Armstrong, PJ: Relationship between inflammatory hepatic disease and inflammatory bowel disease, pancreatitis, and nephritis in cats. *JAVMA*, 1996, 209(6)1114-1116.

Williams, DA: Feline pancreatic insufficiency. *Kirk's Current Veterinary Therapy XII Small Animal Practice*, JD Bonagura, Ed. WB Saunders Co., 1995, pp. 732-735.

Dr. Robert B. Koch

Dr. Robert B. Koch received a Bachelor of Science degree in Bioagriculture from Arizona State University in 1976 and a Doctor of Veterinary Medicine degree from Colorado State University in 1980. He is a Diplomate of the American Board of Veterinary Practitioners, specialty Canine/Feline and Feline. Dr. Koch is the owner of a companion animal multi-veterinarian practice in Phoenix, Arizona.

URINARY TRACT PROBLEMS

By Robert B. Koch, DVM
Diplomate, American Board of Veterinary Practitioners

East Maryland Animal Hospital
529 E. Maryland Avenue
Phoenix, AZ 85012

INTRODUCTION

Urinary tract health is a very important concept in cats. As in all animals, the urinary system of the cat is responsible for the elimination of body wastes, for controlling water distribution in the body, and for regulating the composition and the volume of body fluids. In addition, the kidneys produce several hormones that regulate the red blood cell number, blood pressure, and vitamin D metabolism. The importance of the kidneys is demonstrated by the fact that they receive 25 percent of the total blood volume.

ANATOMY AND PHYSIOLOGY OF THE URINARY SYSTEM

The urinary system consists of the two kidneys that form urine from the blood, the ureters, which are tubes that pass urine from the kidneys to the urinary bladder, which stores the urine, and the urethra, which is the tube that passes urine to the outside. It is important to remember that in the male, the reproductive tract shares a common pathway with the urinary tract.

The kidneys are loosely attached to the body wall near the spine. They are somewhat bean shaped and are enveloped in a fibrous membrane. The kidneys contain thousands of tubes called nephrons. These nephrons filter blood and form urine.

The urine passes from the kidney into the ureter. Regular progressive contractions of the ureter help push urine into the urinary bladder. Filling, storage, and elimination of the urine from the urinary bladder are well controlled by a number of nerve reflexes.

DIAGNOSTIC TESTING

Although history and physical examination can provide presumptive evidence of urinary system abnormalities, laboratory tests, radiography (x-rays), and biopsy procedures are necessary to confirm the diagnosis and ultimately the prognosis.

Blood tests are extremely important in the diagnosis of kidney disease. Measurement of urea (also known as blood urea nitrogen or BUN) and creatinine is very useful in determining kidney function. Urea is formed during protein breakdown, and creatinine is a product of skeletal muscle metabolism. Because both urea and creatinine are filtered through the kidneys, when both values are increased, kidney malfunction is indicated. Creatinine is a more specific indicator of kidney abnormalities, as urea can be affected by outside influences such a dehydration.

Other blood tests assist in providing evidence of kidney malfunction. Increased phosphorus

CAT HEALTH ENCYCLOPEDIA

levels in the blood (hyperphosphatemia) are often seen with kidney disease and are associated with decreased excretion of the mineral. Decreased levels of calcium in the blood (hypocalcemia) may be noted due to increased excretion. In certain diseases where the kidneys are losing excess protein, decreased blood protein may occur.

Urine examination (urinalysis) is often quite helpful in the diagnosis of both kidney and lower urinary tract disease. The concentration of the urine (specific gravity) can be measured and if in a certain range, kidney disease may be present. When the kidneys are functioning properly, they should be able to produce dilute and concentrated urine. Chemical evaluation of the urine is extremely important in the determination of urinary tract disease. The pH of the urine can be an indication of infection (increased pH) and can help determine the type of bladder stone (e.g., struvite stones are associated with increased urine pH). As mentioned previously, excess protein loss can occur with specific kidney diseases. This excess protein can be measured with specific tests. The presence of blood, glucose (sugar), and bilirubin (associated with liver disease) can also be detected quite easily.

The urine can be spun down in a centrifuge and the resultant material examined under the microscope to look for evidence of infection (white blood cells, red blood cells), tumor cells, and kidney damage. Infection can be confirmed by culturing the urine, and special tests can indicate which antibiotic will work the best.

Radiographic examination of the urinary tract can demonstrate kidney size and the presence of certain stones. Special studies are often necessary to further evaluate certain conditions. An intravenous pyelogram (IVP) in which a special dye is given intravenously and then radiographs are taken will outline the entire urinary tract. This can be useful to identify certain stones, tumors, and congenital malformations.

Biopsy of the kidney is often necessary to pinpoint the diagnosis. This can be done during an exploratory surgery or by the use of special biopsy needles that require a much smaller surgical opening. Ultrasound is now being used to evaluate kidney size and consistency. It can also be used to guide a biopsy needle, thus requiring minimal surgery.

KIDNEY DISEASE

Congenital Abnormalities

True congenital (present at birth) kidney abnormalities are very uncommon in cats and are often incidental findings during routine abdominal surgical procedures. Examples include kidney agenesis (lack of one kidney) and fusion (both kidneys are attached to each other). In both situations the affected cat is usually clinically normal.

Polycystic Kidney Disease

Polycystic kidney disease is usually an acquired condition in which the formation of fluid-filled cysts (cavities) leads to progressive enlargement of one or both kidneys. The problem may be present at birth or acquired from the blockage of urine flow through kidney tubes due to infection, inflammation, or scarring. As these cysts enlarge, normal kidney tissue is damaged; and if both kidneys are affected, kidney failure may develop.

Polycystic kidney disease has been seen in mixed-breed kittens. These kittens had swollen abdomens and all ultimately died. The two breeds most

URINARY TRACT PROBLEMS

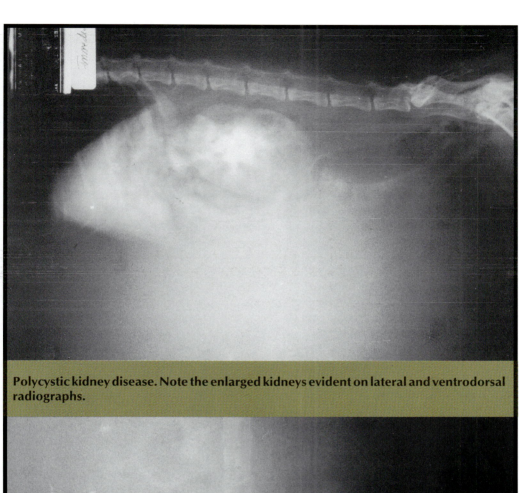

Polycystic kidney disease. Note the enlarged kidneys evident on lateral and ventrodorsal radiographs.

commonly reported with acquired polycystic kidney disease are the Persian and Himalayan. In the Persian cat, this condition is inherited as a dominant trait.

The clinical signs (symptoms) of this disease largely depend on whether one or both kidneys are affected. If only one kidney is involved, there may be no abnormalities noted. If, however, both kidneys are affected, kidney failure may eventually develop. Symptoms may include increased water intake, increased urination, decreased appetite, vomiting, weight loss, and lethargy. Sometimes the kidneys become so enlarged that they can be felt during an examination.

Treatment for polycystic kidney disease is largely medical, as described later in this chapter. In breeds other than the Persian cat, if only one kidney is affected, and the opposite kidney is determined to have normal function, the diseased kidney may be removed. Because this condition is inherited in Persian cats, those affected should not have surgery since both kidneys are likely to be diseased. In addition those affected should not be bred.

Perinephric Pseudocysts

One of the more uncommon reasons for an enlarged kidney in cats is a perinephric pseudocyst. This occurs when one or both affected kidneys are surrounded by a fluid-filled sac. Although pseudocysts can result in apparent massive kidney enlargement, rarely does impairment occur. The cause of this condition is unknown, although trauma may be involved.

Perinephric pseudocysts can easily be diagnosed with radiographic dye tests or ultrasound. Treatment is usually quite effective and involves surgical removal of the cyst wall.

Hydronephrosis

Hydronephrosis results from enlargement of the kidney pelvis due to blockage of the ureter. If this occurs in only one kidney, extreme enlargement may occur. Unfortunately, if present in both, kidney failure will result due to the destruction of kidney tissue from pressure build up. Numerous causes have been found including cancer, injury, and stones.

Diagnosis of hydronephrosis is usually made by radiographic dye tests or ultrasound. Treatment involves early surgical removal of the blockage. If the condition is found to be irreversible and the other kidney is functioning properly, removal of the affected kidney is recommended.

Pyelonephritis

Infection and inflammation of the kidney (especially involving the kidney pelvis) is called pyelonephritis. The source of infection can be from the blood stream or from an infection that has ascended from the lower urinary tract (i.e., urinary bladder). Blockage of the urinary tract, such as that seen with urethral stones, may contribute to the development of pyelonephritis.

The symptoms of pyelonephritis can include fever, loss of appetite, lethargy, dehydration, enlarged and painful kidneys, and increased water intake and urination. Unfortunately, most cats with this disease do not have symptoms that point specifically toward kidney infection. Diagnosis is made with blood tests, urine examination, and urine culture.

Treatment involves antibiotics, correction of the blockage, and fluids. Treatment is often continued for one to two months. If the infection is diagnosed and eliminated before permanent damage occurs, recovery is possible.

Urinary Tract Problems

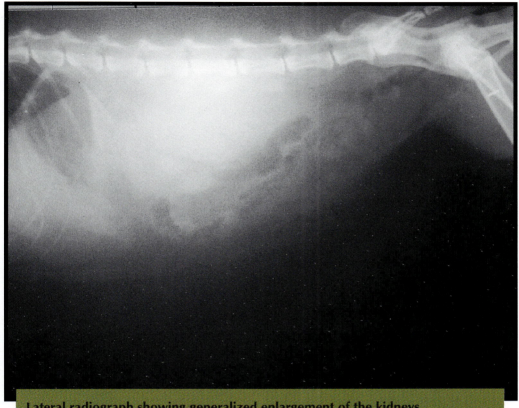

Lateral radiograph showing generalized enlargement of the kidneys.

Amyloidosis

Amyloidosis is a disease in which specific types of proteins called amyloid build up in various body organs. Although this build-up can occur in any organ, amyloid seems to cause the most problems when it involves the kidneys. When enough normal kidney tissue is replaced with amyloid, kidney failure results.

Although the type of inheritance is unknown, inherited amyloidosis has been observed in Abyssinian, Oriental Shorthair, and Siamese cats. Symptoms of this disease mimic those seen with other forms of kidney failure, including decreased appetite, weight loss, and increased water intake and urination. Diagnosis of this disease first involves identifying the presence of kidney failure and then kidney biopsy for confirmation. Special stains usually are required to identify amyloid in the tissue samples.

Treatment of amyloidosis involves the same principles discussed in the "Treatment of Chronic Kidney Failure" section. In addition, identifying and eliminating any concurrent diseases that might lead to the build-up of amyloid, and usage of specific medications that may help prevent the build-up and increase the elimination of amyloid can be beneficial. Specific drugs that may work against amyloid include DMSO and colchicine. DMSO given orally early in the course of the disease may decrease the build-up of amyloid and lower the inflammation resulting from its presence. Colchicine has been used in humans but has not yet been evaluated in cats.

Immune-mediated Kidney Disease

Immune damage to the kidney is termed glomerulonephritis. This occurs when antibodies produced by the cat combine with antigens such as those from tumors or viruses. This combination (complex) is trapped in the filtering mechanism of the kidney, causing inflammation that results in damage.

The average age of cats affected by glomerulonephritis is four years, with no specific breed predisposition. Symptoms can include excess fluid build-up (edema), lack of appetite, weight loss, and lethargy. Diagnosis is made by blood and urine tests. Screening tests usually identify low blood protein, anemia, excess protein in the urine, and at times kidney test abnormalities. If glomerulonephritis is suspected, any underlying disease processes need to be identified. Specific tests for feline leukemia virus (FeLV), feline infectious peritonitis (FIP) virus, and feline immunodeficiency virus (FIV) are performed. Careful examination for cancer and inflammatory diseases is done. Ultimately, the only way to confirm the diagnosis of this disease is through kidney biopsy, including special immunological tests.

Treatment involves correction of any underlying disorders if possible. Drugs to remove excess fluid (diuretics) and corticosteroids to reduce inflammation are often used. High-quality, partially restricted protein diets can be helpful in the early stages. Depending on the stage of the disease and the remaining renal function, cats with glomerulonephritis can do well for extended time periods.

Kidney Stones

Kidney stones are very uncommon in the cat. When stones occur in the urinary tract, they are usually located in the urinary bladder. Kidney stones can be made up of magnesium-ammonium-phosphate (MAP or struvite), calcium oxalate, urate, bile pigment, and calcium phosphate. Diet and possibly underlying urinary tract infection may predispose to kidney stones.

Symptoms of kidney stones can include abdominal pain. If enough kidney tissue is destroyed from urine blockage, kidney failure will occur. In some cases, kidney stones are incidental findings during radiography and necropsy.

Traditionally, treatment has been surgical removal of the stones. Special prescription diets have been used to dissolve specific stones (struvite). If bacterial infection is detected, it is important to treat with appropriate antibiotics. Drugs to lower urine pH (acidifiers) have been used in certain cases involving struvite stones to help increase the effectiveness of treatment.

If a specific stone type is found, prevention of recurrence may be achieved with specific prescription diets.

Tumors of the Kidney

Cats rarely are affected by tumors that arise in the kidneys. However, lymphosarcoma (cancer of the lymphoid system) commonly involves the kidney when it occurs in other parts of the body. This disease occurs in middle-aged to older cats, with males affected more than females. About half of the cats are positive for feline leukemia virus.

Symptoms of kidney lymphosarcoma include all those that are seen with kidney failure. Dramatic bilateral kidney enlargement is often seen.

Once kidney failure is recognized, specific diagnosis of lymphosarcoma is made by taking a sample directly

Urinary Tract Problems

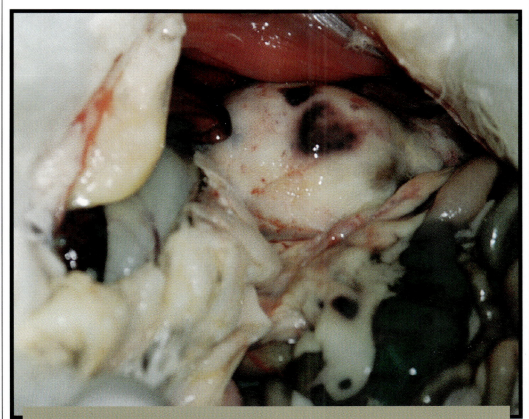

Same cat as in previous radiograph of enlarged kidneys. The cause of the kidney enlargement was renal lymphosarcoma.

from an affected kidney with a small needle (for cytologic assessment) or a full biopsy.

Treatment involves chemotherapy. Statistics have shown poor long-term survival; however, there have been anecdotal reports of cats living longer than two years.

Acute Kidney Failure

Acute kidney failure is a sudden loss of kidney function. Unlike chronic kidney failure, it is potentially reversible. Because of rapid onset, the cat is often unable to compensate and is usually much sicker when noticed by its owner.

Acute kidney failure may begin with factors involving the circulation to the kidneys, the kidneys themselves, and elimination of urine from the kidneys. Severe dehydration can reduce the blood supply to the kidneys and if persistent long enough can result in acute kidney failure. The two most common causes of direct kidney damage leading to acute failure are toxins such as ethylene glycol and blockage of the kidney arteries due to blood clots caused by heart disease. Obstruction of urine excretion caused by stones or urine leakage from injury will ultimately lead to acute kidney failure.

This form of kidney failure, if diagnosed early enough, is potentially reversible. Cats suddenly become ill with symptoms including depression, vomiting, and weakness.

Cat Health Encyclopedia

Treatment involves neutralizing specific toxins, surgery to relieve blockages or repair injuries to the urinary system, and fluid therapy to correct dehydration and electrolyte abnormalities. Fluids are given intravenously and are continued until kidneys can heal. As the kidneys heal, certain electrolytes such as sodium and potassium are lost, so deficiencies may occur. Replacement of these electrolytes is necessary to avoid complications. Other medications are used to provide support for the kidneys. Although the chance for recovery is always guarded, with early recognition and treatment, partial or complete reversal of kidney damage may occur.

Toxic Kidney Failure

Due to the cat's finicky appetite, kidney disease caused by toxins is relatively rare. There are numerous potential kidney toxins recognized, including certain heavy metals (e.g., arsenic) and organic compounds (e.g, pesticides, herbicides, and ethylene glycol). Interestingly, the cat's fastidious nature will at times lead to problems when it licks toxic chemicals that may have contacted its feet and coat. Pet owners may unknowingly cause problems by administering certain drugs to their cat (e.g., aspirin and acetaminophen).

By far the most common example of kidney failure due to toxins is caused by ethylene glycol. Ethylene glycol is found in numerous products, but the most common source of poisoning is the ingestion of antifreeze. Unfortunately, antifreeze is odorless and cats seem to find it pleasant tasting. Antifreeze ingested in even very small amounts is extremely toxic to the kidneys. Symptoms of poisoning include vomiting, depression, difficulty walking, and coma. Unless immediate treatment is given, irreversible kidney damage will occur. Treatment involves the induction of vomiting followed by the administration of ethanol (alcohol). This treatment is successful only if begun within six hours of ingestion and requires several days of intensive care.

The other relatively common kidney toxicant involving cats is that caused by aspirin administration. Although aspirin can be very useful for certain inflammatory and heart conditions, the dosage must be calculated carefully since aspirin is eliminated through the urinary system. Symptoms of poisoning include panting, weakness, high fever, and collapse. Treatment involves intravenous fluid therapy.

Chronic Kidney Failure

Chronic kidney failure, defined as failure present for more than several days, is the most common form of kidney disease in cats. Most studies indicate that chronic kidney failure occurs in cats over seven years of age. Siamese, Abyssinian, and Russian Blue cats may be affected with increased frequency.

There are numerous causes of chronic kidney failure, including all of the conditions discussed so far. The diagnosis of chronic kidney failure indicates that the initial disease process has resulted in injury, permanent damage, and ultimate loss of various structures that make up the filtering system of the kidney. After approximately 75 percent of the kidney filtering system is damaged, signs of kidney failure become evident.

The symptoms of chronic kidney failure include decreased appetite and weight loss. Commonly, during the initial stages, increased water intake and urination are observed. Progression of this disease is

Urinary Tract Problems

Abyssinian cats appear to be more susceptible to amyloidosis and chronic renal failure.

extremely variable, as some cats can be affected for several months before symptoms become severe.

Diagnosis of this disease is made by identification of kidney failure through blood and urine tests. Specific diagnosis requires a kidney biopsy. Many times the specific cause of the kidney failure is indeterminable. The most common biopsy finding is chronic tubulointerstitial nephritis, which indicates abnormalities of the tissue surrounding the filtering mechanisms (nephrons) themselves.

TREATMENT OF CHRONIC KIDNEY FAILURE

Treatment of chronic kidney failure begins with identification and correction, if possible, of the cause of failure along with any underlying factors such as infection, stones, tumors, or toxins.

Specific treatment begins with correction of fluid and electrolyte imbalances. Correction of fluid deficiencies is usually done by administering fluid solutions under the skin (subcutaneously) or by the intravenous route. Unless the cat's condition is extremely critical, the goal is to achieve correction over the first 24 hours.

Electrolyte abnormalities are common with chronic kidney failure. A syndrome of excessive potassium loss has been recognized. Loss of potassium can be so severe that the blood level may drop to dangerous levels. Symptoms can include generalized weakness and a peculiar posture where the head is held down and the neck arched. Treatment involves potassium added to the fluid as well as oral supplements.

Once a cat with chronic kidney failure is stabilized, long-term

CAT HEALTH ENCYCLOPEDIA

management is begun. Dietary manipulation, specifically protein intake regulation, is an important factor. Although somewhat controversial, restriction of protein intake while providing a high-quality protein source appears to be beneficial in the management of chronic kidney disease. Unfortunately, due to the cat's finicky nature, dietary restriction can be somewhat frustrating. Phosphorous restriction coupled with medications to reduce phosphorous absorption also appear to be beneficial. Anemia can become a significant problem with chronic kidney failure. Use of human recombinant erythropoietin (Epogen®) has proved to be consistently effective in treating this complication.

Although the management of chronic kidney failure can be exceedingly time consuming and labor intensive, the results can be quite rewarding. Despite poor laboratory test values, many cats can have very satisfactory lives for long periods of time.

LOWER URINARY TRACT DISEASE

The lower urinary tract consists of the urinary bladder and the urethra. There are numerous diseases of the cat's lower urinary tract, and symptoms can include blood in the urine (hematuria), straining to urinate (dysuria), and increased frequency of urination (pollakiuria). Because diseases of the lower urinary tract can include most or all of these symptoms, it can be difficult to make a final diagnosis without several diagnostic tests.

Feline urologic syndrome (FUS) was a term used in the past that included all conditions in which hematuria (blood in the urine), dysuria (difficulty voiding), and pollakiuria (voiding only small amounts of urine, but frequently) were present. Recently a concerted effort has been made to use FUS only when the cause is unknown or to substitute the term "idiopathic lower urinary tract disease."

Infection

Although not very common, infection of the lower urinary tract can involve viruses, bacteria, fungi, and parasites. Specific viruses such as the feline calicivirus have been identified in the urine of cats with disease of the lower urinary tract. Unfortunately, it has not been proven that these viruses actually cause disease. Further work is being done to determine the significance of these viruses.

Unlike dogs, bacteria as a cause of lower urinary tract disease in cats does not appear to be significant. Cats seem to have a natural resistance to bacterial infection. This resistance may involve the cat's tendency to produce concentrated and acidic urine. When infection does occur, there is often an underlying cause such as recent medical treatment (catheter) or surgery. Diagnosis is confirmed by examination and culturing of the urine. Once identification of the type of bacteria is made, sensitivity tests are done to determine the type of antibiotic required. Any underlying cause is corrected if possible.

Rarely, infections of the lower urinary tract caused by fungi have been identified in cats. Again, underlying causes often lead to this type of infection. Prolonged treatment with antibiotics and catheter use are examples. Diagnosis is made by urine culture. Unfortunately, not much is known about the safety and effectiveness of drugs available to treat these fungal infections.

Parasite infection is uncommon in

Urinary Tract Problems

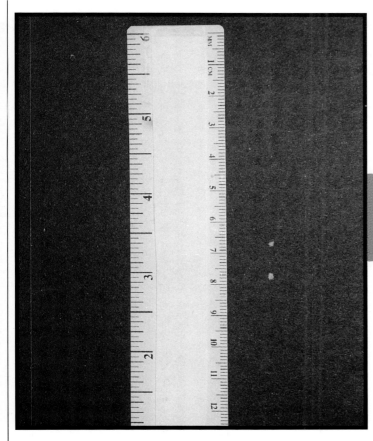

Urethral plugs can effectively block the outflow of urine through the urethra.

cats. The nematode *Capillaria feliscati* has been identified in the urinary bladder of cats. Symptoms of infection are minimal. Treatment is usually unnecessary.

Stones of the Lower Urinary Tract

Stones of the lower urinary tract are composed of varying amounts of minerals and organic matrix (protein substances). Since stones can form in the urinary bladder and the urethra and because the makeup and cause appear to be different for each location, each will be discussed separately.

STONES OF THE URINARY BLADDER

The primary symptoms seen with stones of the urinary bladder include hematuria (blood in the urine) and dysuria (difficulty urinating). Most stones cannot be felt during physical examination. Fortunately, radiography (x-rays) can often detect these stones.

Currently the two most common types of urinary bladder stones are struvite (magnesium-ammonium-phosphate-hexahydrate) and calcium oxalate. Interestingly, struvite stones are becoming less common and calcium oxalate more common, possibly due to dietary changes that were designed to reduce the incidence of struvite stones. Stones form because of the presence of excess quantities of specific minerals in the urine. Other factors that may influence the formation of stones include the urine pH and the presence of infection and organic matrix. The treatment and possible prevention depend upon its composition. After the diagnosis of bladder stones is made, determination of type is done through blood tests, urinalysis, and determination of the stone's composition.

Struvite Stones

There appear to be two categories of struvite urolithiasis: infected and sterile. The infected type results from bacteria that produce a specific enzyme (urease) that raises the urine pH (alkalinize) and increases the amount of ammonium and phosphate in the urine. Because lower urinary tract infection is uncommon in cats, this type is less common than sterile.

Many infected struvite stones occur when there are abnormalities of the lower urinary tract (congenital, previous surgery). These stones tend to grow faster and are usually larger than the sterile type. They also show up better on radiographs (x-rays).

Although there are likely numerous factors that lead to the formation of sterile struvite stones, studies indicate that diet may be involved. Specifically, diets containing excess levels of magnesium may lead to an increased incidence of this type. There is no evidence of breed predisposition. It is possible that reduced water intake leading to less urine formation and increased food consumption leading to increased mineral excretion in the urine may also be factors. Studies also seem to show that a lower urine pH reduces struvite stone formation.

Diagnosis of struvite stones depends on radiographs and evaluation of the composition of a stone obtained during surgery. An "educated guess" can often be made without surgery by evaluating the radiographs and analyzing the urine (especially the pH).

Treatment involves two basic approaches. In the medical approach, an attempt is made to identify the presence of infection by urinalysis and urine culture. A specific prescription diet (Prescription Diet S/D, Hills, Topeka, KS) is available that can be successful in dissolving struvite stones. It is possible to feed low-magnesium diets and administer urinary acidifiers (medications that lower the pH of the urine) that may also dissolve this type of stone. Response to stone-dissolving diets usually takes two to three weeks, with total stone elimination often occurring in several months. Unfortunately, these diets are not 100 percent successful.

Surgical removal of these stones has the following advantages: 100 percent success, very rapid elimination of the symptoms, and the ability to confirm the type of stone.

Prevention of these stones includes complete eradication and prevention of recurrence of lower urinary tract infection in the case of infection-induced stones. Specific diets that keep the urine pH lower and have restricted magnesium levels may help prevent struvite stones.

Calcium Oxalate Stones

The second most common urinary bladder stone in cats is that containing calcium oxalate. In a recent study it was seen 27 percent of the time. It is more common in male cats, and the Burmese, Himalayan, and Persian breeds may be predisposed.

Although increased levels of calcium in the urine may lead to this kind of stone, most cats affected appear to have normal blood calcium levels. However, when this type of stone is found, measurement of serum calcium is done as a screening test.

URINARY TRACT PROBLEMS

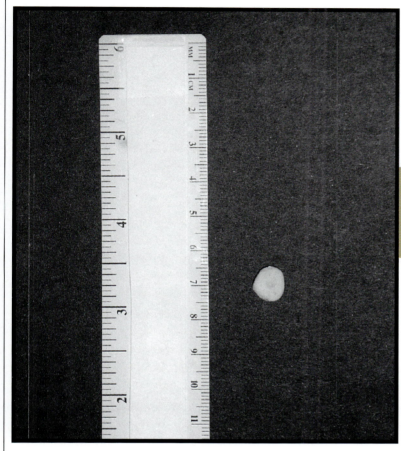

A struvite "stone" removed from the bladder.

In cats with normal calcium levels, it is theorized that some of the recommendations for prevention of struvite stones may predispose to the formation of calcium oxalate stones. Studies are currently being done to determine the effects of lowering the pH of urine and magnesium restriction upon the formation of the stone type.

Treatment of this stone involves primarily surgical removal. Unfortunately, there are no diets that will dissolve calcium oxalate stones.

Prevention of recurrence includes identification and correction of increased calcium blood levels. In cats with normal calcium levels, using a diet with lower levels of sodium, calcium, protein, and one that does not lower the urine pH may help prevent the formulation of calcium oxalate stones. Other medications such as potassium citrate may also be helpful.

OTHER URINARY BLADDER STONES

Other less common bladder stones include calcium-ammonium-phosphate, urate, cystine, and compound (those containing different minerals).

Ammonium urate stones can result from a congenital liver abnormality. In addition, diets high in liver may increase the formation of this type of stone. Predisposing factors for the other types of stones have not been determined. At this time, surgical removal of stones is the treatment of choice.

Tumors of the Lower Urinary Tract

Tumors of the lower urinary system are very uncommon in the cat. The primary location of these tumors is the urinary bladder, although the urethra may become involved, especially as the tumor enlarges. The mean age for cats with bladder cancer is 9.7 years. In a previous study, males were affected more than females.

The most common symptom of a bladder tumor is hematuria (blood in the urine). If the tumor becomes extensive, dysuria (difficulty urinating) may be observed.

There are many kinds of bladder tumors. Transitional-cell and squamous-cell carcinomas are the most common malignant tumors. Leiomyoma is the most common benign type. Little is known about the causes of bladder cancer.

Diagnosis is by clinical symptoms, palpation of a thickened or nodular urinary bladder, radiographs (including dye studies), and surgery. In certain cases, an abdominal mass may be felt.

Treatment involves surgical removal of the tumor and the affected bladder wall. With benign tumors, if diagnosed early, the prognosis is good. With malignant tumors, however, the prognosis is poor due to a high probability of recurrence and spread beyond the bladder.

Idiopathic Lower Urinary Tract Disease

When urinalysis, culture, radiography, ultrasonography, and possibly surgery are unable to determine the cause of hematuria and dysuria, the term FUS or idiopathic lower urinary tract disease is used. Studies have shown that some of the cats with this syndrome have remarkably similar urinalysis and biopsy findings to the inflammatory disorder of humans called interstitial cystitis. Unfortunately, the cause of the condition is also unknown.

The symptoms of idiopathic lower urinary tract disease are often self limiting. Unfortunately, recurrence is common.

Diseases of the Urethra

Diseases of the urethra occur primarily as an extension of conditions of the urinary bladder. These can include idiopathic inflammation, infection, urethral stones or plugs, and cancer.

The principles discussed relating to idiopathic, infectious, and cancerous conditions of the urinary bladder are basically the same as those affecting the urethra. Urethral stones (plugs) often have a very different makeup compared to bladder stones. In most cases, urethral stones are made up primarily of matrix mixed with smaller amounts of minerals. The predominant mineral combination (as with bladder stones) is magnesium-ammonium-phosphate (struvite). In addition to minerals and matrix, these plugs can include red blood cells, white blood cells, bacteria, and non-specific debris.

The primary symptoms of urethral stones relate to irritation and obstruction. Since the diameter of the male urethra is considerable smaller than that of the female, urethral obstruction is seen almost exclusively in males. In the initial stages, pollakiuria (frequently voiding small amounts of urine) and hematuria (blood in the urine) are the primary symptoms. With complete obstruction, vomiting, progressive depression, weakness, paralysis, and coma will develop unless the blockage is relieved.

Treatment of urethral obstruction initially involves gentle attempts at

URINARY TRACT PROBLEMS

If you suspect that your cat is not well, do not hesitate to contact your veterinarian. Veterinarians are trained to recognize problems early, before they become more serious.

dislodging the plug manually. If unsuccessful, backflushing the urethra with saline solution to break down the material or pushing the plug into the urinary bladder where it may be dissolved by repeated flushing is attempted. Once the obstruction is relieved, continued flushing of the bladder until the urine is clear may reduce the possibility of reobstruction.

Aggressive intravenous or subcutaneous fluid therapy helps to correct fluid deficits and electrolyte imbalances, and improves kidney function. Complete blockage of the urethra for longer than 24 hours results in acute kidney failure. If correction of the obstruction and fluid balance is achieved in a reasonable period of time, the kidney failure is potentially reversible.

In a few cases a urinary catheter is sutured in place after the obstruction is relieved. This involves inserting a narrow, non-irritating tube into the bladder; the tube allows for continual emptying of urine. Due to the possibility of causing further damage, this is done only when absolutely necessary.

Fortunately, if discovered soon enough, the prognosis for recovery is good. Once an affected cat recovers, a prevention program is recommended. Since the majority of urethral plugs contain struvite as the primary mineral component, methods previously discussed for the prevention of struvite bladder stones can be used. Surgical modification of the urethra has been performed in intractable cases. However, complications can occur.

Urinary Incontinence

Loss of voluntary control of urination is termed urinary incontinence. Normal storage and elimination of urine is under the control of several nerves that form reflexes that allow the bladder to stretch without excessive pressure and stimulate the bladder sphincter (valve) preventing the loss of urine, except during the voluntary emptying phase. The emptying phase is also under nerve control, with the initial stages usually being voluntary and the continuation a series of reflexes.

Urinary incontinence can be classified as neurogenic (nerve-related) or non-neurogenic. Neurogenic conditions involve those that interfere with the specific nerve pathways that regulate the storage and elimination of urine. Interference can occur anywhere from the brain to the nerves that actually attach to the urinary bladder. Inflammatory disorders, infection, intervertebral disc (IVD) disease, and trauma and tumors are all possible causes. Specific laboratory tests (especially blood tests) and radiographs (including special procedures such as a myelogram) are often necessary to determine a cause. Treatment and outcome depend on the results of these tests with correction of underlying problems the ultimate goal.

Urinary incontinence not related to nerve function can involve the ureters, the urinary bladder, and the urethra. Ectopic ureter is the primary cause of urinary incontinence in a younger kitten. This is a congenital condition in which one or both ureters empty into the urethra or vagina instead of the bladder. About half of the cases involve both ureters. There does not seem to be a sex or breed predisposition.

The symptoms of ectopic ureter are like that of any form of urinary incontinence. Urine dribbling is much more severe if both ureters are involved. An affected cat can usually urinate normally, although if both ureters are affected, there may not be enough urine left in the bladder to do so.

The diagnosis of ectopic ureters requires an IVP, which outlines the ureters and where they empty into the urinary bladder. The surgical correction of this condition requires moving the emptying point of the affected ureters to a more normal location in the bladder. Unfortunately, due to related conditions such as pyelonephritis, the results are not always completely satisfactory.

Rarely, there is no actual obstruction, but the urinary bladder is unable to empty properly. This usually occurs as a result of a prolonged, severe blockage of the urinary bladder with resultant damage to the bladder wall. This condition may be correctable with the placement of a retained urethral catheter and certain drugs.

Urinary incontinence can occur with a partial blockage of the urethra, which may lead to an overly full urinary bladder. In this case, a cat may not be able to empty the bladder completely, even with significant straining (stranguria). Small urethral plugs and tumors located at the entrance of the urethra are two examples of this condition. Diagnosis is usually made by radiographs, with dye sometimes necessary to outline the actual blockage. Surgery or procedures described in the section on urethral plugs are necessary for correction.

The urethra can be responsible for urinary incontinence in cats. In most cases, cats can urinate properly but

URINARY TRACT PROBLEMS

Urinary problems are serious. If your cat is straining to urinate and in distress, an immediate veterinary visit is required.

leak urine when relaxed. Unfortunately, most cats with this type of incontinence test positive for the feline leukemia virus. The actual cause of this incontinence has not been determined.

In cases of urinary incontinence where an actual cause has not been determined, specialized neurological tests can be performed that may locate the abnormality. Based on these tests, certain drugs may be used to correct or control the incontinence.

RECOMMENDED READING
Sherding, RG, Ed. *The Cat: Diseases and Clinical Management.* Second edition. Churchill Livingston, Inc. 1994

W. Jean Dodds, DVM

Dr. W. Jean Dodds graduated from the Ontario Veterinary College, and thereafter spent 25 years in research and clinical hematology with an emphasis on bleeding diseases. She is nationally and internationally recognized as an authority in hematology, immunology and blood banking, and more recently has developed interests in endocrinology, nutrition, and alternative veterinary medicine. Dr. Dodds is President and Director of Hemopet, a non-profit national animal blood bank servicing North America with canine transfusion products and supplies. She also provides consultations to veterinarians and animal breeders in her areas of expertise and lectures widely on these subjects.

IMMUNE DISORDERS

By W. Jean Dodds, DVM

Hemopet
938 Stanford Street
Santa Monica, CA 90403

OVERVIEW OF THE IMMUNE SYSTEM

A normal functioning immune system is essential for maintaining general health and resistance to disease. Immune competence is dependent on two cellular systems that involve lymphocytes. Lymphocytes are cells produced by the body's primary (bone marrow and thymus) and secondary (lymph nodes and spleen) lymphatic tissues. They are descendants of the bone marrow's pool of stem cells and produce a circulating or humoral immune system derived from B-cells (bursa-dependent or bone marrow derived) and a cellular or cell-mediated immune system that derives from T-cells (thymus dependent).

B-CELL IMMUNITY

B-cell immunity includes the circulating antibodies or immunoglobulins such as IgG, IgM, IgA, IgD, and IgE. They present an important defense mechanism against disease in healthy individuals but can become hyperactive or hypoactive in a variety of disease states. Hyperactive, or increased, levels of immunoglobulins can occur in two ways:

- acutely, as a reaction to disease or inflammatory insult (an "acute phase" reaction); or
- chronically, as in autoimmune or immune-mediated diseases, chronic infections, and certain

types of bone marrow and organ cancers.

Hypoactive, or decreased, levels of immunoglobulins can result from rare genetically based immunodeficiency states such as agammaglobulinemia or hypogammaglobulinemia, and from the immune suppression associated with chronic viral, bacterial, or parasitic infections, cancers, aging, malnutrition, drugs, toxins, pregnancy, lactation, and stress.

T-CELL IMMUNITY

T-cell, or cell-mediated, immunity involves T-cells that act as coordinators and effectors of the immune system. Cell-mediated immunity involves the lymph nodes, thymus, spleen, intestine (gut-associated lymphoid tissue), skin, tonsils, and the mucosal secretory immunity conveyed by IgA. The major classes of T-cells are designated as helper, cytotoxic, and suppressor cells. The helper cells "help" coordinate the immune response, whereas the cytotoxic cells comprise the effector network that participates in removing virus-infected cells from the body. The third class of suppressor T-cells is responsible for dampening the immune response when it becomes overactive or out of regulatory control. Finally, cooperation between T- and B-cells is an important component of the

CAT HEALTH ENCYCLOPEDIA

normal humoral and cellular immune response.

Hyperactive cellular immune responses produce autoimmune and other immune-mediated diseases, while hypoactive cell-mediated immunity causes immunosuppression and immune incompetence. The classic examples of this situation occur with retroviral infections such as human AIDS or its feline equivalent, feline immunodeficiency virus (FIV), and feline leukemia virus (FeLV).

Typically, immune-mediated diseases in cats are relatively complex whereby the patient history reveals chronic, relapsing nonspecific clinical signs that are often nonresponsive to standard therapy. Certain breeds or families of cats may be predisposed.

AUTOIMMUNE DISORDERS

The term "autoimmunity" refers to an immune-mediated disease process and literally means the failure to tolerate one's own tissues (i.e., failure of self-tolerance).

In humans and animals, the susceptibility to autoimmune diseases has a genetic basis, but environmental factors also play an important role. Numerous viruses, bacteria, chemicals, and drugs have been implicated as the triggering environmental agents in susceptible individuals. This mechanism operates by molecular mimicry and/or nonspecific inflammation, and the resultant autoimmune diseases reflect the sum of the genetic and environmental factors involved. Autoimmunity is most often mediated by T-cells or their dysfunction.

The four main causative factors of autoimmune disease are: genetic predisposition; hormonal influences, especially of sex hormones; infections, especially of viruses, and stress. The age and sex of the patient can also act as triggers here. Examples of diseases affecting cats include:

- autoimmune, or immune-mediated, hemolytic anemia (AIHA, IMHA) and cold agglutinin disease, which affect the red blood cells, causing anemia and other related signs;
- idiopathic thrombocytopenic purpura (ITP), which is caused by reduced numbers of circulating blood platelets with resultant bleeding into the skin and from mucosal surfaces;
- systemic lupus erythematosus (SLE), a condition in which antibodies are produced against the nuclear protein of cells (antinuclear antibodies, ANA) causing a variety of clinical problems;
- rheumatoid or other immune-mediated polyarthritis of the joints, which can be erosive (positive rheumatoid factor) or nonerosive;
- myasthenia gravis, which results in a generalized weakening of muscles and can also be accompanied by a benign tumor of the thymus gland, known as a thymoma (this same association also occurs in affected human and canine patients); and the immune-mediated skin and eye diseases discussed elsewhere in this volume.

Other conditions believed to have an immune-mediated component in cats include: hyperthyroidism caused by thyroid adenoma or autoimmune thyroiditis (Grave's disease in humans); other endocrine disorders (discussed below); inflammatory bowel disease (IBD); eosinophilic granuloma complex of the skin; ear (aural) hematoma; plasma cell stomatitis and pododermatitis

250

IMMUNE DISORDERS

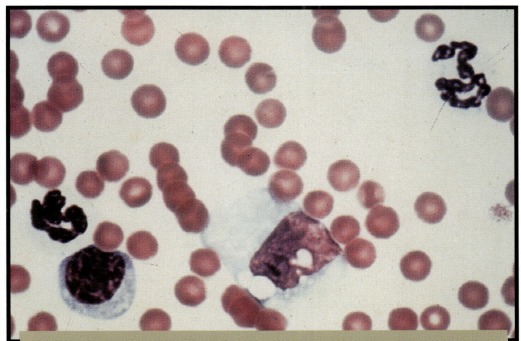

Normal feline blood smear showing the relatively small size of the feline erythrocyte, three neutrophils (multilobulated nuclei), a lymphocyte (large round nucleus), and a monocyte (large cell in lower center).

(footpads); gingivitis, polyarteritis nodosa of blood vessels; and immune-mediated neutropenia of white blood cells.

Treatment of autoimmune diseases usually requires long term use of immunosuppresive drugs (corticosteroids, azathioprine, cyclophosphamide, or cyclosporine), removal of any identifiable contributing agents or factors, and supportive care.

Of the diseases listed above, SLE and the autoimmune endocrine diseases deserve more comment.

SYSTEMIC LUPUS ERYTHEMATOSUS (SLE)

Although relatively rare in the cat, affected cats most commonly have significant skin lesions and elevated ANA levels. The bone marrow (AIHA and/or ITP), joints, and kidney can also be affected.

HYPERTHYROIDISM

Prior to 1979, hyperthyroidism was not recognized as a clinical entity in cats. Today, the frequency of this disease has steadily increased nationally and even internationally, making it the most common feline endocrine disorder. Affected cats are typically geriatric (ten or more years of age), but middle-aged cats are being diagnosed more frequently. Classical signs include progressive weight loss, rapid heart rate (tachycardia), and ravenous appetite. One or both thyroid glands are enlarged, with most cases (70 percent) being bilateral. In rare cases, these nodules are malignant (thyroid adenocarcinoma). Circulatory thyroid hormone levels are usually very high unless some other illness such as liver or kidney disease is present, in which case thyroid levels may be within the upper normal ranges or only slightly elevated. In the latter situation, a T3 suppression test or thyroid scan is performed to confirm the diagnosis. About 30 percent of cats in one study from the United Kingdom had antithyroid antibodies, thereby mimicking human Grave's disease. As retroviruses have been implicated in several human autoimmune conditions and are common pathogens in cats, the potential involvement of retroviruses in feline autoimmune disorders needs to be explored further.

Treatment of feline hyperthyroidism uses three basic approaches:

- medical management with antithyroid drugs such as methimazole or propylthiouracil;
- thyroid destruction with radioactive iodine; and
- bilateral or unilateral thyroidectomy by surgical removal of the hyperplastic or cancerous gland(s).

DIABETES MELLITUS

This is a relatively common disorder of middle-aged and older cats, especially those that are overweight. Obese males are more likely to be affected than females and no breed predisposition has been identified, in contrast to the dog. The cause is currently unknown, but there may be an autoimmune component like that of humans, dogs and mice, with viruses and environmental factors playing some role. Treatment requires rigid dietary control to restrict glucose intake along with daily injections of insulin. Mild cases may respond to dietary management alone.

IMMUNODEFICIENCY DISORDERS

This group of conditions demonstrates impaired host defenses and can be classified as follows:

- defects in the mechanical barriers to invasion by pathogenic organisms or foreign antigenic substances;
- defects in nonspecific host defenses; and
- defects in specific host defenses.

In cats, primary immunodeficiency disorders are relatively rare. They include the Pelger-Huet anomaly, a benign condition demonstrating incomplete segmentation of the nucleus of neutrophils and eosinophils, and the Chediak-Higashi (CH) syndrome seen in blue Persian cats. Affected CH cats have giant, red-colored lysosomal granules in numerous tissues and white blood cells, and the hair and eye color are diluted by large pigment granules. Congenital cataracts, aversion to light (photophobia), platelet dysfunction with resultant bleeding tendency, and impaired neutrophil chemotaxis with increased susceptibility to infections also occur.

Cats more commonly express immunodeficiency disorders as a secondary effect of viral infections from feline leukemia virus (FeLV), feline immunodeficiency virus(FIV), or feline infectious peritonitis (FIP)/enteric coronavirus. In these cases, immunoglobulin and complement deficiencies, and impaired neutrophil, lymphocyte, and macrophage functions may be found.

IMMUNE SYSTEM NEOPLASIA

Lymphomas and Lymphosarcomas

The most common tumors arising from immune system dysfunction in cats typically occur as a consequence of retroviral infections with FeLV or FIV. They can be multicentric, or confined to the skin, thymus, or gastrointestinal tract. Cats develop lymphoid tumors more frequently than any other species and from 1/3

Immune Disorders

Type II hypersensitivity reaction. A kitten showing the icterus of neonatal isoerythrolysis at one week of age (blood type A kitten born to a blood type B queen that was mated with a blood type A tom).

to 1/2 of all feline tumors are hematopoietic in origin. These tumors are often of B-lymphocyte origin. In young adults, lymphomas are usually found in FeLV-infected cats, whereas older cats with lymphomas are most likely to be FIV-infected. The relative risk for developing these tumors is much higher in cats infected with both FeLV and FIV.

Multiple Myeloma and Other Gammopathies

These are more fatal neoplasms of plasma cell origin that produce either solid plasmacytomas or multiple myeloma with significantly increased circulating levels of immunoglobulins (IgG, IgA, or IgM), termed monoclonal gammopathy, or paraproteinemia.

AMYLOIDOSIS

This is a very rare, chronic, progressive disorder of unknown cause that results in deposits of proteinaceous material (amyloid) in various tissues, but especially the liver and kidney. No effective therapy exists, and affected cats are usually given supportive care and immunomodulating drugs.

HYPERSENSITIVITY

Three types of hypersensitivity have been recognized in cats:
- Type I, from allergens that affect the skin, respiratory, or gastrointestinal tracts;
- Type II, as seen with incompatible blood transfusions between cats of blood type B transfused with type A blood, and in neonatal isoerythrolysis (hemolytic disease of kittens born to blood type B queens that were mated with type A toms); and
- Type III, as expressed by

Cat Health Encyclopedia

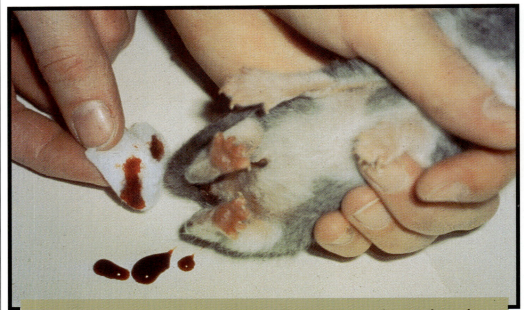

Type II hypersensitivity reaction. Kitten showing pigmenturia at 2 days of age, caused by neonatal isoerythrolysis.

immune complex diseases of the kidney and skin, and the autoimmune skin and joint diseases. In cats, immune complex glomerulonephritis is perhaps the most common and is frequently attributed to deposition of FeLV and FIP within glomerular capillary basement membranes.

IMMUNE DYSFUNCTION

Most of the conditions listed above express a component of immune dysfunction or impairment.

RECOMMENDED READING

Bernard, KA; Schultz, KT: Immune-mediated diseases. *Handbook of Small Animal Practice.* RV Morgan, Ed. Churchill Livingstone, New York, 1992, pp. 835-843.

Day, MJ: Diagnostic assessment of the feline immune system, Parts 1-3. *Feline Practice*, 1996; 24 (2,3 and 4): 24-27, 14-25, 7-12.

Dodds, WJ: Genetically based immune disorders, Parts 1-4. *Vet. Pract. Staff.*, 1992; 4 (1,2,3, and 5): 8-10, 1, 26-31, 35-37, 19-21.

Felsburg, PJ: Immunodeficiency diseases. *Handbook of Small Animal Practice.* RV Morgan, Ed. Churchill Livingstone, New York, 1992, pp. 829-834.

Halliwell, REW; Gorman, NT: *Veterinary Clinical Immunology.* WB Saunders, Philadelphia, 1989, 548 pp.

Tyler, RD; Cowell, RL; Loar, AS: Tests for autoimmune diseases. *Consultations in Feline Internal Medicine.* JR August, Ed. WB Saunders, Philadelphia, 1991, pp. 359-365.

Yamaguchi, RA: Immunoproliferative diseases. *Handbook of Small Animal Practice.* RV Morgan, Ed. Churchill Livingstone, New York, 1992, pp. 843-855.

Immune Disorders

This Japanese Bobtail kitten is the vision of health and vitality; all systems are in good order.

Dr. Bonnie Werner   Dr. Alexander Werner

Dr. Bonnie Werner graduated from the University of California, Davis, School of Veterinary Medicine, followed by an internship at the Coast Pet Clinic in Hermosa Beach, California. She completed a residency in small animal internal medicine at the Louisiana State University, School of Veterinary Medicine. Both Drs. Werner live in Southern California, where they practice together in a referral specialty clinic.

Dr. Alexander Werner graduated from the University of Pennsylvania, School of Veterinary Medicine, followed by an internship at the California Animal Hospital in Los Angeles, California. He completed a residency in veterinary dermatology at the University of California, Davis, School of Veterinary Medicine, where he met his wife Bonnie. Dr. Alexander Werner is a Diplomate of the American College of Veterinary Dermatology.

ENDOCRINE (HORMONAL) DISORDERS

By Alexander H. Werner, VMD, Diplomate, ACVD

and Bonnie E. Werner, DVM

Animal Dermatology Centers
Valley Veterinary Specialty Services
13125 Ventura Boulevard
Studio City, CA 91604

INTRODUCTION

Hormones are chemical messengers that control and regulate the body's metabolism. These messengers are produced by glands distributed throughout the body. The interrelationships and effects that various hormones have on each other and on body systems are complex. Hormones can produce the release of other hormones, can affect specific organs, or can affect the body in general.

Abnormalities are caused by hormonal deficiency, excess, or a lack of the body to respond appropriately to a hormone. Because the function of each hormone differs from another, the specific disease signs seen when problems occur are quite distinct. Unfortunately, the diagnosis of a specific hormonal problems can be complex, requiring specific hormone assays and measured responses to administered medications. As a general rule, hormonal diseases develop in older cats; rarely are animals born with these diseases. The individual syndromes caused by abnormalities of hormones are described below. Examination of your cat, and specific testing by your veterinarian or veterinary internist is required to diagnose these diseases.

HYPERTHYROIDISM

Hyperthyroidism, or having a thyroid hormone (usually T-4) level that is higher than the normal range for a cat, is one of the most common hormonal abnormalities in older cats. The thyroid hormone measurement is performed routinely by veterinary laboratories and is usually part of a general blood profile in geriatric cats.

Almost every case (at least 95 percent) of feline hyperthyroidism is caused by a benign nodule on one or both thyroid glands; only a very small percentage of cases involve a cancerous growth. These nodules can be very small but can be palpable to an experienced veterinarian (normal thyroid glands cannot be detected on a physical examination). In questionable cases, and also as a prelude to treatment, a thyroid scan can be performed at a specially qualified facility.

Hyperthyroidism can affect many body systems. Circulatory system signs may include a fast heart rate, thickened heart walls, arrhythmia, high blood pressure, and heart failure; the skin may be flaky, dry, scaly, or have hair loss; gastrointestinal signs may include diarrhea, vomiting, and a ravenous appetite. The majority of cats lose a

CAT HEALTH ENCYCLOPEDIA

great deal of weight, regardless of whether or not they have gastrointestinal disease. The signs of hyperthyroidism usually worsen over time if not treated appropriately, even to the point of death of the cat.

Therapy includes lowering the level of thyroid hormone produced by the abnormal gland(s) and controlling any secondary diseases due to the hyperthyroidism, such as heart failure. In the past, surgically removing the glands was an option, but this procedure has been replaced by radiotherapy. Radiotherapy utilizes the body's own pathway of thyroid hormone synthesis as a method of destroying the abnormal tissue; it is less invasive than surgery and has many fewer complications. After a thyroid scan, a dose of radioactive iodine is administered. The thyroid gland (and the overactive nodule) scavenges this iodine in order to make thyroid hormone, but in the process the overactive cells are destroyed by the radioactivity. Other organs are not affected because they do not take up the radioactive iodine from the bloodstream, and the animal suffers no ill effects from this small dose. All traces of radioactivity are eliminated in the urine and feces within one or two weeks, at which time the animal can safely return home.

Medical therapy of hyperthyroidism involves oral doses of methimizole (Tapazole®) once or twice daily. This approach is safe in most cats but requires lifelong treatment; the drug does not permanently alter thyroid function. The majority of cats tolerate this drug very well. Some cats will have an unpredictable (idiopathic) reaction to methimizole, which is completely unpredictable. The most common (but still rare) reaction is to stop producing white blood cells or platelets in the bone marrow.

Needless to say, this reaction is very serious, and therefore blood cell counts must be monitored at two and four weeks after initiating treatment, and periodically thereafter. A second, less common, reaction is drug-induced liver inflammation (hepatitis). If liver enzymes are elevated or if the cat appears jaundiced after starting this medication, it must be stopped immediately. Neither reaction is predictable or dose-related; an affected cat can never have drugs of this type again. In these cases, radiotherapy is a good alternative.

Some symptoms of hyperthyroidism, such as ravenous appetite and weight loss, may improve in just a few weeks after treatment. Other symptoms, like heart disease, diarrhea, and skin conditions may take several months to improve. After radiotherapy, 90 percent of cats are no longer hyperthyroid. Very few cats actually become hypothyroid (the thyroid gland makes too little hormone) and require oral thyroid hormone supplementation.

Sometimes, cats with hyperthyroidism also have some degree of kidney dysfunction, as evidenced by high blood urea nitrogen (BUN) or high creatinine levels on their routine blood work. This can be simply a coincidental disease, or it may have to do with hypertension (high blood pressure) or heart disease from the hyperthyroidism. Unfortunately, when a hyperthyroid cat with kidney disease is treated for its thyroid condition, the kidney disease can worsen. One possible theory is that hyperthyroid cats have high kidney blood flow, and this helps the diseased kidney filter more blood than it otherwise could. When the thyroid level, and thus blood flow to

ENDOCRINE (HORMONAL) DISORDERS

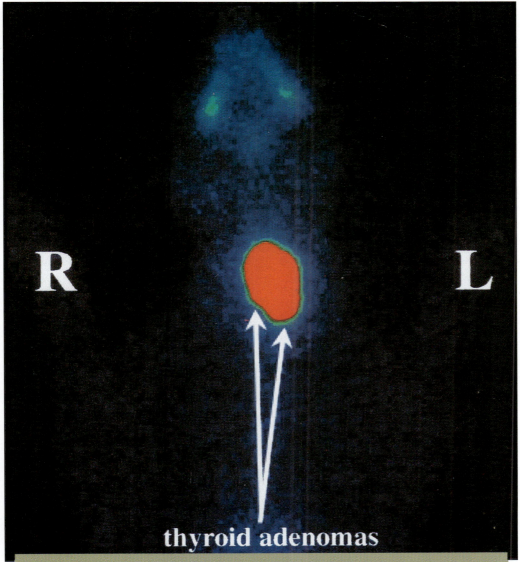

Thyroid scan in a cat with hyperthyroidism. Large thyroid nodules are clearly delineated.

CAT HEALTH ENCYCLOPEDIA

the kidney, normalizes, the true kidney values elevate to the level they would have attained if there were no hyperthyroidism. Whether to treat hyperthyroidism in a cat with kidney disease depends on the degree of kidney dysfunction and on the other symptoms of hyperthyroidism. If heart disease is present, treatment should probably be considered because the heart disease can progress to heart failure, and because heart disease itself can compromise kidney function. Heart disease is diagnosed using chest radiographs ("X-rays"), electrocardiograms (EKGs), and heart ultrasound (echocardiography).

Occasionally, a T-3 suppression test is needed to diagnose hyperthyroidism. This may be necessary in cats that have borderline thyroid hormone levels, or in hyperthyroid cats that are sick from another disease. In these sick hyperthyroid cats, the thyroid hormone (T-4) level is in the normal range because it is temporarily dampened by the other disease. A T-3 suppression test involves giving oral doses of T-3 (another form of thyroid hormone) and then measuring the change in thyroid hormone (T-4) level. Your veterinarian will be able to decide if this test is appropriate for your cat.

HYPOTHYROIDISM

It is unusual for cats to have a lower-than-normal thyroid hormone level. In rare cases, this can be caused by destruction of the thyroid gland by surgery in the neck area, cancer, or severe inflammation. More commonly, a few cats will be hypothyroid following treatment for hyperthyroidism (radiotherapy, surgery, or oral medications). In these cases, thyroid hormone can be given orally; or, in those cats being given methimizole (see hyperthyroidism), the dose is lowered.

Occasionally, thyroid hormone level on a general blood panel will be low. This almost always occurs if the cat is quite ill from another, non-thyroid, disease. In these cases, thyroid supplementation is not warranted, and resolution of the underlying disease usually brings the thyroid level back within normal ranges.

DIABETES MELLITUS

Diabetes mellitus is defined as a persistently high blood sugar (glucose) level with glucose in the urine. Normal blood glucose in a healthy cat is 70-110 mg/dl; however, in a stressed cat (e.g., upset about having blood samples taken), the blood glucose can temporarily increase two or three fold. This problem can be differentiated from diabetes because a stressed non-diabetic cat should not have glucose in the urine.

Signs of diabetes include increased thirst, increased urination, increased appetite, weight loss, weakness (especially in the rear legs), and some greasiness or flakiness of the skin. Diabetic cats are more susceptible to infections and poor healing. There are many other diseases that cause these same signs, so it is very important to have a thorough veterinary examination with diagnostic tests.

Diabetes in cats can be similar to the disease in humans, in that some cats need insulin injections and other cats can be managed with diet, weight loss, and sometimes with oral medications. Differentiating between these two types of diabetes in cats is difficult and may require referral by your veterinarian to a veterinary internist. Most cats need insulin

260

ENDOCRINE (HORMONAL) DISORDERS

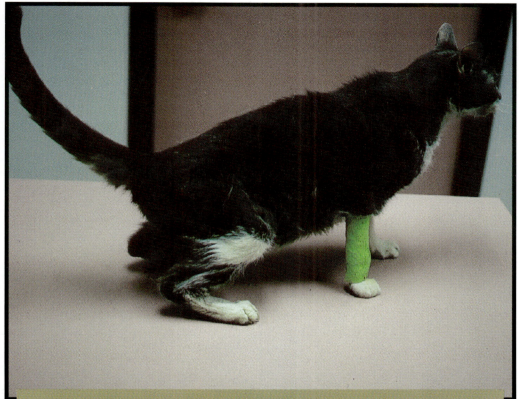

An 11-year-old cat with diabetes mellitus demonstrating weakness of the rear legs by its unusual stance.

injections, but there are some cases in which diet and oral medications may be used initially.

Feline diabetes is caused by many different factors in different animals. Some causes include acute and chronic pancreatitis (inflammation of the pancreas), chronic over-stimulation of the pancreas causing the insulin-producing cells to "wear out," insulin receptors that are not very sensitive (this may be the problem in obese cats), drugs that encourage development of diabetes (especially steroid drugs such as prednisone, methylprednisolone, and megestrol acetate), and high levels of insulin-antagonizing hormones (thyroid hormone, cortisol, adrenaline, glucagon, and growth hormone).

Treatment regimens should include removing any causative or complicating factors. This may involve calming down an inflamed or infected pancreas, eliminating obesity, stopping steroid drugs, and treating any other concurrent hormonal diseases. However, there is no reason to delay insulin treatment while these other steps are being taken. If an underlying cause can be detected and resolved, the insulin injections can be decreased if necessary.

In the past, insulin was scavenged from the pancreas glands of animals; all insulin is now genetically engineered using bacteria to produce large quantities. As human medicine advances, new forms of insulin are produced; and some that were useful

CAT HEALTH ENCYCLOPEDIA

in animals have been discontinued. Almost all of the drug available today is genetically engineered human-origin insulin.

Insulin injections are simple to administer, and your veterinarian will instruct you thoroughly on the proper technique. Most cats are started on low doses of human insulin once daily in the morning. Food is offered prior to the injection in order to ensure that the cat eats; if the meal is not eaten, and insulin is administered, the blood sugar may drop lower than expected during the day. After the first week of insulin therapy, blood glucose should be measured throughout the day (usually every two hours) to determine whether a dosage change is needed and also to determine how long the insulin lasts in any particular animal. This monitoring test is called a blood glucose curve. It can last from 8 to 24 hours depending on the blood sugar level and on how long the insulin lasts.

The only side effect of concern after insulin administration is hypoglycemia, or low blood sugar. This can happen if too much insulin is given, if the cat refuses to eat or vomits its meal, or if the cat's insulin needs have changed. Signs of hypoglycemia include lethargy, weakness, shakiness/tremors, dizziness, incoordination, and, in severe cases, seizures. It is imperative that any of these signs be reported to your veterinarian or local emergency clinic immediately. Do not give any more insulin until the blood sugar can be stabilized. It is also a good idea to feed your cat if you suspect low blood sugar; corn syrup rubbed on the gums and tongue can give prompt, temporary relief if the animal is too lethargic or too weak to eat. Hypoglycemia is easily corrected by repeating a

blood glucose curve to determine a new dose of insulin.

Oral medications are available to help lower the blood glucose level in some cats. In order for these medications to be successful, the animal must have the ability to produce some insulin on its own. The sulfonylurea drugs, especially glipizide, help diabetics by stimulating insulin production in the pancreas and by increasing the sensitivity of tissues to circulating insulin. Side effects include intestinal upset (vomiting, loss of appetite) and hypoglycemia. In many cats, glipizide will not be effective enough in controlling the diabetes; these cats require insulin injections.

Uncontrolled diabetes can be fatal. Although some of the major debilitating symptoms in humans (blindness, kidney failure, poor circulation) are not seen in diabetic animals, serious infections can occur. A severe stage of untreated diabetes is called diabetic ketoacidosis; your veterinarian may also refer to the cat as ketotic. This occurs when the insulin deficiency is severe enough that the body cannot use any carbohydrate as an energy source. Instead, the body begins to metabolize fatty acids (triglycerides) and forms acids and ketones that are toxic at high levels. Symptoms of ketoacidosis may include lethargy, loss of appetite, and vomiting. Diagnosis is made by confirming diabetes, by detecting acidosis (low body pH), and by finding ketones in the urine. Immediate therapy is essential as this condition is life threatening. A less severe variant is early ketosis, in which the only sign is finding ketones in the urine of a diabetic cat. These animals are not usually ill, but they must be started on insulin to prevent progression to ketoacidosis.

ENDOCRINE (HORMONAL) DISORDERS

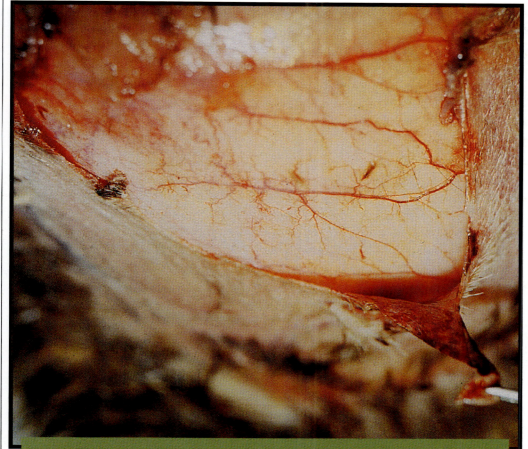

Hyperadrenocorticism in a cat. The skin is excessively thin and has torn away from the body.

Sometimes, a cat that has been stable on a particular dose of insulin will suddenly seem to need a higher dose. This may be discovered because the symptoms of diabetes recur (increased thirst and urination) or because the periodic glucose curves show that the blood sugar no longer decreases in response to the insulin injection. There are many reasons why this may occur. The insulin itself may be expired, damaged by heat or shaking, or administered improperly. Another possibility is that the cat was given a diabetogenic drug. In addition, the cat may have developed a condition that antagonizes the insulin. Such conditions include infections (especially of the urinary tract), other hormonal diseases, liver compromise, obesity, pregnancy, or cancer. A thorough physical examination, radiographs, and blood and urine tests should be performed before adjusting the dose of insulin. It may also be a good idea to switch to a new bottle of insulin prior to adjusting the dose.

It is not uncommon for a cat to suddenly need a lower dose of insulin. This may occur at any time, even months or years after treatment is started. One reason includes the resolution of any underlying or antagonizing factor such as a drug or a hormonal abnormality. In some cases, there is no satisfactory explanation, and the dose of insulin must be reduced or discontinued. It is important to remember that these fluctuations in the need for insulin are usually transient. Cats that do fluctuate may not need insulin for several months or longer, but symptoms of diabetes usually recur eventually and treatment is re-instituted.

Your veterinarian may ask you to periodically check your cat's urine with indicator strips. These strips are used to detect glucose and, sometimes, ketones in the urine. For reasons already stated, you should report any ketones detected to your veterinarian immediately. Most likely, the urine will be positive for glucose at one or more times during the day. This is because the cat's blood sugar usually goes above the threshold level at some point (8-14 hours) after the insulin is given. Persistent glucose in the urine of a treated diabetic cat can mean that the dose of insulin is too low; however, the insulin dose should NEVER be changed based solely on urine glucose measurements because doing so can often result in overdosing. A blood glucose curve should be performed and the dose changed only if necessary. For similar reasons, it is not a good idea to change insulin dosages based on one or two blood glucose measurements because they will not give an accurate picture of the cat's blood sugar levels throughout the day.

Fructosamine levels can be measured periodically in the blood. Higher than normal values indicates that long-term control of diabetes is not as good as it might be. This test is a useful adjunct to blood glucose curves but only indicates trends in diabetes control not daily fluctuations.

Even though your diabetic cat may be generally well-controlled, for one reason or another there may be problems with the appetite or with vomiting. Always check with your veterinarian regarding your individual case; but in general, if your cat seems well but does not eat in the morning, giving half of the usual insulin dose is recommended. If a second meal is not eaten, do not give any more insulin and call your veterinarian immediately as this may indicate a hidden illness. Vomiting food can be a problem if more food is not eaten. Again, if the cat seems well, give half the usual dose of insulin and monitor. If vomiting recurs or if your cat does not want to eat, call your veterinarian.

DIABETES INSIPIDUS

Diabetes insipidus is not related to diabetes mellitus or to blood sugar levels, despite the similarity in names of the diseases. Instead, it is caused by an inability to produce and/or respond to antidiuretic hormone (also known as ADH or vasopressin). ADH is produced in the pituitary gland of the brain and functions to direct the kidneys to retain water in the body. This disease is rare in the cat.

Central diabetes insipidus is the lack of ADH production by the pituitary gland. This condition can be congenital or may occur secondary to any damage to the pituitary gland itself. Secondary (nephrogenic or kidney) diabetes insipidus is the inability of the kidneys to respond to ADH; again this can be congenital or secondary to another disease affecting the kidneys.

Symptoms include markedly increased urine production and compensatory increases in thirst. Some cats may be incontinent due to the remarkable amount of urine produced. Affected animals are

ENDOCRINE (HORMONAL) DISORDERS

ravenous for water and may become aggressive or manic in their search for something to drink; usually they will empty an entire bowl of water without lifting their heads. They should NEVER be left without water, as severe dehydration will quickly occur. Remember, these animals cannot retain any water; it is lost very rapidly through the kidneys.

Diagnosis of diabetes insipidus is made using a modified water deprivation test, but only after other causes of excessive urination and thirst have been eliminated. This is important because other causes are far more common, and water deprivation can be dangerous in some of these cases. Patients must be closely monitored in the hospital during this test in case dehydration begins.

There is no therapy for secondary diabetes insipidus unless an underlying disease such as hyperadrenocorticism can be addressed. It is imperative that water be available at all times. Medication is not effective because the kidneys are unable to respond to ADH.

Primary or central diabetes responds to daily or twice daily administration of synthetic ADH administered using eye drops. The response is dramatic and urine production falls to normal levels.

HYPERPARATHYROIDISM

The parathyroid glands are located in the neck area just above the thyroid glands. They are too small to feel in the normal cat. Their function is to control calcium and phosphorus levels in the body. Parathyroid glands can become overactive in response to dietary calcium deficiency (nutritional secondary hyperparathyroidism), and chronic kidney disease (renal secondary hyperparathyroidism), but in these cases therapy is directed at the underlying disease and not at the parathyroid gland.

Primary hyperparathyroidism (not related to an underlying disease) occurs when the glands become overactive (hyperplasia) or have overactive nodules. Both types are rare in cats.

Diagnosis is made by measuring calcium, phosphorus, and parathyroid hormone levels in the cat. Underlying diseases must be ruled out before a definitive diagnosis can be made. Typically, the calcium level will be high, the phosphorus level will be low, and the parathyroid hormone level will be inappropriately high.

Therapy entails removal of the diseased parathyroid gland. During the surgical procedure, all parathyroid glands should be examined as more than one gland may be implicated. Blood calcium levels should be closely monitored for at least seven days post-operatively.

HYPOPARATHYROIDISM

Hypoparathyroidism, or having a parathyroid hormone level that is too low, is very rare in the cat. It may occur following surgery or radiation to the neck area, or may be a congenital problem. Diagnosis is made by measuring calcium, phosphorus, and parathyroid hormone levels, but in this disease, the calcium is low, the phosphorus is high, and the parathyroid hormone is inappropriately low. Signs include muscle tremors, spasms, and seizure-like episodes if the calcium level is severely low. Treatment includes calcium and/or vitamin D supplementation while carefully monitoring blood calcium levels.

ACROMEGALY

Acromegaly is caused by high levels of growth hormone. It is

CAT HEALTH ENCYCLOPEDIA

uncommon in cats. Usually, the problem is a benign tumor of the pituitary gland that is producing unusually high levels of the hormone. Clinical signs include a large head, thickened tongue, and widely spaced teeth. Typically these cats have large, rather stocky bodies as well. They may also be diabetic, as growth hormone is a diabetogenic hormone.

Diagnosis is made by having typical clinical signs and by measuring growth hormone levels. There are only a few specialty labs or universities that have the capability to perform growth hormone assays. An imaging study of the pituitary gland (MRI or CT scan) may be helpful. Treatment may include irradiation of the pituitary area in select cases. Progesterone, a hormone produced by the ovaries, stimulates growth hormone production; this is why progesterone is important in pregnancy. If progesterone levels are high, then removing the ovaries (spaying) may eliminate the acromegaly.

HYPOADRENOCORTICISM

Hypoadrenocorticism, also known as Addison's disease, is a deficiency of corticosteroids that are normally produced by the adrenal gland. It is extremely rare in the cat but has been seen in animals as young as three months of age. The underlying cause is usually unknown, but any destruction or dysfunction of the adrenal glands could result in this condition.

Corticosteroids are essential for life. A subset of these hormones regulates sodium and potassium levels, which must be maintained within strict ranges. Symptoms of a steroid deficiency include, but are not limited to, loss of appetite, vomiting, diarrhea, arrhythmias, lethargy, shaking, and severe dehydration.

Diagnosis is sometimes difficult because of the nonspecific symptoms but is based on general blood work (sometimes the results mimic kidney failure) and an adrenal function test called an ACTH stimulation test. If the adrenal glands do not respond adequately during this test, the diagnosis is confirmed.

Treatment of hypoadrenocorticism involves administration of the deficient adrenal hormones. It is important to remember that there are literally hundreds of diseases that are more common than Addison's disease that cause the same symptoms. Because Addison's is easily treated with one or more types of oral medications, it should be tested for in appropriate cases.

HYPERADRENOCORTICISM

Hyperadrenocorticism, sometimes referred to as Cushing's disease or Cushing's syndrome, occurs when corticosteroids (especially cortisol) are made in excessive amounts by the adrenal gland or administered orally or by injection. Cats are more resistant than dogs to developing signs of hyperadrenocorticism from steroid drug administration, but this still remains the most common cause of this disease.

In naturally occurring cases, the hormonal abnormality can come from one of two sites. In pituitary-dependent hyperadrenocorticism, a small, usually benign tumor of the pituitary gland produces excessive ACTH. This hormone is the chemical trigger that tells the adrenal gland to produce corticosteroids; with excessive amounts of the trigger hormone, excessive amounts of the product (steroids) are produced. In adrenal hyperadrenocorticism, one or both adrenal glands act independently of the ACTH signal and produce excessive amounts of

266

ENDOCRINE (HORMONAL) DISORDERS

corticosteroids. The affected adrenal gland may have a benign nodule that is responsible for the hormone production, or may have a cancerous tumor, but the difference is sometimes only detectable by removal and biopsy of the gland.

Signs of hyperadrenocorticism include symmetrical hair loss, thin fragile skin, increased appetite, increased susceptibility to infection, and increased urination and thirst. All cases thus far published have also been diabetic secondary to the high levels of diabetogenic (diabetes-causing) cortisone circulating in these cats.

Diagnosis can be difficult but usually involves tests including a general blood panel, urinalysis, urine culture, ACTH stimulation test, dexamethasone suppression test, abdominal radiographs, and abdominal ultrasound. Most cases are detected in diabetic cats that have been difficult to control with insulin.

Treatment in dogs is usually with oral medication, however this is not effective in cats. Therefore, in cats with pituitary Cushing's, surgically removing both adrenal glands is the best option. In those cases in which one adrenal gland has a benign or malignant tumor, removing only the offending gland is necessary. Since a normal amount of corticosteroids is required for life, cats that have both adrenal glands removed will need oral steroid supplementation throughout their lives. Treatment of drug-induced Cushing's simply necessitates discontinuation of the medication.

RECOMMENDED READING
Ackerman, L, Ed. *Owner's Guide to Cat Health.* TFH Publications, Neptune City, New Jersey, 1996.

Lowell Ackerman, DVM, PhD

Dr. Lowell Ackerman is a nutritional consultant in addition to being board-certified in the field of veterinary dermatology. To date, he is the author of thirty-four books and over 150 articles and book chapters dealing with pet health care and has lectured extensively on these subjects on an international schedule. Dr. Ackerman is a member of the American Academy of Veterinary Nutrition, the American Institute of Nutrition, the American Animal Hospital Association, the American Veterinary Medical Association, and the American Veterinary Society of Animal Behavior.

NURTITION-RELATED PROBLEMS

By Lowell Ackerman, DVM, PhD
Director, Department of Clinical Resources

Mesa Veterinary Hospital, Ltd.
858 N. Country Club Drive
Mesa AZ 85201

INTRODUCTION

There have been major strides made in the last few decades in the field of feline nutrition. Manufacturers have come to the realization that cats are not small dogs and that their nutritional needs differ considerably. However, there is still much room for advancement. This chapter deals exclusively with nutrition in relation to disease, but there is an excellent chapter on basic nutrition written by Dr. Rebecca Remillard in *Owner's Guide to Cat Health*. It is a valuable resource for all cat owners.

BASIC NUTRITION

Relative to dogs, cats represent more of a challenge when it comes to formulating acceptable diets. Cats not only require more protein (on a weight basis) than dogs but they have higher specific requirements for a variety of different nutrients, including taurine, arginine, arachidonic acid, niacin, pyridoxine (vitamin B_6), and vitamin A. Cats cannot make adequate quantities of these nutrients so require that they be supplied in a properly formulated diet. Many of these nutrients are found in animals only, so cats cannot survive on strict vegetarian diets.

PET FOOD CERTIFICATION

The American Association of Feed Control Officials (AAFCO) created a Feline Nutrition Expert Subcommittee to establish nutrient profiles for cat foods. Based upon published research data, two nutrient profiles were established: one for adults and the other for both reproducing (pregnant and lactating) and growing cats. Growing kittens have the same dietary requirements as reproducing (pregnant and lactating) queens. These profiles can be found in the 1994 AAFCO Official Publication and are considered the official guidelines, just as the Recommended Daily Allowances (RDA) are the official guidelines for people. The recommendation is to feed only those diets that have been certified by feeding trials to be sufficient for specific life stages. For example, the AAFCO statement, located close to the guaranteed analysis, should read "(Product Name) provides complete and balanced nutrition for kittens as substantiated by feeding tests performed in accordance with AAFCO procedure."

In Canada, pet food certification is carried on by a nutrition subcommittee of the Canadian Veterinary Medical Association. Independent feeding trials and laboratory analysis are required as part of the certification process.

The reason for certification processes is that it is extremely difficult to evaluate a diet simply by

CAT HEALTH ENCYCLOPEDIA

looking at the ingredient list or the percentages printed on the label. There are 43 nutrients considered essential in the cat, and they must be formulated so that certain nutrients are provided as proper ratios of others, in a meal that is both palatable and digestible. This might sound simple enough, but the nutrients need to be provided in such a way that when the cat has finished eating a set amount of food, it has met its requirements for all nutrients.

Although neither AAFCO nor CVMA certification can be relied on entirely to specify that a particular diet is nutritious, it is the best option currently available. Unless you are qualified to assess the nutritional composition of diets yourself, don't take the chance by feeding non-certified diets. Any manufacturer that intends on being around for the long haul will want to see its product meet or exceed the minimal requirements for certification.

Life Stage Requirements

Kittens will begin to eat solid food around three weeks of age, which makes weaning at six to ten weeks a gradual, easy process. Kittens should be fed a food designed for growth and proven so through AAFCO or CVMA growth feeding studies. In general, the growing kitten stage is considered from birth to six months of age. Food should be offered several times each day (free choice is recommended by some), along with fresh clean water for the first year of life. The choice of food is a matter of personal preference. Dry foods are more economical while canned foods are more palatable. Using treats, snacks, and gourmet cat foods only creates finicky cats and contributes to obesity. Semi-moist cat foods are not recommended by this author because of the high sugar content in these products.

At six months of age to one year of age, the young adult cat should be fed a maintenance diet that is moderate in both fiber and fat. Most cats can be fed free choice; that is, food can be put out and the pet will eat the appropriate amount to maintain optimum body weight and condition. The proper amount of food for any cat is that which maintains optimal body weight and condition. However, beware of obesity: It is now quite common in cats. Do not compensate by feeding "lite" diets unless recommended by your veterinarian. High-fiber diets are not recommended for long-term feeding unless absolutely necessary.

Pregnant queens should be offered clean fresh water and free choice adult food the first five to six weeks of gestation and then offered a kitten food the last three to four weeks. In addition, supplementing with some canned diet with a fat concentration of about 20 percent may be beneficial toward the end of gestation. Nutritional requirements increase gradually over the nine weeks of gestation, but good nutrition is most important in the last few weeks of pregnancy. During the first six weeks of lactation, the adult cat should be continued on a kitten food. Inadequate milk production is the most common cause of death in kittens, and most often decreased milk production is related to undernutrition of the queen. Feeding a high-fat growth food will meet her nutritional requirements for nursing. Avoid acidified diets because they have been shown to decrease bone density in the developing kittens and may also affect tooth development.

Opposite: **Nursing queens need high-fat growth food to ensure adequate milk production.**

Nutrition-Related Problems

Weighing neonatal kittens two or three times weekly is an excellent way to monitor the queen's milk production and kitten growth. A steady growth rate and normal stool production are good measures of healthy nursing kittens. A queen should be at optimum body weight and condition at breeding, and ideally she should return to that weight and condition at time of weaning.

When cats reach old age, they benefit from diets designed for seniors. Most indoor cats are considered senior when they reach eight to ten years of age. For the outdoor cat, senior may be considered at five to seven years of age. Geriatric-type diets are often richer in potassium and vitamins, contain more fiber, and have reduced levels of protein and fat. High-protein diets may contribute to kidney disease in the older cat; currently there are many research projects aimed at confirming or refuting this hypothesis. Until more is known, high-protein diets are not recommended for the senior cat.

HEALTH ISSUES AND NUTRITION

There are many ways in which diet and health can be linked, and it is only recently that these have begun to be properly explored. It now appears that some problems may have a nutritional basis, while others are responsive to nutritional manipulation. We'll explore many ways in which diet can impact on health in this chapter. However, this is an area of nutrition that is also quite controversial. Whereas some of the issues have been fully explored and proven, others are more speculation than fact at this time.

Obesity

Obesity is the most common nutritional disorder in North America, outnumbering all deficiency syndromes combined. Clearly, obese pets don't live as long as those of normal weight. They suffer more from heart problems, they fatigue easily, and are at increased risk of developing diabetes mellitus. Obese pets also have a decreased resistance to infection and are more prone to

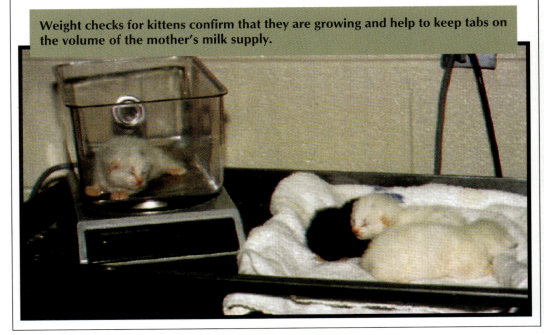

Weight checks for kittens confirm that they are growing and help to keep tabs on the volume of the mother's milk supply.

Keeping cats in excellent condition at their proper weights lengthens life expectancy and reduces veterinary expenses.

CAT HEALTH ENCYCLOPEDIA

anesthetic complications should surgery ever be necessary. A link with many other clinical problems has been suggested but has yet to be clearly demonstrated. Today, more than ever, pets are being "killed with kindness" as their owners allow them to become obese.

Cats are described as obese when they weigh 20 percent more than their ideal body weight. Obesity becomes more common as pets get older. Females are more prone to obesity than are males, and neutered pets are more likely to become obese than are intact pets. This isn't because neutering causes obesity. Rather, neutered animals have lower metabolic rates and require fewer calories than intact animals. If you don't cut back on their calories once they are neutered, obesity becomes more likely. Unfortunately, people that are obese themselves are much more likely to have obese pets, attesting to the significance of environmental factors at promoting obesity. Genetic factors are also contributory, but, although genetics plays a role, clearly the most important factors leading to obesity are providing pets with excess calories and inadequate physical activity. Obesity is rarely seen in wild animals; it is the household pet, rarely exercised, confined to the home and fed a high-fat diet that is most prone to obesity. When one examines the most common brands of cat food, it can be seen that they are often very high in protein, salt, flavorings, and fat (and semi-moist foods are also high in sugars) and contribute to obesity. Feeding gourmet diets only compounds the problem because they are loaded with calories.

Diagnosis of obesity in cats (as well as other household pets, including dogs and other small mammals) is usually not difficult; but if proof is needed, it can be done by comparing the weight with compiled charts or approximated by visual inspection (fat covering of ribs). What is often more critical is to determine the reason for the obesity. In most cases, the owners would rather believe that the pet has a medical problem rather than consider that they are the most important cause. All obese pets should have a thorough physical examination and laboratory profile, but most cases are due to owner feeding practices.

Obesity can be dealt with intelligently and effectively if pet owners are willing to pay attention to the facts. Owners must be committed to helping their pets lose weight and realize that the pet will be healthier and happier if they make the effort. All weight-reduction programs should be performed under the supervision of a veterinarian to reduce the risk of complications from the obesity or the weight loss.

Owners often feel guilty when they start their pet on a weight-loss program. They must be committed to providing a reasonable amount of calories and stopping there. This is often easier said than done. Some cats refuse to be dieted and can make their owner's life miserable. It is not unheard of that cats may have behavioral problems while they are dieting. The cat that is an enthusiastic eater may not appreciate efforts to restrict his caloric intake. Behavioral manifestations of this outrage may include vocalizations, urine spraying, and even aggression. In these cases, owners often elect to have an overweight cat rather than a behavioral basket case.

Together with your veterinarian, determine your cat's ideal weight (often 8-12 pounds for most cats) so that the caloric needs can be

NUTRITION-RELATED PROBLEMS

The litter pan should never be placed so close to the food dish that your kitten gets miffed.

calculated, based on your cat's age, activity level, and health status. Then, select a diet that is moderate in protein and not excessive in fat. Muscle can be lost during dieting, so protein restriction is not desirable. Feed enough of the diet to meet the caloric needs determined. If your cat is obese and needs to lose weight first, it is wise to feed less than required, creating a calorie deficit. This can be done slowly or quickly depending on you and your cat. It takes a deficit of 3500 calories (kcal) to equal one pound of weight loss. Thus, if your cat is fed 50 kcal per day less than its daily requirement, it will take 10 weeks for your cat to lose one pound. In addition, if you currently feed your cat free choice, consider splitting the total meal into three or four servings and only offering them periodically throughout the day for 10-15 minutes at a time. Snacks also contribute to caloric intake, but cat owners are more likely to dispute that their cat gets treats, compared to dog owners. Asking whether they ever give their cat milk, ice cream, cheese, chicken, or stew often prods the memory of many cat owners; these foods count as snacks and need to be counted in the caloric intake.

When dieting your pet, also be aware that things other than food can be just as fulfilling for the pet, including petting, playing, exercising, and other social rewards. When owners are having trouble sticking to diet recommendations, high-fiber "lite" diets may be prescribed. However, the fiber content can interfere with the absorption of other nutrients and is not recommended for long-term use.

Never attempt to starve a cat into weight loss. They are susceptible to a potentially fatal condition known as hepatic lipidosis. Hepatic lipidosis occurs in obese cats that haven't eaten for several days. It might be related to very-low-density lipoprotein (VLDL) mobilization, but this has not been definitively proven. Even the link to obesity is controversial. What is known is that fat accumulates in the liver and becomes mobilized during periods of anorexia. The results can be fatal, but initially cats just appear depressed. Usually it occurs when these cats get sick and lose their appetites. Cats are very susceptible to oxidative stress, and it has been theorized that "free radical" damage is responsible for most of the ill effects. Relative deficiencies of arginine and carnitine have also been hypothesized as causative factors. Treatment is often heroic, and recovery rates may be as low as 10-20 percent. The best chance for success is early intervention with tube feeding (with a high-protein, high-calorie canned cat food), which may increase recovery rates to approximately 50 percent. Adjunctive nutritional therapy with fish oils, carnitine, arginine, inositol, thiamin, and zinc have been advocated. Force-feeding, tempting with baby food, or using appetite stimulants are rarely helpful. In most cases, cats die.

Feline Lower Urinary Tract Disease (FLUTD)

Feline lower urinary tract disease (FLUTD), also known as feline urologic syndrome (FUS), is not uncommon in the cat. The disorder is covered in more detail in the chapter on urinary tract conditions. What will be discussed here is the role of nutrition in contributing to the condition.

Information on FLUTD/FUS has been confusing and sometimes conflicting. Preliminary studies have shown that the cats at increased risk are usually male, neutered, eat dry cat food, drink less than average, and don't exercise much. Long-haired pedigree cats tend to be at higher risk and Siamese-type cats appear to be at lower risk.

The association of FLUTD with urinary tract "stones" (urolithiasis) has spawned many theories linking the condition with dietary components. Struvite "stones" are most common in the cat, followed by calcium oxalate. These were thought to contribute to urinary tract infection and blockage of the lower urinary tract. Early studies seemed to confirm that a high "ash content" could cause crystals in the urine and consequent blockage. Later studies seemed to suggest that magnesium was the culprit. However, there were many facets of these studies that didn't fit well with reality, including the levels and chemical formulation of magnesium found in commercial cat foods and the lack of ammonium in the "stones" (ammonium is a component of struvite). Maybe "ash" isn't as important as originally thought.

Current research seems to suggest that magnesium has some role but is not a major cause of FLUTD. In fact, cats that "block" don't tend to have higher levels of magnesium in their urine than other cats. At this time, the main cause seems to relate to the pH of the urine and the water intake of the cat. When the pH of the urine becomes alkaline, crystals can form in the urine, and the cat is then more prone to blockage. Thus, adding large amounts of magnesium chloride (which contains magnesium but results in an acidic urine pH) doesn't promote FLUTD while magnesium oxide (which causes an alkaline urine pH) does. The studies, therefore, seem to suggest that diet formulations that result in maintaining a urine pH below 6.5 are effective at preventing FLUTD, regardless of ash content. In some cases, veterinarians recommend that acidifiers such as methionine or ammonium chloride be added to diets

NUTRITION-RELATED PROBLEMS

fed to FLUTD-prone cats. These should be used cautiously since they can be toxic and can result in potassium depletion. Acidifying the diet can result in metabolic acidosis, the long-term consequences of which have not yet been sufficiently explored. Increasing water intake, to help dilute the urine, may also be beneficial.

Some researchers have proposed that cases of FLUTD in cats may vary in presentation because they have different underlying causes. For example, some cats may be prone to inflammatory diseases of the bladder (such as interstitial cystitis or viral/bacterial infections), and this may cause protein, mucus, and blood to be passed in the urine. These cats may have no history of crystals or stones in their urine. Other cats may have a history of passing crystals but no real inflammatory component. Finally, some cats may have both conditions, and this results in the formation of urethral plugs that can cause blockages in the urinary tract, especially in males.

What dietary recommendations can be made? At this time, there are more questions than answers, but each case should be evaluated individually. All cats should have constant access to fresh clean water. It is not advisable to put all cats on acidifying diets because this can result in other harmful conditions. Mildly acidifying diets that keep the urine pH around 6.5 are probably advisable in high-risk patients. However, crystals, plugs, and stones should be sent for evaluation to a reference laboratory. One consequence of dietary intervention for struvite urolithiasis is the increased prevalence of oxalate uroliths as the prevalence of struvite uroliths decreases.

Date codes are desirable on pet foods. Even quality pet foods deteriorate over time.

Taurine

Taurine is an essential nutrient for cats, whereas it is non-essential for most other species. Cats can make some taurine, but not enough to meet their nutritional needs. Thus, they must be supplied with adequate amounts of taurine in their diet. This seems simple enough, but it is sobering to think that pet food manufacturers did not consider taurine an essential nutrient in cats until 1975. Cats that receive inadequate amounts of taurine can develop eye problems (central retinal degeneration), heart disease (dilated cardiomyopathy), and reproductive problems. Recent research even suggests that taurine depletion affects immune function and hearing. It is not known how many cats suffered from these problems in years past, when cat food diets were not fortified with taurine. Similarly, dog food is not fortified with taurine, and cats fed dog foods are also susceptible to taurine insufficiency.

In the past decade, most pet food manufacturers have fortified their diets with extra taurine. However,

CAT HEALTH ENCYCLOPEDIA

there are still many unknowns, including the fact that some diets with adequate amounts of taurine can still result in deficiencies. It is also known that cats fed a commercial canned diet have twice the taurine requirement as those fed a commercial dry diet.

Taurine deficiency should now be considered rare, but tests can be run if an insufficiency is suspected. Blood levels of taurine can help establish a diagnosis, and, in the early stages, treatment with taurine can effectively restore health. Which blood tests should be run? Recent studies have shown that taurine depletion shows up more rapidly in plasma than in whole blood, and therefore plasma taurine levels will give the best indication of a recent dietary taurine insufficiency. Whole blood levels give a better indication of long-term taurine status.

If taurine deficiency is diagnosed early, it can be effectively treated with taurine supplementation. This should be done under the supervision of a veterinarian, and periodic blood tests should be taken to monitor effectiveness of the treatment. Studies have shown that the source of dietary protein can also affect taurine bioavailability. Always follow up with blood tests to make sure the dietary therapy is having its desired effect.

Potassium

Potassium is an essential electrolyte that can become depleted in association with several ailments, including kidney disease, diabetes mellitus, liver disease, and lower urinary tract disease. It is also worth mentioning that acidifying diets commonly used to treat lower urinary tract problems in cats can actually promote potassium loss in a cat that is prone to potassium depletion.

Since the potassium requirement of cats is related to the protein content of the food, not just the level of potassium in the diet is critical: higher protein diets require more dietary potassium. Studies suggest that normal adult cats fed diets marginally sufficient in potassium can still develop potassium depletion and kidney disease if those diets are high in protein content or are acidifying.

Affected cats may be lethargic, weak, or listless, but most show no signs until the depletion is life-threatening. Muscle weakness is one of the most prominent clinical signs. Other manifestations include weight loss, poor haircoat, behavior problems (e.g., vocalization, altered behavior, excessive salivation), and anemia. If the potassium depletion is not corrected at this time, muscle dysfunction may progress to paralysis and death. In one study, one-third of all ill cats had hypokalemia (potassium depletion).

Diagnosis of potassium depletion would seem to be straightforward but isn't in all cases. Potassium levels in the blood are low in most, but not all, cases. Urine levels of potassium are often elevated (fractional excretion above 4 percent), which is not what one would normally expect in a deficiency condition. If the depletion is a result of kidney disease, blood tests of renal function, such as creatinine levels, are often abnormal. In cats with muscle weakness (hypokalemic myopathy), creatine kinase levels are often elevated. Other occasional findings are increased blood levels of cholesterol and chloride.

If diagnosed correctly and early enough, hypokalemia can be effectively treated. Although some cats will definitely benefit from fluid therapy, this can also have an

278

NUTRITION-RELATED PROBLEMS

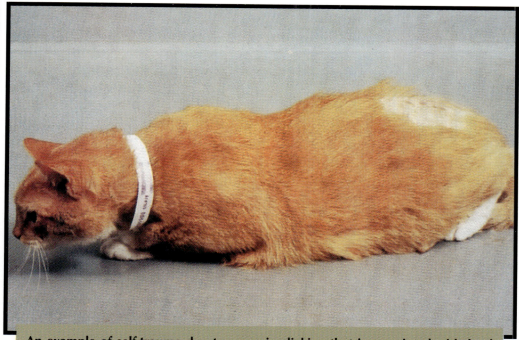

An example of self-trauma due to excessive licking that is associated with food allergies. Notice the hair loss over the rump of this cat.

adverse effect on blood potassium levels. Therefore, unless fluids are needed for treating other conditions (e.g., kidney disease), most veterinarians begin treatment with oral potassium supplements such as potassium gluconate.

Careful attention to diet and potassium supplementation of hospitalized cats are often recommended by veterinarians. Also, those recovering from potassium depletion are often kept on long-term potassium supplementation. Palatable potassium powder supplements are now available.

Iodine

Iodine content of cat foods is now also under scrutiny. It has been theorized that the high incidence of hyperthyroidism (excessive thyroid hormone production) seen in cats may be partially due to high levels of iodine in the diet. Hyperthyroid cats are often overactive and many suffer with heart problems. There is currently no solid link between dietary iodine and hyperthyroidism, but studies are underway.

DIET AND BEHAVIOR

It is not outlandish to assume that some cats might have behavioral problems related to their diet. After all, many cats eat high-calorie, high-protein, high-fat commercial diets, liberally laced with additives, flavorings, preservatives, and other processing enhancements. All of these features have become suspect by different investigators pursuing different aspects of behavior problems. This discipline is still in its infancy and not immune to controversy. However, let's take a look at some of the ways that nutrition and behavior may be linked.

Most veterinary behavior specialists have considered the role of

CAT HEALTH ENCYCLOPEDIA

protein in behavior problems. Both the quantity of protein and its quality and extent of processing have recently become suspect. High-meat diets can result in lowered levels of the neurotransmitter serotonin in the brain, which can make some animals more aggressive. Conversely, high carbohydrate diets result in higher levels of serotonin in the brain. Can feeding high-carbohydrate diets be an effective treatment for some forms of aggression? This concept is being explored, but clear-cut answers are not yet available. Recent studies in dogs have demonstrated a link between fear-induced aggression and dietary protein; such studies have not yet been done in cats. The topic of feline aggression is so complicated that it is difficult to make any generalizations.

Casomorphine is derived from the digestion of casein and exorphines from the digestion of gluten. Together with hormones, hormone-like substances, and pheromones naturally present in many cat foods, all have been shown, scientifically, to alter normal animal behavior. Casomorphine and the exorphines, which would be provided by milk proteins and cereals respectively, can trigger behaviors in cats not unlike giving them morphine or other opioids. The overall effect of casomorphine and exorphines from commercial cat foods has not been adequately investigated.

Another concern is that some problems are more common in cats fed dry food than those fed a canned ration. Individuals often blame moisture content, but there is probably a better explanation. Most dry cat foods are heavily preserved with antioxidants so they can last on store shelves for months without going rancid. Since canned diets are heat sterilized before packaging,

additional use of preservatives is not needed. Some of the preservatives getting increased scrutiny are ethoxyquin, butylated hydroxyanisole (BHA), and butylated hydroxytoluene (BHT). Only recently has any scientific research been directed in this area.

Testing the Theory

It's not enough to make claims and hypotheses about health care issues. There must be a way of proving or refuting such theories for individual animals. This is possible to a limited extent, as long as certain provisions are accepted. The hypothesis of high-protein or preservative-rich diets contributing to behavior problems can be easily tested by feeding a high-quality but low-protein diet for as little as seven to ten days. This time frame is not long enough to uncover adverse food reactions (up to 12 weeks would be necessary) but is sufficient for judging the impact of protein and preservatives on pet behavior. The diets must be homemade protein sources that are suitable. Such diets include boiled chicken, lamb, or rabbit combined with boiled white rice or mashed potatoes. This also limits problems that might occur from high-cereal diets (e.g., exorphines), milk proteins (e.g., casomorphine), and preservatives. The meal should be mixed as one part meat to three parts carbohydrate and fed in the same amount as the pet's regular diet. Only fresh water should be provided during the trial. No supplements, treats, or snacks should be given. This diet is not nutritionally balanced, but that should make little difference for the seven to ten days in which the trial is being conducted. However, it is critical that cats not be maintained on these diets, certainly not for longer than ten days.

NUTRITION-RELATED PROBLEMS

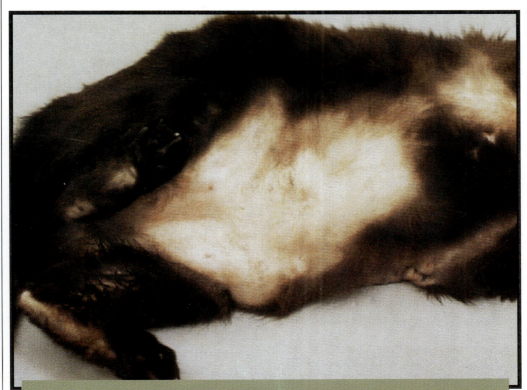

This cat did not exhibit licking in the presence of its owners, but was secretively licking its abdomen. These cats are sometimes referred to as "closet" lickers.

If there is a response to the diet trial, it is advisable to follow up on the process by challenging the pet with specific potential offenders. The first test would be to increase the protein component of the diet (50:50) to see if there is a behavioral change. If so, this helps confirm the suspicion that it is the protein component that is contributory. Adding commercial foods or treats with specific preservatives is the best way of determining the role of food additives in the problem.

What to Do About It

For animals that respond to a homemade low-protein, preservative-free diet, there are many options available. Regular use of a homemade diet should be discouraged unless a completely balanced ration can be formulated. Low-protein diets are commercially available and are the most convenient option. Remember that low protein should not mean low quality. Look for diets with high-quality protein in moderate amounts and an easily-digested carbohydrate source. Cereal-based diets tend to have a lot of exorphines, which may contribute to behavioral problems. Start with canned diets, which tend to have few, if any, preservatives. Dry foods have the most preservatives, and semi-moist foods have too high a sugar content. If the conditions worsen when the pet is put on a commercial ration, there are likely more problems than just protein content to consider. Home-delivered, preservative-free, home-prepared, and frozen pet foods are all options with which the veterinarian should be familiar.

CAT HEALTH ENCYCLOPEDIA

For cats with reactions to preservatives, canned foods are an option, and there are also preservative-free diets commercially available. Both of these are usually acceptable, but current regulations make it almost impossible to be assured that there are actually no preservatives in preservative-free diets. Manufacturers need to list on the label only those preservatives that they add during ration preparation. However, there is no guarantee that the manufacturer did not purchase the raw ingredients already preserved. If a pet responds well to the homemade diet, and challenge feeding fails to uncover a culprit, consider additives as a likely candidate. When commercial diets cannot be used, homemade diets remain a final option. At this point, it is worth having a diet recipe prepared by a nutritionist to ensure that nutritional requirements will be met. Alternatively, computer software is available (e.g., Small Animal Nutritionist: N-squared computing) so that custom diets can be formulated by veterinary practitioners.

FOOD ALLERGY/INTOLERANCE

It is not unusual for pets to react adversely when fed certain foods. Occasionally, diet-related problems can affect systems other than the skin and digestive tract, and behavioral problems have been reported. Some animals can even develop diet-related seizure disorders or urinary tract problems.

When it comes to allergy and intolerance to foods, individual ingredients are always to blame. Pets are likely allergic to specific ingredients in a diet, such as beef, chicken, soy, fish, milk, corn, wheat, etc. In addition, some commercial foods contain high amounts of certain factors (e.g., histamine,

saurine) that can cause problems all by themselves in susceptible individuals. These are referred to as food intolerances. For example, some human baby foods fed to cats have been implicated in causing Heinz body anemia, presumably because they contain onion powder, which is toxic to cats. However, many owners tend to blame brand names, preservatives, or a suspicious ingredient listed on the package. Many others fail to get the correct diagnosis because they refuse to believe that the problem they are seeing is diet related. They may be hesitant because they have been feeding the same diet for years without problems, or they feel that the problems are not worsened at feeding time. It's time to lose all of your prejudices about what you think about adverse food reactions and learn some basic truths.

How Do I Know if My Pet Has a Food Allergy/Intolerance?

It is almost impossible to confirm the diagnosis by switching from one brand of commercial food to another. Since most of the ingredients in pet foods are similar, merely changing brands or types of food is helpful only if you are lucky enough to change to a food that does not include the problem-causing ingredient.

A homemade elimination (hypoallergenic) diet is the best way to confirm a diagnosis. It must consist of ingredients to which the pet has never been exposed. This will diagnose an adverse food reaction in most cases, but it will not differentiate between allergy and intolerance. A single protein source (a protein source to which the pet has not been exposed) can be combined with a carbohydrate source such as rice or potatoes and the entire diet fed for 6-12 weeks. The meat can be

NUTRITION-RELATED PROBLEMS

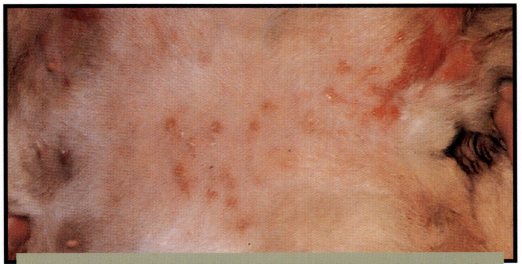

A close-up of the damaged, hairless skin of a "closet" licker. Further investigation must be done to reveal the cause of this compulsion.

boiled, broiled, baked or microwaved (but not fried), and the rice should be boiled prior to serving. They are mixed at one part meat to one part rice or potatoes. The mixed ingredients should be fed in the same total volume as the pet's normal diet. During the trial, hypoallergenic foods and fresh, preferably distilled, water must be fed exclusive of all else. Absolutely nothing else must be fed, including treats, snacks, vitamins, chew toys, and even flavored medications. Access must also be denied to the food and feces of other cats and dogs in the household.

If there is substantial improvement while on the diet, further investigation is warranted. If there is no improvement, diet is not a significant part of the problem, and the diet can be discontinued. The intention is not to feed these diets indefinitely. They are not nutritionally balanced for long-term feeding. They are only meant to be fed for the 6-12 weeks necessary to determine if food is implicated in the problem. If the condition improves while on the diet, challenge feeding will be needed to determine which ingredient(s) is (are) causing the problem.

By now, most pet owners have heard about blood tests that claim to be able to diagnose food allergies. Surely this is a lot easier than having to prepare and feed a homemade diet for many weeks. That would be true if the blood tests actually lived up to their claims. Unfortunately, these tests can be very misleading since the results are often quite inaccurate, being reliable perhaps only 10 percent of the time. This is not surprising because not all diet-related problems are allergic (these tests don't identify intolerance); those that are allergic are not necessarily caused by the antibodies measured in the blood tests. Therefore, blood tests should NEVER replace a hypoallergenic food trial as a screening test. More often than not, the results supplied will not prove helpful and can be misleading.

What Do I Do if My Pet Does React to His Diet?

If there is improvement by the end of the elimination diet trial, further

CAT HEALTH ENCYCLOPEDIA

investigation is warranted. Challenge feeding with individual ingredients should allow you to determine the dietary cause of the problem. This is accomplished by adding one new ingredient each week to the hypoallergenic diet. You then create a list of ingredients that your pet can tolerate and those that it can't. The recommendation then is to feed a balanced commercial ration that does not include the problematic ingredients. Rarely is it necessary for pets to remain on specialty (e.g., lamb-based) diets, nor is it advisable. Commercial hypoallergenic diets are suitable for owners that don't want to determine the specific cause of their pet's problem. These diets are effective about 80 percent of the time, for pets with documented adverse food reactions.

DIET AND DENTAL PROBLEMS

Diet doesn't directly cause plaque and tartar buildup, but it can play a role. Cats that eat only hard or dry food tend to have cleaner teeth than those that eat soft or canned food. Tartar must be periodically removed by veterinarians, and home care involving brushing and cleaning is highly recommended.

Cats develop resorptive lesions on their teeth, and the incidence has greatly increased over the past 20 years. These resorptive lesions are similar to cavities in people, except that they are not associated with caries, as human cavities are. It is very tempting to speculate that this increased incidence is a result of modern feeding practices, perhaps a direct effect of acidifying diets. However, at this time, speculation is all there is. Although dental problems (and decreased bone density) in kittens are more common when pregnant queens are fed acidifying diets, a cause-and-effect relationship

has not been documented for feline resorptive lesions.

SUMMARY

Cats are not small dogs, and they have their own specific nutritional requirements. This chapter reviews life-stage requirements for cats and specific disorders that might be diet related.

ADDITIONAL READING

Ackerman, L: Adverse reactions to foods. *Journal of Veterinary Allergy and Clinical Immunology*, 1993; 1(1)18-22.

Ackerman, L; Lansberg, G; Hunthausen, W (Eds.): *Cat Behavior and Training...Veterinary Advice for Owners*. TFH Publications, Neptune City, New Jersey, 1996.

Atkins, CE; Gallo, AM; Kurzman, ID; Cowen, P: Risk factors, clinical signs, and survival in cats with a clinical diagnosis of idiopathic hypertrophic cardiomyopathy: 74 cases (1985-1989). *Journal of the American Veterinary Medical Association*. 1992; 201(4): 613-618.

Ballarini, G: Animal psychodietetics. *Journal of Small Animal Practice*. 1990; 31(10): 523-532.

Biourge, V: Sequential findings in cats with hepatic lipidosis. *Feline Practice*. 1993; 21(1): 25-28.

Blackshaw, JK: Management of orally based problems and aggression in cats. *Aust. Vet t.* 1991; 21: 122-124.

Buffingtion, CA; Chew, DJ; BiBartola, SP: Lower urinary tract disease in cats: Is diet still a cause? *Journal of the American Veterinary Medical Association*. 1994; 205(11): 1524-1527.

Butterwick, RF; Wills, JM; Sloth, C; Markwell: A study of obese cats on a calorie-controlled weight-

NUTRITION-RELATED PROBLEMS

reduction program. *Vet Rec.* 1994; 134(15): 372-377.

Fernstrom, JD: Dietary amino acids and brain function. *Journal of the American Dietetic Association.* 1994; 94(1)71-77.

Glass, EN; Odle, J; Baker, DH: Urinary taurine excretion as a function of taurine intake in adult cats. *Journal of Nutrition.* 1992; 122: 1135-1142.

Grevel, V; Opitz, M; Steeb, C; Skrodzki, M: Myopathy due to potassium depletion in 8 cats and one dog. *Berliner und Munchener Tierrarztliche Wochenschrift.* 1993; 106(1): 20-26.

Halliwell, REW: Comparative aspects of food intolerance. *Veterinary Medicine.* 1992; September: 893-899.

Hickman, MA; Bruss, ML; Morris, JG; Rogers, QR: Dietary protein source (soybean vs. casein) and taurine status affect kinetics of the enterohepatic circulation of taurocholic acid in cats. *Journal of Nutrition.* 1992; 122: 1019-1028.

Hubbard, BS; Vulgamott, JC: Feline hepatic lipidosis. *Compendium on Continuing Education for the Practicing Veterinarian.* 1992; 14(4): 459-464.

Kallfelz, FA; Dzanis, DA: Overnutrition: An epidemic problem in pet animal practice? *Vet. Clin. N. Am.* 1989; 19(3): 433-445.

Remillard, R: Feline nutrition. Ackerman, L (Ed): *Owner's Guide to Cat Health.* TFH Publications, Neptune City, New Jersey, 1996.

Schoenthaler, SJ; Moody, JM; Pankow, LD: Applied nutrition and behavior. *J. Appl. Nutr.*, 1991; 43(1): 31-39.

Wallin, MS; Rissanen, AM: Food and mood: Relationship between food, serotonin, and affective disorders. *Acta Psychiatrica Scandinavica.* 1994; 89 (Suppl. 377): 36-40.

A healthy, well-fed kitten is a master of the fine art of play. With relatively little effort, your cat will remain healthy and playful throughout its long life.

Dr. Bonnie Werner   Dr. Alexander Werner

Dr. Bonnie Werner graduated from the University of California, Davis, School of Veterinary Medicine, followed by an internship at the Coast Pet Clinic in Hermosa Beach, California. She completed a residency in small animal internal medicine at the Louisiana State University, School of Veterinary Medicine. Both Drs. Werner live in Southern California, where they practice together in a referral specialty clinic.

Dr. Alexander Werner graduated from the University of Pennsylvania, School of Veterinary Medicine, followed by an internship at the California Animal Hospital in Los Angeles, California. He completed a residency in veterinary dermatology at the University of California, Davis, School of Veterinary Medicine, where he met his wife Bonnie. Dr. Alexander Werner is a Diplomate of the American College of Veterinary Dermatology.

FELINE EMERGENCIES

By Alexander H. Werner, VMD, Diplomate, ACVD

and Bonnie E. Werner, DVM

Valley Veterinary Specialty Services
13125 Ventura Boulevard
Studio City, CA 91604

INTRODUCTION

Cats, by their very nature, are mischievous. Perhaps this is a major reason for our tremendous attachment to them. Unfortunately, their insatiable curiosity often leads them into danger. Cats are also very independent. While this can make caring for them on a daily basis easier, it can also make detecting problems more difficult. Cats can, and often prefer to, hide the initial signs of illness. This is especially problematic because, being a small animal with a rapid metabolism, a sick cat often lacks the stamina to tolerate delays in diagnosis and treatment. In general, any change in the behavior of a cat warrants close observation and possibly veterinary examination. Simple alterations in urinating habits, bowel movements, activity, playfulness, breathing pattern, appetite, or drinking habits can be symptoms of serious disease.

The following pages briefly discuss several of the more common reasons why cats are presented to animal emergency rooms. This is, by necessity, an incomplete list. Thus, whenever there is any question about your cat's health, it is always best to have the animal examined by a veterinarian. It is much more comforting (to both cat owner and veterinarian) to have an examination reveal nothing significant than to wait until disease has progressed to become serious or even life-threatening.

FELINE UROLOGIC SYNDROME (FUS)

Feline urologic syndrome (FUS) is a phrase applied to a group of diseases involving the urinary tract of cats. FUS is most often seen as alterations in a cat's normal urinary habits, such as increased urinating frequency, urinating outside the litter box, or the presence of blood in urine, and is an emergent reason for a veterinary visit. In many cases of urinary trouble, male cats can develop a urethral blockage and may be unable to urinate, leading to a painful death within hours. The urethra, the tube through which urine travels from the bladder to the outside, is wider in the female than the male, resulting in less severe disease in females. However, any cat exhibiting difficulties in urinating, straining to urinate, bloody or discolored urine, urinating in unusual locations, or increased visits to the litter box, should be examined by a veterinarian as soon as possible.

Although FUS most likely has several causes, the most common cause appears to be diet related. Cat urine contains ammonia (hence the strong odor) as well as minerals such

CAT HEALTH ENCYCLOPEDIA

as magnesium and phosphorus. If the pH of the urine is low (acidic), these minerals stay dissolved, and are passed during urination. However, if the urine pH fluctuates into the high (alkaline) range, mineral crystals can form (magnesium ammonium phosphate, or "struvite"), much like sugar falling to the bottom of a glass of iced tea when too much is added. These crystals irritate the sensitive lining of the bladder, and bleeding may occur. In males, these crystals, blood, and mucus from the bladder can combine to form plugs that obstruct urination. Cats with FUS tend to urinate frequently, often with blood, but rarely do they have true bacterial *infections*. Rather, they have bladder *inflammation* without the presence of bacteria and therefore almost never require antibiotics.

When symptoms of FUS are observed in a male cat, he may be in any stage of the disease. If his bladder is inflamed or sore, he will strain to urinate and may cry out in pain with even a drop of urine in his bladder. Obstructed cats will act similarly, although they will pass little or no urine. The distinction between bladder inflammation and urethral obstruction must be left to someone skilled in abdominal palpation. The inflamed bladder will be small and often difficult to feel, while the obstructed bladder will be large and the cat will resent the bladder being touched. Often, an owner can be instructed in the proper technique of abdominal palpation, but regardless, any cat exhibiting signs of FUS should be examined by a veterinarian. Female cats, and male cats that are definitely not obstructed, can wait until normal hospital hours to be examined. Male cats that are obstructed, or any cat in which there is a question regarding its ability to urinate, are veterinary

emergencies and must be examined immediately. Waiting until the next hospital day, even if only a matter of hours, can mean the difference between life and death in an obstructed cat.

The obstructed cat quickly becomes ill due to the accumulation of compounds such as urea, creatinine, phosphorus, and potassium, which are normally excreted in the urine. Within hours, the levels of these compounds in the bloodstream can become life-threatening. Typical signs of toxicity include lethargy, hiding, pain when lifted, and loss of appetite. Vomiting occurs rarely. Cats with a history of FUS should be closely monitored for recurrence of obstruction and should preferably become indoor cats.

Treatment of non-obstructed cats mainly involves changes in diet. Treatment of the obstructed cat is more involved, and requires a hospital stay, often of several days. During hospitalization, the cat will be sedated to permit the placement of a urethral catheter, which is a small plastic tube used to open up the urethra. The bladder can then be emptied and flushed with sterile solutions to remove any remaining crystals or blood. An intravenous catheter will also be placed to provide a large amount of fluids to keep up with the kidneys as they flush out the accumulated toxins. The kidneys produce a large volume of urine after an obstruction, thereby increasing the need for intravenous fluid support (subcutaneous fluids, or fluids under the skin, may be sufficient in less ill cats). In addition to catheters and fluids, the severely ill cat may require heart monitoring and assistance with nourishment until normal attitude and appetite return. Unfortunately, many male cats will re-obstruct, usually within

Feline Emergencies

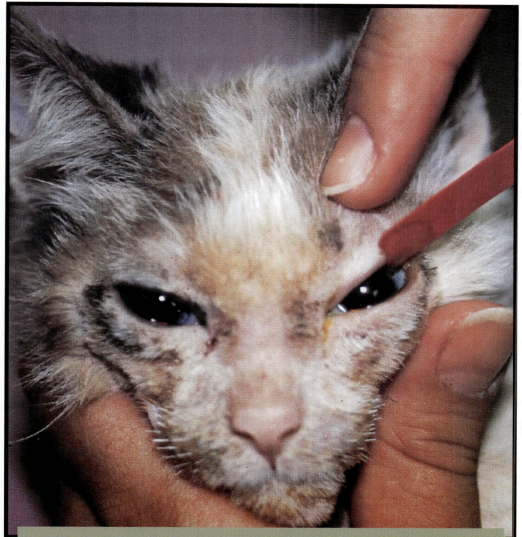

Application of fluoroscein stain to determine if the cornea has been damaged. Corneal wounds stain bright green after application.

days of the primary episode. This reobstruction may be due to the reaccumulation of debris within the bladder, or due to urethral inflammation caused by FUS as well as by urethral catheterization.

Preventing episodes of FUS on a long-term basis requires maintaining a low (acidic) urine pH. This is best accomplished by exclusively feeding an acidifying diet, and prescription diets that can accomplish this are available from your veterinarian. Even a few meals of an alkalinizing (high pH) diet can precipitate FUS symptoms.

Regardless of the exclusive feeding of a special diet, some male cats persistently obstruct. In these cats, a perineal urethrostomy (PU) surgery may be required. This surgical procedure opens the urethra between the bladder and penis, where it is wider, and thereby reduces the

CAT HEALTH ENCYCLOPEDIA

chances of obstruction during future episodes of FUS. The PU surgery is difficult, and it is strongly recommended that it be performed only by veterinarians experienced in this procedure. Possible surgical complications include urinary incontinence (dribbling), stricturing (narrowing) of the remaining urethra, and recurrent bladder infections. However, these uncommon complications are still preferable to frequent episodes of life-threatening urethral obstruction.

OCULAR EMERGENCIES

Any evidence of eye discomfort should be immediately investigated by a veterinarian. A damaged eye can quickly become permanently scarred, or may even rupture. The first signs of eye disease are often swollen or closed eyelids, a discharge on the cat's fur near the inside corner of the eye(s), or a reddened or blood-congested sclera (the white of the eye). There are several possible causes for a reddened eye. In the order of severity and urgency, these include conjunctivitis (inflamed membranes), keratitis (inflamed cornea, the clear surface of the eye), uveitis (inflamed contents of the eye), and glaucoma (increased pressure within the eye).

Conjunctivitis, or the inflammation of the outer membranes of the eye and eyelid, is usually caused by viruses, *Chlamydia* or other bacteria, or foreign objects lodged in the eye. The inner eyelids and third eyelid (the membrane at the inside corner of the eye) may look swollen, red, and angry, and a clear, mucousy, or bloody discharge may develop. Because the condition is usually painful, the cat may hold the eye partially or completely closed, or may blink excessively (eyelid spasms).

Keratitis, or corneal inflammation, is usually caused by infection

(viruses or bacteria), dry eyes (inadequate tear production), wounds (especially scratches or chemical burns), and foreign objects lodged in the eye. This is more serious because the cornea is very thin and easily ulcerated or punctured. Excessive amounts of pigmentation on the cornea may develop during healing and can obstruct vision. Cats with keratitis are very painful and frequently exhibit eyelid spasms. The pupil of the eye may also become very small due to spasms of the iris (the colored part of the eye).

Uveitis, or inflammation of the inside of the eye, is an extremely serious condition. Uveitis can result from infections or bleeding within the eye (frequently from trauma), or from the immune system depositing antibodies within the eye (similar to the deposition of antibodies within the joints of some people with arthritis). The eyesight of cats with uveitis is at great risk; therefore immediate veterinary examination is critical.

Glaucoma is one of the most serious ocular emergencies. Luckily, it is less common in cats than in dogs or people. Sudden onset of glaucoma causes a painful, possibly enlarged, cloudy, or reddened eye. The slow onset of glaucoma is often less painful but is no less serious. Both loss of vision, as well as loss of the eye, are possible with glaucoma.

The diagnosis of the precise cause of any ocular discomfort requires a veterinary examination. Specific tests are often required, such as fluorescein staining (to detect corneal damage), retinal examination with an ophthalmoscope, and eye pressure measurement. The immediate examination of any cat with eye discomfort is paramount if vision is to be preserved. The treatment given to various eye conditions depends upon

FELINE EMERGENCIES

the exact cause and resultant symptoms of the disease.

TOXICITIES

Most of us are familiar with household compounds that are potentially hazardous to humans (especially children), but there are several compounds that are specifically toxic to cats. Cats may exhibit the characteristic signs of a specific poison, or the non-specific and vague signs associated with many toxins. General signs of toxicity in the cat include lethargy, inappetance, vomiting, and diarrhea.

Many common drugs that are used routinely by humans are severely toxic to cats, even in the reduced dosages administered safely to dogs. Cats are particularly sensitive to analgesic (pain) medications such as aspirin and acetaminophen. The feline liver is unable to metabolize these compounds as quickly as the human liver does, and therefore toxic forms of the drugs build up in the feline body. Aspirin can be given to cats in very small dosages, but only every 2 to 3 days because of its slow metabolism, and only when specifically prescribed by a veterinarian. Acetaminophen should never, under any circumstance or in any dosage, be given to cats as it can be quickly fatal. Both aspirin and acetaminophen produce liver and kidney disease; acetaminophen also causes anemia, brown or muddy gum color, and sometimes facial swelling. Treatment of the toxicity produced by these compounds includes lengthy hospitalization and long-term monitoring for permanent organ damage.

Another common source of potential poisoning for cats involves flea control products. Commonly used flea control products contain pyrethrin-derived compounds,

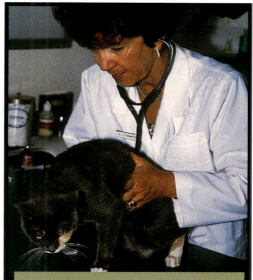

Buffered aspirin is the only non-steroidal anti-inflammatory agent that can be safely used in cats. Check with your veterinarian before use to make sure it can be safely given to your cat.

organophosphates, or carbamates. Only pyrethrin-derived compounds are safe to use on cats; organophosphates, including chlorpyrifos, are labeled for use on dogs only. Signs of organophosphate toxicity include salivation, excessive tear production, urination, diarrhea, and very constricted (small) pupils. A veterinarian might also note such signs as a slow heart rate and fluid accumulation in the lungs. Because early treatment may completely reverse the toxicity of organophosphates, prompt veterinary examination is essential after a potential exposure. Even waiting 24 hours after exposure can produce severe and irreversible harm. If you suspect organophosphate exposure (or know that the wrong flea control product was used), you should rinse the cat off with a mild soap and cool water, and then proceed immediately to your veterinary office or animal emergency clinic. If the cat is already

CAT HEALTH ENCYCLOPEDIA

seriously ill, do not take the time to rinse it off; the veterinary staff will do that after the crisis has passed.

Pyrethrin-derived flea control products are safe to use on cats. In extremely sensitive individuals, or when improperly diluted solutions (i.e. too concentrated) are applied to a cat, toxicity may develop. Pyrethrin toxicity produces signs such as muscle tremors and seizures. If pyrethrin toxicity is suspected or known, the cat should be quickly bathed in a mild soap and cool water, and brought in for immediate examination. Regardless of the slight potential for toxicity with these compounds, the proper use of flea control products represents a safe alternative, rather than risking diseases and possible severe blood loss that can occur from a heavy flea infestation.

Citrus-smelling flea control products usually contain the insecticide d-limonene. Many groomers and cat owners believe this chemical to be safer than pyrethrins; however, recent studies in humans and specific experiences with cats has led this author to strongly recommend that d-limonene products not be used in cats. Adverse reactions to d-limonene in cats have included severe redness and itching of the skin, respiratory difficulty, vomiting, inflamed and damaged skin and, rarely, death.

Ethylene glycol, the active ingredient in automobile antifreeze, is fatal when ingested by any animal or human. As little as a few tongue laps can cause death by either neurologic (brain) toxicity, or by irreversible kidney failure within a few days. The only way to ensure that a cat will not come into contact with antifreeze is to keep it inside at all times. Unfortunately, antifreeze is attractive to cats and dogs, and they will drink it if they encounter it. Only immediate hospitalization (within four to six hours after exposure) and specific treatment offers any hope of survival. Recently, a new company has begun marketing a relatively non-toxic antifreeze that contains propylene glycol as its main ingredient. Although propylene glycol, when ingested in large amounts, can cause anemia in cats, the severity of this toxin is markedly less than that of the quickly fatal ethylene glycol. It is the hope of the veterinary community that this new product, called Sierra® will replace standard antifreeze, and thus eliminate a large number of feline deaths each year.

Part of the natural curiosity of cats is to sample household plants. Unfortunately, many household plants are poisonous to cats. A complete listing of toxic plants is beyond the scope of this book, but a few common examples include oleander and foxglove (including snapdragons), which produce heart disease; dumb cane, which causes numbness and tingling of the mouth and throat, and philodendrons and ficus trees, which contain oxalates and most commonly cause intestinal upset. If you have a question of whether or not your cat has ingested a poisonous plant, you should consult a poison control center in your area.

RESPIRATORY EMERGENCIES

Any abnormality involving breathing should result in an immediate visit to your veterinarian or an animal emergency facility. Common signs of breathing difficulty include open mouth breathing, panting (similar in appearance to panting in dogs, but a very unusual action in normal cats), increased breathing rate (more than one breath every two to three seconds), increased

292

breathing effort, especially with exaggerated movement of the rib cage, or loud breathing sounds.

Diseases associated with signs of respiratory distress in the cat include feline allergic bronchitis (asthma), pneumonia (lung infection), heart disease, fluid or air within the chest cavity that restricts lung movement, airway obstruction (choking), and upper respiratory (nose and trachea) infections. Differentiating between these and other less common conditions always requires a veterinary examination, often requires chest radiographs (X-rays), and sometimes requires special tests to detect heart abnormalities (such as EKG and heart ultrasound). Any breathing pattern that is not normal for a particular cat necessitates an emergency veterinary visit.

The most common respiratory disease in cats is the upper respiratory infection (URI) syndrome. This syndrome is usually caused by viruses (rhinopneumonitis, calicivirus) or *Chlamydia*; the yearly combination vaccine helps prevent or ameliorate the disease. Signs of URI include sneezing, head shaking, clear or mucousy discharge from the eyes and/or nose, congested breathing, fever, and inappetance. The condition is very similar to a common cold in humans and is just as contagious (from cat to cat). The disease course can be mild or severe and usually lasts from three to ten days, with more severe infections lasting longer. Treatment is symptomatic, as there are no effective anti-viral drugs to cure the common cold, although antibiotics are usually administered when severe signs indicate a possible secondary bacterial infection. Symptomatic treatment includes rest, a warm quiet environment, and tempting the cat's appetite, which may involve hand feeding or watering.

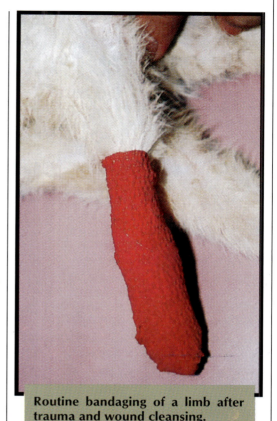

Routine bandaging of a limb after trauma and wound cleansing.

A veterinarian may hospitalize cats for fluid therapy if they are dehydrated because they will not drink, tube feeding for anorexic cats, antibiotics for secondary bacterial infections, decongestants for severe congestion (and to improve the sense of smell, which is very important to the feline appetite), or oxygen therapy (for only the most extreme cases). The dangers of dehydration cannot be overemphasized; kittens are the most susceptible to URI, and their extremely small body size leaves little reserve when they refuse to drink. Even 24 hours of decreased water intake may require your veterinarian to administer fluids.

Preventing URI is as difficult as preventing the common cold. Common sense should prevail, and such measures as reducing exposure

CAT HEALTH ENCYCLOPEDIA

to other sick cats and keeping upper respiratory vaccines current are important.

CARDIAC (HEART) DISEASE

In general, the manifestations of cardiac disease are very similar to the signs of respiratory emergencies (distress, weakness, labored breathing, coughing, pale or blue gums). It can be difficult to differentiate the two problems unless more specific signs are present.

Cardiac abnormalities can be divided into three broad categories:

- diseases of the heart itself (heart muscle and valves);
- rhythm or rate disturbances (fast, slow, or irregular); and,
- combinations of these categories.

Sometimes, a very fast or slow heart rate is obvious by watching the cat's chest wall (just behind the elbow), or by placing your fingers over the chest so that the heartbeat can be felt. Any abnormal heart rate is an urgent problem until a cause can be discovered.

One unusual sign that is associated with heart disease in cats is sudden, painful paralysis of the rear legs (one or both legs). These cats are unable to use their rear legs and may drag them. In addition, the rear legs may be painful and cold to the touch. Specific heart diseases cause these symptoms by producing blood clots that travel directly from the heart and lodge in the area where the arteries separate leading to the rear legs. The veterinarian can diagnosis this syndrome by the lack of pulses in the rear legs and an abnormal heart rate or rhythm, or ultrasound findings.

Cats do not suffer "heart attacks" in the classical sense because they do not develop artery-clogging plaques (a common cause of heart attacks in humans). However, cardiac emergencies can appear suddenly even though the heart disease has been progressing for a long time. Regular veterinary examination and auscultation (listening) to the heart can catch heart and other diseases early. An examination, most often at the time of yearly vaccinations, is the best preventative available.

TRAUMA

Injuries and accidents are almost exclusively problems of cats that venture outdoors. The most common incidents involve encounters with automobiles or with larger or stronger animals (dogs and cats, particularly). A notable exception involves felines who reside in multilevel dwellings, such as high-rise apartments or condominiums, and who venture outdoors through an open upper-story window. The pattern of injuries that these cats suffer after falling has been termed "high rise syndrome" and involves injuries to the chest (lungs, heart, and diaphragm), forelimb fractures, and broken jaws. These varied injuries cause swollen faces, inability to walk, and moderate to severe respiratory compromise. In general, cats are amazing in their ability to survive large falls and walk away unharmed from smaller falls.

Cats suffering blunt-force trauma from automobiles can have injuries ranging from cuts, bruises, and frayed toenails, to serious fractures (especially of the pelvis and legs) and less apparent internal organ injuries (lungs, heart, diaphragm, spleen, liver, kidneys, bladder, and brain). Although the cat may seem initially to be uninjured after being hit by a car,

Chest radiograph of a cat with an enlarged heart. The heart is the round object in the center of the chest and should normally be less than 2/3 of the width of the chest.

294

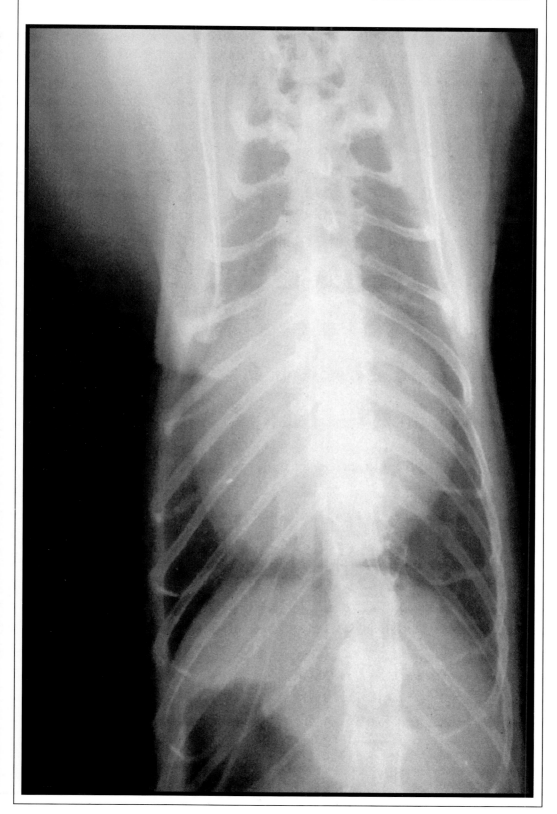

CAT HEALTH ENCYCLOPEDIA

pelvic fractures and internal damage may have occurred, and diagnosis may require radiographs, blood tests, or even just observation by a veterinarian. Any cat who is out of doors is at risk of automobile injury and should be examined at the first sign of pain, lameness, lethargy, or unexplained absence.

In general, the treatment of cats experiencing blunt-force trauma is directed towards stabilizing the animal and diagnosing potentially dangerous or hidden injuries. Although repairing a broken leg may seem the most important treatment to the cat owner, the emergency room veterinarian is often most concerned with being sure that signs of shock and internal organ damage are assessed and stabilized. Most often, stabilization, or shock, therapy includes placing an intravenous catheter, administering large volumes of intravenous fluids, giving medications aimed at reversing or preventing further signs of circulatory or respiratory instability, and protecting open wounds from further damage. The first 24 to 48 hours after any trauma are the most critical. This is the time period during which most signs, both initial and delayed, will manifest. Therefore, any cat with signs indicating possible trauma should be hospitalized and observed for at least one day. In severe cases, the veterinarian may choose to monitor particular body systems for signs of delayed shock. The heart is particularly sensitive to trauma and may beat in an irregular and dangerous manner, necessitating continuous monitoring with an electrocardiogram (ECG). In addition, damage to internal organs can take time to manifest itself. For example, a small tear in the bladder may permit some urination while allowing urine to leak into the body, producing both

toxicity and severe abdominal inflammation. Also, a small rupture in a blood vessel or organ can seep blood slowly. Only after several hours may either of these injuries be detected.

Encounters with larger animals (sharp-force trauma) can produce signs of shock similar to blunt-force trauma. However, the additional damage caused by sharp teeth can be significant. The least severe and most common sharp-force trauma is the cat bite. Any cat bite, to human, dog, or cat, should be considered a medical emergency. A cat carries many bacteria in its mouth; thus most cat bites will result in infection and, without proper treatment, abscessation. A large, painful, fluid-filled, rapidly enlarging swelling, particularly on the head, forelegs, or tail of an outdoor cat is likely to be a developing abscess. Left untreated, these abscesses will burst and ooze a large quantity of pus. Eventually, many will heal without treatment, but with tremendous scarring. Prior to bursting, and during healing, the cat will often have a fever (over 102.5°F) and feel generally ill (malaise). Abscesses are best treated by having a veterinarian open and drain them and by administering antibiotics until healing is complete. Most abscesses can be avoided if the bite wound is immediately cleaned and antibiotics are administered within eight hours of the injury.

Dog bites can be much more serious. The sharp teeth of a dog can penetrate through the skin and into any of a cat's organs with tremendous crushing force. Additionally, most dogs will shake their victims around while biting down. This shaking causes both bodily trauma from the swinging force and ripping of the tissues between the teeth. Often the skin

Feline Emergencies

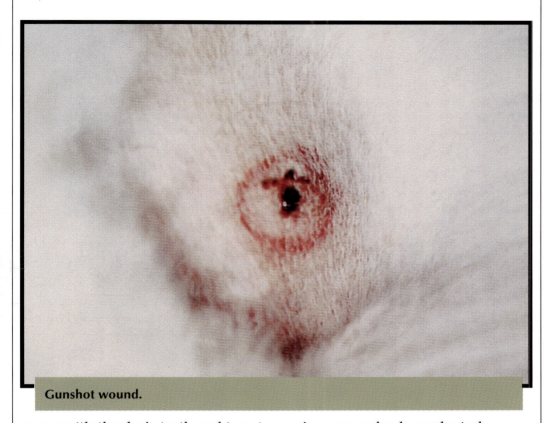

Gunshot wound.

moves with the dog's teeth and is not lacerated, so that the only obvious wounds a cat owner may notice are small puncture marks. However, the damage beneath these punctures, from the excessive shaking, tearing, and crushing can be life-threatening. Punctures of lungs, intestines, kidneys, bladders, livers, and spinal cords are possible and common. Treatment of these injured cats includes the same methods of stabilization as for automobile trauma, as well as specific treatment aimed at stabilizing the particular wounds suffered from the bites. Immediate surgical exploration is indicated in every case of sharp-force injury to the abdomen or chest. A torn intestinal segment will bleed or leak intestinal contents continuously until repaired. Left uncorrected, severe infection (peritonitis) and blood loss, leading to death, will result.

As a general rule, exclusively indoor cats live much longer and healthier lives than do outdoor cats. Besides the constant dangers of trauma and attacks that outdoor cats face, they also are at risk for contracting infectious diseases such as the feline leukemia virus and the feline immunodeficiency virus. It is also fairly obvious that the only way to lose your cat is to have it go outside. All outdoor cats should be given collars with identification tags in case they are injured or lost. It is a good idea to have your veterinarian's telephone number on the tags as well as your home and work numbers. However, during any type of trauma, or even by simply climbing a tree, an outdoor cat may lose its collar and identification tags. New systems of animal identification, using electronic implants, have been developed to allow identification of animals by a simple scanning device, much like an airport metal detector. Several of these devices are currently available, and with further refinement and availability, should make it easier to locate a lost pet. It is best if more than one method of identification is used in case of a lost collar or if a scanning device is not available. Having the cat tattooed with a registration, license, social security number, or telephone number is another alternative. Telephone numbers are the least preferred unless you subscribe to one of the new permanent telephone numbers that will always be current. The tattooed area (usually an inner thigh) must be kept shaved so that the numbers will be highly visible.

SEIZURES

True, generalized seizures are relatively rare in cats because the incidence of epilepsy is much lower in cats than it is in dogs. Seizures can occur from many causes, such as toxins, low blood sugar, low blood calcium, severe liver disease, severe kidney disease, head trauma, brain infections, and tumors (benign or malignant).

If your cat has a seizure, you may see uncontrolled movement of one or all limbs, marked stiffness, breath-holding, vocalizations, urination, bowel movements, vomiting, and partial or complete loss of consciousness. Most seizures last from 5 to 60 seconds but can be longer. During a seizure, do not attempt to restrain your cat unless it will otherwise severely injure itself (e.g. fall from a high place). Simply remove objects that might harm the animal from the immediate environment and bring the cat to your veterinarian as soon as the seizure stops. Seizures lasting less than three minutes are not

intrinsically dangerous, but the underlying cause may be serious. If the episode lasts for more than three minutes, bring the animal to the hospital immediately, if you can do so without injuring yourself. Long and continuous seizures result in dangerous elevations of body temperature from extreme muscle activity. Also, if respiratory compromise occurs during a seizure, death from asphyxia can result. A veterinarian will be able to administer medications to stop a prolonged seizure and then begin the diagnostics necessary to determine the cause. Episodes of disorientation, depression, or abnormal, or "spacey," behavior can precede and/or follow a seizure. These episodes are normal and can last from just a few minutes to more than two hours. Aside from the need to control active, prolonged seizing, it is very important that the cause of the seizure be found (or obvious reasons ruled out) so that treatment and prevention can be initiated.

GASTROINTESTINAL EMERGENCIES

Gastrointestinal (GI) disturbances in cats are arguably the most common reasons that cat owners seek veterinary care. Just as in humans, GI diseases can range from mild to severe, and can result from literally hundreds of causes. Gastrointestinal manifestations usually take the form of either vomiting, diarrhea, or inappetance; disease of the intestinal tract itself, or of other non-intestinal organs, can produce very similar signs. The cat seems somewhat unique in that GI signs seem to accompany almost any disease state, physical or emotional. Emergency veterinary care should be sought if vomiting is of sudden onset and is associated with inappetance, fever, abdominal pain, or lethargy, or

Feline Emergencies

Chemical or thermal burn on the side of a cat.

if it contains blood. Diarrhea is seldom an emergency by itself unless it is profuse, associated with pain or bleeding, or causes dehydration (an especially common condition in kittens). Inappetance alone often represents disease in other organ systems, and the degree of urgency depends on the underlying disease and whether dehydration ensues.

True GI emergencies include ingestion of foreign objects, especially strings or other linear objects; twisting or telescoping of the intestinal loops; acute pancreatitis (a very difficult diagnosis in the cat), which involves inflammation of the pancreas, an organ that sits next to the stomach and upper small intestine; puncture wounds or other penetrating injuries; and acute, severe inflammation of the intestines such as seen with parvovirus infection (termed panleukopenia or "kitty distemper", although it is not a distemper virus). Differentiating between these diseases involves a thorough veterinary examination, radiographs (X-rays), one or more blood tests ("blood panels"), and sometimes exploratory surgery. Although an owner's initial reaction is often to avoid surgery at all costs, it is sometimes safer and better for the cat to undergo an exploratory operation and find nothing than it is to let a cat die from an intestinal puncture or blockage while waiting for a firm diagnosis.

Vomiting or inappetance can result from non-GI diseases. Other organs (when diseases) that commonly result in GI signs are the liver, kidneys, pancreas, adrenal glands, thyroid glands, and possibly heart, lungs, and central nervous system. Since it can be difficult to ascertain whether the primary problem lies within the intestines or in another organ, your veterinarian must rely on many different diagnostic tools. For instance, even though it may seem pointless to perform X-rays on a cat with kidney disease, it is important to rule out other conditions that cause the same signs.

Chronic intermittent diarrhea or vomiting is rarely a dire emergency unless dehydration ensues or unless there is a sudden exacerbation of the condition. These diseases, however, can be serious, and veterinary attention should be sought early on in the course of any GI disease.

SUMMARY

Feline emergencies are common. The nature of the cat, with its independence and curiosity, is partially to blame for the problems that occur. Abnormal changes that we force upon the domestic cat, such as urban environments and feeding mass-produced, commercial diets, produce further stress. In general, indoor cats are less likely to suffer dangerous trauma and are more likely to be presented to the veterinarian for examination earlier, due to their increased observation by owners. The outdoor cat is at risk of contracting infectious diseases, suffering traumatic injuries, and

Outdoor cats have many opportunities to get into trouble even with their formidable self-defense tactics. If you have an indoor/outdoor cat, be sure to check it over every day.

Feline Emergencies

In addition to the dangers of trauma and attacks outdoor felines face daily, they are also at risk for contracting infectious disease. Indoor cats live longer than outdoor cats.

more significantly, disappearing during the initial period of time following an illness or injury, resulting in a delay in diagnosis and treatment. If there is any alteration in your cat's normal behavior, or if your cat returns home following an abnormally long absence, an immediate trip to the veterinary office is your best assurance that any developing problem will be detected early and treated before it becomes serious.

ADDITIONAL READING

Ettinger, SJ: *Small Animal Internal Medicine*. Third edition. WB Saunders Co, Philadelphia, 1990.

Kirk, RW, Ed.: *Current Veterinary Therapy IX: Small Animal Practice*. WB Saunders Co., Philadelphia, 1986.

Kirk, RW, Ed.: *Current Veterinary Therapy X: Small Animal Practice*. WB Saunders Co., Philadelphia, 1989.

Kirk, RW, Ed.: *Current Veterinary Therapy XI: Small Animal Practice*. WB Saunders Co., Philadelphia, 1992.

Oliver, JE Jr.; Lorenz, MD: *Handbook of Veterinary Neurologic Diagnosis*. Second edition. WB Saunders Co, Philadelphia, 1993.

Dr. Lester Mandelker

Dr. Lester Mandelker has been a private veterinary practitioner in Largo, Florida for over 25 years. He is the owner and director of an American Animal Hospital Association Member Hospital, a Diplomate of the American Board of Veterinary Practitioners, board-certified in feline and canine practice. Dr. Mandelker has a special interest in pharmacology and has written over 100 scientific articles on pharmacology and has co-authored three books, including Burns Pharmaceutical Index. He is the Pharmacology Consultant for both the American Veterinary Medical Association's Network of Animal Health and the Veterinary Information Network.

PHARMACOLOGY

By Lester Mandelker, DVM
Diplomate, American Board of Veterinary Practitioners

Community Veterinary Hospital
1631 West Bay Drive
Largo, FL 34640

INTRODUCTION

Cats are unique in their ability to handle and utilize various drugs. The cat lacks certain enzymes or has lower amounts of these metabolic enzymes (such as glucuronyl transferase) needed to metabolize many drugs, and that makes them more susceptible to adverse drug reactions and drug toxicity. In addition, the half life (the time it takes for 50 percent of a drug to leave the body) is often much different in the cat than in humans or other animals. For example, the drug aspirin has a half-life of six hours in dogs and people while, in the cat, the half-life is around 36 hours. Furthermore, the liver alters chemical compounds absorbed from the gastrointestinal tract into more stable forms so that the body can utilize them. Since the liver detoxifies various drugs, animals require a healthy liver to reduce toxicities. The cat commonly has liver ailments including lipidosis (fatty liver) and cholangiohepatitis (bile duct and liver disease) that would affect drug metabolism.

DRUG DISPOSITION

Diseases of body organ systems can alter dramatically the effect drugs have in the body and how they are eliminated. For example, gastrointestinal disease will affect the absorption of oral medications, and kidney disease often will affect the elimination of certain drugs. Cardiovascular disease may alter the regional distribution of drugs to their targeted organs. Some of the more common factors that affect drug reactions in the body include: physiological factors such as age, sex, body weight, diet, temperament, environment, and route of administration. Pharmacologically important factors include drug interaction with diet and other drugs. Pathological factors such as gastrointestinal or kidney disease will modify drug action and drug levels in the blood. Therefore, it is of prime importance not to indiscreetly give drugs to sick or even healthy cats without the advice of a veterinarian. That simple desire to give some aspirin could have far-reaching effects.

PRESCRIPTION AND OVER-THE-COUNTER (OTC) DRUGS

Drugs that can be obtained without a prescription are called over-the -counter (OTC) drugs. There are OTC drugs in the drugstore that can be safely given to cats under the direction of a veterinarian. There are also many that are very dangerous and should never be given to your cat. A brief listing of such pharmaceutical agents will be discussed in this chapter. Generic drugs are drugs that no longer have a patent on them from the original manufacturer. Generic names are often synonymous with the chemical name of the drug. Often, generic drugs are just as effective as the brand name product, but occasionally this is not so. Even though the generic is exactly the same chemical, absorption and uptake by the body may differ due to physical differences in the final product.

There are many OTC drugs that can be given to cats under the direction of a veterinarian. These include antihistamines, such as diphenhydramine, baby aspirin (but only 2-3 times per week), hairball remedies, diarrhea treatments, vitamins, some worm preparations, certain laxatives, and topical agents such as antibiotic creams, cortisone ointment, vitamins and various medicated shampoos.

DRUGS, VACCINES, TOPICAL AND INJECTABLE AGENTS

Drugs and various pharmaceutical agents can be given in a variety of ways. Injections of drugs are most often given intravenously, intramuscularly, intraperitoneally, or subcutaneously. Injections such as these should be given by a veterinarian. In some situations, like diabetes, knowledgeable owners must learn to give daily injections. But in general, it is not recommended that owners give injections without a veterinarian's knowledge so that if any adverse reactions occur they can be more easily handled.

Vaccinations are often given by veterinarians for safety and efficiency. However, there are many owners and cat breeders that give their own vaccines. Vaccinations that are necessary include distemper,

rhinotracheitis, *Chlamydia*, and rabies, as well as feline leukemia and occasionally feline infectious peritonitis. Recently, we have had a vast amount of vaccine reactions that has manifested as a local cancer called fibrosarcoma. It is not known why this rare vaccine reaction has occurred, but it is always in the same place where the vaccine had been given. It is thought to be caused by a chemical additive that is used in some vaccines to increase the immunity of the vaccine. If any swelling occurs locally where a vaccine had been given, it is most important to seek veterinary care immediately. These local cancers can be fatal. This is good reason for cat owners to have their veterinarian administer vaccines, as vets have more knowledge about these vaccine reactions. The feline infectious peritonitis vaccine has been a focus of dispute and disagreement concerning the need of vaccination. Many veterinarians feel this vaccine offers less-than-optimum effectiveness. Recently, there also has been introduced a new vaccine for ringworm. Ringworm is not a worm but instead a surface fungal infection. This vaccine has not proved its full effectiveness, but some claim it has been most useful in catteries. Ringworm has been more apparent in the Persian and Himalayan breeds.

Drugs can also be given orally, rectally, nasally, via inhalation, and topically. Some of these methods are much easier for an informed owner to administer. It occasionally becomes a problem giving cats oral medication. Pills or tablets can easily be resisted and rejected by an unwilling feline. In these situations one can try to mask the pill in some human baby food (i.e. chicken or beef), or coating it with butter or another such food substance. Some tablets can be

Pharmacology

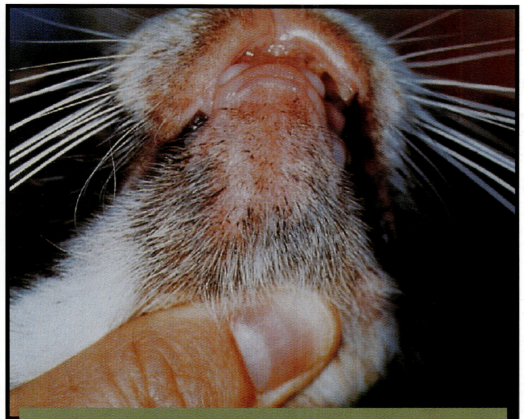

The ringworm affecting the chin and muzzle of this cat could easily be mistaken for simple feline acne.

crushed and mixed with baby food, tuna or tuna/beef juices, even some favorite food. Other times it may be easier to administer liquids to cats. If the taste is objectionable, it should be disguised by adding to milk or tuna juice and/or adding a pinch of Sweet&Low® to detract from any bitter taste. The once-monthly flea pill (liquid) called Program® has been a welcome addition to flea control for many cat owners. This drug is helpful in controlling fleas by making the adult flea sterile so as not to lay viable eggs in your house. The net effect is to reduce the life cycle of the flea so no new hatchings occur. This drug is effective only where there is not a new source of adult fleas entering the house.

Nasal application of drugs is often given for local diseases of the nostrils, for allergies, or for flu-like conditions. Occasionally, use of drugs like Neosynephrine® (1/4%) can be given for short intervals of one or two days to reduce sneezing and nasal congestion. It is best to consult your veterinarian before attempting such a remedy. Rectal application of drugs offers another possibility but is used only in a veterinary office situation. While enemas are often given to constipated cats, other drugs are more difficult to administer to a conscious feline.

Topical agents are also given to cats, and products like flea repellents and flea collars have been used for many years. In general, cats do not

CAT HEALTH ENCYCLOPEDIA

like flea preparations applied to their haircoat. This is especially a problem in the fastidious feline that grooms itself regularly. On rare occasions, flea collars can cause a localized allergic reaction evident by severe inflammation around the neck. If this occurs, seek veterinary care as soon as possible. The new topical flea agents (e.g., Frontline® and Advantage®) have revolutionized flea control. Both products are safe, but the use of Frontline® spray can be more unsettling with cats; and some can get ill from licking the spray before it has dried. Some flea repellents, like permethrins found in certain flea sprays, are also more toxic to felines. It is most important to read labels on the flea spray or consult your veterinarian if you are using daily flea sprays for flea control. Today, with the new monthly flea products there has been diminishing use of daily flea sprays.

Drugs can come in several oral forms including tablets, capsules, liquids, and oral powders. Cats are one of the hardest pets to medicate safely since they often resist anything given orally and may even salivate profusely when approached in this manner. If you have trouble medicating your cat, contact your veterinarian, as he/she may suggest different forms of administering these pharmaceutical agents. Some people try wrapping the cat up in a towel while medicating; others disguise medication in meat-type baby foods.

NEW BREAKTHROUGHS IN DRUG THERAPY

There are several new drug therapies that appear to be significant additions to therapy for cats. The once-monthly flea products, as mentioned, have been nothing short of miraculous in aiding flea control. There are some topical flea repellents available that utilize insect growth regulators to reduce flea burdens on the pet. They do not appear to be as beneficial as the new products such as Advantage® or Frontline®. The use of heartworm preventative is another method of preventing a deadly disease in endemic areas. Heartgard® is now approved for use in the feline and is given once monthly as it is in dogs. Feline heartworm disease is quite different in cats compared to dogs. Cats less often display microfilariae (larval stage of the worm) in their blood, and yearly testing is not often required as it is in dogs. Heartworm in cats is often responsible for more respiratory problems, such as wheezing, than the typical heart-affecting symptoms in dogs. The heartworm preventative is called Heartgard® and contains the drug called ivermectin.

There has been an increase in the use of behavioral drugs in cats for such conditions as aggressive behavior, compulsive behavior, and anxiety. These new drugs block uptake of the brain's neurotransmitters and in so doing, alter behavior. Human drugs like Buspar®, (busiprone), and Elavil® (amitryptylline) are examples of what many veterinarians are using in such situations.

POISONING

Poisoning is a common problem in feline practice. Some of the more common poisons include: household plants, insecticides, rodent poisons, human medicines, fertilizer, and various other chemicals found in the house, such as antifreeze. I would like to first list those chemical agents that are most commonly seen in practice.

PHARMACOLOGY

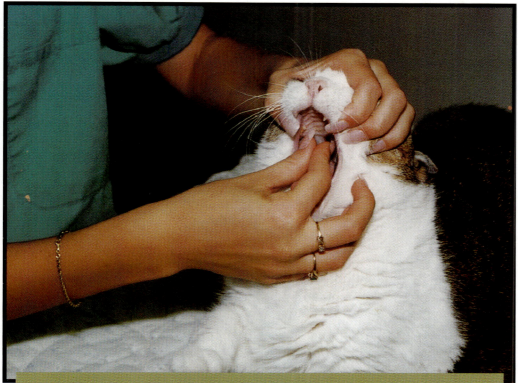

Coating the tablet with baby food makes "pilling the cat" a bit less of a challenge.

1. Insecticides. Organic phosphates such as malathion, chlorpyrifos, dichlorvos, diazinon, phosmet, cythioate, fenthion, carbaryl, lindane, and chlordane are particularly toxic for cats. Many varieties of the pyrethroid class, d-limonene and piperonyl butoxide can also be toxic in some circumstances. Sugar-based insecticides often contain arsenic and are toxic. Boric acid insecticides can make some cats ill.
2. Plant chemicals, including herbicides and various fertilizers. This area might also include household plants like dieffenbachia and philodendron, which are known to be toxic if ingested by cats.
3. Human medicines, such as acetaminophen (Tylenol®), aspirin, other anti-inflammatory agents such as ibuprofen, decongestants, bronchodilators such as pseudoephedrine, anti-clotting agents such as warfarin, and topical agents such as zinc oxide and 5-fluorouracil.
4. Miscellaneous chemicals such as antifreeze, turpentine, lead from paint, motor oil, cosmetics, graphite, slug bait, and various other agents. If any cat ingests or comes in contact with the above-mentioned chemicals, it should be taken to a veterinary hospital for immediate treatment. One can also contact the poison control center in your area. There is also a national poison center (1-800-282-3171) that can be consulted regarding treatment of various poisons.

ADVERSE DRUG REACTIONS

Adverse drug reactions can occur in cats and can take the form of allergic reactions, drug fever, cardiovascular reactions, liver, bone and kidney toxicity, and gastrointestinal disturbances. Sometimes, the practice of giving more than one drug at a time will increase the likelihood of adverse drug reactions. The occurrence of adverse drug reactions increases greatly with dysfunction of various organs, such as in kidney or liver disease.

Any drug can cause an adverse reaction and can end up being dangerous or even toxic to cats. It is important to consult your veterinarian concerning any drug that makes your pet act sick or depressed. Any cat that vomits, acts depressed, or strange in any manner after specific drug therapy should be presented to a veterinarian for investigation of possible drug toxicity. Over-the-counter medications or human-labeled drugs can often be a source of toxic drug exposure. Examples of common OTC human drugs that should be avoided include acetaminophen (Tylenol®) and any other pain relief agents like aspirin, ibuprofen, etc. There are some drugs, like human antihistamines, that are more safe to give to cats, but you should always consult your veterinarian for dosages and frequency. Most adverse drug reactions occur due to problems with absorption, metabolism, or kidney excretion of the drug. Certain drugs are more toxic when there is concurrent kidney or liver disease; and some drugs, like the Valium®-type agents, can cause a fatal liver-failure syndrome. Drugs like phenobarbital, which are given for seizure control, often need blood monitoring to check proper dosage and avoid toxic blood levels.

DRUG PROFILES

There are many drugs that are used in feline medicine, and a brief discussion will follow. These drugs are given therapeutically by veterinarians in disease situations.

Antibiotics are among the most common drugs given to cats for bacterial infections and include various types of penicillins (such as amoxicillin), sulfas, cephalosporins (such as cephalexin), tetracyclines, quinolones (such as enrofloxacin), and certain aminoglycosides (such as gentamicin).

Antifungal agents are used to treat various fungal infections such as ringworm and deeper infections such as cryptococcosis. Drugs include griseofulvin, ketoconazole, fluconazole, etc.

Antihistamines include chlorpheniramine, diphenhydramine, and clemastine. They are often used to treat allergies, car sickness, excessive grooming, and to initiate mild sedation. Consult your veterinarian for the dosage and frequency of administration.

Analgesics lessen pain and are occasionally given to cats. Be aware that they can also be extremely toxic to cats. Baby aspirin is the only type recommended and should only be given at least three days apart. This is sufficient for short-term needs. Acetaminophen (e.g., Tylenol®) is extremely toxic to cats and should never be given to cats under any circumstances. Other pain medications such as ibuprofen, naproxen, ketoprofen, etc., are not useful for treating cats because they have too many potential side effects.

Anti-inflammatory agents may be given for allergies, immune-mediated diseases, and inflammatory bowel

PHARMACOLOGY

Beware of poisonous houseplants like this philodendron.

disorders. Corticosteroids may be given orally (prednisone, dexamethasone) or by injection, depending on the duration of action needed. Progestational compounds are occasionally used, but they have too many side effects for routine administration.

Several drugs are used for treatment of routine problems in cats. For example, Kaopectate® or loperamide (Immodium®) may be recommended by your veterinarian to treat occasional diarrhea. Laxatives such as petrolatum or dioctyl sulfosuccinate (Colace®) can be used for cases of constipation. Syrup of ipecac is a common household remedy when cats ingest various poisons. However, contact your veterinarian or poison control center before inducing vomiting. B-complex vitamins are often used as appetite stimulants for cats. For cats with systemic illnesses, there are a variety of prescription medications that can be used to stimulate appetite.

Nutritional supplements represent an important class of medications that are often administered at home. Please remember that most nutrients can function as drugs within the body and should not be used indiscriminately. Taurine is an amino acid that can cause heart, eye, and reproductive disturbances if not provided in adequate quantities. Virtually all commercial diets are fortified with taurine. Supplementation is used if there is any question as to the adequacy of a cat's diet. Similarly, many cats that are ill develop deficiencies of potassium. Supplementation is often given to cats with a variety of illnesses. Although there are many skin and coat care supplements available OTC, contact your

CAT HEALTH ENCYCLOPEDIA

veterinarian before you use them in your pet.

There are a variety of drugs used to treat systemic diseases. Insulin is most commonly used for diabetes, but there is some research to suggest that drugs like glipizide may help lower blood sugar by increasing the output of insulin by the body. Ulcer medications like cimetadine (Tagamet®) and famotadine (Pepcid®) have been used to treat gastric ulceration. Bronchodilators such as albuterol are sometimes needed to treat cases of asthma and bronchitis. Hyperthyroidism may be treated with methimazole (Tapazole®). Heart disease may be treated with digitalis, enalapril, and various diuretics such as furosemide (Lasix®).

NATURAL AND HERBAL REMEDIES

Herbal remedies for people can also be dangerous for cats due to the species' unique metabolism of drugs. Therefore, while some herbal drugs are useful, it would be wise to contact a veterinarian familiar with these drugs before one gives them to their cat. Some natural vitamin and nutrient therapies have proven useful in the feline. Vitamin E has been useful in therapy for certain inflammatory and heart conditions. Co-enzyme Q has been used in therapy for cardiac disease as has the amino acid taurine. This amino acid has been proven to reduce a fatal form of heart disease called cardiomyopathy. Vitamin B complex is rarely toxic, but human doses are often too high for a feline. When providing these nutrients for a cat, it is best to use a product specially formulated for cats. Vitamin A can be toxic at higher doses, and therefore it should not routinely be added as a supplement. Cats often get sufficient vitamin A in their diets. Vitamin C is rarely used as therapy in cats since they produce much of their own. It has been suggested that vitamin C will reduce urinary symptoms associated with infection or the presence of small crystals in the urine (feline urologic syndrome). The use of vitamin C in this capacity has not been shown to be effective. Minerals like potassium and magnesium have been utilized in therapy for conditions involving the heart muscle or for a deficiency syndrome called hypokalemia. Cats with low blood potassium (hypokalemia) often display a weakened condition, muscle fatigue, and hold their head in an unusual position called "ventroflexion." Calcium has also been given to cats to combat imbalances in the body. Such minerals as potassium, magnesium, and calcium should not be given to your cat without medical knowledge, since high blood levels of these minerals can be very dangerous to the health of your pet.

SUMMARY

An informed cat owner is better suited to discuss various drug options when the need arises for their use. This chapter may be helpful in understanding some of the pharmacological agents routinely given cats in the treatment and prevention of disease. For further information regarding these drugs, please contact your veterinarian.

RECOMMENDED READING

Mandelker, L: *Burn's Pharmaceutical Index*. 1994.

Papich, M; Boothe, D: *Current Drug Therapy*, 1992.

Kirk, RW: *Current Veterinary Therapy*, WB Saunders, Co., 1996.

Consumer's Guide: Prescription Drugs, 1995.

INDEX

Page numbers in **boldface** refer to illustrations.

A

Abdominal wall hemorrhage, **155**
Abscesses, 296
Abyssinian, 10, 80, 115, 192, 235, 238
Acetaminophen, 139, 291, 307, 308
Achondroplasia, 70
Acquired valvular disease, 141
Acromegaly, 265
Actinobacillosis, 25
Actinomycocis, 24
Acute gastritis, 215
Acute kidney failure, 236
Acute pancreatitis, 299
Addison's disease, 266
ADH, 264
Adrenal glands, 266
Agenesis of upper eyelid, 96
Agglutinin disease, 250
Albino, 109
Allergic bronchitis, 168, 293
Allergic pneumonitis, 168
Allergy, 11, 168
—flea, 11, 12
—food, 13, **37**, 282
—skin testing, 15
Alopecia areata, 22
Ameloblastomas, 202
American Association of Feed Control Officials, 269
American Curl, 70, 71
Amino acid, 141
Amlodipine besylate, 134
Amyloidosis, 234, 253
Analgesics, 308
Anemia, 36, 147, **150**, 151, 152
Angiocardiography, 132
Anorexia, 141
Anterior uveitis, 109
Anti-inflammatory agents, 308
Antibiotics, 308
Antidiuretic hormone, 264
Antifreeze, 205, 238, 292, 307

Antifungal agents, 308
Antihistamines, 16, 308
Appetite stimulants, 309
Arrhythmia, 131, 141
Ascites, 141
Aspergillosis, 31, 206
Aspirin, 80, 139, 291, 303, 307
Asthma, 168, 293, 310
Atenolol, 134
Atopy, 14
Atrioventricular valve malformations, 124
Auscultation, 141
Autoimmune diseases, 18, 155, 205, 250
—oral manifestations, 205
Autoimmune hemolytic anemia, 156, **157**, 250
Autoimmune thyroiditis, 250
Automobiles, 294

B

B-cell, 249
Baby aspirin, 308
Bacteremia, 149
Bacterial endocarditis, 130, 141
Bacterial enteritis, 216
Bacterial folliculitis, 23
Bacterial pneumonia, 172
Bacterial skin diseases, 22
Bartonella, 118
Beta-adrenergic blocker, 141
Birman, 10
Bladder
—cancer, 244
—cystine, 243
—ruptured, **66**
—stones, 243
—urate, 243
Blastomycosis, 31, 172
Bleeding, inherited disorders, 151
Blepharitis, 98
Blepharospasm, 92, 107

CAT HEALTH ENCYCLOPEDIA

Blindness, 95
Blood pressure, 126, 141
Bobskill, Lorie, 70
Bone marrow, 145
Bone plating, 61
Bowel disease, 216
—inflammatory, 250
Breast cancer, 173
British Shorthair, 152
Bronchitis, 310
Brushing, 207
Burmese, 10, 38, 106, 124, 242
Burns, 42

C
Calcium, 310
Calcium channel blocker, 141
Calcium oxalate, 241, 242
Calculus, 208
Calicivirus, 162
Campylobacter, 118, 216
Canadian Veterinary Medical
   Association, 269
Cancer, 220
Candida albicans, 206
Candidiasis, 206
Canned foods, 270
Capillaria feliscati, 241
Cardiac arrhythmias, 128
Cardiac disease, 294
Cardiac ultrasound, 141
Cardiomyopathy, 114, 124, **127**, 142,
   310
Cardiopulmonary resuscitation,
   137
Cardiovascular disease, 128
—early signs, 128
Casomorphine, 279
Cat bites, 23, 50, 296
Cat scratch disease, 118
Cataracts, 94, 113, **113**
Catteries, 198, 221
Central corneal ulcer, **93**
Cerclage wiring, 62
Cervical line lesions, 190
Chediak-Higashi syndrome, 10, 153,
   252
Chemical burn, **299**
Cheyletiellosis, 38

Cheylettiella blakei, 37
Chiggers, 37
Chin edema, 200
Chlamydia, **93**, 101
Chlamydia psittaci, **102**, 103, 118,
   163
Chlamydial conjunctivitis, 103
Cholangiohepatitis, 303
Chondrosarcoma, 76
Chorioretinitis, 114
Chronic kidney failure, 238, 239
—treatment, 239
Chronic progressive polyarthritis, 52,
   56
Chronic tubulointersitial nephritis,
   239
Chyle, 180
Chylothorax, 180
Claws, 45
Clot, 126
Clouding, 94
Coagulation, 150
Coaptation devices, **53**
Coccidia, 218
Coccidioidomycosis, 31, 172
Coccidioides immitis, 50
Cold agglutinin disease, 20
Collagen defects, 10
Colonic motility, 220
Color changes, 94
Congenital abnormalities, 232
Congenital heart problems, 123
Congenital hypotrichosis, 10
Congenital portosystemic shunt, 228
Congenital skin disorders, 9
Congestive heart failure, 128
Conjunctivitis, 96, 100, 163, 290
Constant licking, 40
Constipation, 220, 309
Contact dermatitis, 16
Cornea, 107
—degenerations, 109
—dystrophies, 109
—inflammation, 290
—nigrum, **106**
—sequestrum, **106**, 108
Coronaviruses, 217
Corticosteroids, 12, 80, 266, 309
Cortisone, 8, 31

INDEX

Creatinine, 231
"Crossed eyes", 109
Cruciate ligament, 68
Cryptococcosis, 30, **33**, **34**, 54, 172, 206
Cryptococcus neoformans, 30
Cryptosporidium, 218
Ctenocephalides felis felis, 34
Cushing's syndrome, 31, 158, 266
Cuspid extrusion syndrome, 194
Cutaneous amyloidosis, 22
Cutaneous asthenia, 10
Cutaneous tuberculosis, 23

D
Deciduous teeth, 189
Declawing, 82
Degenerative arthritis, 79
Demodex cati, 38
Demodiocosis, 38
Dermanyssus Gallinae, 36
Dermatophyte infection, **25**, 26
Dermatophyte lesions, **26**
Devon Rex, 10, 71, 80
Diabetes, 310
—insipidus, 264
—mellitus, 32, 252, 260
—ketoacidosis, 262
Diaphragmatic hernia, **49**, 186
Diarrhea, 299, 300, 309
Diet, 14, 279, 287
—behavioral problems, 279
—dental problems, 284
—FUS, 287
Digoxin, 134
Dilated cardiomyopathy, 124, 132
Dilitiazem, 134
Dirofilariasis, 126, 134
Displaced lens, 114
Displacement behaviors, 40
Disseminated intravascular coagulation, 154
Dog bites, 296
Drugs, 303
—reactions, 20
—toxicity, 303, 308
Dry foods, 270, 281, 284
Dwarfism, 70
Dyspnea, 142

E
Ears, 45
—cartilage anomalies, 70
—hematoma, 250
—mites, **36**, 37
Ecchymoses, **155**
Echocardiogram, **138**
Echocardiography, 131, 141
Ectopic ureter, 246
Ectrodactyly, 71, **73**
Electrical burns, 201
Electrocardiogram, 131, **135**, 142
Electrolyte abnormalities, 239
Endocardial fibroelastosis, 124
Endocardiosis, 130
Endocrine, 142
Endodontic disease, 196
Endoscope, 162
Enophthalmos, 116
Enteritis, 216, 221
—inflammatory, 216
Entropion, 97, **101**
Environmental skin disease, 41
Enzyme, 142
Eosinophilia, 149
Eosinophilic granuloma complex, 12, 43, **43**, **44**, 45, **45**, 199, 250
Eosinophilic keratitis, **97**, 108
Eosinophilic plaque, 43, **42**, 44, 199
Eosinophilic pneumonitis, 168
Eosinophilic ulcer, 199
Epidermolysis bullosa, 9
Epilepsy, 298
Epiphora, 106
Epistaxis, **155**
Epulides, 202
Erythematosus, 18
Esophageal stricture, 213
Esophagitis, 213
Estropia, 109
Ethylene glycol, 205, 238, 292
Eumycotic mycetoma, 29
Evan's syndrome, 156
Excision arthroplasty, 80
Exocrine pancreas diseases, 222
Exocrine pancreatic insufficiency, 223
Exophthalmos, 116
External coaptation, 59

313

CAT HEALTH ENCYCLOPEDIA

External fixators, 60
External odontoclastic resorptions, 190
Eye emergencies, 290
Eye hemorrhage, 110
Eye weight, 87
Eyelid, 96
—diseases, 96
—neoplasms, 99
—tumors, 99

F
Facial dermatitis, **11**
Factor XII deficiency, 151
Feeding, 270, 281, 284
—kittens, 270
—pregnant queens, 270
—seniors, 272
Feline asthma, **173**
Feline calicivirus, **29**
Feline immunodeficiency virus (FIV), **19**, 102, 110, 158, 252
Feline infectious anemia, 148
Feline infectious peritonitis (FIP), 110, 180, 217, 221, 252
Feline leukemia virus (FeLV), 56, 76, 102, 110, **150**, 151, 158, 178, 252
Feline lower urinary tract disease (FLUTD), 240, 276
Feline urologic syndrome (FUS), 240, 287
Fertilizers, 307
Fiber, 275
Fibrinolysis, 150
Fibrosarcoma, 77, 202, 304
Fibrosing pleuritis, 182
Fight wound lacerations, 107
Fleas, 34, 148
—allergy, 11
—bite allergy, 12
—bite hypersensitivity, **9**
—control, 34, 291, 304, 305
Follicle cysts, **8**
Food, 270, 281, 284
—allergy, 13, **37**, 282
—allergy dermatitis, **12**, **13**
—canned, 270
—dry, 270, 281, 284
—intolerance, 13, 282

—poisoning, 216
—semi-moist, 270, 274, 281
Foreign bodies, 43, 166, 204, 219
—oral, 204
Fractures, 59
—femur, **59**
—forelimbs, 59
—hind limbs, 59
—lower leg, 65
—mandible, 64
—rib, 66
—scapula, 66
—spine, 63
—tibia, 60
Frostbite, 42
Fulminant pulmonary edema, 133
Fundus diseases, 114
Fungus
—arthritis, 54
—infections, 29, 206
—paronychia, **29**
—pnuemonia, **177**
—skin disease, 26
Fur mites, 36
Furunculosis, 23

G
Gammopathies, 253
Gastrointestinal emergencies, 298
Gastrointestinal neoplasia, 220
Gastrointestinal ulcers, 214
Geotrichosis, 31
Giardiasis, 218
Gingiva, **195**
Gingivitis, 192, **193**, 250
Glaucoma, 111, **113**, 290
Glipizide, 262
Globe, 116
Glomerulonephritis, 236
Grave's disease, 250, 252
Grooming, excessive, 40

H
Hair follicle disorders, 9
Hairballs, 214
Hairlessness, 10
Harvest mites, 37
Haw, 104
Heart, 123

—disease, 294, 310
—failure, 130, 142
—hypertensive disease, 128
—hyperthyroid disease, 125
—murmurs, 124, 130, 142
—sounds, 142
Heartworm, 126, 132, 142
—preventative, 306
Heinz body anemia, 282
Helicobacter infection, 214, 215
Hematopoieses, 145
Hemobartonella felis, 148, **153**
Hemophilias, 152
—A, 151
—B, 151
Hemorrhage, 95
Hemostasis, 149, 150
Hepatic encephalopathy, 227
Hepatic fibrosis, 227
Hepatic lipidosis, 225, 275
Herbal remedies, 310
Herbicides, 307
Hereditary disorders, 9
Hereditary myopathy, 71
Herpesvirus, 101, **103**, 107
Heterochromia, **98**, 109
High blood pressure, 116
High rise syndrome, 294
Himalayan, 10, 27, 106, 108, 152,
192, 234, 242, 304
Hip dysplasia, **76**, 79
Histopathology, 73
Histoplasmosis, 31, 54, 172
HIV, 118
Hochenedel, Sandra, 70
Home care, 207
Hookworms, 218
Hormones, 31
Household plants, 292, 307
Human medicines, 307
Hydronephrosis, 234
Hyperadrenocorticism, 31, 158, **263**,
265, 266
Hyperkalemia, 126
Hyperlipidemia, 158
Hyperparathyroidism, 265
Hyperphosphatemia, 232
Hyperpigmentation, 33
Hypersensitivity, 11, 253

—reactions, 206
Hypertension, 116, **118**, 126
Hyperthyroidism, 32, 126, 132, 134,
142, 250, 251, 257, 260, 279, 310
Hypertrophic cardiomyopathy, 125,
134, **137**, 140
Hypertrophic osteopathy, 82
Hypervitaminosis A, 79
Hyphema, **95**, 110
Hypo-allergenic, 14
Hypoadrenocorticism, 266
Hypocalcemia, 232
Hypoglycemia, 262
Hypokalemia, 278, 310
Hypokalemic myopathy, 278
Hypoparathyroidism, 265
Hypopigmentation, 33

I
Icterus, **157**, 221, **226**
Ideal weight, 274
Identification, 297
Idiopathic lower urinary tract
disease, 244
Idiopathic thrombocytopenic
purpura, 156, 158, 250
Immune complex glomerulonephritis,
254
Immune dysfunction, 254
Immune system neoplasia, 252
Immune-mediated hemolytic anemia,
156, 250
Immune-mediated kidney disease,
236
Immune-mediated polyarthritis, 250
Immune-mediated thrombocytopenia,
158
Immunodeficiency, 11, 252
Inappetance, 299
Indolent ulcer, 43, 44, 199
Indoor cats, 297
Infectious disease, 22, 50
Inflammatory diseases, 50—58
Inflammatory polyp, **167**
Insect allergy, 11
Insect-growth regulators, 34, 306
Insecticides, 307
Insulin, 262
Interfragmentary techniques, 62

CAT HEALTH ENCYCLOPEDIA

Intestines, 146
—parasites, 217
Intradermal allergy test, **16**
Intramedullary pins, 61
Intraocular hemorrhage, 94
Invasive resorptions, 190
Iodine, 279
Iridocyclitis, 109
Iris, 109
—melanoma, **107**
Iritis, 109
Ischemia, 142
Ivermectin, 306

J
Japanese Bobtail, 69
Jaundice, **157**, 221, **226**
Joint dislocation, 66
Juvenile hyperchylomicronemia, 158
Juvenile osteoporosis, 78
Juxtacortical osteosarcomas, 74

K
Keratitis, 107, 290
Keratoconjunctivitis sicca, 106
Ketotic, 262
Kidneys, 146
—disease, 154, 232
—failure, 79, 126, 204
—secondary hyperparathyroidism, 79
—stones, 236
—tumors, 236
Kinked tail, 71
Kitty distemper, 299

L
Lacrimal system, 104
Large intestine diseases, 219
Lens diseases, 112
Lens luxation, 114
Lentigo, 33
Leprosy, 24
Lesions, 43, 142, **195**
Leukemia, 158
Lice, 40
Lidocaine, 134
Ligamentous injuries, 66
Linear granuloma, 200
Lipidosis, 303

Liver, 146
—disease, 154, 224
Lungs
—aspiration, **178**
—cancer, 173
—collapsed, **49**
—infection, 293
Lyme disease, 35
Lymph nodes, 146
Lymphocytes, 249
Lymphocytic-plasmacytic
  cholangiohepatitis, 226
Lymphocytic-plasmacytic
  gastroenteritis, 216
Lymphocytosis, 149
Lymphomas, 252
Lymphoplasmacytic colitis, 219
Lymphosarcoma, 111, **111**, 158, 166,
  178, 202, 220, 236, 252
Lysosomal storage diseases, 109

M
Magnesium, 276, 310
Maine Coon, 70, 80, 140
Malassezia, 28, **30**
—dermatitis, 28
Malignant melanomas, 202
Malocclusion, 202
Mange, 39
"Manx" gene, 69
Markers, 9
Mast cell tumors, 202
Maxilla fractures, 64
Membrana nictitans, 90
Metabolic acidosis, 277
Metabolic musculoskeletal disease,
  78
Methimazole, 134
Microchip identification, 297
Microphthalmos, 118
Microsporum canis, 26
Miliary dermatitis, 12
Mineral oil, 170
Minerals, 310
Mites, 34, 36
Mononuclear-phagocyte system, 146
Mosquito, 126
—bite allergy, **10**, 13
Mucopolysaccharidosis, 70, 78

INDEX

Multiple myeloma, 253
Multiple osteocartilaginous exostosis, 76
Multiple-cat households, 221
Munchkin, 70
Musculoskeletal cancer, 72
Myasthenia gravis, 72, 250
Mycetomas, 207
Mycobacterium, 23, 118
Mycoplasma felis, 101, 104
Mycoplasmal arthritis, 54
Mycotic stomatitis, 206
Myositis ossificans, 82

N
Nail caps, 83
Nasopharyngeal polyp, 202
National poison center, 307
Natural remedies, 310
Neck lesions, 190
Neonatal conjunctivitis, 96
Neonatal isoerythrolysis, 253
Neoplasia, 72, 110, 116, 142, 213
Neurodermatitis, 40
Neutropenia, 149, 251
Nigrum, 108
Nocardiosis, 25
Non-infectious inflammatory disease, 55
Norwegian Forest, 70
Nose diseases, 161
Nosebleed, **155**
Notoedres cati, **38**, 39
Nuclear scintigraphy, 132
Nutrition requirements, 269
Nutritional musculoskeletal disease, 78
Nutritional secondary hyperparathyroidism, 78
Nutritional supplements, 309

O
Obesity, 252, 270, 272
Obstipation, 220
Ocular diseases, 95
Ocular fundus, **91**
Onion powder, 282
Onychectomy, 82
Opacity, 94

Oral tumors, 202
Orbit, 116
Organophosphates, 291
Oriental, 235
Orthopedic disorders, inherited, 68
Osteochondromatosis, 76
Osteodystrophy, 71, 78
Osteomyelitis, **48**, 50
Osteosarcoma, 73, **74**
Otobius megnini, 36
Otodectes cynotis, 37
Otodectes mites, **35**
Outdoor cats, 297
Owner's Guide to Cat Health, 217

P
Paecilomycosis, 31
Palpation, 142
Pancreatitis, 223
Panleukopenia, 198, 217, 299
Paper-bone disease, 78
Paralysis, 294
—rear leg, 294
—tick, 35
Parasites, 34, 217
Parasitic skin disease, 34
Parathormone, 79
Parathyroid glands, 265
Parvovirus, 299
Patellar luxation, 80
Patent ductus arteriosus, 137
Pathogenic, 142
Pectineal myectomy, 80
Pectus excavation, 70
Pediculosis, 40
Pelger-Huet anomaly, 252
Pelvic fractures, 62
Pemphighus vulgaris, 18
Pemphigus complex, 18
Pemphigus foliaceus, **14**, 18, **20**, **21**
Penicillinosis, 206
Pericardial disease, 142
Perinephric pseudocysts, 234
Periocular whitening, 34
Periodontal osteomyelitis, 50
Periodontal probe, **199**
Periodontitis, 192
Peritoneum diseases, 221
Peritonitis, 219

CAT HEALTH ENCYCLOPEDIA

Persian, 9, 10, 26, 97, 106, 108, 113, 192, 234, 242, 252, 304
Pet food certification, 269
Pets Are Wonderful Support (PAWS), 119
Pflueger, Dr. Solveig M.V., 70
Phaeopyphomycocis, 29
Phthisis bulbi, 117
Pigmentation abnormalities, 32
Plague, 25
Plant chemicals, 307
Plaque, 192, 208, 284
Plasma cell pododermatitis, 43
Plasma cell stomatitis, 250
Platelet dysfunction, 151, 153
Pleural effusion, 128, 142, 177, 180, 182, **184**, 185
Pneumonia, 170, 293
Pneumothorax, **49**, 184, **187**
Pneumonitis, 163
Pododermatitis, 250
Poison, 291, 306
Pollen allergy, 14, **15**
Polyarteritis nodosa, 58, 250
Polyarthritis, **47**
Polycystic kidney disease, 232, **233**
Polydactyly, 69, **70**
Potassium, 278, 310
Preservatives, 282
Primary teeth, 189
Progressive retinal atrophy, 115
Propranolol, 134
Proptosis, **119**
Propylene glycol, 292
Prototothecosis, 31
Psychogenic hair loss, 40
Pulmonary edema, 128, 142, 175, **181**
Pulse rate, 129
Pupil size, 94
Pyelonephritis, 234
Pyothorax, 182
Pyrethrin, 291, 292
Pythiosis, 29

R
Radial fractures, 60
Regurgitation, 213
Relapsing polychondritis, 21

Renal failure, 79, 126, 204
Renal secondary hyperparathyroidism, 79
Resorptive lesions, 190
Respiratory emergencies, 292
Reticuloendothelial system, 146
Retina, 142
Retinal degeneration, 114
—inherited, 115
Rheumatoid, 250
Rhinotracheitis virus, 162
Rib cage, 66, 70
Ringworm, 26, **28**, 304, **305**
Rochalimaea henselae, 118
Rodent ulcers, 199
Root resorptions, 190
Roundworms, 218
Russian Blue, 238

S
Salmonella, 118, 216
Scabies, 39
Schiotz tonometer, 112
Schirmer tear test, **105**, 106
Scottish Fold, 70, **72**
—gene, 71
Sebaceous adenitis, 43
Seborrhea, 9
Seizures, 298
Semi-moist foods, 270, 274, 281
Septic arthritis, 52
Serum, 142
Shaft disorder, 10
Shock therapy, 296
Shorthair, 235
Siamese, 10, 24, 33, 34, 38, 41, 70, 109, 114, 152, 235, 238, 276
Skin lesions, **27**
Small intestine diseases, 216
Solar dermatitis, **40**, 41
Solitary osteocartilaginous exostosis, 75
Sphynx, 10
Spiders, 34
—bites, 39
Spina bifida, 69
Spleen, 146
Sporothrix schenckii, 30
Sporotrichosis, 30, **31**, **32**

318

INDEX

Squamous cell carcinoma, 41, 42, **44**, 78, **101**, 202, **156**
Stabilization, 296
Starvation, 275
Steroid, 31
Stomach, 146
Stomatitis, 194
Stones, 241
—struvite, 241, 242
—urinary bladder, 241
—urinary tract, 241, 276
Sunburn, **40**
Supperative cholangiohepatitis, 226
Symblepharon, 102
Syncope, 128, 142
Syncytium-forming virus, 56
Systemic diseases, 204
Systemic fungi, 172, 206
Systemic hypertension, 126
Systemic lupus erythematosus, 18, **22**, 56, 250, 251

T
T-cell, 249
Tail sucking, 41
Taillessness, 69, **71**
Tapeworms, 218
Tartar, 284
Tattoos, 298
Taurine, 114, 132, 135, 277, 309, 310
—deficiency, **115**, **117**, 124, 130, 132
Teeth, 189, 203
—devitalized, 201
Tenectomy, 83
Tension pneumothorax, 185
Therapy, 133
Thermal facial burn, **39**
Third eyelid, 90, 104
—prolapse, 92
Thoracocentesis, 142
Thrill, 142
Thrombocytopenia, 153, **154**, 156, **157**
Thromboembolism, 128, 140, 142
Thrombopathia, 153
Thrombosis, 125, 134, 149, 154
Thrombus, 132
Thymoma, 250

Thymus, 146
Thyroid adenocarcinoma, 125, 251, **259**
Ticks, 34
—paralysis, 35
Toes, 69
Tonometer, 112
Tooth super-eruption syndrome, 194
Torovirus, 105
Toxemia, 149
Toxic epidermal necrolysis, 206
Toxic kidney failure, 238
Toxoplasma gondii, 110, 118
Toxoplasmosis, 218
Tracheal stricture, 165
Tracheal wash, **174**
Transtelephonic ECG monitoring, **133**
Trauma, 58, 294
Trichobezoars, 214
Trichosporonosis, 31
Trochlear groove, 81
Trochleoplasty, 82
Tumors, **179**, 243
Tylenol®, 139

U
Ulcer, **169**, 310
—linear, **104**
Ulcerated lesions, **41**
Ulcerative dermatitis, 45
Ulceroproliferative cheilitis, 199
Ulceroproliferative faucitis, 194
Unilateral anterior uveitis, **99**
Upper respiratory infections, **92**, 162, **169**, 293
Urethral diseases, 244
Urinary incontinence, 246
Urinary tract stones, 276
Urine, 287
Urolithiasis, 276
Urologic syndrome, 126, 276, 310
Uveitis, 114, 290

V
Vaccinations, 304
Vascular problems, 125
Vasculitis, 21, 58
Vasopressin, 264

Vegetarian diets, 269
Ventricular fibrillation, 143
Ventricular septal defect, 124, 135, **139**
Ventricular tachycardia, 134
Ventroflexion, 72
Vertebral fractures, 63
Viral arthritis, 52
Viral enteritis, 216
Viral infections, 198
Viral-associated bone disease, 52
Vision loss, 95
Vitamin A, 79, 310
Vitamin C, 310
Vitamin E, 310
Vitamin K deficiency, 154
Vitiligo, 33
Vomiting, 213, 299

Von Willebrand's disease, 151, 152

W
Waardenburg-Klein syndrome, 33
Walking dandruff mite, 37
Warfarin, 154, 307
Wounds, 50, 296

X
Xanthomas, 32

Y
Yeast, 28
Yersinia pestis, 25

Z
Zoonoses, 118, 217
Zygomycosis, 29